BREAKING
THE LIMIT

BREAKING
THE LIMIT

*One Woman's Motorcycle Journey
Through North America*

KAREN LARSEN

 HYPERION NEW YORK

Library of Congress Cataloging-in-Publication Data

Larsen, Karen
  Breaking the limit : one woman's motorcycle journey through North America / Karen
Larsen—1st ed.
    p. cm.
  ISBN 0-7868-6870-8
  1. United States—Description and travel.   2. Canada—Description and travel.   3. Larsen,
Karen—Travel—United States.   4. Larsen, Karen—Travel—Canada.   5.
Motorcycling—United States.   6. Motorcycling—Canada.   7. Women
motorcyclists—Biography.   I. Title.

E169.04.L365 2004
917.304'931—dc22   2003056763

Hyperion books are available for special promotions and premiums. For details contact Michael Rentas,
Manager, Inventory and Premium Sales, Hyperion, 77 West 66th Street, 11th floor, New York, New York
10023-6298, or call 212-456-0133.

FIRST EDITION

10 9 8 7 6 5 4 3 2 1

For my families.
All of them.

| ACKNOWLEDGMENTS

IT WAS NOT POSSIBLE TO TELL the tales of every kindness, from New Jersey to Alaska and back, that was offered to a leather-clad motorcycle stranger that summer of 2000. What follows is only a selection of roadside happenings, but it should be understood that there were many unmentioned people who helped to make this journey a deeply affirming one.

Without the prodding of John, another continental wanderer, this book would never have been. My families, all three of them, generously gave their love, support, and permission in the telling of these stories, for which I am deeply grateful. I am also indebted to Meagan Hoak, who refused to stop calling, and to Virginia Barber, who took a chance on the unknown. William Bolger suffered through black flies and the first draft and gave me shelter and friendship when I most needed it. I will remember. Peternelle van Arsdale, wielding her editorial machete, helped to hack away the unruly growth of early work. Thank you. Finally, to my beautiful husband, Brad: with you I have found my place, my always, and the beginning of a whole new set of adventures.

"Aren't you afraid?"

Sometimes when people asked, I suspected that they had seen too little. Their question sprang from a provincial sense of safety at home and from a fear of the unknown. Who knows what dangers exist *out there*? Stay home. Stay safe.

"Aren't you afraid?"

Sometimes when people asked, I suspected that they had seen too much. Their question transferred their fear for wives, for daughters, for themselves, onto me. Look at what is in the papers and on television. The world is full of psychopaths, deviants, and criminals, to say nothing of long-haul truckers doing ninety. You might get hurt. You might be killed. Stay home. Stay safe.

"Aren't you afraid?"

The question seemed to transcend age, gender, race, and class. Strangely, however, the question of vulnerability, of the unknown, did seem to be mitigated by region and landscape. I heard it frequently in the densely populated metro corridors of the East and West Coasts. I heard it less often on the huge green surges of the Great Plains and the Canadian Shield. In the overwhelming glaciated landscapes of the far North and West I heard it only rarely. What is a motorcycle road trip to someone who lives alongside silvertip grizzly bears? What is solitary travel to someone who hauls a living over the rail of a crab boat amidst the churning seas of the Bering Strait?

"Aren't you afraid?"

I suppose it is a natural question to ask of a young woman driving alone in a great circle through the far reaches of the North American continent, from New Jersey to Alaska and back on a motorcycle. Not too many men, and fewer women, attempt such things. Had I answered honestly, which I did only rarely, I would have said, "Yes, I am afraid. I am afraid of *not* living before dying. I am afraid of *not* seeing, of *not* knowing. There is fear in living this way, in traveling this way, but there is a greater fear to be found in *not* doing it."

Before that summer on the road, I had never seen my own country, or rather, countries. Born in Ontario and raised in Massachusetts, my sense of nationality has always been dual. I have traveled widely, although not with any sense of home, personal place, or territorial intimacy. Work, as well as simple curiosity, has taken me from the oil fields of the South Caucasus through the deserts of the Middle East. I've lived in the Balkans and seen their beauty as well as their madness. I've walked the gold sands of the beaches in Mozambique and have seen the basalt columns of the Giant's Causeway stretching out into the North Atlantic. However, before the summer of 2000 I had never actually seen the vast spaces or the geographical features of either of my home countries. I knew something of the American East Coast, having visited her cities and walked her mountains, but of the Great Plains, the deserts of the Southwest, or the Oregon coast, I knew nothing. I had a sense for Ontario and the lake country that stretches north from Killarney Provincial Park, having spent summers there, but I knew nothing of the great Canadian Shield, the High Rockies, or the long days of a far north summer.

I did not, for the most part, drive my motorcycle to Alaska in the attempt to somehow "find myself" along the way. There is a long and wonderful tradition of people taking to the open road, both spiritually and physically, as seekers of self and identity, but this was not my primary purpose. At thirty-one, I was already a woman whom most would consider tough and self-assured, and I was certainly independent to a fault. For the most part I know who I am, what I am capable of, and where my strengths and weaknesses lie. In the early spring of 2000 I was near to completing my master's degree. Although I struggled with some of the academics and a few of the personalities, as I neared the end of my second year of studies I felt fully in control and was looking forward to a summer exploring the continent before a new job began in September.

In late March, however, just two months before I was to leave for my trip, my illusion of complete self-determination was obliterated by a small soft mass, growing just to the left of my sternum. It became, as foolishly as I tried, impossible to ignore. My boyfriend, seething with rage that I had not told him or anyone else earlier, packed me off to the campus health clinic. From there I was sent to an oncologist to discuss possibilities associated with a genetic history of cancer. It was a history that was not immediately available as my parents had adopted me as an infant.

"It's probably nothing," the doctor said, "but it would be helpful to have as much information as possible. You should consider making some calls."

Over the course of the next few weeks I pieced together what medical background I could. Although the subject matter was horrifying, some of the calls were simple. I had met my biological mother, Gloria, five years before and we were good friends. She told me that there was some history of melanoma and breast cancers on her side of the family but nothing epidemic. Other phone calls were incredibly difficult. The process that had introduced Gloria and me, mutual and independent registration at the agency through which my adoption had been facilitated, had not been available to my biological father. To get the information I needed I had to invade—as I saw it at the time—the life of a man, possibly intruding upon his family, who had given me up thirty years before. I lacked the mutual permission that I had from Gloria when she and I had met, but I had no choice, and all of us would have to cope with the emotional repercussions later. The news from my biological father's side of the family was not reassuring. Incidents of breast and bladder cancer as well as brain tumors marked their lineage for three generations or more. The most recent victim had been my biological aunt, a strong young woman who had lost her battle with breast cancer shortly after her fortieth birthday.

Within the swirl of emotions that surrounded contacting my biological father was a very personal and deep-seated fear. I had watched my dad, the man who raised me, and the person whom I loved and respected more than anyone else in the world, struggle through bladder and prostate cancer four years before. He had been stoic, incredibly resilient following the surgery and chemotherapy, and as always he had conducted himself with a grace and dignity that was reassuring to all of us who lived through it with him. But it was an awful thing: painful, debilitating, sickening, and I felt sure that I could not have endured what he did. For the very first time in my life, looking at the specter of the same disease, I was genuinely afraid; afraid of a situation that I did not choose, a course of events that I was unable to extricate myself from, and the possibility of a malignancy that I could not control.

A week after contacting my biological father for the first time, my surgeon removed the mass, pathology came back with a nonmalignant diagnosis, and I took a deep breath for what felt like the first time in weeks. An odd growth, in an odd place, a small scar slicing across my upper chest, and a warning from my doctors to watch for this sort of thing in the future. Bullet dodged, for now.

I had told only one of my professors, a kindly and intelligent man, about what was happening, and only then because I had to miss his class for the surgery. He summed it up best:

"When you're my age, you expect things like this, but the *first* time something like this happens, when you're young, it stops you short." So it does, and such stops often bring reevaluation along with knowledge. In my case, the possibilities associated with a frightening medical history forced open doors closed since the winter of 1969. The desire to travel the continent, as well as the recent contact with my biological family, brought me to the conclusion, more than ever, that I needed to go; to set out and learn some small part of what the open roads of America and Canada had to teach.

Megalopolises and the homogenizing influences of urban culture held no great appeal when I planned my explorations. I wanted to see the continent on its back roads, to stop in the smallest of towns and experience the intimacy of local cultures where the flow of the land met people who lived in concert with their neighbors and their region. I also wanted to meet, face to face and for the first time, some of the blood relatives who, when I called, generously gave not only the information that I needed, but invited and encouraged me to become part of their lives. It was not too late to do all of these things now, but one day it might be. Individual time, and life itself, is not in fact endless.

Driving a motorcycle is a sensual, visceral, and immediate experience. It's the blast of air parting in an almost physical way around your body. It's the feel of heavy steel machinery between your thighs and knees as you move through turns, running a good road on a clear warm morning. It's the taste of wet grass, deep woods, damp riverbanks, and freshly cut hay that finds its way to the back of your throat. You know and experience what is around you and feel the very sensation of motion itself, in a way that you never can behind the wheel of a car.

In a car you drive a road, on a motorcycle you feel it. On a motorcycle every rise and dip, every change in surface or cant, every turn and straightway, is a temporal and physical experience. In a car you are enclosed, removed from what is without by the machinery that moves you. The windshield, the air-conditioning, the heater, the radio, the upholstered cradle of your seat, the locked doors, the surrounding frame, they all separate you from the reality of the road and weather. On a motorcycle the machine and the environment are an integral part of the experience. As you come home in the afternoon, the sun touches your shoulders with great warm hands. Somewhere in the middle of a long day of riding—especially on curves, where lean and torque, body and bike angle, gravity and speed, determine the physics and the line of movement—the machine becomes an extension of the body, a melding of what is human and what is mechanical.

I have heard the criticisms and they are true: on a motorcycle you trade safety for sensation, enclosure for exhilaration. A steering wheel, an airbag, and a roll cage are, however, poor substitutes for the motion and the freedom of a motorcycle.

I was fifteen when my love affair with motorcycles began. Part of it, I must admit, was rebellion. "Nice" girls in the insulated suburban town near Boston where I grew up did not drive motorcycles. Then there was my brother—solidly built, more man than boy, sporting a shaved head and well into his own teenage rebellion—who came up the driveway one Saturday afternoon on a black and chrome Yamaha 650 Special. He never took me for a ride and after a minor accident a short time later, he sold the bike and never drove again. Just a brief look at that machine, however, and I knew that this was something I just had to try.

When I was sixteen, I bought myself a secondhand Honda scooter with hoarded baby-sitting money. At the time my parents were pleased that I had my own transportation and that I had not gone after a "real" motorcycle. My Honda was small, red, "cute," and presumably safe. Unfortunately, scooters of the time had three major design flaws: a high center of gravity, small wheels, and high torque. In combination with youthful inexperience, these three things resulted in disaster one June day when, wearing no protective clothing, driving too fast, and cutting a corner too sharply, I lost control. My fingers wrapped around the handgrips, I panicked and froze, and rode the machine all the way down, shattering an elbow on impact. The sound of my skin and muscles tearing while tendons pulled away from disintegrating bones is one that will stay with me for the rest of my life. My mother watched as an orthopedic surgeon picked bits of sand and gravel out of my mangled arm and listened to him explain how my triceps had been ripped off the skeletal structure and would have to be surgically reattached with titanium screws. Small wonder that any enchantment my family might have felt with my choice of transport—and admittedly there was never very much—disappeared that day. It was different for me though. Months of physical therapy followed reconstructive surgery, and as my arm healed and strengthened, I worked toward the day when I could ride again. For reasons that I could not articulate at the time, I had to get back to the flow of the road beneath two wheels, the rush of the wind, and the pulse of four-stroke, two-piston engine. The next time, I knew, it would be on a full-sized motorcycle.

At nineteen I moved to Maine for college and stayed to teach high school social studies in Presque Isle, a small town near the Canadian border. I bought a motorcycle there—a Honda Shadow 500. She was a spunky little low-slung machine: five gears, a loose clutch, a burgundy tank, and a black seat. I had "Rosie" for years. Together we drove at speed through the low rolling potato and timber districts of Aroostook County, Maine's largest and most sparsely populated region. The riding season was short and the winters were long, but roaming the border country until the day ice seized the road was important to me.

Presque Isle, as well as the hamlets that surrounded it, was a safe, traditional, white, religious, and staunchly conservative community. Although I was warmly welcomed by my colleagues, students, and community as a whole, I was—and knew that I would always be—"from away."

The superintendent of schools admitted that one of the reasons he had hired me was because I was "different" and an outsider. He felt that it was good for students to have contact with someone who might have viewpoints foreign to those typically generated in a lovely yet isolated district. Before I taught my first class, however, my principal pulled me aside and warned me about the dangers of "radicalism," and the need to "uphold community values and standards." I walked a fine line as I taught. I loved my classroom and my students, but it was often mentally exhausting work. On the bike, however, out there with Rosie between the fields and the forests, I could leave the restrictions of my classroom behind. Out there, with four hundred pounds of machinery humming beneath me, my thoughts would center on what was immediate—the road and the surrounding environment—and my mind would relax and renew. Out there, hundreds of miles of secondary road riding later, I came to know, and to love, a region that was not my own.

Occasionally I took my students out. It was mostly young women who rode "up back" on Rosie, and usually I took them up along the river or out to the border. They knew at sixteen what I knew: that they wanted to create something different in their lives, something that they suspected they might not find there in the bucolic and insulated society that was northern Maine. I took them riding because I hoped they would feel an inkling of what motorcycles like Rosie have taught me: that fear can be managed and freedom can be achieved whether one stays within one's own region or leaves it entirely.

There were contradictions, however. As much as my motorcycle life was meant to be lived on my own terms, to some extent I hid the fact that it existed. I rarely drove my bike to school, as I sensed that my administration would not approve of the flaunting of such a thing. I also successfully hid Rosie from my parents for a couple of years, until my father, visiting for Thanksgiving, took an impromptu poke around the barn where I had her stored for the winter. He and my mother were not amused. They thought that what they referred to as my "latent death wish" had been buried a long time ago. What I could not explain to them at the time, what they were unable and unwilling to listen to, was that the machine they saw as destruction—unenclosed, unsafe, frivolous—I saw as liberation.

In 1995, my father was diagnosed with cancer and I resigned my teaching position at the end of the school year so that I could return to Massachusetts to help my mother care for him. Knowing that having a motorcycle would only strain an already emotionally stressed household, I took one last ride along the river and sold Rosie to my boyfriend. A year later, and with Dad much improved, I joined the Peace Corps and left for Eastern Europe. There was no motorcycle in my life for three years and I missed it terribly.

From this hour I ordain myself loos'd of limits
And imaginary lines....

—Walt Whitman
Leaves of Grass, "Song of the Open Road"

BREAKING
THE LIMIT

WE SAT ON THE OUTDOOR TERRACE of a Chinese restaurant that overlooked the broad, tree-shaded boulevard of Princeton's main street. Sergio was from Mexico. Tall and slim, he had a diplomat's resumé and a quick mind. We had met a few hours before during the midmorning break of a three-hour calculus class and had made plans to continue our conversation over lunch. Tea arrived, a small stainless steel pot and delicate porcelain cups that fit into the curvature of a palm. I poured while Sergio spoke of life in Mexico City and how violent it had become in recent years. He paused, watching a blonde woman with a baby carriage cross the street at an intersection as traffic came to a stop for her.

"It's different here. Silent, peaceful. You know what will and will not happen." The woman guided the carriage up the beveled curb and onto the sidewalk. Traffic resumed. "But it's somehow sterile, don't you think?" I nodded.

"It's good though," I said. "It's easy to live here, don't you think? You don't have to constantly be watching." I told him about the street life in Eastern Europe that had become normal to me: the noise of the bazaars, the grit, the beggars and the livestock, the undercurrent of instability and struggle that sometimes flashed to violence. For good or ill, what roiled in the streets of many other nations was not here in New Jersey suburbia. Our present reality was a different one, controlled and sterile perhaps but "this will all be normal soon."

"Yes, I expect so. I think we're all adjusting well." A vintage car rolled slowly, unnoticed, up the street. It passed the restaurant, momentarily hesitated for a left-turning vehicle, accelerated, and backfired with the explosion of a handgun. The metal teapot fell to the flagstones and the porcelain cups overturned on the table, drenching everything as Sergio and I ducked toward the shelter of the low wall that encircled the terrace. Halfway off my chair I stopped, paused, and straightened.

"It's a car. It's only a car." I mopped at the table with shaking hands, righting the cups. Sergio's face was white and a vein pulsed visibly in his temple. He stared at me, slouched in his chair, his brown eyes gone nearly black with the dilation of his pupils.

"Yes, I think we're all adjusting well, don't you?"

Despite what I told Sergio, as the weeks stretched on, things did not feel ever-more "normal" and I was having a hard time adjusting to a culture and a country that was my own, but was also fantastically alien. "Culture shock," I discovered, was not something that just affected foreign students. Princeton, New Jersey, and the graduate school program for which I had moved there, had little that I recognized.

The previous two and a half years I had been based in a small city near the Serbian border, working in Bulgaria and Macedonia with the Peace Corps. During the time I lived there, street demonstrations over mismanagement and corruption had eventually led to the collapse of the national government. Skyrocketing inflation had meant that fuel, food, and medicine were scarce or simply unavailable for weeks or months at a time. My one-room apartment was in a Stalinist concrete high-rise and I hauled water by the bucketful from a spring bubbling up under a railroad trestle on the other side of the city when the heating system failed and the pipes froze and split. Through two long Balkan winters I taught English and history in an often unheated building where meltwater from the cracks in the roof ran down the stairwell. My spare time was spent coordinating relief and aid programs for two local orphanages, where children lived, and died, in the most squalid of conditions. Life there had not been easy but it was a life I had grown used to.

I felt I was ready to come back to the States, at least temporarily, when I left the Peace Corps, and looked forward to the prospect of graduate school. What I expected at Princeton's Woodrow Wilson School of Public and International Affairs was a profound study of issues of social justice, politics, and policy, and an examination of practical stratagems for how to create effective programming. What I got, especially that first year, was theory, lots of it, and what seemed to be endless required courses in statistical analysis, economic theory, and political utilitarianism. I missed my friends and my colleagues half a world away. I dreaded the cocktail parties and the loud campus bars. The joyful gatherings of song and homemade wine drunk in small, cold rooms made warm by laughter and stories were gone. I was miserable. At three in the morning I would often sit on the carved stone benches in the formal gardens behind what was once Woodrow Wilson's home, wondering where I was and why I had come there. I felt like I was living in a movie set, something that would crack and fall away in a few moments. The sense of unreality and dislocation continued for weeks, and sometimes I wondered if I might have gone a little insane.

Things began to change on the day a new friend invited me to go look at airplanes at a landing strip twenty miles north of Princeton. It was on the way back to campus that I saw a motorcycle parked on someone's front lawn with a FOR SALE sign tucked between the handlebars and the windshield. I pulled over and walked across the grass to look at a piece of machinery that somehow had just started a song playing inside my mind. She was a Harley-Davidson 1200 Sportster, red with chrome accessories, black leather saddlebags and seat, custom straight pipes, a peanut tank, and less than three thousand miles on the odometer. I wrapped my right hand around the throttle and immediately realized that this motorcycle was something I recognized. Maybe she could teach me—as Rosie had taught me—love for, and connection with, a region that was not my own. Maybe this motorcycle could, as Rosie had done years ago, open a whole new landscape of thought and motion.

Lucy, as I came to know that Sportster, did all of that and more.

. . .

I left New Jersey the day after I finished my master's degree. The photographs had all been taken, my dormitory room was occupied by another graduate student, and most of my few possessions were stored in a warehouse in Trenton. My family had come down from their homes in Massachusetts and New Brunswick for the three days of commencement celebration. Gloria, my biological mother, had come from Quebec to be introduced to my parents for the first time. They were all very proud and it had been an emotional weekend. My mom put twenty-four roses into my arms, but no one brought any sort of graduation gift. It was in part because I asked them not to. I would be moving to a new city for a new job after the summer and I didn't want to have to move or store extra "stuff." My mother also genuinely feared that I would not survive my motorcycle adventures. What would she do with my graduation gift then? We actually had a brief conversation, which I truncated with a dismissive laugh, about what color my casket should be.

My mom is a strong and intelligent woman, with a sense of humor and a deep devotion to her family that smooths occasional fractures and keeps us all, however far we may travel, connected. She and I do not, however, always hold the same viewpoints and values. The volatility of our relationship was such that I left home a few weeks after graduating from high school and did not return for anything more than a holiday for the seven years that followed. I was the second child my parents adopted and am ten months younger than my brother. My brother always seemed to find the common ground with Mom that I lacked, and I most often speculated that our clashing personalities were due to typical mother-daughter conflicts. In darker moments, however, I also wondered if it had to do with the fact that we were genetically different, that this tall, dark-haired, home-centered woman saw little in her petite, pale, willful daughter to remind her of herself. We are better now, my mother and I, much more accepting and loving of one another as individuals, and we spend as much time together as possible. But I am still willful and she still worries about me.

My friends and family were generally fearful about this whole project although I had traveled alone many times before and my ability to take care of myself in places foreign and far away for months and years at a time had been amply demonstrated. Their pessimism involved the combination of the usual list of hazards supposedly inherent to a woman traveling alone superimposed upon their general horror of motorcycles. Mom put it succinctly: "You're going to be raped, robbed, and run over by an eighteen-wheeler."

"Can't you go with a group?" she asked. "Can't you get one of your biker friends to go with you?"

If there was a group of bikers leaving New Jersey for points west and north the first week of June I was unaware of it. It is also not a light thing to ask someone to share weeks of travel. I know married couples who would never attempt such a thing, the stresses of the road and constant movement being what they are. I do have many friends who drive motorcycles, several who would have loved to do a long-distance trip like this one, and a couple of whom I would have actually asked to come with me. The problem was that they all worked, had families, spouses, and children, and none of the ones that I would have asked to come and spend three months on two wheels could have taken the time. My boyfriend had a bike. I asked him to come, but along with a lower back that did not tolerate long days on his Kawasaki, he had a start-up company to run. As it turned out, there were other reasons, too.

I must admit that I did not search especially thoroughly in the attempt to find a companion. It is a character flaw that I find it difficult to ask for help, to admit weakness, to be honest about fear. Entwined in all the other reasons for wanting to attempt such a trip, I wanted to be able to do it alone, to be strong and capable enough not to have to ask anyone's permission or aid.

Of course, the whole concept did make me nervous. I am not a fool, I would very much like to live a long and healthy life, and I had never attempted a motorcycle trip that lasted more than a long weekend before I set out for Alaska. Although I can do my own basic motorcycle maintenance, upkeep, and some troubleshooting, I am not a good repair mechanic. The Harley Owner's Group and Road America membership cards in my wallet would get me the same benefits that a AAA membership has for those on four wheels, but motorcycle parts and repair shops are not as closely spaced as those that deal with automobiles. The distances on the maps looked so huge: Kansas,

Montana, the Yukon, Alaska. What would happen if I found myself on the side of the road with a major mechanical problem?

Driving motorcycles does have an element of danger to it. Although motorcyclists statistically have 50 percent fewer accidents per mile than people who operate cars, the fatality rate in collisions is three times higher. I am a careful and experienced driver, but crosswinds, truck blast, animals or objects in the road, as well as other drivers who simply do not "see" motorcycles are always a risk.

The last of my nervousness came from the stereotypes that are sometimes associated with women on motorcycles. Unfortunately, popular culture, such as it is, often portrays a woman on a motorcycle as a sex kitten, dominatrix, lesbian, or whore, and the prevalent image is more about high heels and bikinis and women draped over the backseat of a bike driven by some large—and often hairy—man, than it is about capable women who drive their own bikes wearing sensible boots. B-grade Hollywood films and magazines targeted for the male audience often objectify women associated with motorcycles as "biker babes," "fender bunnies," or "biker chicks." There are elements of biker culture that perpetuate these myths. When riding two-up, the person on the back is often referred to as "riding bitch," and I have often seen bikers wearing T-shirts that proclaim: "If you can read this the bitch fell off."

Thankfully, I have only rarely had encounters with negative prejudicial behavior based on what I drive or the leather jacket that I wear. Strangely enough, the few times that it has happened, it has tended to be other women who assumed that I was either a slut or a renegade and they didn't want their sons, husbands, or boyfriends anywhere near me. Fine. I am capable of dealing with that on an individual and aberrant basis, but what would small-town America and Canada generally think of a lone woman, dressed in black leather, rolling into town?

It was time to find out.

I WOKE UP EARLY ON THE morning of June second, having slept badly. Too nervous to eat much breakfast, I checked over my bags one more time as Dave dressed and put in his contact lenses. We had been together for the better part of a year; he was a good man and a good friend. I listened to him running water in the bathroom sink, the sound of his bare feet, muffled but still audible on the plush carpet, and felt my chest constrict and the loneliness begin. I would miss him more than I cared to admit, and although I wished it otherwise, I knew instinctively that the moment I walked out the door, the end of our relationship would begin. Feeling slightly nauseous, I looked over my things, willing strength and toughness, now and for the coming months.

You can do this.

There wasn't much in those two bags, but the essentials were there for fairly comfortable, self-contained travel: a tent, a ground sheet, and a thin, inflatable sleeping pad would be my house, and a blue construction tarpaulin would be Lucy's garage. A Gore-Tex jacket and rain pants, thin polypropylene gloves for layering under one of two other pairs of heavier gloves, a fleece hat, socks, underwear, a tank top, nylon shorts, a pair of jeans, long underwear, nylon running pants, a T-shirt, a silk scarf, a bandana, a fleece jacket, and running shoes would be my supplemental wardrobe. An ankle-length black knit skirt was tucked at the bottom of the bag, insurance for an unexpected occasion in some town where bug-splattered blue jeans might be inappropriate. I was wearing everything else: a black hooded zip-front shirt, black tank top, green army pants, and heavy black boots, belt, and leather jacket. Walt Whitman's *Leaves of Grass* shared space with my journal, a guidebook, a Rand McNally road atlas, a few photographs of friends and family, and a tiny address book. For Lucy's upkeep there was a tool kit with the usual assortment of wrenches, a tire pressure gauge, a can of Fix-a-Flat, extra spark plugs, rubber tubing, electrical tape, and a quart of oil. Tucked between the leaves of my road atlas I also carried an eagle feather. A friend who visited the far north every year had found it in the Yukon and had given it to me as a sort of talisman. He thought it would keep me safe.

Dave came out into the bedroom and we sat together for a few more minutes. He seemed to have trouble meeting my eyes so I dropped into a chair across from where he sat on the corner of the bed and propped my boots up on the frame next to his bare feet. I looked at them, our feet resting there on the dark mahogany, and thought of how this one visual snapshot, Dave shoeless and Karen booted, said so much about who was staying, who was leaving, and the very different places that we were in our lives. A few miserable tears slipped down my nose.

We had met the September before at a street-side picnic table beside a local sandwich shop where he sat alone with his newspaper and hoagie.

"Could we sit with you?" my girlfriend Sondy asked him. He nodded. We sat down and Sondy and Dave began an easy conversation. Dave was bright, articulate, and had a hockey player's body: broad shoulders, narrow waist, and powerful legs. Sondy liked what she saw. She fished a little: "So what do you do in your free time?"

"I have a motorcycle." I looked up from my Greek salad with new interest.

"Karen has a motorcycle, too." Sondy nudged my leg under the table, an almost imperceptible signal between women—*well go on, this one's for you.* "You should go riding together sometime."

The next weekend we did take the bikes out; over Sourland Mountain and across the long rolling gradual drop through open farm country toward the tarnished silver line of the Delaware River. Dave was a cautious rider. He was scrupulous in the maintenance of his Kawasaki and, even when the road opened up to mile-long views of asphalt free for the taking, he obeyed every posted speed limit. The way a person drives a motorcycle reveals something of their personality, and perhaps I would have protected my heart better had I remembered this as our motorcycle friendship became a romance.

Never an ardent or spontaneous man, as the months slipped by, Dave's lack of obvious enthusiasm for our relationship slid toward apparent disinterest. He always seemed glad to see me when I knocked on the door of his third-floor condominium, provided that I called first, but he rarely came to see me at my university dormitory and never met me for coffee without scheduling it at least two days in advance. He was consumed with running his new company, I told myself. He's a somewhat shy and restrained person, I thought. Most of all, I believed that the death of his father in December of that year, a loving parent with whom he had been extremely close, had left him temporarily bereft of the capacity to feel deeply connected to another person. Although I was in love with Dave, and told him so, I never asked for a commitment, a future plan, or talked of a life together after I finished school. All I wanted was for him to want me in his life as much as I wanted him in mine. However, as spring came and went Dave showed no more—although no less—interest in our relationship than he had on our first awkward dinner date.

Now it was June, and I was ready to leave, both New Jersey and a relationship that, as much as I wanted it, seemed to be over. Surprisingly, in those last minutes in his apartment as I reached for my jacket and scarf, Dave told me that he wanted to give it another try.

"Don't give up on me. I'll try and come see you, maybe in Oregon."

I nodded, unable to speak, wanting to trust what he said, wanting to believe that if I only waited long enough, told him how I felt, how much I desired him in my life, that he would someday feel as strongly as I did.

We carried my bags down the stairs and he watched as I adjusted the straps and buckles that secured my T-bag—a piece of motorcycle luggage topped by a sleeping bag roll—to Lucy's frame. A soft-bodied backpack followed, lashed to the T-bag with three compression straps. Both bags rested on an eight-inch steel rack bolted to the saddle frame. I checked the saddle-bags where I kept most of my tools and spare parts, along with the things I needed more frequently: wallet, guidebook, and journal. Finished, I turned to Dave and he wrapped his arms around me in a hard embrace, his breath soft in my ear.

"Goddamn . . . you're going to Alaska." He held me for a few moments, kissed me quickly, then released me with "Ride safe," turned, and was gone.

I had asked him to leave me there and go back upstairs before I finished suiting up. There are few things worse than crying inside your own helmet and I was not sure how much longer my remaining shreds of composure were going to last.

Lucy started quickly and cleanly, idling with a soft, deep pulse while I inserted foam earplugs and buckled the strap of my full-face helmet. Over the protests of some of my biker friends, I had traded the powerful explosive roar of customized straight exhaust pipes for the quieter and lower rumble of factory stock exhausts. Before the change, I had occasionally taken perverse pleasure in gunning the throttle just to hear her roar as I drove up the refined stillness that is Princeton's main thoroughfare and had learned that some of the expensive cars parked on Nassau Street had alarm systems sensitive enough to be activated by a carefully timed blast of sound. It was great fun. Juvenile prankishness in Princeton was one thing, but there was no sense in horrifying half the continent with an overly loud exhaust system and making myself more conspicuous than I already was. I swung my leg over the saddle, took a deep breath, pulled the kickstand up, and drove out into the rising heat of the day.

At first the roads were familiar. In the last two years, I had driven most of the secondaries that sweep out of central New Jersey and into the low rolls and folds of the Delaware Valley. People who have never traveled through New Jersey except via the concrete, steel, and industry-lined perversions of landscape that flank the Parkway or Interstate 95 often do not realize that there are regions of New Jersey where "The Garden State" motto is well given. The Delaware Valley, marked by long swathes of open farm country, tiny historic villages, and roads that follow the contours of the land, is one of them. In Newton, I stopped at an Exxon station for gas and water. The air was heavy, white-hazed, and humid. According to a bank clock, at 10:15 A.M. it was eighty-eight degrees.

Sheer adrenaline had kept me going for an hour and a half, but as I stepped off Lucy, peeled off a couple of sweaty layers of clothing, and adjusted a compression strap, the reality of what had just begun set in. *This is lunacy. What am I doing?* Every negative thing—and there were so many—that people had said when they heard about what I was planning for the summer came flooding back in a cacophony of internal chatter. *This is insane, a deathwish. You can't drive all that way. It's not the right bike, it's too small. Do you realize how far away the West Coast is?* My mother's voice rang in my ears: *You'll be robbed, raped, or run over by an eighteen-wheeler.* My hands shook as I held the pump nozzle and I spilled gasoline over the tank exterior. Swearing softly, I took the bandana from around my neck and carefully wiped up the gas. Splashed fuel can do ugly things to a paint job and I was bike-proud enough to want to protect mine.

The man behind the register had steady eyes, brown skin, and a sweet smile. He took my five-dollar bill and, looking through the window at the bags on Lucy, asked me where I was going. I almost didn't believe the unnatural squeak of my own voice when I heard the word "Alaska." Two minutes later, out on the pavement by the pumps, I was wedging my water bottle between the T-bag and the backpack when the attendant appeared.

"Here," he said, pressing a tiny tiger-tail keychain into my hand. "You should collect something from each state that you go through." He cast no judgment on my destination or choice of vehicle and in that gift, a promotional Exxon key chain, and the small suggestion to gather mementos along the way, was the implicit statement that such a journey was possible. My mind quieted and my confidence returned as he shook my hand and wished me luck.

I crossed the Delaware River at Dingmans Ferry and headed up the opposite side of the valley on Route 739 into rising wind, oppressive heat, and gathering clouds. Thunder rumbled a deep bass undercurrent that I could feel in my chest, a frequency below the rumble of Lucy's exhaust but palpable as my own heartbeat. The storm was coming. I crested a ridge near White Mills and as the pavement swung around the slashed outcrop of a road cut, I looked straight into a black-purple, sickly yellow-edged mass of clouds. The gloom of late twilight was beneath boiling clouds too heavy, too saturated, to let even the feeblest ray of sunshine through. Route 6 is a ridge road, too high and too exposed for comfort when the storm began. In a thunderstorm, a motorcyclist is not protected from lightning strike as she would be in a car. A single bolt would fry a rider for sure, and what the electricity did not do, the impact of being thrown from the bike would finish. The lightning came in disconcerting and irregular combinations of huge, jagged white bolts and flashing incandescent sheets as the wind began to howl and fat raindrops exploded off my faceshield.

Twisting the throttle and leaning hard, carving bike and body into the curves, driving aggressively for speed and descent off the exposed summit of Salt Hill, I looked for something, anything, that would provide cover. An open garage door fronted a darkened house with no lights halfway down to the valley, and as a particularly vivid flash of purple-white light lit the storm from beneath, I ducked in like a rabbit diving for cover, not caring whose garage I was invading. Beside the looming hulk of a tarp-draped motorhome I shut Lucy down and dropped her kickstand to rest on the concrete floor. The full fury of the storm broke seconds later in a deluge of rain hammering in a deafening timpani roar off the metal roof of the garage, explosive lightning, and violent crashing thunder. There was no movement from the house and no car in the garage, so I assumed that the owners were temporarily away and mentally thanked them for sheltering uninvited guests. Munching on a few half-melted chocolate-covered pretzels I leaned against the door frame and watched the weather, mesmerized by the storm, and grateful that I was not out in it. Torrents of water turned the road into a shallow, swift-running stream in a matter of minutes.

"Staying dry?" The voice was low and measured, totally unexpected, and right behind my left shoulder. Pretzels scattered all over the floor and I whirled to face the owner of the voice, and presumably the garage.

"Terribly sorry. Didn't realize you were home . . . lights out in the house . . . should have checked . . . the storm." I babbled on until his slow grin and raised hand stopped me.

"It's OK, not a problem. You can wait it out here as long as you like." Ed, as he introduced himself, was tall, gray, lanky, retired, and the owner of the garage.

We shared what remained of my pretzels and talked of families and travel. Ed was looking forward to his own summer journey: a monthlong, cross-country ramble in his motorhome, to visit far-flung children and grandchildren. He wished me well before returning to the house to check on his electronics.

A Harley-Davidson Electra Glide pulled up at the gas station in Troy, Pennsylvania, where I stopped for fuel and water, and a bearded biker with tattoos and a tight Harley T-shirt stretched over his broad chest swung off. Electra Glides are big cruising bikes, outfitted for long-distance comfort. They often have the latest in motorcycle electronics installed—everything from radio and CD players to hand warmers in the grips—and come with a price tag that can exceed twenty-five thousand dollars. The bike was new, gleaming dark forest green, immaculately maintained, and driven by a man who looked critically at mine.

"You call that a tourer?" He was clearly skeptical of a Sportster carrying the baggage that bespoke a long trip. Sportsters are the smallest of the Harley line, and although mine, with 1200ccs, was one step up from the smallest 883cc model, it was still not considered a bike for long-distance riding. At approximately five hundred pounds, Sportsters have a lot of power relative to their mass, which makes them agile and extremely maneuverable. They are excellent street bikes for town and city driving but they do not have any of the things that the larger cruising bikes like the Honda Gold Wing or the Harley Electra Glides have: wind fairings, heavy frames, sophisticated electronics, or hard luggage. To make mine a little more distance friendly, I had added a three-quarters windshield—tall enough to take most of the force of the wind off my chest—and had changed the original "peanut" gas tank for one with larger capacity. Loaded, with a full tank of gas, I could drive more than 130 miles in normal conditions before I had to refuel.

"Well no, but that's what it's going to be." Tired, and at the end of a long, hot, and weather-filled first day on the road, my hackles were up and I was ready to dislike this man for his implied judgment of Lucy. However, as we stood talking about motorcycle touring, I found my irritation dissipating with the friendliness and candor that was just below his rough exterior.

"I have only one rule," he informed me. "Always wear gloves!" He peeled off one of his gloves to show me the deep scars that creased his palms from fingers to wrist. "I laid the bike down a couple of years back. No gloves and skidded to a stop on my hands." He tapped one of his palms lightly with the fingers of the other hand and then wiggled all ten for my inspection. "Everything works, but I can't feel too much there anymore." The fact that he wore only a T-shirt on his upper torso, leaving most if not all of his epidermis above the waist exposed to road rash, did not concern him. He loved two things: women and driving his motorcycle. Living close to the Jersey shore, he was retired military and liked to spend weekends in Atlantic City. There he met "lady friends" who were strategically located: geographically close enough to visit in a pleasant day's motorcycle drive, and far enough from one another that the chances of them meeting and sharing information was minimal. He was heading back to Jersey now after a few romantic days with a widow out near Warren and I was laughing by the time he left.

The sun was lowering and the weariness of the day was setting in when I climbed back on Lucy. The aftermath of the storm was written at roadside; detritus from uprooted trees, collapsed fences, and broken branches littered the fields. At one intersection, where the traffic lights had failed, firemen in yellow overalls directed the flow of cars around a heap of shattered window glass and by the time I passed the wreckage of another three-car accident strewn across a field I was again thankful for Ed, his garage, and the general kindness of strangers.

Hills Creek State Park was a gorgeous little spot with a small clear blue lake tucked into the low rolling hills west of Mansfield, Pennsylvania. Wooded tent sites with pine-needle bases went for sixteen dollars a night; more expensive than I thought camping should be, but I was too tired to think of going elsewhere. The ranger was a friendly man who spent time helping me choose a spot that he thought would be quiet and comfortable.

"Where'd you come from today?" he asked.

"Central Jersey."

"You've come quite a ways."

It was the first of many times that I would hear that phrase.

THE BIRDS WERE CHIRPING WHEN I woke snug and warm in my sleeping bag with the cool breath of damp forest air on my face. I looked through the mesh net of my tent door and it took me a moment to remember where I was and why I was sleeping in the middle of the woods rather than in the dormitory. *Ah yes, the road to Alaska.* My hands were sore and I flexed them, gingerly massaging what felt like bruising in the fleshy parts of my palms. I sat up and stretched forward, tensing as muscles, unaccustomed to sleeping on the ground after three hundred motorcycle miles, seized in a brief, painful spasm.

It was misty and chilly and the concrete floor of the shower house was freezing on my bare feet. The air temperature was perhaps twenty degrees colder than it had been the evening before. Instead of the full immersion of a shower, I opted for a quick splash of cold water over my face and hands, pulled on a clean pair of socks, stepped into yesterday's clothes, and didn't bother with a hairbrush. Life on the road was so much simpler.

I was pulling the tarpaulin from Lucy's frame when a juice box and granola bar that had been tucked into the folds fell to the ground. Who had put them there, and when? I looked around, but the few campsites that were visible through the trees and the mist were still and silent in the early morning light. Was it the family of the four-year-old who had come the evening before to stand and stare at Lucy as I set up my tent? He had shaken his blond head in wide-eyed shyness when I asked if he'd like to sit on a motorcycle. Was it the ranger? He knew that I was tired after a long day. Years ago, walking the long green tunnel that is the Appalachian Trail, one of my hiking buddies coined the term "trail magic" to put words to phenomena that all of us had experienced. When the sky was about to open up and a long day's walk had just begun, or we were so tired that we felt we couldn't go another step, there it was, trail magic: the kindness of a stranger, an unexpected clearing of clouds, a sheltered campsite, a fantastic view, or a perfect crocus growing from a split rock. Something would happen that reminded us of where we were, why we were there, and how lucky we were to be living and breathing that experience. Trail magic apparently works on motorcycle trips, too.

At Smethport, I left Route 6 and wound my way north through light rain on twisting, scabby, frost-heaved Routes 59 and 646, up the low ridges of the Alleghenies and through small, shabby, and undeniably lovely backwoods towns: Cyclone, Aiken, Derrick City, and Knapp Creek. Chilled from the rain and a fifty-degree start to the morning, I stopped in Franklinville, New York, at the Gates Creek Café. The café was small and cheery, with lemon-colored walls, blue-flowered curtains, and sun-filled booths pressed against the windows. Sue was the waitress. She was a tired-looking woman with lively blue eyes edged with thick, black mascara that did not match the fatigue in the rest of her face. Motherly and chatty, she put coffee, biscuits, and sausage gravy in front of me along with a bill for just over two dollars. Wiping her hands on her apron, she pointed to my helmet sitting in the corner of the booth.

"My husband and I had a bike," she said, "but we sold it." She paused for a moment. "It's my dream to have my own bike. Ride it myself I mean."

Motorcycling is still very much a man's world. Although there are a growing number of women who ride, race, and tour, it is still perceived in many circles as somehow "unladylike" or not suited to what women should be capable of. No one finds it odd when I step out from behind the wheel of a car, but when I step off my motorcycle and the helmet comes off, releasing a shoulder-length tangle of hair, people stop and stare. Sue was the first of many women I met on the trip who looked at me in part as some sort of affirmation that riding a motorcycle, without a man doing the driving, was possible.

A little later, dropping the change from my ten-dollar bill on the table, Sue leaned close and whispered, "I wish I were coming with you . . . you be careful, honey."

As I came into Niagara Falls, the mist from the cataract rose like smoke above the river, visible from two miles away. Closer, the fine gauze of water was palpable in the air. A green park with mature trees, wide lawns, and rainbowed flowerbeds lined the waters' edge, but downtown Niagara Falls was much less appealing. Abandoned buildings with gaping broken windows watched over entire city blocks given to grass and garbage. I drove down Ferry Avenue looking for the youth hostel where I would spend the night and found it tucked into a neighborhood where modest but well-constructed single-family detached homes were falling into total disrepair. The guidebook recommended, ". . . avoid walking alone on Ferry at night."

Despite the decayed backdrop, the park area along the riverbanks was spectacular. After all those hundreds of miles on the bike, it felt good to walk for a while, and I did; for miles along the park pathways tracing the riverbank, weaving my way through bridal parties toward the river overlooks. It was a sunny Saturday in June and the brides and grooms were out in force to have their pictures taken with the rushing water in the background. Three young women in yards of white lace, chiffon, and satin stood smiling into a battery of cameras while groomsmen in identical rented tuxedos and bridesmaids in dresses as colorful as the flowerbeds waited for their photo opportunity. I looked down at my heavy boots and blue jeans, thought about my hair carelessly pulled into a ponytail, and felt rather out of place. Not uncomfortable exactly, in my solitude and my functional clothing, but certainly different. I moved toward the falls' edge, away from the laughing groups, and into the hanging mist.

Just beyond the fragile barrier of two slender bars held between wrought-iron poles no more than three feet high, the Niagara River dropped over the edge of the chasm, 675,000 gallons of water per second, in blue-green torrents. The jagged rocks below were softened, almost lost, in rainbow mist. I leaned out over the balustrade. The spectacle, the draw to the edge, was compelling and mesmerizing; the same beckoning that one feels on the observation deck of a tall building or standing on the edge of a subway platform. Edgar Allan Poe once referred to this self-destructive impulse as the "Imp of the Perverse," and the Imp stood beside me as I leaned out over the water, my weight balanced on my hands and rib cage, staring into the torrent falling away, into oblivion, a few feet below. What would it be like to just step over the edge and into that water? In 1901, at the age of sixty-three, Annie Taylor had gone over these falls in a well-padded barrel. She survived the experience. Could I? Gulls floated, webbed feet paddling lightly, toward the precipice, looking for what I imagined were rapidly back-finning fish trying to escape the edge. The gulls took flight just before the drop, launching themselves out and off the verge, soaring through the spray over the void before wheeling back to float down again. Now that, I thought, would be the way to do things. Over the edge, but still in control.

EXHIBIT A: *Instructional Interlude*

A family of four piled out of the blue Windstar minivan, hustling to trot around the archeological site. They stopped and stared at me where I sat in the shade of an oak eating my lunch on the grass, as if I were another interpretive plaque.

Father: "It is a her!"

Mother: "I told them it was a girl." This was directed at me.

The little round boy, a floppy, round-brimmed hat perched above small, round glasses, paused to consider me for a moment.

"I didn't know that girls could ride motorcycles."

I repeated him to make sure I had understood: "You didn't know that girls could ride motorcycles?" He shook his head. "Girls can do nearly everything that boys can do," I told him quietly and, I hope, gently.

Mom spoke loudly as she herded her children down the path. Was it for my benefit or theirs? "Girls can do *anything* that boys can do!"

. . .

At a gas station in Canada I heard disturbing reports out of Detroit, my destination for the next day, from an eastbound biker. An Organization of American States meeting was taking place in the city and would continue through the early part of the week. Protesters had tried that day to block the Ambassador Bridge, which I had to cross on the next day. Detroit was reported to be under heavy security in an attempt to avoid a violent showdown. To make matters worse, another biker told me that the police were being overly zealous in stopping people who looked "suspicious." He told me to have my documents in order when I crossed the bridge and to expect to be searched as thoroughly as he had been.

Near Point Pelee I started looking for a campground and found nothing that was both affordable and *not* perched on a gravel pad surrounded by motorhomes. The one promise regarding travel safety that I had made both Dave and my parents was that I would stay in campgrounds or parks and not set up my tent alone in wilderness areas or farmers' back fields. It was a simple promise to make, but it meant that as afternoon stretched into evening I had to start searching for a place to stay. With nothing reasonable at Point Pelee, I backtracked fifteen miles and ended up at Wheatly Provincial Park. It cost nearly twenty-two dollars for a campsite, but in the evening I had a cheerful, if not entirely smoke-free, campfire, sputtering and hissing a few yards from my tent. The smoke was welcome as it seemed to keep away the mosquitoes, which rose in clouds from the flat shallow ponds that made this park a haven for migrating birds. Later that evening, I sat on the ground by the fire, feeding sticks slowly into it, writing, and eating cheese and crackers. Below was the sound of large carp splashing in the silver ponds and above the soft twittering of birds as they winged through the trees hunting for insects. Four Canada geese flew by in a low and abbreviated V-formation, the sound of their feathers brushing through the wind in gentle counterpoint to the alto of their honks. Such peace. I could almost hear the earth breathe in deep, slow rhythms.

AT THE AMBASSADOR BRIDGE BETWEEN WINDSOR and Detroit, the
border patrol was only marginally more thorough about checking my papers.
When I had crossed the border before, either by car or motorcycle, the most I
had ever had to produce was a driver's license. This time, in addition to the
license, they wanted a passport and vehicle registration as well as answers to
questions concerning my point of origin and destination. The point of origin
was easy, New Jersey still did not seem that far away, but to give "Alaska" as a
destination seemed ridiculous, even suspicious. I told the officers that I had
come to Detroit to do some interviewing in the city, and that this was my destination. It was partially true.

I asked the border patrol official in the booth at the bridge for directions
to the street address of an organization in the northeast part of the city that
did work similar to the firm I would be joining in September, and he sent me
to talk to a cluster of police officers in black jumpsuits. They stood, with seemingly little to do, in front of the steel doors of the immigration office. It had
been a quiet day, as the people protesting the OAS conference were in other
parts of the city. The officers were bored and a little cold standing there in the
wind, but the city was paying them overtime and they would stay throughout

the afternoon. Helpful and friendly, they seemed to be glad of the distraction of my questions and gave me detailed directions to a side street off East Jefferson Avenue, even calling the dispatch office in that part of the city to check on the route. They were hesitant, however, about the neighborhood where I was going.

"If you get lost or miss your turn," one told me, "don't stop. Don't ask anyone for directions. Go straight to the precinct on East Jefferson, it's on the northwest corner. If you were a guy, I'd say just turn around and do your thing, but as you're a white woman alone . . . well, you know."

I didn't get lost, and although northeast Detroit clearly has its problems—the usual sights associated with a declining and depopulating industrial city—I've seen and been through worse, much worse, in other places and in other countries. Try Bucharest in Romania, Sumgait in Azerbaijan, or Maputo in Mozambique for true poverty, desperation, and lack of opportunity. What I noticed most about the street life near East Jefferson was the lack of it. Gaping, glassless windows of deserted homes and businesses looked out onto fissured sidewalks and empty lots where prairie grass grew thigh high. A solitary elderly black woman shuffled slowly toward a corner bodega, a plastic shopping bag clutched tightly in one hand, a purse slung bandolier style across her chest. Once this had been a prosperous and bustling district. The history showed in the quality of the architecture and in the ornamentation of wood and stonework visible under sagging eaves. I had no concept of what those streets might be after dark fell, but as I moved through them on a late weekday morning, the sense was of decay rather than violence.

I left Detroit late that afternoon as the rain was just beginning to spit from pendulous ugly clouds, retracing my route back toward the bridge and the intersection of Route 12 headed south. At a stoplight on East Jefferson a police cruiser pulled up next to me. Both officers were white and the one in the passenger seat had his window rolled down and was staring at me. I flipped up my helmet shield and returned his gaze.

"Are you lost?" he asked.

"No. Just headed down toward Twelve."

"Then you know where you're going?"

"Yes." Like his brethren at the bridge, I got the distinct impression that he thought a white woman alone in this part of the city was something of an anomaly. I wondered if they ever got out of their cruisers in those once-beautiful neighborhoods where it seemed that suspicion, stereotype, and poverty shaped the relationship between those who lived on these streets and those who policed them.

The rain started in earnest as I drove out of the city, past what seemed to be the largest collection of topless bars and triple-X-rated video stores east of the Mississippi. The number and variety were truly astonishing. Hard-faced men slouched down the street hunched under jacket collars while shivering women in tight cocktail dresses stood outside the black painted doors of windowless bars. For sheer seediness, the east side of Detroit that my officers at the bridge were so worried about had nothing on the south.

As the afternoon progressed, the road conditions went from bad to worse as high winds joined drenching sheets of cold rain, and oncoming rush-hour traffic hurried over slick, ill-repaired roads. I drove through Inkster, Wayne, Ypsilanti, and Saline in a southwestern slant with the force of wind and rain coming in from the west beating on my right shoulder. By the time I reached Clinton, the sensation in my hands was almost gone and I was half blind from driving with my faceshield partially up so that I could have some visibility in the torrents of water. When a northbound eighteen-wheeler plowed through a deep puddle and threw something akin to a tidal wave up and over me in a buffet of exploding water and sound, I knew that it was time to stop before I hurt myself.

I pulled into a gas station and peeled gloves off hands that were strangely purplish red from the combination of wet windchill and black dye bleeding out of soaked lambskin. I wrapped my fingers around a steaming cup of coffee as Stan, a slim man with a straggled mustache who was also sheltering out of the rain, came over to talk about motorcycles and traveling. He prattled on about the weather, a grown son in a different part of the country, and a bike he had as a teenager. I nodded dumbly, so numbed and saturated that it was a few minutes before I could actually hold a coherent conversation. Clarity slowly returned with the humid warmth of the station. Stan told me about his dreams of building a truck and going to Alaska. *So go,* I thought. Despite the horridness of the afternoon's weather, there was, strangely, no place else that I would rather have been.

Putting up a tent in the middle of a deluge—which I later found out dumped an inch and a half of rain on the country south of Detroit inside of three hours—seemed an unnecessarily damp and foolish proposal, and I began the hunt for a hotel in Clinton. Actually finding a bed with a roof over it was more difficult than I thought it would be, however. Clinton's single B&B was closed and dark, as was the grand old hotel in the center of town. Driving conditions had not improved on Route 12, and the light was beginning to fail, but I felt confident, even as I plowed back into the downpour, knowing that I would not be spending the night in a tent huddled against the driving rain. This was, however, little consolation half an hour later—and I could feel a prickle of rising panic—as I stood before the cold eyes of the woman behind a reception desk in Springville. She scanned my dripping jacket, muddy boots, and rain-matted hair.

"No, we're completely booked."

This was strange considering that there were a total of two pickup trucks and one car parked in front of her string of small cottages and row of motel doors. Did she think I was an outrider for a whole pack of dripping and muddy bikers? There was nothing I could do but step back into the rain. In the lowering dusk and worsening visibility, I pulled into my last option in that township: a tiny place called Brunner's. It was a small residential house with a FOR SALE sign out front and three upstairs bedrooms converted to en-suite rooms. Mrs. Brunner, a heavy, blonde German woman, was brusque at first. Along with a credit card I had twenty-five dollars in cash in my pocket and she was asking for thirty-five in cash.

"No, vee don't take credit cards," she told me.

"Is there an ATM nearby?"

"Oh . . . five miles up this road, left, and then right, I tink there's one dere at the store."

My stomach knotted as I looked out the window at the deep gray sky and the rain hammering against the glass. I had an awful intuition that I should not get back on Lucy. My voice shook as I explained to Mrs. Brunner about the weather, and proposed that if I could just give her the twenty-five in cash now, I would leave whatever she wanted as a deposit in the morning while I drove to the ATM. She considered this for a moment, scowling and staring directly into my eyes. I'm sure I looked pale, pinched, and thoroughly miserable because, seconds later, the hard lines of her face softened and she agreed. Lucy, I was told, should be pulled up onto the concrete walkway under the eaves of her home and I was to go change into something dry immediately. By the time I brought my bags in there was a cup of hot coffee and a cellophane-wrapped cheese pastry sitting on the small table beside my door. With maps spread out and drying on a chair, I took a hot shower and climbed into bed. The crisp sheets smelled of cedar chests and mothballs and I was asleep before many minutes had passed.

SHE WAS DEAD, OR NEARLY SO, by the time I reached her. She shuddered once, spasmodically, as her nervous system reached the electrical and chemical conclusion that all the other organs that sustained it had ceased to function. She had no pulse and the already thickening blood that clogged her nose and matted her hair had stopped flowing. Later I kept thinking, *What if that girl in the road crew vest hadn't come out of the store to talk to me about motorcycles? What if that red light hadn't held me at the intersection for just those few critical extra seconds? What if my still-wet gloves had been easier to pull on as I left Mrs. Brunner's? That would have been me, dying at the bottom of an embankment in the tangle of an eighteen-wheeler and a red sedan.* As it was, I missed being in the middle of a deadly wreck by what I estimate to be about thirty seconds.

The morning had a cold beginning, but the landscape sparkled in the clean washed sunshine that follows a storm and I was delighted to be out, on the road, and moving through clear still air into a day that looked as if it might just be perfect. The tourist maps labeled this part of southern Michigan as "The Irish Hills" and it was well named for its emerald slopes, tree-edged fields, and tiny jeweled ponds caught in the hollows. Traffic was light and Route 12 rolled and lifted, following the contours of the land, as the best roads do, rather than arrowing the shortest distance between points. I passed through Springville and Somerset, angling toward the Indiana border. I hummed an old Eagles tune inside my helmet, held an easy fifty-five, rounded a long, slow corner near the village of Moscow, and started down a gradual slope with another curve at the bottom. It was just before eight in the morning when I saw it, and the song died with what came into view around that next corner.

In the middle of the road, two hundred yards ahead, a jackknifed eighteen-wheeler blocked the road. Something was wrong, very wrong. I let up on the throttle, slowing rapidly, not fully understanding what had just happened until I saw the red sedan, crushed and burning, lying in a field at the bottom of an embankment. Braking hard, I came to a shuddering halt at the side of the road, dropped the kickstand, and ripped my helmet off. I was the second to stop, and the first to step over the pieces of wreckage, running toward the car.

The door was open and she was alone; a deployed airbag filled the space between her body and the steering wheel. The roof of her car buckled inward and I think that it had rolled before coming to rest on its wheels. Flames were spilling out from beneath the crumpled hood when I reached her but I ignored them as two other truckers were coming across the field at a sprint from their stopped rigs, extinguishers in hand. The wreckage of the roof had severely gashed the right side of her head and the only indication of the life that had just been wrenched from her body was the rattle and choked gasp of her final breath. Acrid dust filled the air, and I wanted to reach over and close her staring eyes, not yet glazed in death, as the tiny particles came through the smashed firewall and settled on her face. Her skin was still warm as I checked for a pulse in her neck and her open eyes looked like they might flicker back to seeing at any moment, but the congealing blood in her nose, ears, and mouth told me otherwise. The small knot of people who gathered in the next few minutes was strangely silent. There was nothing that any of us could do; the immensity, immutability, and finality of death was before us.

The trucker whose rig was jackknifed in the road said that she had drifted across the centerline, without warning, and without slowing. His voice was low, tight, and choked. "I locked it up, but I knew she was gonna hit." He was in his early fifties, a big, broad-shouldered man in a white short-sleeved dress shirt, blue jeans, and a blue baseball cap. His hands shivered slightly as he slid the Buck knife that he had used to cut through the web of the woman's seat belt back into its leather holster on an embossed belt. I put a hand on his shoulder and could feel the muscles, bunched and tight beneath the thin fabric of his shirt. He had gone silent, but his eyes were filled with agony and confusion. At that moment I wished that I knew him well enough to put my arms around him. The most I could offer was a quiet "Are you all right?"

"Yes," he said. "I'm OK."

The woman was in her late thirties, heavy-set, with frosted and permed light brown hair. She was wearing a plaid shirt and leggings and looked as if she might have just been going down to the corner store where I had stopped for gas minutes earlier, to buy a quart of milk. The fourth finger of her left hand bore a starburst cluster of tiny diamonds, a wedding set, that had sunk a bit into the flesh of her finger. I breathed a silent prayer of thanks that there were no children in the car with her. Where was she going? Who was waiting at home for her?

My knees were shaking badly as I walked back to Lucy after the EMTs arrived. Tremors ran through my hands as I fumbled with the chin strap on my helmet, my keyring rattled against the engine head as I reached to turn the key, and I took several deep breaths before twisting the throttle to pull Lucy back onto the road and away from what lay twisted and finished in the field. A local wrecker had angled across the road a quarter of a mile back, stopping and diverting traffic onto graveled farmways that right-angled their way around the field in half-mile stretches. He stood on the centerline directing the big-rig trucks in slow, roaring turns off the main pavement, and I surprised him as I pulled up from behind to ask about the detour.

"Holy smokes, where did you come from?" I could think of nothing to say and motioned back toward where the twisted eighteen-wheeler still blocked the road.

I drove only a few more miles before stopping in Jonesville at a Dutch Uncle coffee shop. Inside it smelled like hot oil, coffeepots that were always brewing, and glass cleaner. It felt warm, sunny, and safe where I crawled into the last booth in the back. Old men in ball caps sat gossiping around a large table in the front corner. They flirted gently with the young waitress, told jokes probably heard a hundred times before, and poured sugar into spoons poised above the decaf in their white stoneware mugs. I sat hunched in my back booth, ran my hands through my hair, felt the pulse in my own neck as I massaged fingertips into knotted muscles, tried not to cry, and felt guilty for feeling good to be alive.

I had seen violent death before. Local criminals had beaten one of my neighbors to death in the apartment building where I lived in Bulgaria. "A bad loan," his mother's friends had whispered, taken out with the wrong people. There was no electricity to run the elevator and his mangled body lay in an open casket outside my entryway door for two days so that elderly relatives would not have to climb the stairs to the fifth floor. In Azerbaijan, I did photography and the interviewing in support of a United Nations landmine and unexploded ordnance removal program on the Ngorno-Karabakh border. Leveled cities, minefields, and missing limbs filled my camera lenses and film canisters for weeks. That morning in Moscow, Michigan, was different, however. Michigan is not in a war zone or a developing nation. That woman died as I stood over her, and her life ended as she did something that I expected to do every day for the next three months: drive. Her death was sudden, random, and easily could have been my own.

SILVER SILOS, RED BARNS, AND WHITE farmhouses dotted the land-scape. The towns on Route 52 were not much more than clusters of houses and grain silos built alongside the railroad: Brookville, Lanark, Mount Carroll, and finally Savanna, which sits on the right bank of the Mississippi.

Savanna is a pretty little town with broad, white-painted verandas fronting brick homes and mature trees lining the streets. Children on their bikes waved to me as I came through. They pumped their arms—elbows crooked and fists moving vertically—asking the big-rig truckers and passing motorcyclists to honk their air horns. In that quiet river town none did. Half an hour later, I was standing in a grocery store parking lot and finding places for a few canned goods and a yogurt in my saddlebags, when three teenagers, a girl and two boys, walked by. They passed me, too polite to stare directly, but cast quick glances at Lucy, the leather, and my dusty and sweaty self. They were no more than ten feet away when the girl turned to her companions.

"It's so weird to see a woman driving a bike."

For a moment I was angry and felt the fierce rush of blood to my face. Did she think that perhaps I wouldn't hear her? Worse yet, was I so bizarre to her understanding of the proper place of women in society that she thought it didn't matter if I did? I stared after her as she slid into the backseat of her friend's car—young, slender, a light brown ponytail swinging down her neck—and felt my anger shift to something like sadness. This girl, in one sentence, had told both me and those boys—who would soon be men—that she was not able to understand or appreciate anything but a traditional model of womanhood.

There is strength and power in being a wife, raising a family, pursuing a profession, and contributing to a stable community, if this is what one does freely and with knowledge of options. Spatial freedom does not necessarily mean intellectual liberation and narrow-mindedness can just as easily be found in a blanket rejection of all that is suburban and entrenched, picket-fenced, and socially insular. Every woman does not need to drive a motorcycle, or to necessarily make choices that lie outside of a traditional value system, in order to feel strength, power, or personal liberation. However, each of us needs to search for—and hopefully find—those things somewhere. It is not important whether a woman is a housewife or a peregrine, if she wants to fit in or stand out, if she would rather hold her own counsel or express it loudly. What is important is the understanding of options and the courage to explore them. Could that girl in Savanna, Illinois, do that? For her sake, I hoped so.

The Mississippi was broad and blue at Savanna, clear for the top foot or two, but clouded by muddy brownish silt just beneath the surface. The river there was a fraction of what its girth was a thousand miles south, and the span was crossed by a steel bridge that joined Illinois 52 and Iowa 64 in a narrow, high, graceful arch. The metal grating that formed the roadbed of the arch was like that of the bridges that I had driven many times before across the Delaware River between New Jersey and Pennsylvania, but the span was longer, and not flat. I can understand why bridge builders like metal grating: it's relatively cheap, strong, and will not collect pooled water, or ice and snow, like solid surfaces. The problem with metal grating, however, is that its rough corrugations pull the wheels of motorcycles from side to side. It's an unnerving feeling to have a bike shift unbidden beneath you, and for a moment, coming over the uphill slope toward the apex of that bridge over the Mississippi, I felt the hairs rise on the back of my neck as Lucy slid toward the guardrail. In the shift of the bike one must consciously control the instinctive reaction to set a foot down hard to correct an unexpected sideslip. I know people who have done this on metal grate bridges and have had broken ankles to show for it. *Feet on the pegs, feet on the pegs.* The words ran through my mind, a self-repeating mantra, and I tried to consciously relax and let Lucy run between my hands, guided yet loose, slow enough to keep control, yet fast enough to keep a driving forward momentum. We passed into Iowa without incident and I stopped to take a picture of that Mississippi River bridge: the divide between the eastern and western United States as well as a tiny personal victory.

The road beyond the bridge was built on a causeway running between small floodplain lakes. There were more hills and subsequently less wind, and I pulled into a picnic site with a boat ramp that jutted out into a lake to eat a sheltered lunch. With Lucy parked under the shade of a spreading oak tree, I walked for a bit to stretch my legs and then perched on the picnic table watching fathers with young sons coming to launch their fishing boats. The water birds were there, too. A cormorant fishing in the shallows disappeared in repeated sleek dives that raised little more than ripples on the surface. An incoming great blue heron, wide wings fully stretched, played a soft whistle of wind between dusty bluish-gray feathers as he dropped toward the frog-populated banks.

In the shelter of the river hills I thought that the morning wind might have diminished, but there was no such luck. As I climbed up and out of the valley and made my way through Nashville, Baldwin, and Wyoming, Route 64 rolled upward, built on exposed ridges high above the fields. This made sense from a farming perspective—low land for agriculture, high land for roads—but the blasting crosswind coming out of the south, varying in gusting duration and intensity, was merciless. I was shocked by its force. The physics of motorcycles are such that as speed and torque increases, the friction created between the tires and the road becomes less. This destabilizing effect can be counterbalanced with weight, but Lucy, at five hundred pounds, was not a heavy bike. I weighed in at just over a hundred pounds and our combined mass was not enough to keep the bike on the road in high winds and at top speed. I slowed Lucy to thirty-five miles an hour to keep control and had genuine difficulty when the road turned slightly into or away from the wind and the force shifted from square on my left shoulder to buffeting my torso and back.

It was painfully slow and, with the constant adjustment of machinery, body, and bike angle, physically exhausting. In the small communities the bank clocks were registering temperatures in excess of ninety-three and a humid haze hung heavy on the hills. An hour and a half of hard driving later, still struggling with the heat and the wind, I left the openness of 64 to roll down Main Street in Anamosa to look for a coffee shop and hiatus from the road.

Tucked into the shelter of the valley where the Buffalo and Wapsipinicon Rivers come together, Anamosa is where the painter Grant Wood, creator of the famously stoic *American Gothic,* was born on a farm in 1891. It is a sheltered, contained, and thoroughly charming small midwestern town. The Memory Café was open, and I liked the look of the oak-topped tables, the wrought-iron stools, and the old-fashioned soda fountain bar. Painted knick-knacks, Victoriana, and displays of dried flowers and candles stood in racks, filling the precise corners of the walls with soft floral scents where they met the black-and-white tiled floor. Entering with my helmet in one hand and my leather jacket draped over an arm, the waitresses looked at me curiously, but with welcome. Two women worked there: one was older, with a warm smile and a motherly way; the other, a slightly shy yet truly beautiful blonde girl with huge eyes and long fingers, served from behind the counter. I took a corner table near the window, where I could see Lucy and the street beyond, as well as observe the comings and goings in the café. A few minutes later a piece of thick, flaky-crusted peach pie that had been made by the owner's mother was in front of me, along with strong black coffee and a tall glass of ice water. An old man with work-thickened hands sat at the counter, a thirty-five-cent green phosphate soda before him. The waitress didn't have to ask what he wanted before she set it down on the scrubbed surface.

Suddenly it struck me just how happy I was to be there. Not in that café specifically, as friendly and cool and sheltered as it was, but just to be *there;* traveling with no immediate destination, learning something of a country in which I had grown up but that I knew very little about. Many years on the road in other people's nations had made me a tourist and outsider in my own. In those tiny communities, where everyone seemed to know everyone else, where retired farmers drank their phosphates at soda fountains or gossiped with friends that they had known for half a century and more, I was a complete foreigner. Generally people's faces were kind, welcoming, and curious, rather than hostile or distrustful as I had feared in my bleaker pre-departure moments. In places like Anamosa, Iowa, where the population thinned and the miles between towns increased, brief conversations showed me that I was not the faceless stranger that I might have been in a major metropolitan area. People were open to my questions, no matter how silly they might have seemed; they were willing to talk about their lives, to take the time to tell me their stories, their histories, and to ask about mine.

What people asked, however, was a different set of questions than I was used to in the frenetic transient social spaces of the East. They asked where I was from, where I was going, how I chose my route, what it was like to travel alone, to live on the road, to see new places and new people every day. But I was rarely asked the standard Eastern questions: where I had gone to school and what it was that I did for a living. Was it because there, in the midst of the great open spaces of the country, where people were more settled, and where communities—for better or worse—did know each individual member with the intimacy of generational understanding, that education and profession became less critical than character? Was it because I was a drifter, clearly not attached to place and presumably profession, that people were reluctant to ask what might be a potentially embarrassing question? I never figured it out. By Iowa, however, it was becoming clear to me that on this trip I had no past and no future that was important to anyone, even to me. There was only today and the immediate concerns of taking care of myself and Lucy, of making sure that neither one of us got damaged in the chance happenings of the road, and of experiencing what the continent had to show. There was no real agenda, nowhere that I had be at the end of the day, the week, or the month. In The Memory Café, in Anamosa, Iowa, I knew that I would not have traded that life, as I lived it then, for any other. It was the time and the place for that journey and I was free.

I kept telling myself that there was no time schedule; that I didn't have to be anywhere anytime in the immediate future. Still, it was frustrating to be grounded, to not be able to ride as much or as far as I would have liked to because, of all things, of the wind. Such a force it was; silent until it exploded on my shoulder and chest, mercurial in its change of direction and velocity, but still, it was just *air*. Who would have thought that a little over six hundred pounds of moving steel and woman could be effectively halted in the middle of Iowa by something that seemed so inconsequential? Inconsequential until the force of the blast hit. At two in the afternoon I had given up on trying to tear my way through the gale and was instead pitching a tent near Creston, Iowa, in the Green Valley State Park campground, all of 150 miles from where I had camped the night before.

The day had started off well. After dodging trucks and windblast on Route 92 for a few miles early in the morning, I stopped in Knoxville for breakfast. My morning routine was to drive thirty or forty miles before pulling over at some tiny eatery where cholesterol was not a concern. I was beginning to develop an eye for where to get the best flapjacks and biscuits and often it was in the most nondescript places, which advertised only through the rows of pickup trucks that lined the street out front. After various artery-hardening combinations of eggs and toast, pancakes, hash browns or grits, sausage and bacon, I would spend the rest of the day doing the long miles on cheese and crackers, fruit, granola bars, yogurt, the occasional piece of chocolate, water, juice, and coffee. For reasons both financial and social, breakfast was the main meal of the day. With a slender budget to cover what I expected would be close to three months on the road, restaurant dinners and hotels, even campgrounds with swimming pools, were luxuries I could not afford. It was also easier to walk alone into a strange café early in the morning, ask for a cup of coffee, and strike up a conversation with the waitress on the early shift or whoever happened to be sitting at the next table. Dinner was a time for couples and families to be together and I felt awkward sitting alone in restaurants where the lights were dim and conversation swirled around, but did not include, strangers on motorcycles.

Route 14 contours south out of Knoxville, a stretch of pavement with long, slow green curves through protected hilly country. Unfortunately the shelter was temporary. As the landscape flattened, and I turned Lucy west on Route 92 out of Winterset, the wind began to blast again. Try as I might,

I could not find another road snugged into a valley and there was no body position that would lessen the impact of the wind. Getting blown all over the road, I dropped Lucy's speed to a painful thirty miles per hour. Leaning hard off the natural centerline of a bike, constantly adjusting balance and speed as the wind blows and shifts, is a physically exhausting way to ride and it wasn't long before I began to think of the wind as an almost personal malevolency. Its scream was in my ears, dulled only slightly by my helmet, and its huge fists pummeled my shoulders and torso in an attempt to tear me from Lucy. From Stanzel I cut directly south from 92 toward Zion and across the Grand River, hoping to find the wind directly in my face; an easier point of physical negotiation compared to side-blast. According to my map, the road to Zion was supposed to be a blacktop, but what materialized was a long stretch of winding crushed gravel linking remote farms.

Driving in gravel has its own dynamics. The surface—such as it is—is loose and the stone tends to collect more deeply on the corners. Traction is generally worse and control is more difficult. A road base of peanut-sized stones did not improve Lucy's handling in the wind and I was glad to hit blacktop again near the coal and grain elevators that marked the entrance to Creston.

At the public library I stopped to check e-mail, collapse into an armchair, and consider options. The next camping spot listed on my map after Creston was seventy agonizing miles away. Although it was still early in the afternoon I was exhausted, windblown, and sunburned. I decided to stay the night and hope for better driving conditions the next day.

Green Valley, the local state park and recreation area, looked as if it had fallen on hard times. The lake had dropped twenty feet in recent years, mostly due to ongoing repair work on the containment dam. Left high and dry, thousands of large sunbleached clamshells littered the shore. The earth at the water's edge was cracked and drying, and the view, combined with what had been an excruciating day, brought on a bout of depression and loneliness. I avoided conversation with other campers, wrenched my tent upright in a wind that tried to flatten it before I even set the stakes, and was personally and irrationally resentful of every gust that blasted through the trees. Negativity whipsawed through my brain. *What a godforsaken place. This is not fun, this is not an adventure, and this is not travel. This is survival. What the fuck am I doing in the middle of Iowa on a motorcycle?* My hair had come loose from its clip and was whipping around my face. I tried to push it back with fingers black from road grit and engine grease but they immediately tangled in the sweat that caked the ropey strands. It was almost funny, and I had to sit down with both hands stuck near my temples to work my fingers and rings free of my hair. Crumpled on the ground, I realized that my attitude was neither healthy nor helpful. I had only been on the road a week but I knew that there were going to be days in the months to come that were completely atrocious, when movement was painful, and when miles that were usually given freely by the road had to be earned. I had to find a way to relax and find a little peace in motionlessness as well as motion.

A family of four, two women and two children, were breaking down their pop-up camper as I put up my tent. One of the women, struggling with the trailer hitch on the camper, called over to me.

"Hey! You got a husband?" She wanted help with the mechanics and muscle of torquing the hitch around.

"Nope." She snorted in disgust and turned back to her camper. Both annoyed and amused by her question, I went over to have a look at the hitch and offered to help but she had already cranked up her cell phone to call in a male reinforcement. Her children, adorable with dirty knees and elbows and a yellow Lab puppy on a string, came to visit as I returned to my site. They were fascinated with Lucy and reached out tiny filthy fingers to touch the leather saddlebags and seat and to feel the still-warm chrome of the exhaust pipes. For my part, I was delighted with their curiosity and with the soft ears and tiny pink tongue of their pet, who was valiant in his efforts to scramble up my chest and lick my face. Maybe when things got difficult in the larger sense of travel it was best to focus on the smaller elements of the same: children, puppies, shelter, and motionlessness in blasting wind.

I crawled into my sleeping bag that night feeling more rested and having accepted my static afternoon, but it had been a rough couple of days in Iowa, and I was more than a little afraid of Kansas. If the wind was this bad here, what would it be like as I crossed the Great Plains?

THE WIND SNAPPED AND STRAINED AT the tent fabric and I felt a deep weariness before I even rolled over to unzip the screen door. Would it ever stop? Out of my sleeping bag at 5:30 in the morning, I hoped to get an early start before the wind rose in earnest but I wasn't exactly sure of which road to take. The day before, pulled over at roadside to reposition the flat plastic-fronted map pocket lashed to my gas tank, my roadmap of southern Iowa and north-western Missouri had blown out. The last I saw of it, it was moving at a good forty miles an hour, gaily flapping up and over a cornfield. I would just have to connect the spaces in a southwest run to the Kansas border, not an overly diffi-cult challenge in a region where most of the roads ran at right angles.

It was a good ramble south down to the Missouri border on a road that had the direction but none of the curves of the Platte River. Across the state line I picked up Route 169 and drove through low rolling hills on gray corru-gated pavement patched with broad black bands of tar through Grant City, Carmack, and into Stanberry and Liz's Diner.

Liz's was warm and bright, with white linoleum floors and tables. Black booths and raised bar stools fronted a long counter, and mirrors covered the walls that did not have windows, making the inside space look bigger than it was. Conversation stopped as I walked in, and I was greeted by silent watchful stares that were not hostile, just not friendly. Clearly not too many travelers came through Stanberry. I sat down in the silence, taking a booth facing the window where I could see Lucy over the lifted rim of my coffee cup. The boy serving was young and shy, with a brown ball cap that inched down over his wide and shifting eyes each time he spoke to me. Three older farmers sat drinking coffee and resumed talking as I got out my surviving maps and pieced together a route into Kansas that would cut between St. Joseph and Leaven-worth while avoiding both. The conversation at Liz's was of hunting season, turkey, pheasants, the exploding deer population, and the problem of the crea-tures stepping into the road. I eavesdropped and dug into a mountain of pan-cakes that I knew I would not be able to finish. One man, tall and spare with gray stubble on his chin and a dark blue ball cap, had hit a deer with his truck the week before.

"It was a six-point buck, all in velvet. By golly the prettiest thing you ever did see, them antlers. Back all busted, jaw all busted, them big eyes just a-lookin' up at you. I had to shoot it, put it out of its misery." His friends nodded in silent sympathy.

If there is a prettier rural road than Missouri 116, I don't know where it is. Dipping into hollows, 116 bent and twisted under the spreading boughs of massive trees, through floodplains bordering the Missouri River. A roadside marker with vertical hash marks read "water level 1–2–3 feet" and I was glad for the smooth dry sweep of asphalt beneath Lucy's tires. Orange tiger lilies perfumed the air, blooming in clumps by the roadside, and small holdings set back from the thruway dotted the roll of the hills: white farmhouses, red barns, scatterings of outbuildings.

After I crossed the roll of the Missouri River on the Amelia Earhart Memorial Bridge, leaving the Victorian mansions of Atchison behind, Kansas opened up in earnest on Route 16. Expansive grasslands lifted to a huge hazy white sky, and the emerald corn that had painted Iowa and Missouri shifted to wheat that ranged in color from pale gold to deep bronze. Sometimes the road arrowed in an unbroken line to the horizon, ascending and challenging the hills in graduating humps. Other times it flowed around the rises, contouring with the land, dipping into streamed washes and tracing the edges of hollows, as gentle and accommodating as asphalt can be. Midday brought passing showers heavy enough to soak my clothes but not carrying enough rain to break the humidity or end the drought in the fields. With temperatures hovering at just over ninety degrees, it was too warm to bother hauling out rain gear, and I drove straight through the weather, drying in the wind within half an hour of each shower. As Atchison County gave way to Jackson, the towns got smaller and distances between them larger. Holton, Jackson's county seat, punctuated the grasslands with quaint brick paved streets, tree-lined boulevards, and a population of just over three thousand. It was the most bustling place for a hundred miles.

Between Wheaton—aptly named—and Fostoria I stopped for gas in Blaine. The man at the station had white-blond hair, blue eyes just a shade deeper than colorless, an easy smile, and a gentle way about him. He was taller than me but managed to look straight into my eyes. I wished that I had the courage to ask his name. Every now and again intuition tells us that a stranger is a kindred soul. How many of these would I meet in a motorcycle summer in my own continent? I had met a few, very few, in ten years of traveling in other countries. That intuition, a flash between people that begins with a glance, deepens with a look, and is fixed within sentences, is a rare and dangerous thing. In that flash of understanding, your life and that of another can become entwined, and you know within seconds that even though you did not grow up within the same household you are from the same family. I stepped away from him, lacking the confidence to begin a conversation that I might not be able to stop.

In the late afternoon I traveled west out of Beloit toward Glen Eder and Waconda Lake, where I would stop for the night. The last ten miles of the day were deliberately slow ones and I drove with just one hand loose on the throttle, feeling each pulse of Lucy's engine up my spine, each slow corner as it arched the back of the road. Waconda is a state park area and has at its heart a massive reservoir with a surface area of more than twelve thousand acres, which was created by a dam built in 1968 at the place where the north and south forks of the Solomon River came together. The shores hosted a campground and man-made sand beaches for swimming and boating. I was exhausted, overheated, and dehydrated, so camping on the banks of a lake sounded like a fine idea. I pulled over at the registration booth, deposited the camping fee, lashed helmet and jacket to the T-bag, and drove the mile or so down the park road wearing just my sunglasses and gloves for protective gear, hair flying on the wind. Helmets and jackets are so very necessary but after a long hot day the wind buffeting on bare arms and shoulders feels like a cool caress. I felt strong and capable at moments like that—riding a beautiful machine, covering the last mile of a day filled with good roads, small towns, and fine people—and I could feel my spine straightening. The wind was still a presence, pulsing in on my left shoulder as I drove to the lakeshore, but it did seem to be less fierce, and I had gotten in 350 steadily rolling miles and had thoroughly enjoyed each one.

My tent site was at the water's edge. It was a treeless, windy spot, but had a gorgeous view across the whitecaps on the lake. I slid into the water, cooling my parched skin and letting the liquid wash away the weariness and road dust of the day. Noisy families shouted to one another across the shoreline expanses of grass and I paddled just enough to keep afloat while letting my head and ears slide below the silence of the surface. In the middle of the Great Plains, on the shores of an artificial but beautiful construct of a lake, I spent the evening in contemplation of water and waves and fell asleep listening to the wind and slap of ripples on the sand.

EXHIBIT B: *Frame of Reference*

Paul's Café is a friendly spot with none of the small-town silence that sometimes fills a corner diner when a stranger walks in. The waitress, a tall handsome woman in her forties, rolled a yellow pencil between her fingers.

"Are you on a motorcycle?" The pencil eraser rotated toward the leather jacket slung over the back of the chair.

"Yes."

"Traveling through?"

I nodded. "Headed toward Colorado, just seeing the sights. You've got some beautiful country around here."

"And have you been up to see the Center of the World?" There was no irony in her question and I looked at her with genuine confusion.

"The Center of the World?"

"Oh . . . I mean the country . . . you know what I mean." She tucked an auburn curl behind one ear, laughed, and turned to go find me a couple of scrambled eggs and some hash browns from a kitchen just south of where the north-south-east-west lines of a nation crossed.

· · ·

Lebanon, Kansas, is the geographical center of the lower forty-eight United States and there wasn't a car or truck on the road as I swooped over low rolling hills toward the U.S. Geological Survey marker. White gravel secondary roads fell away from the main paved thruway that stretched directly north toward Red Cloud, Nebraska. The Center sits betwixt a wheat field rolling up a gentle slope to the horizon and a desolate end-of-the-road farm called Hub Dairy, which had no immediately visible bovine residents. Apart from the wind, there was silence and an emptiness of human movement at the spot where the lines between Maine and California, Florida and Washington crossed. I've always thought of America as a cultural concept, an amalgamation of peoples, histories, cities and towns, traditions, and productions of both physical and intellectual material. Here, however, at the "center" of America, there was none of that, there was only the land, and the wheat, and a few imported referrals to the society of people who called themselves "Americans." A burr oak had been planted near a truncated stone pyramid marker. It was a stunted-looking thing, young and struggling, a few dozen leaves heaving against the wind. Perhaps one day it will grow into something representative of the U.S. Forest Service plaque that marked it: "forestry . . . at the hub of America." A small portable chapel stood nearby, a tiny church on wheels complete with a miniature steeple. This was the U.S. Center Chapel, constructed and donated by a local man who wanted people to have the chance to think on their relationship with God as they thought upon their relationship with America. Much is said about the separation of church and State in this country, but it often seems to me that this separation is at best a narrow one. The strong religious thread that winds through the fabric of domestic American culture and politics is especially fascinating as much of the rest of the world—judging by the media and entertainment that the United States produces—considers America to be a "godless" and amoral place. How many bus and train conversations had I had in how many countries with people who were genuinely surprised to hear that large percentages of Americans went to church or mosque or temple, and that the majority of Americans believed in some concept of God and attempted to structure both private and public life around that concept? Not a church, temple, or mosque-goer myself, I did not stop to meditate in the chapel but instead climbed atop the survey marker, spread my arms into the wind, took a deep breath of warm, wet, wheat-scented air, inhaled the center of the country as best I could, and jogged back to Lucy to continue the exploration of the same.

Paul's Café is in Smith Center, just down the block from where an 1870 Dutch-style windmill that used to grind grain into flour still spreads its wooden sails. Smith Center is the county seat, has a population of 2,016, and boasts three intersections. Paul's sits on the northeast corner of one of those intersections and is, along with the farm equipment dealership just across the street, the spot where farmers meet friends in the morning. The younger men linger in the parking lot before heading out to the fields; a booted foot resting on the front bumper of a truck, the last five minutes of companionship before a long solitary day on the tractor. The older men, their tractors passed on to their sons, or the bank, sit inside gossiping with friends over three-hour cups of coffee. Mr. Burgess sat to my right. A retired farmer with hair that was moving from steel gray to snow white, Mr. Burgess was one of the founding members of the "As The Bladder Fills" Club, a cohort of similarly retired farmers who agreed to a strict schedule of who was to buy the coffee for the rest on any given morning. From time to time Mr. Burgess Xerox-published *The Echo*, a four-page newsletter subtitled "The people's choice for a newspaper voice in the heart of the Heartland Empire," which detailed the news and events of Smith Center as gleaned from his extensive network of sources, most of whom drank coffee at Paul's. With solemnity he presented me with a copy of *The Echo*. It included such news as: "Charley Cole showed up at Paul's Café early Tuesday morning. Was sunburned on his arms. Said he got it from helping hold some stuff that was being welded. I thought at first he was

kiddin' but he assured me that he wasn't. You can get burned from a welder."
The next editorial piece concerned the rising price of fuel: "I tell you, the guy
that is responsible for the current gasoline prices ought to have his bag slit and
his leg run through it."

To my left was a younger man, a farmer from Gaylord, a hamlet of three
hundred people just down the road. His hair was the color of the wheat that he
grew, and his bright blue eyes twinkled in the deeply lined face of one who has
spent many years working in the sun. I asked about farming, what it meant to
live here, in Kansas, near the geographical center of the lower United States
and far from any major urban center. He was thoughtful, direct, open, and
generous with his time and his stories and considered each thing that I asked
for a long, silent moment before answering. He told me that the drought was
becoming problematic. The normal average annual rainfall was twenty-four
inches, most of it falling in May and June, and there had been less than four
inches of rain so far that year. He had two children, a boy and a girl, eight and
ten years old, and when he spoke of them his face creased in love and concern.
He told me that he was happy with his life but that he would never encourage
his children to go into farming.

"There are other jobs where you can retire at fifty-five, maybe earlier. It
used to be that you could make a good living farming. Now we struggle. And
the small places, well, if they're not gone already, they're going."

"And the subsidies from the government," I asked, "do they help?"

"They help a little, but what with the costs: seed, fertilizer, equipment, and
fuel . . . and then wheat is $1.80 a bushel on the market?" He laughed ruefully.
I'd never seen a bushel of wheat but I knew what bushel baskets of apples,
lined up in New England orchards in the autumn, looked like—heavy and
round, their strip-wood diameters too big for me to encircle with my arms. I
thought about the amount of wheat that it would take to fill one of those apple
bushel baskets. One dollar and eighty cents? He loved his community, though,
where "everybody knows everybody," spoke with pride of his home, and told
me to look for his house as I left Smith Center. I drove out under lowering
clouds and took 281 through Gaylord toward Route 9. It was there as he had
described it, a small white farmhouse tucked into a hollow fronting a low hill

with a short silver silo beyond it. I passed, giving the people inside a mental wave, thinking, *What is this place, who are these people, that a man—knowing his family was alone—would happily tell a stranger on a motorcycle exactly where his home is and encourage her to look for it as she left town?* Like so many people that I met that summer, I had not earned his trust, he simply gave it, freely.

ROUTE 9, FLOWING THROUGH THE SEAS of grain and prairie in the northwestern part of Kansas, was unexpectedly beautiful. This was Kansas, after all, and it was supposed to be flat, boring, nothing to see. "Just drive through it as rapidly as possible," I had been told. "There's nothing there." I slowed down instead and watched the low rolling hills, following a road that vaguely mirrored the winding course of a river a couple hundred feet below the pavement bed. The hills were gentle, sheltering, lessened the buffet of the wind, and were colored in spectrums that ran from the pale gold of early wheat to the soft sage green of the scrub and prairie grasses. Human habitation was scarce. Although much of the land was under cultivation, farm families lived isolated from one another and from the tiny towns that appeared every twenty or twenty-five miles.

I had not gassed up in Smith Center as my Rand McNally indicated that small towns were scattered up the length of Route 9, but by Kirwin gas was becoming a problem. Although each settlement did indeed have a gas pump, it was just that: one pump that required a co-op card to activate it. By Logan I was getting nervous. I had driven eighty miles on my tank and the map implied that the next town of any substantial size was another eighty miles up the road. Logan was the same as the other hamlets before it: a tiny town, with a single co-op pump, and streets—paved in the town center and shifting to dirt at the edges—deserted on a Sunday afternoon. I parked Lucy in the drizzling rain and walked over to the diner to ask about where the nearest gas could be found. Conversation ceased as I walked in the door and every head turned to examine my dripping presence. I stood there confused; my boots and lower legs were wet and none too clean, and the floor of the diner was covered in, of all things, thick plush white carpeting. If I moved I would leave muddy bootprints all over the carpet. Eight people looked at me, I looked at the carpet, and no one moved or said a word. Finally the owner broke the silence: "You can come in and sit down, anywhere's fine."

"Thanks. I'm just worried about tracking up your nice clean carpet."

He laughed. "Oh, don't worry about that."

"Actually, I just came in to ask where the next gas station would be."

"About a hundred yards up the road. Course, you need a card. You got one of them?" I admitted that I did not. "In that case, the next gas is Colby, 'bout eighty miles away." My heart sank. In this kind of wind, the luggage strapped to Lucy increasing the resistance and lowering fuel efficiency, there was no way I was going to make it. A tiny woman, sitting with her husband at a sparkling white Formica table onto which sandwiches had just been deposited, stood up.

"C'mon, honey, I'll take you down to the pump and you can use my card."

"No, I'm interrupting. Please, sit down, finish your lunch, I can wait."

"No, no, it's not going anywheres. C'mon, I've done this for others before, and I can certainly do it for you." Pat was in her late fifties with twinkling green eyes, carefully arranged hair, green slacks, and a white sweater so spotless it glowed in the misty afternoon light. At five feet three inches I towered a good head above her, but she seemed a woman who, for whatever she lacked in stature, more than made up for it in warmth and kindness. At the pump she ran her card through and we talked about her part of Kansas and my desire to see the country as I ran a little less than two dollars' worth of gas into Lucy's tank. I asked if she had ever done any traveling around the States.

"No," Pat said. "I'm not one of those traveling folks, going here and there. I like it here, the furthest I been away from Logan is Colby, and I don't want to go anywheres else. Some people they go here, they go there, but me, I like to stay home, and I've never really wanted to go and see . . . you know . . . the Grand Canyon . . . or Las Vegas." The pump stopped. I screwed the cap back on the tank and reached for my wallet.

"Now you put that away," Pat said. "What is it, all of two dollars? I'm not going to take that from you." She wished me good luck, told me to be careful, and stepped back into her white Cutlass to drive up the street to where her lunch waited. I pulled my driving gloves back on, watching her taillights and thinking about the people who spent years, and sometimes their entire lives, searching the world for what Pat knew she had in Logan, Kansas: an understanding of place, a sense of belonging.

EXHIBIT C: *A Sense of Place*

His suit was custom-tailored, double-breasted, with the easy sophisticated drape of an Italian design house, and a subtle gray stripe barely noticeable in the richly colored midnight blue wool. He handed me a glass of champagne and motioned to a waiter who arrived with toast points heaped with sliced egg and black beluga caviar. It was a casual conversation and we both scanned the room looking for the people who we were really there to talk to: the oilmen who had flocked to Azerbaijan after the former Soviet republic declared independence.

"Where is your home?" I asked. We moved through a group of Azeri, Japanese, Dutch, and English diplomats and businesspeople toward a marble courtyard fountain.

"I live here, in Baku," he said. "I've been here for a year and a half."

"Yes, but I mean your *home*, where are you from?" He looked over my shoulder, scanning the crowd for his business contacts.

"Well, before this I was in Venezuela for four years, and before that South Africa and Saudi." He listed off a handful of other countries, his voice flat and his eyes vacant. "I was born in Kansas. But that was a long time ago."

. . .

The clouds dissipated by early afternoon and the heat returned with the sun. Through Densmore, Edmond, and Lenora, I started passing cyclists coming the opposite direction up Route 9. First there were single people, young men and women pedaling strongly, then pairs, then small groups, and finally long lines of all kinds of people: old and young, men and women, on mountain bikes and ten speeds, all moving toward the east. *Where were they going?* The hills were long and rolling, wave crests on the sea of the prairie, never steep, but never flat. I could see their faces: red, sweating under helmets, working with the effort of hauling bicycle and body up and over a rise, down a dip, and up the next rise. Feelingly vaguely guilty, I twisted the throttle and sailed effortlessly over the land, slowing only slightly as wind, or gravity on the inclines, decreased my forward momentum. A few miles later I pulled over at an intersection to remove a layer of clothing, and a bicyclist rolled to a stop near Lucy. He reached for his water bottle and I nodded a hello. A gruff man in his early sixties with powerfully corded calves and a bristling thatch of iron-gray hair that rose vertically above his deeply tanned face, Mr. Gage, as he introduced himself, told me that this was the annual "Ride Across Kansas," a cycling tour where the route changed every year but which always stretched over three hundred miles from one end of the state to the other. He told me that some riders did the tour for charitable causes while others, like himself, just rode.

"I'm not saying that charity riding is bad. It's not," he said. "But sometimes, I think it's good to just ride!" Gage had been cycling Kansas for more than a decade, enjoying the camaraderie of the road and happily sleeping on the floors of community centers and high school gymnasiums in the small towns that hosted the riders as they passed through. He was solo now but used to cycle with a group of friends. He laughed and referred to those early rides as "Beer Across Kansas." He told me that it was less rowdy now that his aging friends had stopped cycling, and that there were more families with children who participated.

"Ah, it's different," he growled, "but I still love it, and for one week every year, I get to see a new part of the state. I've lived here all my life, but every year I see something different." He swung into his saddle, I swung into mine, and we each pulled out in opposite directions with a wave.

On the far side of Selden, a mile past the way station for water and bicycle repairs, three women were struggling with a punctured tire on the side of Route 83. The sun was blazing, and they looked unsure of what they were doing, so I pulled over to ask them if they were all right and if they would like me to ride back to Selden to let people know that they were having some trouble. There were grateful nods all around, so I pulled Lucy into a tight U-turn and rode back to the way station. Several local, and not very sober, men were leaning against a shaded wall as I pulled in. One immediately crossed the dusty lot as I pulled off my helmet.

"You"—he grinned at me with a mouth long on spaces and short on teeth—"are the second best-lookin' woman ever to come to Selden." I thanked him for the compliment and refrained from asking who the best-lookin' woman had been. After letting the ride coordinators know about the women with the flat tire and watching the support truck pull out, I was just getting back on Lucy, when my toothless admirer came back.

"Where you from?"

"New Jersey." He looked at me as if he couldn't quite believe what he was hearing.

"New Jersey?!"

"Yes." He stopped to consider this, looked at Lucy, squinted at me again, and wheeled on one booted heel, striding back toward his friends.

"Get the rope, boys, she's from New Jersey!" I didn't stay to continue the conversation.

From Gem I ran directly south to Oakley and west again on Route 40. Away from the roll of the river hills, the country opened out into the hugeness of the prairie, the wind picked up, and a dreadful afternoon began. Once again I was down to thirty-five miles an hour in the interest of keeping Lucy on the road. It was exhausting and frustrating to crawl along at half speed on gorgeous open pavement with a seventy-mile-an-hour posted speed limit that invited an unchecked throttle and the full-throated roar of a galloping motorcycle. Instead I crawled painfully, slowly, across golden grasslands that stretched to a horizon that receded a mile for every mile traveled. The wind was always there, but never with a steady tension that I could lean into and keep a consistent speed or angle of machinery. It was instead a random shifting of pressure at my left elbow and shoulder. Sometimes small puffs would force my shoulder back a few inches; sometimes a full-body explosion of force that ran from my ankle to helmet would slam into the side of the bike, forcing a sideways slide across the lane. With my jacket opened to rib-cage level, the blast of the south wind rolling across the plains was a physical and bruising presence on bike and body. *Christ, this is awful.* Where had the wind come from? Had it rolled up over the heated spaces of the Yucatan Peninsula, picking up the moisture from the Gulf that now made my skin feel damp and sticky even in the blast of oven-hot air? It was definite and tangible, a physical force moving through space, and as the hours wore into exhaustion, an invisible malevolent presence. Momentarily, the pressure of the wind might drop for a few seconds, and I would lean Lucy back to an upright position, easing her forward to perhaps forty-five miles per hour. Then, a gentle superheated damp caress would stroke my neck: a wet kiss and a warning. Another second, a slow count of one-one-thousand and it would be there: an explosion of pressure and sound, a solid wall of moving air, an impact with a howl of white noise and a rush of force. Once I recognized the pattern it was more manageable, never enjoyable but bearable. That wet kiss on my neck and I would immediately drop my speed, shift weight and machine to counterset the force of the wind that was coming, and stop the slide across the pavement before it began. Once, however, the wind hit me like a fist, a sucker-punch with no warning. I heard the crunch of air against my body in the same moment that Lucy slid toward the verge of the road and the ditch beyond. I corrected, letting all torque off the throttle and leaning hard into the wind, regaining control just inches before the pavement ended. I could do no more than drive the white line at twenty miles an hour, adrenaline flowing purple-silver through my veins, until the velocity of the wind dropped again and I could shift back out toward the centerline. Thankfully the traffic was light, but the occasional eighteen-wheeler, with enough mass to push through the gale without slowing, would pass me in a rush of tons of metal to my left. I actually looked forward to the shriek of the diesel engines coming up behind me and to the crosscurrent of air as they passed. For a few brief seconds I was sheltered behind a twelve-foot wall of metal moving at seventy-five miles an hour and the scream of the south wind was silenced. Only once I saw a trucker struggle with the wind, and unfortunately it was from much too close a vantage point. The long white trailer was just pulling by me when a particularly powerful gust of wind caught it broadside. The taillights, even with my left knee, slid toward my leg at an alarming rate as the trailer swayed and the trucker decreased his speed, moving back into the right lane much too rapidly. I hit the brakes, hoping the truck would keep its forward momentum, and watched the tailgate clear Lucy's front tire by no more than twenty-four inches. It was exhausting, frightening riding and at each small prairie town I set a new goal: the next small prairie town. The focus was just on getting there, moving through the force of the wind for another twenty-five or thirty miles, clawing my way west, from Oakley, to Monument, to Page City. In the vast reaches of the prairie the grain elevators of each town rose like small Emerald Cities on the enormity of the land. Like a mocking reminder of the distance left to travel, or a sign of encouragement, the tallest elevator in each municipality was emblazoned with the name of the town in huge white or reflective gray lettering that could be seen from miles away. I pressed slowly toward each one. It was excruciating.

I made Colorado on principle that evening, rather than need, running hard and thinking that if I got across the state line that somehow the wind would be less. Everyone knows that Colorado is mountainous and Kansas is flat. I had seen photographs that proved it. There would be less wind in Colorado, I was sure of it. Of course there wasn't. It should have been no great surprise that Eastern Colorado was remarkably similar to Western Kansas and that the vast flat reaches of prairie swept by howling wind flowed onward into the deepening light of the evening.

In Cheyenne Wells, a few miles past the state line, I pulled over and considered my options for the night in light of the weather. The wind had not diminished as the day faded and looming anvil-shaped clouds were building over the plains. They were purplish black, with sulfur-yellow edges and sheets of rain blurring the horizon beneath them some miles away, miles that seemed to become fewer even as I watched. The wind was shrieking, and lightning bolts began to drop with disturbing regularity onto the exposed landscape.

This was not a night to put up a tent. Cheyenne Wells consisted of a gas station, general grocery, and liquor store, all in the same building, and a single-story, bile-green establishment called the Ranch Motel. At the store I bought a can of chili, another of spinach, and two strips of beef jerky from the large glass jars by the cash register. The array of chewing tobacco for sale was impressive but I left the assortment of tubs, tins, pouches, and sticks of chew where they lay. From the pay phone outside I called Dave, and as I shouted at him over the keening of the coming storm and the passing roar of the big-rig trucks, telling him of the heat, the wind, and how amazingly and strangely beautiful the Great Plains had been, I tried to pretend that he wasn't as uninterested as he sounded.

"It's great, Dave, you should be here! You're missing out!"

"Uh, yeah. I know."

I booked into the Ranch Motel, establishing a price for the night based on a combination of my broken Spanish and the halting English of the proprietors. Twenty-five dollars did not seem too much to pay to get out of what was blowing in from the south. The motel walls were built of green painted cinderblocks. Cattle brand decorations rodeoed the upper perimeter of the room in a strip of wallpaper just below the ceiling, and a floridly colored picture of the Sacred Heart hung by the door. I pulled Lucy up and onto the narrow concrete porch that fronted the motel and tied her tarp down. There, under the overhang, she was partially sheltered and I could see her through my room's picture window. Perhaps three minutes after closing the door on the dust devils in the parking lot, the rain began in opaque slanting sheets and hazelnut-sized hail pelted down in a snare drum of noise on the metal roof. There are few things so blissful as to be dry and safe and sheltered when storm rages just inches away. With Lucy parked just outside the window, shedding rain and out of the worst of the weather, country music videos on the television, and a can of chili for dinner eaten cold with a spoon, I was content.

GIVEN THE HEAT OF THE PRECEDING days, it was surprisingly cold as I saddled up to leave Cheyenne Wells at 5 A.M. It was, however, a blessedly windless ride across the prairie, passing through Kit Carson and Wild Horse on the way to the day's first gas and coffee stop in Hugo. I was alone in the pink-and-gold wash of early morning light save for the occasional antelope lifting its head at the sound of Lucy's engine. On the outskirts of Hugo a repair shop advertised on a peeling wall, "We fix ANYTHING—from daybreak to heartbreak." It was closed.

Route 24 followed the curves of the Big Sandy Creek in a southwestern slant into Colorado Springs. The pavement was patched where frost heaves had been dug out and resurfaced, which made for less than smooth riding, but there was no traffic and I was able to maintain a steady sixty miles per hour; fast and free, the very antithesis of the previous day's crawl. Pikes Peak, gateway to the Rockies, rose like a huge headland in the distance as the last undulations of an enormous sea of grassland flowed under Lucy's wheels. I felt like a sailor who sees the pier in the distance as we roared toward the beachhead of the mountains.

Looming red sandstone formations towered over Colorado Springs and the 7-Eleven parking lot where I pulled in to remove a layer of clothing in the rapidly warming day. A cyclist, a dark wiry man with deep-set eyes and a hawk nose, walked across the pavement to look at Lucy. He had recently arrived from Cincinnati, he said, to train in the mountains for two weeks. The lower levels of oxygen at high elevation could lead to better cardiovascular conditioning and an "edge" in the low-altitude amateur races he rode.

"This is my vacation," he said. "The rest of the year I work on the rails."

"Really? What's that like?"

"Well . . ." He paused for a moment and looked at me with eyes that suddenly seemed hard. "There are women moving into our jobs and it really burns some of the guys up . . . can't say I blame them."

"Oh? Why is that?"

"Well, there are some things that women shouldn't do." He stepped back and looked at Lucy again, critically. "It ages them." There was challenge in his voice, bait, and an argument that I had not started. I lifted my coffee cup to him in a mock salute and gave him the biggest, most false smile I could muster.

"Here's to staying young." I took a last sip and tossed the dregs into the shrubbery.

A fantasyland of bizarre and wonderful soaring shapes of wind-carved red sandstone encircled by the softening arms of dark green pinyon pine and juniper, the Garden of the Gods is wedged between the city of Colorado Springs and the mountains behind it. A railroad magnate named Perkins bought hundreds of acres of the surrounding land in the last decades of the nineteenth century for a summerhouse that he never built, and in 1909 the Perkins family donated the land for use as a public park. The Garden of the Gods Park now covers fourteen hundred acres and is shot through with both roads and hiking trails that bring people to see the strange, bulbous, leaning, and sometimes improbably balanced spires of rock.

Colorado does not have a helmet law and it was more than eighty degrees in the bright midmorning sun, so at the entrance to the park loop I stopped, took off my helmet, and drove the slow curves of the park roads in my tank top, mirrored sunglasses, and gloves. I felt strong, free, and was relieved to be in the shelter of the mountains again. As magnificent as the Plains had been, they were like an ocean—vast, treeless, and exposed—and there in the shadows of those red spires, I felt like I was once again on terra firma. The sun stroked huge warm fingers across the bare skin of my shoulder blades and back, and in Lucy's side mirrors I could see the curve of newly defined muscles in my upper arms and shoulders. Was it the oxygen deficiency of the altitude that fueled the intoxication of those moments, that feeling of earthbound flight, that joy of solitude, that perception of strength, and the slow steady heartbeat that drummed in my ears? The insinuations of the cyclist drifted away.

Helmet and jacket back on, I left the park and headed for the high country. On the edge of an open meadow dotted with wildflowers, the trees began again. They shifted with the altitude from firs to aspens until nearly all the vertical forms at roadside shimmered in gray bark, slender and crowned in a flagellation of tiny rounded leaves that flashed silver and green. In Florissant I stopped to eat lunch, sitting amidst the dry crackle of parched vegetation on an embankment beside a church. Despite the dryness of the soil, the carpet of sage that surrounded my picnic spot was fresh and fragrant. I lay back, stretching out on the ground, rolled a bit between my fingers, and inhaled.

Most motorcycle trips are olfactory experiences. I think it's true what I've heard said: that only bikers genuinely understand why it is that dogs like to ride with their heads, tongues lolling, ears flapping, and noses sniffing, out the windows of cars. The wind carries with it a thousand observations of the land that it brushes over. I had spent the last eleven days breathing the continent in. The forests and lakes of the east left the perception of dying pine and soft wet leaf mould in the air. Corn, springing from the black earth of Iowa and Missouri, had a heady, fecund scent. The smell of growing wheat is different when a cool breeze shakes the heavy dew from its golden heads early in the morning and when it bakes in the sun late in the afternoon. It is the same plant but each scent is entirely different. In Colorado, what filled the air in the climb up toward the central ridge of the Rockies were the clean dry scents of meadow grasses in the sun, sage at roadside, and the upwelling of fir trees from the valleys.

Wilkerson Pass, at 9,500 feet, lays out a prospect of the whole of the western Rockies below. I took a short walk up a gravel path near the closed visitors' center to Puma Point to see the view. Gasping like a rabbit on the gentle uphill grade, my heart jackhammering in my chest, I began to question my physical stamina in air that lacked the oxygen-rich mix that I was used to at lower elevations. Breathing heavily I reached the overlook and caught my breath again, this time in wonder. The valley below commanded the middle distance and was perhaps fifty miles long and thirty miles wide. An entire mountain range reared out of the central plain like castle ramparts surrounded by a moat of prairie. The South Platte River glittered; a snaking stream that connected the still blue pools of the Antero, Spinney Mountain, and Elevenmile Canyon Reservoirs. The dark firs of the Pike National Forest swept down the sides of the mountains to meet the gold of the valley grasses. It was spectacular country.

EXHIBIT D: *The Far Valley*

Hartsel was a tiny place: population seventy, a gas station and store with one bench and view to hundreds of miles of timber and territory, a widening in the road that crossed the valley bisecting Pike National Forest. Two men, both in their late sixties and dressed in layers of heavy brown and green clothing, sat together in the sun on the bench. Coffee in hand, I asked if I could join them and received a silent, but not unfriendly, nod in return. They were quiet men who only rippled the silence with a few pebbled words from time to time. I eavesdropped on what was not said: that they had known one another, and had been in this valley, a very long time. After a few minutes of stillness I spoke to the man next to me.

"Can I ask how long you have lived here?"

He thought for a long moment. "I arrived here forty-two years ago, from Charleston, West Virginia, and haven't left yet."

I nodded and we drank our coffee in silence for another few minutes before he spoke again. "You from the far valley?"

"New Jersey."

"New Jersey." He paused a moment longer and nodded his head slowly. "Well, that's in the far valley, all right."

. . .

It was only thirty-five miles from Hartsel to Buena Vista, but Route 24 narrowed and twisted up and over 9,300-foot Trout Creek Pass in a series of turns that tightly scribed the corners of rock cuts and copses of trees, and I was seriously fatigued by the time I got there an hour later. The elevation and a long day in the saddle were taking their toll. A light headache was coming on, my entire body felt heavy, and a glance in Lucy's mirror showed a pale face and weary eyes.

A frothy Oregon chai, drunk on the outdoor deck at a place called Bongo Billy's in Buena Vista, perked me up a little. Sitting there, hands wrapped around the mug, I meant to write postcards, but ended up leaving the pen idle on the table and just stared at the mountains lost in thought. It was amazing the difference that a day's drive could make in the landscape. Just that morning I had been twenty miles from the Kansas border, surrounded by the swells of the prairie, and now, late in the afternoon, I was in the heart of western Colorado's mountain kingdom, surrounded by the fourteen-thousand-foot spires of the Collegiate Peaks.

The Collegiates were one of the most magnificent and the most inappropriately named group of mountains that I had ever seen. They rose wild, barren, full of the power of the land, and with frigid winds blasting across their naked summits, out of the valley that held the tangled icy swirl of the headwaters of the Arkansas River. In a fantastic irony of nomenclature, various surveying teams had given those grand monuments of the wilderness the place names of the safest, most elite, and most gentrified of the Anglo-European academic institutions. Mounts Harvard, Yale, and Princeton stretched south in a jagged line just east of the Sawatch Range, which marked the ultimate loft of the Continental Divide, while Mounts Oxford and Columbia stood near. I laughed, thinking of smooth green lawns and gothic architecture, carefully pruned trees and forced bulbs in well-tended gardens, classrooms stifling with dry heat and professors working in their cramped offices. It all seemed so far away.

I drove out of well-named Buena Vista slowly, looking for a campground and watching the light, fractured by scudding clouds, slide and shift across the naked rock of the peaks. At a national forest campground at the foot of Mount Princeton I stopped for the night, giggling at having driven 3,500 miles to get to a place that bore the same name of the place where I had started.

My tent site was beside the flow of an icy crystalline brook that had all the marks of a good trout stream and I wished for a fishing pole. The earth was rocky and hard, and I bent several tent stakes as I hammered them into the ground. It was a difficult setup and blasting gusts of wind blew the tent down just as I pulled the roof poles to vertical. I had to scramble to catch the parachuting fabric before it blew into the stream and to rehammer all the stakes. Exhausted in the aftermath, I dug through my saddlebags for food and realized that I had only one small can of spinach and several caramel toffees with which to create dinner. I wasn't really hungry anyway and the altitude was making me feel vaguely intoxicated so, after spending the evening staring at the swirl of water and listening to the wind sing in the trees, I fell asleep over the fragmented lines of Whitman and dreamed of oceans that became mountains that fell once again to the sea.

MORNING CAME, COLD AND MISTY, AND I rolled out of my sleeping bag feeling dizzy, nauseous, and loose in the knees. Altitude and lack of nutrition were beginning to take their toll and food had to be the first priority of the day. Bongo Billy's seemed as good a place as any, and after breaking camp and packing up, I headed back into town, concentrating hard on the road through vision that occasionally swam. Oblivious to anything but protein and carbohydrates, I wolfed down the first half of a burrito stuffed with eggs, bacon, beans, potatoes, and guacamole without looking up. Feeling better, with things coming into focus, I lifted my head and looked around Billy's, wondering at all the people I had not noticed before. Boys with sun-lightened hair, pierced ears, tribal band tattoos, and shorts hanging long and loose over lean, corded, brown legs milled about, laughing and talking, gentle and boisterous. A crowd of puppies. Billy's was where the local raft guides came for huge cups of strong coffee before heading out for the tumble of the Arkansas' rapids. I smiled and listened.

"Meanwhile, I was just like playing volleyball . . . and it was like . . . *dude!*"

"There's that gnarly spot, man, you know the one that chutes the boulders and drops into the hole . . ."

From Buena Vista, still on the curving valley run of Route 24, I headed northwest for Aspen. Lucy was running smoothly through early morning showers, her engine firing with a steady, even pulse as I climbed toward the Continental Divide and Independence Pass, but I was worried by the drops of engine oil seeping from beneath her air filter, dripping and smoking on the hot exhaust pipes. My left directional signal was also working only sporadically so I decided, halfway up the eastern side of the Continental Divide, that a stop at the Harley dealership in Glenwood Springs on the other side of the pass was in order. The rain stopped, the clouds began to lift and split, and despite the continuing cold and wind, the ride was pure pleasure, and the road sheer drama.

A family of three from Texas drove the pavement to Independence slowly with the occasional puff of diesel smoke belching from their massive, laboring, white pickup truck. Like one of Hannibal's soldiers crossing the Alps by hanging onto an elephant's tail, I slotted in behind them, afforded some shelter from the wind. They crawled around corners with cliffs on one side and drops of several thousand feet on the other, at speeds that might have annoyed the people in the cars backing up behind us, but at a pace that gave me time to gawk at the landscape and the road. Route 82 is magnificent as it twists up through the highest peaks in Colorado before plummeting down into Aspen. For grandeur, I had never seen anything like it. Independence Pass, a half-mile stretch of meadow sitting atop more than twelve thousand feet of thin air, blasting wind, and soaring landscape, is the apex of the road and of that part of the Divide, and we all stopped there to look at the view. Snowfields still remained on the meadows and the weak sunshine filtering through the bright air was just beginning to raise new green shoots through the winterkill of last year's grass.

The Texan father was a bull of a man with big hands and a silver windbreaker and shirt unbuttoned at the throat. The fabric gaped enough to expose the top of a livid purple scar, a souvenir of recent open-heart surgery. Although he was concerned about "young ladies" traveling around the country on motorcycles, as I listened to the oxygen-deprived hammering in my own chest, I was more nervous about the immediate state of his heart. We agreed to drive down to Aspen together and on the other side of the pass I once again slotted in behind them and descended slowly into the valley, into warmer temperatures and sunshine.

Aspen was too rich and too perfect to be real. Pulling into town, I parked Lucy next to a wine store to peel off my rainsuit and repack clothing that was no longer needed in the valley heat. Up on the Divide my hair had been blown into odd protruding bits and with my bright yellow rain jacket and purple rain pants I must have looked an odd sight indeed. I knew this, but it didn't make me any less annoyed when a man with an asymmetrical haircut stepped out of a shiny Jeep Grand Cherokee, pushed a few gelled strands from where they blocked the vision of his left eye, and examined me like a zoo exhibit.

"You look like a piece of Americana stepping off that dusty motorcycle."

He was the only one with a comment, but not the only one who openly stared in the few minutes I stood rearranging clothing and baggage. The expressions of the wine store patrons ranged from blatant curiosity to bald disgust. Their faces told me that I was unwelcome and ragged, an interloper with engine grease on her trousers. Across the street my Texas family was at the gas station, filling up for the homeward leg of their journey. I walked over to say good-bye. The father squeezed my hand in a powerful and lasting shake.

"God bless you," he said, "and be careful." I thanked him and assured him that I would be.

Route 82 continued in a long sloping drop that followed the Roaring Fork River to Glenwood Springs. At the Harley dealership the mechanics replaced my rear directional signal. They also suggested that my oil leak problems were due to failing umbrella valves. They could fix the valves, they said, if I left Lucy and a few hundred dollars in the repair bays on the following day.

"Could I use your phone to call my mechanic in New Jersey?" They were surprised by my question but graciously let me call from the office. Steve Scherer was in the shop when the call went through to Trenton, but he left what he was doing to come and talk with me. Five-foot-eight, all attitude and lean muscle, heavy on tattoos and light on patience for casual chatter, Steve had overhauled Lucy before I left. He was a good mechanic and I trusted him implicitly. I explained the oil, Independence Pass, and what the mechanics had said about the umbrella valves.

"Oh fuck, Karen, them guys are just trying to make a buck. How high did you say that pass was? It's the pressure change, man, not the valves. Have them drain off some oil, change the filter, and if you're still having problems in a couple of days, then do the valves. Unless you want to spend a shitload of money and time? No? All right then. How's the trip, good? Good. Now put those assholes on the phone and call me back if you have problems."

I turned to the mechanic with a smile. "Steve would like to speak to you."

The hostel at Tenth and Grand in Glenwood Springs was run by Gerry, a slight, funky, bald man who had spent much of the early seventies in Nepal and India: one of the original hippies. He had a slow smile and skin weathered to walnut brown from years spent in the sun of half a dozen subtropical countries. The walls of the hostel, which was also Gerry's home, were painted every shade but white and more than three thousand vinyl records sat in crates on the living room floor. A coffee table fronted a sofa covered with a printed tapestry, and photographs had been tucked under the glass top; Gerry in an ashram, with beads, with hair, with friends whose faces spoke of their many nationalities. Other photos were there, too, evidence of the international band of vagabonds, tourists, and travelers that had come through Glenwood Springs. We walked through the hostel, Gerry explaining the layout and the rules, which lacked structure but emphasized consideration for others. He also told me a little of his life and travels and as he spoke I realized that I knew him well. He was one of perhaps twenty different people with whom I had spent hundreds of hours on the roads of a dozen different countries.

They are out there, men and women who travel ceaselessly, not as tourists do—to see a sight or a particular foreign city and then come back to a clearly defined home—they travel because that is what they are, that is how they live, and that is what feeds their souls. They are creatures of every city, of every nation, at home everywhere, and homeless always. They are rare. Most people, myself included, even if they are on the road for months or years at a time, know that eventually they need to "go back" to something; back to some sense of country and culture, some personal understanding of stability and order. I've met only a few people who do not share this sense of placement, and they move with a special kind of energy; an energy of simultaneous restlessness and temporal peace. Gerry was one of those people. In the middle of a story about Thailand I interrupted him.

"When are you leaving?"

He stared at me. "How did you know?"

I shrugged.

"No, it doesn't matter. I want to go now," he said, "this week. The problem is the hostel. I need someone reliable to run it for me while I'm gone and I don't know when I'll be back. Maybe six months?" He paused for a moment, smiled, and looked straight into my eyes. "What about you? You could take it. Live here, manage the hostel. What do you think?" Gerry had known me all of five minutes and was offering me his home and his business. It was tempting. It would be a whole other way of life with people from all over the globe coming to stay with me, but I knew that I couldn't. I had the rest of the continent to explore, and a family that I had yet to meet. It wasn't the right time.

"I can't, Gerry, it's not yet time for me to stop." He nodded, understanding implicitly, as I knew he would, that journeys have a life cycle of their own that must be followed.

I spent the evening sitting on the porch, drinking beer, and chatting with the rest of the hostel residents. William and Larissa, native Coloradoans on a three-week bicycle tour of the high country, looked happy and windblown. Larissa was warm and vibrant, with long, brown, athletic legs and an easy laugh. William was more silent, had a "vote for Ralph Nader" hand-lettered sign pinned to his bicycle backpack, shaggy white hair that drifted over his collar, and eyes as pale as a malamute's. They made a great couple and I loved watching the small messages, a glance or a word or a touch, that passed between them. Roy, an intense and darkly quiet divorce attorney with glittering eyes and two failed marriages to his own credit, gave us a recitation of reasons *not* good enough to get married for. "I'm pregnant" and "she's so hot" topped the list. John, a tall blond man who bore more than a passing resemblance to the late John Denver, had left Point Pleasant, Pennsylvania, a dead-end job, and a failed romance the week before, after becoming "finally sick of everything." What he did not sell or give away, he loaded into the back of his pickup truck before heading west to make a new start. Rick, a nineteen-year-old boy from Rhode Island who spoke a trucker's dialect with the accent of a Portuguese seaman, told us that in the middle of one of his delivery runs it struck him as strange that he drove all day everyday and had never seen any part of his country but that which bordered his run. At the end of the shift, he went back to the dispatch, quit, and started driving west. The last of our little group was Daisia. She lived in Glenwood Springs and had a soft voice that did not match her aggressively shaved hairstyle that left only a tiny forelock of bleached-blonde hair spilling down to one eyebrow. Kasha, her huge, fawn-colored dog, slept at her feet, motionless, as our conversation swirled from the coming political season, to places each of us had seen, to life's pivotal moments.

"Delight in the world's good things, at the very most can only tire the appetite and spoil the palate; and so, not for all the sweetness will I ever lose myself." As I fixed a breakfast of leftover pizza, Roy stood behind me in the hostel kitchen quoting long passages of St. John of the Cross. Imprisoned for his extreme religious views, John was a sixteenth-century Spanish ascetic who wrote poetry about the search of the soul for union with God. In Roy there was a search of a different sort, for peace, wholeness, and family stability, but it was a search nonetheless. The cadence of four-hundred-year-old poetry seemed to bring him comfort and I watched his shoulders relax and his wide, bright eyes dim and close as he spoke.

In the afternoon, I took Lucy up the road to see the Maroon Bells. The exposed red of the mountains' rocky slopes closing off the end of a green valley was so dramatic and perfect as to be unreal. The small, symmetrical, oval, blue lake in the foreground, the snow-capped rocky peaks behind, the fir trees blanketing the slope to the upper valley, and the lush green grass carpeting the lower areas below, was like a picture off a Swiss chocolate box, artificial somehow. I took a short hike on the lakeshore path and wondered if at some point I would crash into frame and canvas daubed with paint.

Back in Aspen I stopped in at the library to read and respond to e-mails. Aspen's attitude had not improved in the twenty-four hours since I had been there last. The librarians were rude, blunt to the point of nastiness, and peered over my shoulder for much of the time that I sat before the terminal to make sure, they said, that I was not accessing pornographic sites. I was not bothering anyone, I had taken a shower that morning, and was as presentable as possible considering the circumstances, but these ladies looked at me like I had stepped in something and was tracking it all over their carpet. I came very close to reminding one unpleasant lady in a pale gray twinset and pearls that public libraries were just that. Public. Mind and body tired, my e-mails done, I left the library and bought an overpriced cup of coffee at a café called Zele. At an outdoor table I sat glumly musing about nasty Aspenites. How could it be that people who had every material thing, and who lived in such a spectacularly beautiful place, should be so poor in spirit and human kindness? Aspen felt a lot like Princeton shifted west; the same aggressively wealthy, rather unfriendly atmosphere permeated the street. God help you if you weren't white enough, rich enough, or well dressed enough to match their standards. The café tables were filling up; it was late in the afternoon and Zele was a central place for people to meet, greet, see, and be seen. A couple approached. I was alone at a table that could seat at least four.

"Could we share your table?"

"Of course. Please, sit down." George, as he introduced himself a few minutes later, sat where, like me, he could see the street. While his wife, Marlena, went to chat with someone else, we began a conversation. George was originally from New York City. A powerfully built man in his early sixties with steel-gray hair caught in a ponytail, he still exuded street smarts and urban edginess. He had come to Aspen more than thirty years before because he loved the thrill and the wildness of downhill skiing on soft powder in the high peaks. An early version of what today would be called a ski bum, George started taking on construction projects to support himself in the summer while waiting for the first snowfall. Over the years the summertime one-man contracting operation ballooned into a large company as Aspen became the winter retreat of the rich and fashionable, and he was now wealthy from the habits and houses of people whom he didn't seem to like very much. His most scathing indictment was: "These rich people don't have the strength to ski well." He was talking about more than the physical aptitude of the healthy and well-shod people whom we watched passing in the street. Marlena came back to join her husband. Tiny, blonde, and very pretty, Marlena was an interior decorator in her late forties who was successfully fighting the good fight to remain twenty-nine for as long as possible. She exuded wealth and social ease, he energy and initiative. If I ever needed to get through the mountains, I would want a man like George around. If I ever wanted to get through a fancy cocktail party, it would be Marlena whom I would wish for at my side. They were quite a pair, obviously devoted to one another, and were probably the ideal combination of what one needed to be successful in Aspen. Feeling a bit quiet and watchful, I spoke only infrequently, asking a few questions about their lives and community, as they told me about themselves. They used to ride motorcycles, too, and George had courted Marlena while driving a huge Harley, but they didn't anymore. George had broken his back in a construction site accident a few years before and Marlena had asked a single question that spoke volumes about her feelings regarding the additional risk of the bike: "OK, do we walk on the beach later, or do we ride the bike now?" Marlena began asking me about my own trip, machine, and gear. She raised one perfectly shaped eyebrow as she fingered the battered leather of my comfortable ten-year-old jacket and was horrified to hear that I did not wear leather pants or chaps when I rode.

"I have a set that I don't wear, a new jacket and leather pants, you must take mine!" The gift of leathers would have been an extravagant one, and I told her that I couldn't possibly accept. She insisted, gave me her telephone number, and told me that she would be terribly offended if I didn't at least try on the leather pants considering that I did not own a pair. As she and George left to meet friends for dinner, I promised that I would call.

COOL AND ELEGANT IN TAILORED LINEN trousers and a crisp white shirt, Marlena was waiting when I arrived at Zele's. The leather pants that she offered were top quality, nearly new, and didn't fit—too slender at the thigh for my build—but we sat and had coffee together, talking of the road, of the men in our lives, and of this fantastic mountain kingdom. A tall woman, Marlena's friend and travel agent who happened to be passing in the street, came to sit with us. Giovanna was handsome, olive-complexioned, slender, and also permanently twenty-nine. She had just been to the dentist, she told us, but hadn't really enjoyed the experience. I sympathized, thinking of drills and novocaine, but for Giovanna the problem had been much more fundamental.

"I haven't had my hair done recently, he's so handsome, and I spent the entire time worrying about my roots." She turned slightly in her chair, recrossed her long legs, looked at me for a long moment out of dramatic kohl-rimmed eyes, and turned to Marlena. "Isn't she beautiful?" she said. She turned back to me and said with a mock stage whisper, "We only associate with beautiful people." I got the disturbing feeling that this just might be true.

I'm not sure what it was that made me so uncomfortable about the attitudes, wealth, and light gossip of Aspen. Marlena especially was trying to be kind and generous and, regardless of the lifestyle choices that I had made as an adult, my own upbringing had been in a suburban Boston community that in recent years had become almost as exclusive, white, and privileged as Aspen was. Granted, my cocktail dress and little suits with their accompanying high heels were stashed in an urban warehouse half a continent away, but I did own such things and could function well in the settings where they were required. The conversation at Zele's was facile and filled with light laughter and amusing allusions to people that I didn't know. It should have been relaxing but instead I could feel the tension crawling up my spine and gray-edged depression swirling through my thoughts. Perhaps it was the contrast between the rawness and immediacy of the lifestyle that I was beginning to feel comfortable with—always moving, accepting conditions, human or atmospheric, at face value, reveling in the solitude and the temporal nature of the road—and Aspen, which was the antithesis of all of that. In Aspen people lived, or aspired to live, established lives where relationships were crucial, the social hierarchy of the community was clear, and conversations were the sum of more than the words of which they consisted. Discourse and interaction was neither direct nor immediate and sentences were multilayered things filled with innuendo, applause, and sarcasm that writhed just beneath the placid surface of well-educated diction. There was nothing raw, immediate, or accepting about any of it.

We did spend a few minutes talking about the beauty of the valley and the contrast in the lives that people lived here as compared to the lives that people on "the outside" experienced. Marlena's voice was soft, strangely hesitant. "I dream," she said. "Sometimes I dream I see the mobs coming over the mountains with torches. They're pissed. And they should be." I think that both she and Giovanna knew that this life they led, Giovanna booking resort holidays and Marlena decorating the chalets and summerhouses that her husband built, was somehow artificial. It was, however, a refined and beautiful artificiality.

I said good-bye to the women, left them with their lattes, and, suddenly sick of civilization, hustled down the hill to where Route 133 breaks west of Route 82. I needed to get back to the road, back to the woods, and back to the solitude and silence that was within the rumble of Lucy's engine.

Route 133 snakes out through Carbondale and follows the frothy greenish-blue tumble of the Crystal River, up through a gorgeous, heavily wooded valley, toward the heights of McClure Pass. At only nine thousand feet, the ridge that marks the pass was not particularly lofty by Colorado standards, but it was dramatic in how the landscape and vegetation changed from one side to the other. Within the space of a hundred yards of the crest, I left behind the climbing depths of the forest and descended onto hot, dry, buff-colored slopes covered in semiarid sage and low-growing vegetation. Without the shade of tall fir trees, the air temperature rose immediately and a pleasant day turned into a hot one.

After skirting the edge of the Gunnison National Forest in a crescent moon arc, I spent the afternoon running the lip of Black Canyon. The occasional guardrail did little to hide the yawning drop into the abyss below my right boot. The Canyon looked like it was the product of a lightning bolt that had split the ground open, charring the rock all the way down, but it was actually the Gunnison River that had cut the volcanic crystalline schist and gneiss into a chasm that reached depths of almost three thousand feet. The interior was craggy, wild, nearly impenetrable, and completely deserted. The Denver and Rio Grande Railroad that used to snake through fifteen miles of the upper canyon was long gone and only a handful of fools and adventurers had ever dared to navigate the tangle of the Gunnison as it roared through the Black Canyon, tearing itself to froth over a dragon's mouth of jagged rock. A little tired in the heat and preoccupied with negotiating the tight turns of a road that fell away to oblivion just to the right of Lucy's exhaust system, I moved slowly and stopped frequently at the overlooks to roll fragrant sage between my fingers, lean on splitrail guard fences, and admire the view. At the Curecanti Needle overlook, where the green river water swirled and surged around the base of an eight-hundred-foot spire, Poe's Imp of the Perverse came to find me again. I stood alone, peering over the drop, and wondered what it would be like to just walk over the edge of that black void. I could take two more steps, disappear, and my body would never be found. Shaking off my dark little companion, I moved back from the edge.

The speeding trucks on Route 50 made the forty-mile run from the

Morrow Point Reservoir into Montrose a little less than relaxing, but it was dazzling country. The road into Cimarron, looping and curving through rolling foothills, might as well have been built through a kaleidoscope. Green, gold, and crimson highlights flashed across the slopes and dry washes, kicked up by the rays of a falling, blistering sun. Traffic thinned and I slowed, watching the light burst on weather-beaten ranch houses and barns, turning dry, gray board to bonfires of flashing purple and orange.

EXHIBIT E. *After the War*

Ridgeway State Park is twenty-five miles south of Montrose on Route 550, nestled at the base of the San Juan Mountains. Winnie was the ranger at the entrance station. A bright, laughing woman with vivid blue eyes, she was in her seventies, but her back was straight and her shoulders were broad and strong. She was writing my license plate number on the registration form when she looked up and smiled.

"You're from New Jersey?"

"Yes."

"I once knew a boy from there, this was during the war. He was from Mount Holly." She laughed, suddenly girlish. "Oh, the dances we went to. We had such a good time!" Winnie's New Jersey soldier was stationed at the airbase in Ridgeway in 1943. She told me of long walks and how much he loved the mountains.

"Was there a little romance maybe?"

"Maybe. Maybe. But when they get married, you'd best forget all about that." She was silent for a moment and continued a little wistfully. "I did think he might come back, though, he liked it here that much . . . lots of boys came back after the war."

. . .

THE PREVIOUS DAY'S HEAT AND LONG miles had left me feeling a little frayed, but I packed up and headed out at 7 A.M. into a crystalline, windless morning. The San Juan Mountains soared in grand, snow-crested ridges, a massive rampart crowning the already elevated country. Two hot air balloons, bubbles of yellow, blue, green, and orange silk, rose in airy grace before a mountain backdrop that was as enduring as the balloons were ephemeral. I pulled to the side of the road, knowing before I released the shutter that the photographs I took would fully capture neither the contrast nor the expansiveness of the landscape beyond.

Past Ridgeway, the San Miguel Canyon road, which tacked west toward the Utah border, was a narrow strip of tar twisting beneath red-rock walls and built just above the river that bore the same name. I followed it for miles as the watercourse narrowed, splashing over slabs of burgundy sandstone. When the road veered away from the river, everything associated with flowing water—damp air, trees, stands of dark green grasses—disappeared in seconds. I drove into a long, low valley, patchy with dusty brush and fist-sized rocks scattered across the red sand, stretching uninterrupted toward distant ridgelines already shimmering in the rising heat. A few miles east of the state line, where

I suspected the rapidly drying country would soon give way entirely to desert, I stopped in Bedrock to top off Lucy's gas tank and call home.

If the community of Bedrock was more than a store at the crossroads where a single dirt track leading to Uravan and the blacktop leading to Paradox came together, I was not aware of it. The singular building was an antique one-room affair with a steel-rimmed bushel barrel of antlers on the front porch and jars of mayonnaise neatly lined up where bolts of calico had once been stacked. The sign above the door read BEDROCK STORE SINCE 1881 and I doubted that renovations had altered much in over a century. I paid for my gas and borrowed a roll of toilet paper for use in the "ladies' room," a weathered gray outhouse thirty yards off the northwest corner of the store. A few minutes later, stepping back into the glare of desert light, I noticed that a truck had pulled in and was waiting near the single pump, which was blocked by my motorcycle. Hustling to move Lucy, I swung into the saddle and was tilting her center of gravity to the right so that I could lift the kickstand on the left, when my right boot slipped on the loose gravel of the pad surrounding the pump. I felt a sickening surge of adrenaline as Lucy heeled far past her central balance point, beyond recovery. Five hundred pounds of metal rolled toward the crushed rock and the only thing I could do was step out of the way and try to guide her somewhat more gently to the ground. With gas splashing from the full tank, soaking my hands and trousers, I picked her back up, horrified by the possibility of damage. *What am I going to do way out here if I've mangled something major?* I was quite sure that there wasn't a repair shop for a hundred miles. Frantically I checked her over, straightening a side-view mirror, looking for wires ripped loose, bent hardware, and snapped brackets, but there was nothing. No damage. Not even a scratch. A short cut on my palm leaked blood into my glove where handlebars and rock had come together with my hand between them, but it was a tiny thing and I much preferred to see a minor laceration on me than major damage to Lucy.

Colorado Route 90 met Utah Route 46 as I crossed the state line. The fantastical beauty of the Southwest began somewhere around La Sal, where rising mesas and fins of colored rock, shaped into arches, pinnacles, smooth curves, and falling cliffs by wind, water, and ice, jutted from the desert floor. Park service signs at Wilson Arch, where a cobalt sky glowed through a gaping yet graceful hole in the red stone, explained the process: "This formation is known as entrada sandstone. Over time the superficial cracks, joints, and fissures of these layers were saturated with water. Ice formed in the fissures, melted under extreme desert heat, and winds cleaned out the loose particles. A series of free-standing fins remained. Wind and water attacked these fins until, in some, the cementing material gave way and chunks of rock tumbled out." Whatever the science, what resulted from these forces was a sculptors' garden of shape and color lit from all sides in the clear blaze of desert light.

At the Edge of the Cedars State Park and Museum in Blanding, I pulled over to look at a collection of art and artifacts from the many native peoples who had lived in what is now southeastern Utah. The twentieth-century buildings of the museum had been erected not only to house the collection, but also to protect and frame the ruins of a pueblo inhabited by the Chacoan people between the ninth and thirteenth centuries. The wings of the building stretched out, flanking the rubble foundations of a village that included homes, storerooms, and a kiva—a circular ceremonial room dug deep into the earth. I walked streets abandoned for centuries and climbed down a wooden ladder into the kiva. It was cool and dim inside, and I sat on the packed earth floor, breathing the faint odor of old wood smoke. Fires had burned in that earthen womb for a thousand years and their redolence was still in the walls.

A ponytailed boy of perhaps twenty stood smiling in the brilliant light as I emerged from the kiva. He had a red bandana tied around his forehead and ripped blue jeans tucked into high, black motorcycle boots. On his T-shirt a yellow smiley face with a bullet hole through its forehead leaked painted blood down his chest. Black leather cord necklaces dropped past his rib cage: two slices of geode, a tiny white skull, and a pentagram. Despite the toughness in his dress, his speech was gentle, and as we circled back toward the museum buildings, I found out that he was a traveler, too, but a more serious one than I will probably ever be. Ezra lived in a van painted with a Tree of Life design, worked as an auto mechanic when he needed money or found a place where he wanted to stay for a few days, and was slowly making his way toward a family reunion in northern California. I thought about my own family and their distinct lack of enthusiasm for some of the travel and lifestyle choices that I had made.

"What does your family think about the way you live?" I asked him.

"Them? Oh, they're thrilled. I'm actually one of the more normal people in my family."

Our loop around the village completed, we went to look at the interior collection. The walls were decorated with reproductions of art found carved or painted in the surrounding canyons. Geometric shapes of people and animals hunted, played pipes, and danced, fanning out across the vertical space. One group showed a family: a man and woman holding hands, their bodies each a single trapezoid. Within the mother's trapezoid was the upside down figure of a baby. White Anasazi pots, smooth shapes highlighted by overlays of black geometric designs, stood graceful and spotlit in stark glass cases. Intricate baskets, so tightly woven in the twelfth century that they could still hold water when they were discovered eight hundred years later, rested near them. From the modern period of the Navahos and the Utes there were wonderful beaded moccasins and fringed shirts and pipes carved from juniper. The pipes were traditionally fashioned by a young man who would pitch the instrument to match the timbre of his voice so that his sweetheart would recognize it when he played in the dark.

EXHIBIT F: *Risk*

"I hope you are careful driving your motorcycle. We just saw a really bad accident at the Grand Canyon." The young man was tall, strongly built, blond, and a total stranger. I was reading about geology in the lobby of the visitors' center at Natural Bridges National Monument when he launched, unasked, into tales of motorcycle carnage, crumpled fairings, bloodstained pavement, and EMT crews.

Why do people feel compelled to tell motorcyclists this sort of thing? Tens of thousands die in car crashes every year, far more than die in motorcycle accidents, and I have yet to see anyone approach a stranger driving a car and caution them to "be careful." Yet these unsolicited warnings happen all the time to motorcyclists. How are we supposed to respond to: "I hope you are careful"? Perhaps: "No, I'm not careful. In fact, I drive like a complete lunatic and have a secret wish to become one with the front grille of a Cadillac DeVille." That is, after all, the implied message—that one is somehow self-destructive, reckless, a needless risk-taker if one drives a motorcycle. Cars—as anyone can see—are so much safer. Safer, that is, until one thinks of the more than forty-five thousand Americans who die in car crashes every single year despite their airbags and roll cages.

"Yes," I said, "always." I was annoyed, but understood that he was associating me with some horrible scene of wreckage. Maybe he thought his warning would save my life, and for that I tried to find gratitude. He had an accent, and in the short conversation that followed, he told me that he was from Estonia, and that he went to university in Texas, where he was on an athletic scholarship. He spoke of the beauty of the Southwest and told me how much he had enjoyed learning outdoor pursuits that he had not experienced in his home country.

"Scuba diving," he said. "I especially like scuba diving in caves."

. . .

Partially because it was a blisteringly hot day, partially because the park loop road that runs through the Bridges area had speed-limit restrictions of twenty-five miles an hour, but mostly because the feel of sun and hot motorcycle-driven wind on skin is something that warms the senses right to the bone, I left my jacket off and strapped my helmet to Lucy's frame before setting off into the park.

Natural Bridges National Monument was established thanks to the discovery and publicity efforts of a prospector named Cass and the support of President Teddy Roosevelt. Different from free-standing arches like Wilson, the bridges were formed where rivers cut into, and beneath, canyon walls. The rock spans were graceful, almost delicate where they stood, far below the rim level of the twisting buff, cream, and white-walled canyons. The tallest bridge, two hundred feet from arch to riverbed, was called *Sipapu*, the Hopi word for "the opening between worlds."

I had left Ezra still gazing into the cases at the Edge of the Cedars Park, but I met him again at one of the pull-offs in Bridges, and we walked together to look over the yawning edge of the rim at the Horsecollar cliff dwelling ruins. The small stone homes had been snugly built beneath the lower lip of the canyon a thousand years before. To get down from the rim, or up from the riverbank, to where the cluster of buildings sat several hundred feet above the floor of the canyon, must have been extremely difficult. I wondered if it was fear or necessity that made people choose that perched, protected, and precarious spot. Ezra and I stood on the edge and talked of freedom and travel. I knew it to be true when he said that as much as he enjoyed what he did and how he lived, his gypsy existence was sometimes a lonely life.

"Maybe we could travel together for a few days?" he asked. I smiled and declined, not because there was anything off-putting about Ezra; he was curious, capable, bright, and—despite the bleeding smiley face on his T-shirt—soft spoken and gentle. I said no because I still wanted to be alone for a while and to see the emptiness of the desert in solitude. After two years of graduate school, where the voices of hundreds rang clear and sharp every day, to listen to nothing more than the rumble of a motorcycle and the beating of my own heart was something that I needed to do. I told him all of this, but I think Ezra would have understood without my explanation; he was a wanderer, too.

After the Bridges, the ride and the road heated up. Lucy and I snaked our way across inhospitable and incredibly beautiful canyon, mesa, arch, and natural bridge country. The air was dry, the breeze a blast furnace, and sweat dried instantly to a flaky layer of white powder on my jawline and collarbones. I passed weather-sculpted rock in fantastical formations that bore strangely civilized names; names that fit the shapes but not the feeling of this land, names like Cheese Box Mesa and Jacob's Chair.

At 7 P.M. the sun was still high, but I was getting tired and decided to pull into the Lake Powell area and shut Lucy down for the night. With my tent pitched on a moonscape of soft red desert sand and powdery earth, I followed a sloping wash down to the opaque yellowish green waters of the Powell Reservoir.

As welcome as the sight of cool water at the end of a dusty day was, I knew that this broad expanse of artificial lake was the product of a massive dam that had stopped the free flow of the Colorado River and had drowned the natural magnificence that used to be Glen Canyon. Ironically, Lake Powell was named for John Wesley Powell, a Civil War veteran who had explored the reaches of the Colorado River in 1869 and who had especially loved "the curious ensemble of wonderful features—carved walls, royal arches, glens, alcove gulches, mounds and monuments" of Glen Canyon. The 710-foot Glen Canyon Dam, which created a lake 560 feet deep that took eighteen years to fill, had destroyed forever what Powell had loved. I slid into the water and lay on my back, paddling slowly to keep afloat. Although refreshing, there was something eerie about the experience; like swimming over the site of a shipwreck, or walking through a Civil War battlefield. The landscape felt negatively disturbed and unnaturally altered in important ways.

The next morning I stopped in Hanksville for breakfast. Vicky was the waitress in the combination hotel/restaurant on the right side, if one was headed west, of that one-street town. Her hand was tattooed with a floral design that curled from her wrist and sent tendrils of roses growing up fingers that were already heavy with silver rings.

"Good morning."

"What do you want?"

"Pancakes, a short stack, and coffee please." She sniffed and turned away in silence broken only by the chime of her bracelets. A few minutes later she was back. The plate dropped to the table along with the check.

"Here. You can pay on the way out." I slid the check to the inside of the table, stirred half-and-half into my coffee, and eavesdropped on the conversation a few tables down, where Vicky talked and laughed loudly with local men about the Harleys that she and her boyfriend were rebuilding together. Was there room in Hanksville for only one motorcycle woman?

With little wind and temperatures that stayed below eighty-five degrees right through the afternoon, it was a rare and perfect driving day. Lucy galloped effortlessly through jaw-dropping scenery on smooth roads. Route 95, coming out of Glen Canyon and through Capital Reef National Park, was a labyrinth fantasy of red walls that give way to beige and rose mountains devoid of any visible greenness or human settlement until the Freemont River came down through the washes in green and silver clarity. Where there was water, human habitation had flourished for centuries, and I stopped to look at the petroglyphs in the Fremont River Valley. Big-horned sheep, hunters, and human figures topped with elaborate headdresses danced across the smooth face of a rock wall, inscribed eight centuries before by a people whose name has been forgotten. More recent was the settlement at the little town of Fruita. Mormons had arrived a century before and planted the orchards that still stand: peach trees, row upon row. The Fremont River kept them watered and lush, an oasis in the midst of thousands of square miles of harsh and beautiful land.

Dave's Country Store and Trading Post sits at the crossroads where Routes 89 and 24 come together, just past a sign that reads LAST CHANCE FOR NIGHT CRAWLERS. I filled Lucy's tank and went inside. A sign hung near the door: PRICES SUBJECT TO CHANGE DEPENDING ON CUSTOMER'S ATTITUDE. Dave stood behind a cash register that had a poster taped to the front: a monkey morphing into Bill Clinton in a series of Warhol-bright prints. The embodiment of his business, and a possible character out of a gunslinger paperback, Dave wore a black cowboy hat low atop his ears. Broad, gray mustaches swept across his face and joined forces with the substantial sideburns descending from his hat brim. His legs and hips were slim within dark blue jeans, and a huge "Dave" belt buckle sat at the bottom of a line of neat pearl buttons that closed his blue-green shirt. I handed him two dollars for the gas.

"Would you pour me a cup of coffee? I'm just going to go out and move the bike. I'll be right back."

"Sit down," he growled, not unkindly. "It can stay where it is." There was one pump and Lucy was blocking it. I mentioned this to Dave. It was the wrong thing to say. Bushy gray eyebrows dropped over narrowed eyes. "This is my place, ain't it? If I say it can stay where it is, it can stay where it is. *Sit down.*"

"OK," I squeaked and dropped onto a stool. Dave poured my coffee. I reached for one of the spoons bundled in a mug near the register and looked down to see a fund-raising letter from the National Rifle Association. The return envelope was sealed and stamped.

From the overhead beams hung a collection of hard-used baseball and cowboy hats. Most were ragged, sweat-stained, misshapen, and frankly filthy, mute testimony to the lives of the men who once wore them. He collected them from his patrons, Dave explained, sometimes forcibly removing the hats from their heads once he deemed them to have enough "character" to hang beside the rest of the collection. Five were nailed slightly lower than the rest: the headgear of deceased, but not forgotten, friends. Dave was gruff, yet warm, concerned, and curious about my trip. We talked for a while about my route through Utah and where I was going next. Then he reached behind the register and his hand reemerged holding an enormous heavy pistol. Crafted from solid steel, it was an evil-looking thing, a six-shooter with a long barrel and bone inlay grips.

"You carry one of these?"

"No." I thought it might not be prudent to mention how much I disliked firearms and how I thought that carrying one tucked away in a saddlebag would be one of the more useless things that I could do.

"You should. I don't leave home without it."

CHARLIE HUNT HAD THE TOP-OF-THE-LINE BLUE BMW R 1150RT, complete with CD player, and was the best-looking septuagenarian that I have ever seen. Only a few gray streaks peppered his thick auburn hair and the muscles of his chest and shoulders moved visibly beneath his tight black T-shirt. Charlie Applebaum had a Honda ST 1100 ABS with sleek lines and a candy-apple red finish. A decade younger than his friend, Honda Charlie was no slouch either, and although he claimed that BMW Charlie could out-ride and outrun him, he seemed to be holding his own.

We rode out of Delta together, bounding over the open expanses of the flats and the hill country approaching the Nevada border at speeds in excess of eighty miles an hour. It was a glorious run; the roads wide and straight across the flats, banked and well turned up through the hills. We were in the high desert, sage green and buff colors in the foreground, the white of salt flats gleaming like snow on the dry reaches of Sevier Lake to the south. The purples and blues of the Confusion Range shifted toward deep greens as the low-growing pines came closer and the land rose a few thousand vertical feet. An hour and fifteen minutes and a hundred miles from Delta, we pulled into the next town, Baker, which sits astride the Nevada/Utah border. As one Charlie went inside the gas station for coffee, the other sat and talked with me about international relations, the status of the post-Soviet republics, and the conservative versus liberal political and social agendas. By the time we were saddling up, the Charlies had decided they would take me out for a "real" dinner and continue the conversation in Ely, the town toward which we were all headed that night. Heavy on the throttles, we crossed the Snake and Schell Creek Ranges, flew over Conner's Pass, and dropped into Ely in the late afternoon.

The men were staying at a hotel in town. As my budget was tighter than theirs, I went looking for a place to pitch my tent. Ely's KOA, at almost eighteen dollars a night, was too expensive for a patch of chemically treated grass wedged between motorhomes, so I backtracked out of town to look for a spot at Cave Lake State Park. The centerpiece of that limestone valley, with its green meadows shot through with daffodils, was a small lake that turned dark agate green in the lowering light of the evening. The camping ended up being free thanks to a couple of friendly Californians who, when they saw me circling the packed tenting area for a second time, searching fruitlessly for an unoccupied space, came out and offered me part of their site, as well as a cold Budweiser out of an ice-filled cooler.

I met the Charlies at the Jailhouse Restaurant, where we devoured mountains of potatoes, steak, and grilled chicken. The conversation ranged from second wives—each of the Charlies had one of those—to our jobs "back in the real world," where one Charlie was a professor and the other a financial planner, to motorcycle lifestyle issues, to global warming, politics, and foreign aid. The men had been friends and traveling companions for many years, and every summer, usually in the company of a third biker buddy, they carved out time to take long road trips together. The third friend had been with them on this trip, too, until the day before. He had continued on Route 66 and was going all the way to Chicago, while the Charlies were on a shorter loop and had to return home to work and family obligations. We spoke of why we continued to ride, despite the hesitations of our families, despite the occasional risk: each of us sought a sense of place within our nation, each of us tendered enormous curiosity about the diversity of people and lifestyles to be found where the towns were few and the roads stretched long, and each of us had a visceral appreciation of the solitude and the sensation and the rush of motion as asphalt flowed beneath two wheels. Honda Charlie stabbed the last wedge of potato on his plate and considered it a moment.

"Your senses return out here," he said. So they do. I had noticed it especially that afternoon, riding through the parched and unforgiving landscape of eastern Nevada. A small pond was caught in a hollow on the outskirts of Ely and I could smell the water, wet and green and hanging in the desert wind, miles before seeing it.

I said good-bye to the Charlies at the end of the evening and promised to send a postcard when I returned home. I was sorry to see them go, kind and generous men that they were. I liked my solitary ways, but conversation like that was a rare treat.

It was a slow drive back to Cave Lake. A full moon was rising and the dark, open landscape began to shift and streak with long, nickel-plated washes of light. A combination of the night's beauty and my concern about the browsing elk that I had seen at roadside earlier in the day kept my hand on Lucy's throttle light. By the time I got back to my tent the moon was huge and full, a shining sphere that shimmered like mercury in the soft clear air and brushed the landscape with silver.

Months later, a letter from BMW Charlie arrived in New Jersey and, looking back on that evening in Ely, that conversation took on extra importance. As each of us attempted to articulate what it was that brought us to ride that high, hot, desert country, as we agreed that moving across America with the flow of the land beneath our wheels was an awakening of sorts, we did not know that their friend, riding Route 66, had been killed that afternoon. He had crossed an intersection and did not see the oncoming truck.

The next morning began cool and windless and I was back in Ely early for coffee and a few attempts to call back East. Maybe it was the openness of the desert or long conversations with strangers, but I wanted to hear a familiar voice. There were only answering machines picking up at Dave's, my parents', and an old friend's, but I listened to the recorded messages right to the end, just to hear the cadence of familiar tones. I left a message with Dave, wanting to update him on where I was, and thinking that Oregon wasn't so far away. Reconnected again, I hung up the phone and stepped outside, into the rising wind.

Out in the parking lot, unwrapping a cellophaned Danish, I looked up toward the slopes of the White Pine Mountains. Storm clouds were building, rolling in from the east and south, boiling over the ridges in heavy black and gray masses. *Oh Christ, here it comes. Time to get the hell out of Dodge.* With one more burning gulp of coffee, I stuffed the remaining half of my breakfast in the saddlebag and set out on Route 50, driving west at speed in an attempt to outrun the far edge of the storm.

Route 50 stretches more than three thousand miles from Ocean City, Maryland, to Sacramento, California. Thanks to a *Life* magazine article, the three-hundred-mile section that crosses Nevada, roughly following the path of the Pony Express riders, bears the appellation "The Loneliest Road in America." The route bisects the state, cresting a series of grassy mountain ranges and dropping into valleys five to ten miles across that are oriented in long, unpopulated north–south sweeps. There is no tree cover, just low growth composed mostly of sage, a few scruffy bushes, occasional stunted pines, and tumbleweeds drying in the wind and heat. It is not the sort of landscape where one wants to be caught by a storm.

The blast of wind that fronted the violence of the weather system began a few miles from the immense sand heaps and craters of the Ruth Copper Pit. Lucy bounced across the road with the gusts, and the specter of the Plains wind rode with me. Would this day be like the one I spent in western Kansas, grinding through the miles, remote town by remote town? I dropped my speed to keep control and swore softly at the coming storm. Where the asphalt ended in loose gravel at the shoulder, triangular orange signs began to appear, advising of "fresh oil," recently sprayed on the chip-sealed road. *Wonderful. High winds, a bouncing motorcycle, and a slippery surface, could there be a more enjoyable combination?* An hour later, travel on the Loneliest Road became a wild ride of deceleration, speed, and body and bike adjustment, made even more dramatic when lightning started to flash across the open valleys in gigantic, ragged bolts.

A pulse of greenish-yellow electricity scissoring from the pendulous clouds to the valley floor upped a tickle of fear to a full-fledged adrenaline rush in the middle of the Butte Valley. The storm had caught me. There wasn't a house, barn, or gas station anywhere nearby and I was driving a large chunk of metal at forty miles per hour. What did it feel like to get blown off a bike by a hundred thousand volts of electricity? The scrub brush got no higher as the road lifted into the low ridges of the Diamond Mountains and the gentle contours of the ancient eroded slopes could provide no overhang or shelter. Eureka, billed as "the loneliest town on the loneliest road in America," was the only option for getting out of the weather and I leaned hard into the wind, twisted the throttle, and carved the turns as close to the centerline as possible. Showers blew over in stinging points of wind-driven rain, each drop a tiny needle on my bare wrists and neck. It was strangely beautiful in the Diamonds, moving through the shriek of wind and the greenish light that slanted beneath the dark underbellies of convulsing thunderheads. For a moment, as the air moved and heaved, the electricity of the storm lit the rain from within, and the clouds shifted in a dark and moving ceiling, I wondered if I had somehow driven beneath the surface of an ocean.

Set into a sheltered valley on the western side of the Diamonds, Eureka was an old silver and lead town and seemed to me a bastion of civilization and shelter. At the Owl Club Café, with Lucy tucked in against the lee wall of the gas station across the street, I waited out the weather over a bowl of oatmeal. It was a fruitless wait, however; the storm never fully came down off the ridge, and after an hour of restless sitting, I decided to try the next seventy miles into Austin.

Initially there was no storm, but the wind was just as violent and Lucy was down to thirty-five miles an hour most of the way. The pavement was deserted, silent but for the scream of the gale. Twice, caught in a blast, we skidded dangerously close to the edge of the road and the ditch beyond. Another thunderstorm rolled over fifty miles out from Eureka. Bolts burned through the agitated air, brilliant and uncomfortably close. After one particularly proximate flash left the palpable taste of sulfur hanging in the wind, I decided that I had had enough and would be staying in Austin for the night. Getting fried in the middle of Nevada, somewhere between the Shoshone and Stillwater Mountains with the sole goal of trying to make a few more miles, simply wasn't worth it.

Austin was once a silver-mining town of ten thousand. Now maybe two hundred people live within the municipal limits, the graveyards are more heavily populated than the homes, and most of the houses and buildings that are not recently arrived trailers are boarded up or abandoned and have porches and picket fences that tilt crazily into the dust. Fifty million dollars in silver had been dug from the hills around Austin in the later years of the nineteenth century, but the silver is gone, and only small and faltering turquoise extraction operations keep Austin's reputation as a mining center alive.

As the mines gasp their last breath, tourist dollars help to keep Austin's short commercial district respiring, if only barely. Three turquoise stores on Main Street sold a variety of glittering jewelry and art pieces, although most were set with stones that originated from places other than Austin. One store belonged to Jim, a huge man who wore a silver watchband five inches broad and set with large chunks of fine turquoise. He told me that the annual Rock and Bottle show, where sales of turquoise and antique glass merged with a community party that welcomed any and all travelers, had taken place in Austin the day before. Apparently a lot of bikers had shown up.

"Are you riding with any of those guys?"

"No, I'm alone." I thought of the Charlies and the two hundred miles that we had ridden together the day before. What I did not know then was that those two hundred miles were the most that I would ever travel with other bikers over the course of the summer. The report from the Rock and Bottle show was that it had been a good party, although things had gotten rough at the bar as the evening progressed. Jim spoke of the local people who came into town from isolated homestead sites and of the woman who arrived in Austin each year with a load of homemade pies for sale. According to Jim the lemon meringue alone was worth waiting twelve months for.

"I ate that whole pie yesterday," he said. "It was so good I just kept going back for another piece." He patted the strain of the purple shirt that covered the swell of his waistline. "It's a good thing I don't do that too often."

Jim's counter help, a petite woman in her early forties, was devoted to Austin. She talked about a young man who, just passing through on a road trip from Florida to California, had at first sight fallen in love with the crumbling little town and had returned a few months later with all of his possessions. He found work as a carpenter and rented one of the slanting little houses perched on the hillside. "He loves it here," she said. "Maybe one day you'll come back to stay, too."

It happens sometimes: the heart beats slowly with a pulse of belonging, for different people in different places, and I wondered if I too might find a place for myself like that one day. It would not be in Austin, however. True it was isolated and very beautiful, just the sort of community that I liked best, but there was a sense that Austin was hanging on by its fingernails. The townspeople, while so kind and welcoming to vagrant carpenters and motorcyclists, encouraging us to stay, were abandoning their own homes. In ones and twos, family by family, they were leaving, moving toward less lonely communities, better schools, better jobs, somewhere, anywhere, else. As one woman, a slender blonde with sun-leathered skin, told me later that afternoon as she came into a bar to collect cardboard boxes to pack her things, "It's hard to live a hundred and twelve miles from the nearest grocery store."

In the late afternoon I left my rented room and crossed the street to the International Hotel to spend the evening listening to a jukebox replete with George Straight, Hank Williams Jr., and Eagles tunes, music that fit the feel of the old pineboard floors, the peeling pool table, and faded dart board. Broad gold bands of late western light spilled across the front porch and flooded through tall windows, illuminating motes of dust floating in the dry air.

Although a large room with a high ceiling is where most of the drinking happens at the hotel, the bar at the International is not a place. It is, rather, a grand and marvelous piece of furniture. Fifteen feet tall, it had a central mirror and two side panels that were just beginning to bronze with age, but that still reflected the motion of the room beyond. It was the sort of massive, heavily carved and ornamented installation designed for grand salons with thick red carpets, sweeping gowns trimmed with marabou feathers, and the silver-headed canes of the gamblers and mining magnates of another era. Shipped out of New York in 1860, the massive expanse of mahogany and glass had sailed around The Horn and was carried overland to Austin by wagon from San Francisco. The bar arrived in pieces and was reassembled and installed in the hotel in 1863, where it has sat, glowing and undisturbed, for generations. The grinning face of a satyr leered down from the center section. What had it seen in the last century and a half? As the rest of Austin, the churches, the homes, and the hotels, crumbled into dust, this piece—formidable and incongruous—looked as if it had arrived yesterday.

Neil, the local electrician who wore an impressive turquoise and gold ring on his pinky finger, payment for a complex wiring job, bought me my first beer. He was from Fallon but drove the hundred-plus miles to Austin for work and stayed days or weeks until the jobs were finished. He told me that he was a former karate prize fighter, something that sounded very much like a bar story, but that I came to believe as I watched his quick hands and the whippet energy that pulsed through his mastiff-sized frame. A biker named Jazz came over to talk when Neil went outside to join other recently arrived friends on the porch. Jazz was from California. Every year he came to Nevada, he said, usually to Austin, to ride dirt bikes through the mountains, high desert, and open sage with a couple of buddies. He pointed them out: two men inexpertly throwing darts in the adjoining billiard room.

At the door there was a flurry of sound and motion and Neil came bounding back in. "C'mon! You've got to see this!" He took me by the hand and pulled all of us, locals and newcomers, out onto the porch to watch the sunset. Pink, orange, and gold washed over the landscape in broad bands of light, the pale colors of the mountains deepening and holding the last of the daylight in their slopes. The sky shifted to a palette of darkening and intensifying violet, blue, and burgundy as, one by one, the stars appeared and brightened. We sat, transfixed, watching that simple, yet most dramatic, show of light and color and space. Low voices and raised arms pointed out constellations, the lights of a jet, a satellite. Jazz sighed from where he sat perched on the railing beside me. He stared out over the desert and spoke without turning, his voice pulling between appreciation and wistfulness.

"The country is all filling in. This is one of the last really *open* states."

I thought again about the Florida carpenter and his rented house on one of the little streets just above where we sat. I could see why a boy from the closed, smoggy, dense, flat places of Florida would want to come back here to settle in where the landscape was vast and high and the sunset heroic.

Austin was silent and the road was empty when I packed up Lucy in the early morning light. My fear of rising wind and more storms proved unjustified and only the breeze created by the movement of machinery blew the ends of my scarf back from my neck as I left town. Route 50 spilled downhill, past the graveyards and the ruin of Stokes Tower, a turreted Italianate structure that was the former summer home of a wealthy mining financier, and within half a mile I could not find Austin in my rearview mirror.

The terrain was much the same as the day before: low ranges, broad valleys, and single-track dirt roads heading out at right angles for the horizon, some labeled with tiny signs for mines or communities that may or may not still exist. Is Antelope, Nevada, a living place? Fallon was the next town, more than a hundred miles away across flattening, alkali-encrusted country. The track of the Pony Express riders, who pounded across that landscape for less than a year beginning in 1860, was still visible at roadside; a bare path cut through the sparse vegetation and the fragile wafer of desert topsoil to the dusty earth. The pavement was wide, in good repair, and there was no traffic. I let Lucy's speed drift upward to sixty, seventy, eighty miles an hour, galloping through clean air that lacked any hint of moisture to haze or mute the intensity of the midmorning light. Sand Mountain, a looming, rust-colored dune, rippled in the northern distance, its ruddy hue in stark contrast to the white of the alkali flats at its base. Lonely white crosses stood thirty yards into the dust and the sage, appearing from time to time, memorials to pioneer travelers and modern traffic fatalities. It was not a landscape without life, however. A jackrabbit bounded down into the ditch, absurdly long legs pumping, ears slicked back against his delicate head. Pigeon-sized birds swooped suicidally across the road, startled from their hiding places in the low grasses at the pavement's edge by Lucy's rumble and motion. One bird finally made good on a mad flight, bouncing painfully and fatally off my ankle in an explosion of dun feathers.

The irrigated greenness of Fallon's lawns could be smelled from three miles out. Fallon is the base of operations for a U.S. Navy air station and hosts one of the country's largest bombing ranges. People in Austin who knew Fallon well—it was after all the home of the nearest grocery store—told me that on some nights the vibrations of the passing planes, to say nothing of the munitions that they fired, could be felt through every home in town.

I stopped at one of the gas stations on the main strip. A barrel-chested man dressed in full leathers was fueling up a powerful new Kawasaki. The bike had Pennsylvania plates.

"'Morning," I said. He nodded wordlessly and gave me a tight smile. "Nice day for it." I gestured at his bike. Something that sounded like a snort was his reply before he launched into a monologue of just how miserable he was riding his motorcycle, across Nevada particularly, and America generally. This was his first cross-country trip and he had planned it to spend time on his new machine, to visit with his family in California, and to be able to tell his friends that he had ridden all the way across the country. The last reason was a bad one and he was not happy. He'd been riding interstates as rapidly as possible for the last six days and had seen nothing but wind, miles, highway embankments, and the taillights of trucks in his hustle to get from one coast to the other. He had found the previous day's storms as unnerving as I had, and he had little that was good to say about the enormous landscape that let wind roar unchecked across its incredibly open spaces. Not even to his destination, he dreaded the trip home.

He shook his head in utter disgust. "So where've you been?" I gave him a synopsis of my winding route of the previous three weeks and watched as his face took on a sickened aspect. "God, that's even worse!" he croaked. He paid for his gas and was gone, riding hard out of town before I finished pulling my gloves back on.

I thought about the unhappiness of that biker from Pennsylvania for a long time and wondered why, despite the occasional rough stretch of road or weather, my own experience had been so positive. It was late in the afternoon before I finally figured it out. Although both of us were going coast-to-coast and back again, we had vastly different agendas: I had no real destination, just a journey; he had no journey, just a destination.

INTERSTATE 80 IS THE ONLY ROAD that runs west through the high pass
north of Reno. It was, as expected, four lanes of tarred manic hustle, all speeding trucks and high embankments. The gentle colors and contours of the landscape, the sweep, silence, and clarity of the desert, were gone in a mass of
moving metal, restricted sightlines, and fume-belching vehicles. Past Sparks, I
cut north on I-395 and then took the rapidly quieting Route 70 west into the
foothills of the mountains. Secondary and tertiary roads are designed for half
the speed but have twice the enjoyment of interstate travel.

Route 89 snakes through Quincy on its way to Lassen Volcanic National
Park. Dense groves of fir trees lined the undulating pavement, which occasionally leapt onto the graceful and dizzying trestle bridges arching Spanish
Creek. Stark testament to the power of volcanic activity, Lassen was a magnificent place. More than ten thousand feet high, Lassen Peak, a volcanic cone
that last erupted in 1914, towered over the landscape. Route 89 ran through the
park in a tangle of tight corners and switchbacks, passing through icefields at
the higher elevations and blooming meadows at the lower. Even in late June,
so much snow lay piled in bluish heaps beside the roads—the banks were eight
feet high and more in places—that it did not surprise me to learn that the park

used GPS satellite technology to find and clear the pavement as spring turned to summer. It was a clear day, and Lucy moved in the shifting pocket of air that was the interface between the coolness of the snow at roadside and the warmth of the sun above. Fir trees bent and shaped by the wind filled the air with a green, woody scent and thrust their hoary arms and soft needles toward the sun for their brief season of growth. Looking at their twisted boughs, I knew that Lassen must be an unforgiving place in the winter. Emerald and Helen Lakes, edging the feet of steep-walled rockslides, were just beginning to melt with hints of electric blue mineralized water showing at the edges and center of crystalline snowfields. The only places clear of snow in the upper reaches of the park were those where geothermic vents and sulfur springs spangled the earth in shades of yellow and orange and filled the air with a warm, eggy mist. Running low on gas, I took the turns and straights through the "Devastated Area" at slow to moderate speed, keeping Lucy's rpms relatively low to conserve fuel. It was there that the 1914 eruption swept every blade of greenery and topsoil from the mountainside in a torrent of boiling mud and exploding gasses. Eighty-six years later, only small shrubs, tiny pines, and low-growing grasses were beginning to regain footholds in the blasted sand and gravel. It was not a place I wanted to run out of gas.

At the western entrance of the park I coasted into a station almost on fumes, fueled up with a sigh of relief, and spent a few minutes looking out over the placid waters of Manzanita Lake before dropping out of the restless heights of the volcanic mountains on Route 44, headed west toward Redding and the Sacramento Valley. At Shingletown the construction began, as did the heat, rising in heavy waves out of the valley below. The traffic was thick and slow, moving across the uneven black surface at a crawl that did nothing to displace the shimmering, stagnant air. In the lowest and hottest part of the valley, Redding was a blast furnace. A bank clock on the far side of the bridge that crossed the turquoise waters of the Sacramento River read 108 degrees. Mount Shasta, another snow-clad volcanic cone of more than fourteen thousand feet, loomed over the valley to the north, something of a Japanese painting in its outline, incongruous in its airy iciness when viewed from the concrete and heat below. Sweat dripped down my back, soaking my tank top and the waistband of my trousers. Slowly parboiling, I mumbled unkind things inside the oven of my helmet at the air-conditioned, cell-phone–chatting, radio-fiddling, and traffic-jamming SUV drivers of central Redding. Getting out of the Sacramento Valley, away from the congestion, and up into what I assumed would be the cooler and higher reaches of the Trinity Mountains, became my only ambition.

Throughout the afternoon I followed the shimmering pavement of Route 299 and climbed into the Trinities through a haze of sharp corners and inescapable heat, my vision blurred by the sweat dripping into my eyes. The altitude never brought the relief of mountain coolness or a single breeze to shift the dry air. As the light began to fade I pulled into a deserted national forest campground on the edge of the Trinity River Canyon and dropped Lucy's kickstand into the desiccated crackle of last season's fallen leaves near a large sign warning against fires or any sort of open flame. It had been a hot, dry spring in the west. On a sheltered, level spot several hundred feet above the river, I set up my tent, swatted a few mosquitoes, and ate cheese and crackers topped off with a can of spinach. Too tired to do much more than stare into the trees, I watched the shadows lengthen and deepen from my perch atop a picnic table, listening to the low vibration of insects singing beneath the stirring of the pine boughs.

In the clear gold slant of the morning light, the upper slopes of the Western Cascades flashed in jewel-box hues of malachite, emerald, topaz, and amber. Farther below, pink-edged fog blankets softened the deep valleys and rugged canyons. The road banks had recently been mown and the clippings released an herbal perfume of mint, rosemary, and thyme, as they dried in the light and heat of the rising sun. Following the final run of Route 299 to the sea, I descended into the clinging and clammy embrace of the fog. Visibility was poor and what had been a cool morning in the sunshine above the clouds became a bitterly cold and damp one in the shadows beneath. My hands ached and my teeth were chattering by the time I reached the foot of the mountains and pulled into the town of Blue Lake. It was one of those mornings that occasionally made me question the wisdom of motorcycle travel, given the vagaries of atmospheric conditions; the day before I had fried in hundred-plus-degree heat and withering sunshine, and twelve hours later I was freezing in forty-degree coastal fog. At a gas station, I wrapped my hands around a very large cup of coffee and stood immobile, as close as possible to a hot-water radiator, betraying silent, faithful Lucy with thoughts of cars with windows that rolled up, stereos that played, and heat vents that opened.

Just north of Orick, where 101 sweeps back from the coast toward the stands of old growth redwoods, I turned up the Bald Hills Road following the signs for the Lady Bird Johnson Grove. The pavement skimmed the bank of a broad gravel wash that edged Redwood Creek before climbing the ridge into the forest. Through the mist, a hundred yards away, I thought I saw large creatures standing in the stream. U-turning back, I pulled Lucy to the side of the road, took off my helmet, and peered through the wraiths of fog that trailed across the water. There, a whole herd of Roosevelt elk was crossing the gravel wash on the far side of the creek. They were enormous animals with heads and necks of deep chocolate brown that faded to dun bellies and cream-colored rumps. The bulls had racks of antlers that twisted up and back between their ears, a crown of thorns atop massive skulls. The park rangers said that they often grew to twelve hundred pounds and, looking at the heavy, bunched muscles of their haunches and chests, I believed it. The cows, wide-set eyes shining black in delicate faces, were smaller and more numerous. They crossed the stream on slender legs, each hoof precisely placed. Sitting on the bank, I watched them for half an hour, the silence disturbed only by the occasional logging truck roaring out of the hills.

The elk were heralds to a different world. At the Lady Bird Johnson Grove, the parking lot at the trailhead was empty and only the scream of a brilliant blue jay winging over a cluster of bright orange lilies toward the shelter of the great trees broke the silence. The redwoods were a gate and as I stepped away from Lucy, walking a path soft with moss, needles, and loam into the mist of the forest, I entered an ancient world. Irises so pale as to be almost white bloomed at the feet of the great trees. The understory of plant life was delicate and diverse. Rosebay rhododendrons bloomed in pale pink clusters that crowned sprays of deep green waxy leaves. Soft, pale green sorrel grew sheltered under the thorns and tri-fingered leaves of thimbleberry bushes. The thimbleberries were ripe, blushing orange, with a sweetness that lacked the tart edge of their eastern red raspberry cousins. Shafts of sunlight dropped through the heavy moist air in beams distinct enough to curve a hand around. The very trees seemed to breathe in green exhalations of oxygen and water. Five to seven hundred years of old growth towered three hundred feet above my head, heavy green boughs tier upon tier, disappearing upward into an unseen canopy, while twisting, gnarled, and knotted roots spread in mats over and into the forest floor. In that grove I could hear the breathing, the music, the age, and the majesty of the earth. At the feet of those shaggy, red-barked giants, in the presence of such towering existence, I knew that I was insignificant, my life ephemeral and evanescent. I wandered slowly through the grove, listening to the great trees, grazing on berries, feeling my heartbeat slow and peace drop into my chest like the beams of light falling through the mist.

I drove slowly out of the park and up the coast, stopping in Klamath in the hunt for afternoon coffee. A solitary bar, the post office, and a casino were the going concerns of downtown Klamath; everything else was boarded up and silent: the beauty parlor, the market, even a storefront church, all closed. The desertion was due, at least in part, to the Klamath River, which had been a fickle neighbor. In 1964, a massive flood completely destroyed the downtown and swept away the local school as well as the bridge on Highway 101. The bridge was rebuilt but Klamath never recovered. I walked into the dim bar where four loggers just coming off shift drank and talked quietly, large pitch-stained hands cradled around their draft beers, and sat at the far end of the counter.

"Do you have any coffee?"

"Coffee?" Marilyn, a tired-looking barmaid with two gold chains draped over the front of her white sweatshirt, turned to look at the black sludge that filled the bottom few inches of a cold glass pot. "Not just now, but if you wait a couple of minutes I'll put a fresh pot on." I thanked her and sat eavesdropping on the conversation of the loggers, thinking how strange it was that while some people cut trees down to make their living, others, like those in the recreational and environmental industries, depended on the preservation of the trees to do the same. Marilyn returned with a Styrofoam cup, chemical creamer, and sugar. She nodded toward my leather jacket. "Where're you going?"

"Just up the road a bit I think. Is it true there's a hostel outside of town?"

"Hostel? Is that what it is? I never been there myself but it looks real nice from the outside." We talked for a bit about small things: the beauty of the coast, the quietness of Klamath, and my plans to drive up through Oregon toward Washington. Unless questioned directly, I had given up on telling people that I hoped to make it all the way to Alaska, as what generally followed were questions regarding the status of my mental health. I finished my second cup of coffee and slid two dollars across the bar. Marilyn looked at the money and slid it back. "It's on the house. Now you have a good trip. And be careful."

AS TWO LANES NARROWED TO ONE, the white sedan squeezed by Lucy on the right, nearly forcing me into oncoming traffic. With little time to react, I kept my front tire on the centerline and flashed my best New Jersey one-fingered salute. Driving the Redwoods Highway, the northern tip of California's Route 101, was something like being trapped inside a fast-moving arcade game. Much-needed construction and partial patching of the road surface, to say nothing of the burlwood souvenir stands that attracted buslike RVs into shuddering stops and impossibly tight turns, made hair-trigger awareness on the brake and throttle a necessity. On the whole, I had not been impressed with the conditions of the roads in northern California, or the natives who drove them. The scenery was fantastic, the trees especially, but the roads, from Route 70 climbing into the Sierras on the western side of the state, to Route 101 sliding up the coast past Crescent City, were lumpy, grooved, potholed things driven by destination-obsessed lunatics. The theory that I had developed, in my albeit brief experience on the state's northern roads, was that Californians were a strange breed: friendly and welcoming when met in cafés and gas stations, on hiking trails or along the beach, but put them behind the wheel of a car and an ugly and inexplicable transformation occurred. The sign that marked the Oregon border was a welcome sight.

. . .

"The Oregon Coast is the most beautiful in the world" the man at the Visitors' Center said, and an hour's drive later, moving past Brookings, Pistol River, and Gold Beach, I was inclined to agree. Magnificent pearl and silver rocks jutted up from the western sea, guarding the sloping expanses of gray beaches where the Pacific rollers banked and crashed while stands of bluish-green Douglas firs swept up the mountains to the east. A bruising headwind was blasting but thankfully it came straight down the coast, impacting Lucy's windshield before it got to my chest. I could feel the pressure and watched my fuel efficiency decrease dramatically, but at least I was not side-blasted all over the road in shades of Kansas and Nevada.

In Bandon, a hamlet of not-quite three thousand people, I stopped for a not-quite New England clam chowder lunch. A former port on the shipping run between San Francisco and Portland, Bandon now owed more to tourism, fishing, and cranberry harvests than it did to the seaport, and the jumble of boutiques, fresh-fish markets, and small restaurants that lined modern Bandon's few narrow streets was low built, charming, and eclectic. Stretching my legs, I walked around town, people-watching and window-shopping, and stopped in front of a jewelry store to admire gold rings set with firestones and green amber. They were nothing that I could afford, but the metal and jewels flashed with a magpie attraction. The woman behind the counter saw me looking through the picture window and motioned me inside.

"Would you like to see something?"

"Just browsing, really. Your rings are beautiful." The amber winked and glowed emerald and honey in the sun and the firestones seemed lit from within by smoldering streaks of red and gold.

"Well, try one on! C'mon, let's see how one looks on your hand." She slid the velvet tray from the case but I thrust my hands into my trouser pockets, embarrassed to lay them out in front of her. My fingers were red and cold from the coastal wind, weeks of constant travel had left my fingernails dirty and ragged, and the lines of my palms were creased with black grease that would not wash away. I muttered something about engine grease and balled my fists deeper into hiding.

"Hey, it's OK," she said. "That's my favorite moisturizer, too." In addition to running the shop, her interests lay, she said, in auto mechanics and electrical work. "I was so proud when I finished rewiring my trailer and didn't have to ask anyone's help." She was a single mom and we talked about living in Oregon and about her family situation, raising two teenage sons on her own. "I always tell my sons: be proud of where you come from because this is the most beautiful place in the world."

Back in the parking lot, the proprietor of a small seafood shop saw me adjusting my saddlebags and came out to ask about Lucy. A few minutes later he was joined by a friend in a wheelchair. The man in the chair had long curls whipping on the wind, an army jacket, and wore fingerless gloves like the ones I had for driving on hot days. There was something in his manner, in the way he looked at Lucy, guiding his chair from one side of her to the other to examine the crankcase, the front forks suspension, and whether she ran with a chain or Kevlar drive belt, that told me this man knew something about bikes, and that once, maybe before whatever had left him in that chair had happened, he had driven one, too.

"Where are you comin' in from?" His voice was low, soft.

"New Jersey."

"New Jersey." He nodded twice, resting his hands on his immobile thighs, then looked up, smiled, and extended one gloved palm. "I'd like to shake your hand." His grip was strong and warm. He squeezed my hand, nodded one more time, and turned his chair to go. I finished adjusting the straps on my saddlebags, pulled on my helmet, and fired up Lucy.

"Hey! New Jersey!" The shout was from behind me. I turned to see the man in the chair raise his fist in salute. "It's a great trip! Good luck!"

The Dixonville road was the best sort of motorcycle run: a snaky little two-lane humming under arching trees and singing through a Gloria of hayfields. On roads like that you lean hard into the curves, accelerate up and over the rises to the straights, and feel like a bird coming to rest on a branch, wings and feet outstretched, when, all too soon, it comes time to stop.

At Dixonville I stopped for gas before making the seventy-mile run up toward Crater Lake. Oregon, like New Jersey, is one of the few states that do not allow people to self-serve their own gasoline. A man came out of the store as I reached for the pump handle.

"No, it's OK, I got it." Normally, regardless of state regulation, bikers will pump their own gas.

"I know what you're thinking," he said. "But look over there." He pointed to a trashcan standing beside the store's entrance. On it was a finely detailed airbrushed portrait of his own face. "My brother did that. He does all the custom work on all the bikes around here. Been around bikes all my life, your paint is safe with me." I stepped back. In fifteen thousand miles of riding that summer, and God knows how many stops for fuel, he was the only person I ever allowed to put gas in my tank.

Route 138 east to Crater has a beauty of stupefying proportions. The road runs above the silken flow of the Umpqua River, which spills in green whorls over black stone ledges. Towering volcanic rocks and immense trees loomed over the pavement, as did tall hexagons of basalt columns peeking from ash-layered road cuts.

Twenty miles west of Diamond Lake, tired and needing to stretch my legs and back for a few minutes, I stopped by the side of the road to rest and collect some of the cool spring water spilling across a black rock face. A passing green pickup, the first vehicle I had seen in many miles, slowed, stopped, and turned around, pulling to the side of the pavement behind Lucy. A tiny woman, beautiful with blonde ringlets framing her face, stepped out from behind the wheel. A massive, dark-bearded man sat watching from the passenger side.

"Are you all right?" she asked. "We passed and thought, 'We can't leave her sitting out here alone in the middle of nowhere.'"

"I'm fine, thanks, no problems, just resting for a minute. I'm only going another twenty miles tonight."

"OK, good, we just wanted to be sure." I thanked her and she slid back behind the wheel, waved, and pulled out onto the road again. As I watched them go I saw the flash of yellow license plates. License plates from Alaska. Brought with the kindness of strangers, it was an omen from the North.

. . .

The campground was quiet, shaded, and green and I was pleased with my little spot tucked in under the tall firs; just enough room for a tent set on a soft bed of needles, the bike, and a picnic table. Across the silver sparkle of Diamond Lake, snowcapped Mount Bailey loomed eighty-three hundred feet into a blue pearl sky. At a little store half a mile down the road I bought myself fixings for a lake picnic dinner: a beer and a tin of kippered snacks. Sitting atop a hummock of grass at the water's edge, I managed to spill a third of the beer on myself as my fingers slipped while opening it, but between the heavy smell of hops and the fishy odor of the sardines, it seemed to keep the mosquitoes away. The sun dropped and I watched the snow-sheathed slopes of Bailey shift from icy white to a soft rose pink in the fading light; a gentle end to a spectacular day.

ROLLING OVER FOR ANOTHER NAP ATOP the pine needles, I swore that the watchword of the day was going to be "leisure" and not "mileage." Finally in Oregon, running north alongside the Pacific, and a continent away from where I had begun, thoughts of a meeting with Dave seemed real and close. I had left it to him to resurrect his promise, but he had said that it was in Oregon that he would try to come and see me. I expected that one day soon, maybe in the next phone conversation, he would tell me when he was coming and where I should meet him. I was also only one U.S. state away from British Columbia, where my biological mother, Gloria, had invited me to visit with her family for the very first time. The tendency was to push rapidly north, twisting the throttle and collecting the miles in a headlong rush to see a man I missed and a family I had never met. The road sometimes gets lonely. There was, however, another guiding reality: in my lifetime I expected to have exactly one chance for a trip like this and was consciously reluctant to rush anywhere for anything and risk missing what I had only one opportunity to see. I had heard rumors about the blueness and beauty of Crater Lake and did not want to scramble by it.

At the edge of Diamond Lake I spent a little time with my journal as the sun came up, writing and eating chocolate-covered raisins as a breeze turned the dark face of the water to silver glitter. It was a cool morning, a good driving day—clear, with no promise of clouds on the horizon. An hour later, I packed up Lucy and started toward the remains of Mount Mazama, the blown-out volcano that held Crater Lake.

The road moved through the wide valley that fronted what remained of the peak across a barren plain called the Pumice Desert. Mazama had lost four thousand feet of elevation in seconds and the devastation of the cataclysmic explosion was still evident in the denuded and nearly treeless features of the Desert. Eight thousand years ago the valley had been an inferno and although the fires had ceased to burn, the scarred earth had yet to heal. Any tiny shreds of green were in vivid contrast to the pinkish dun of fist-sized, half-melted rocks, gravel, and dust. The pavement snaked up in slow curves through the valley, climbing into the trees past snow patches that rapidly become banks, and up to the lip of the caldera that held the lake within. I pulled Lucy to the side of the road at the first pull-off, stepped to the edge, and looked down through a thousand feet of atmosphere to the surface of the water. The lake was a sheet of cerulean blue, mirrorlike and reflective of the sky, although just a shade paler. Standing on the edge and looking down toward the calm water, space was reversed: what was sky and what was water, what was liquid and what was atmosphere, was somehow unclear. It was perfect: a pale sapphire caught in a setting of oxidized black rock, God's mirror, the bluest eye unblinking and gazing at the sun. Only Wizard Island, the cinder cone of a new volcano, rose from the depths and broke the surface: an almost perfect circle on the eastern side.

Ancient people held the lake as sacred. Only holy men were allowed to go there to pray and speak with the gods and spirits. When the Europeans arrived, the natives kept their silence about the location of the lake and it was not found by whites until 1853. It is a stunning spot, nearly indescribable in its beauty; one of those places that must be seen to be even partially appreciated. A soft peace slid down my spine as I sat on the ledge. The slide of breath into lungs became an almost deliberate thing. For a few minutes the air was silent save for the twitter of a small bird resting in the gnarled branches of an ancient juniper that had twisted its roots into the fissures of rock. There was no wind.

The lake was still and smooth, its iridescent and gelatinous surface undisturbed by the tiniest ripple. At my feet a golden-mantled chipmunk scampered over and between my boots, looking for a handout, and spiritual contemplation turned to the temporal.

The only access point to the lake itself is the Cleetwood Trail. It writhes down the north caldera wall, switching back through tall stands of fir trees in a mile of long, well-graded turns, passing tiny resting benches at overlook points, and dropping seven hundred vertical feet to the water's edge. The lake, if possible, was even lovelier at close range. The water, two thousand feet deep, was clear and topaz blue. Fish slid through the depths, visible as if they were caught in glass, reflecting gold and green with every movement of their lithe bodies. A group of college students sat on the rocky shore, paddling their feet in the shallows and talking about the biology of the lake. Later I asked a boy with waist-length hair and a slim, strong frame about the clarity of the water. He told me that Crater is "allotropic."

"What does that mean?"

"The lake is young and has only the beginnings of the plant life that will one day cloud its waters like any other normal, healthy lake. But the process here is slowed. The lake has filled gradually only with rain and snowmelt. There are no streams or rivers to bring minerals, plant life, or nutrients from other places." There was some photosynthetic life, however, enough to oxygenate the water and provide "atmospheric" support for the schools of fish swimming in the depths. The fish were human introductions; nearly two million kokane salmon and rainbow trout have been stocked in the lake since 1888. I put my hand into the water. It was cold, the snow was still melting on the rim, but it was less frigid than I expected and I dropped both hands, then arms to the shoulder, through the glassy surface, reaching for the unreachable bottom.

From a ledge some fifteen feet above the surface, two girls shrieked and danced, finding the collective courage to jump in. For me, there was no choice, only a need to be inside all of that blueness, to swim, like the salmon, down into that icy volcano. I left my belt and boots on the ledge, stepped past the girls and dove straight down off the rocks into the soft embrace of the lake. There was no shock, only wonder, as I opened my eyes and looked into a watery, cobalt-colored world. Below, the ledges dropped straight down into the abyss of the crater, level upon level of blue water to infinite spaces, flashes of yellow, green, or turquoise marking the outcrops of ledges hundreds, or perhaps a thousand feet beneath me. How far I could see I do not know, but the clarity of the water, like something out of a *National Geographic* spread of the world under the ice of Antarctica, was astonishing. For a moment I was weightless, clean and whole, peace dropping—not slowly here, but all at once, total and enveloping. Every ugly thing I had ever seen, every compromise I had ever made, every crack in my heart, every chattering voice in my psyche, was gone. I wondered if I could just inhale and stay there, beneath the shimmering surface, sliding through the noiseless light of blue and gold water. The silence and the wonder lasted for just a minute, maybe two, and my lungs stared to burn. I lacked the courage to breathe and had to surface, reluctantly. Back in the unfiltered light, treading water, I looked up to the ledges and to questioning eyes.

"Is it cold?"

A swim like that comes once in a lifetime and makes you feel alive and whole. Five thousand miles is not too far to drive a motorcycle if that was the experience at the end.

"No. You should try it."

Coming down from Crater I crossed back over the Pumice Desert toward Mount Thielsen, which loomed above the blasted plain at ninety-two hundred feet. Thielsen is fantasy mountain, something out of a Tolkien book: a central barren twisted spire supported by lower buttresses reaching into the sky. The gray stone might have been hewn; it was treeless, forbidding, and fascinating.

Route 97 runs directly north. Although flanked by tens of millions of blooming grape hyacinths, which filled the air with a delicate perfume as the miles spooled out, 97 became increasingly unpleasant. Speeding trucks, badly rutted and potholed pavement, temperatures rising to inferno levels, and a lunar landscape marked by ancient lava flows that poured in frozen black masses across the scrub country, made me wish for the green silence of the mountains. One of the major benefits of solitary travel was that I could make wishes become reality almost immediately, without consulting anyone or worrying about deviating from a planned itinerary. Fifteen miles later, I turned west onto Route 20 and headed toward the verdigris of the rising Cascades and the town of Sisters. It was a good choice, I later learned, to get off of 97. Another fifteen miles north of the Route 20 intersection, wildfires were burning through the scrub and the road had been closed as flames licked across the pavement.

The afternoon slid into early evening as I pulled into Sisters and the sun flashed through the tall pines sheltering the municipal park and campground. After depositing my fee in the unmanned and carefully labeled "Honesty Box," I headed into town for a beer and a little company.

Sisters is named for the three-peaked mountain that rises to the southwest. It has a strange history of development: from a sawmill and transit point for westward-bound travelers in the late nineteenth century to its present incarnation as a tourist destination. Local industry was beginning to die when a resort hotel built a golf course and luxury accommodations west of town in the late 1960s. Sisters' storeowners on Main Street were offered a fifteen-hundred-dollar incentive by the developers to false-front their businesses with an 1880s style veneer. What was incentive rapidly became ordinance, and as the resort drew in tourists—as well as their spending habits—Sisters adopted its new image with a vengeance. A rodeo now draws thousands annually, and the narrow streets of the town are lined with pricey Old West–style saloons, restaurants, and country decorative boutiques.

There was a low brass rail at the bar and I propped one boot up and watched the swinging saloon doors admit golfers, retirees, vacationers, and the rare person that looked as if they just might live in Sisters. I had come for conversation but somehow, once inside, sitting under the pressed-tin ceiling and soft glow of faux gas lamps, I was content to listen to the swirl and laughter of the bar, to watch the motion and color of people as they moved in and out of the restaurant, and remained largely silent, immersed in the crowd but somehow apart. I stayed for a second, silent beer, walked back to my tent in the park, crawled into bed, and dreamed of blue water.

SANTIAM PASS MARKS THE SADDLE BETWEEN Three Fingered Jack Mountain and Hoodoo Butte. It separates the Mount Jefferson Wilderness in the north from the Mount Washington Wilderness in the south at a wooded junction where Route 20 cuts through the forest in two lanes of black asphalt beneath a dense canopy of Douglas firs. After Santiam, Route 22 branches north and west, falling toward the river junction town of Detroit on pavement that curves against heavily forested mountainsides, sliding over ridges and dipping into rocky depressions where icy streams tumble frothy white. Deep in the valleys, where vapor settled atop shaded stream banks—damp, turgid, and frigid in the quiet morning air—it was bitterly cold. I was shaking by the time I pulled into a café in Detroit and most of the sensation in my hands was gone. The host took one look at me, my red nose, bluish lips, and the bike beyond, smiled broadly, and sat me in a booth beside a sun-filled window. He poured out a steaming mug of coffee before I even had the chance to ask for it and set it wordlessly on the table. Huddled inside my jacket, I gratefully wrapped my hands around the cup and leaned my face into its vapor.

A toasted cinnamon bun and a quart of coffee later I stepped back out into the sunshine and the rising warmth of the day. Slouched against the wall of the restaurant was a man in a green army jacket. He was tired and dusty-looking, his eyes mostly dead when he raised them to meet mine. He had the look of someone who had been beaten badly by most of the important things in life. He looked at my jacket and then at Lucy, with her bags strapped tight to her frame.

"Where're you going?"

"Alaska." Something in his eyes flickered to life.

"Alaska." His half-lidded gaze shifted past my shoulder, to the bike and the road beyond. "After graduation, sixteen of us all drove our bikes to Alaska." They were young Californians then, just eighteen, and had traveled north to work on pipeline construction. With a short riding season, and backcountry employment, all had sold their bikes and settled in for what was supposed to be just one winter. They stayed nearly six years before returning to the lower forty-eight. When they did finally come south, none of them returned to California. Each man instead chose the state or province that he had liked best on his motorcycle journey north. This man had chosen Oregon.

"Why Oregon?"

"It was the greenest." He smiled a crooked half smile. For whatever else had happened in his life, he still believed in his choice.

From Detroit it was sixty miles of deep woods through the Mount Hood National Forest, following first the Breitenbush and then the Clackamas River. The road moved over low ridges, sometimes dropping with the rush and fall of the river, sometimes shooting into green-tunneled, dense-foliaged avenues, where shafts of sunshine scattered like gold pieces over the road. Lucy sang and lifted easily over the rises, and my speed crept up as I watched the flash of light and shadow and breathed in the wet leaf mould and warming fir-needles smell of the forest. Oregon. The Greenest State. Maybe one day I would come back here, too.

The overturned wreck of a car in a ditch interrupted my leafy relocation thoughts. I was moving too quickly to get a good look at it, but I saw that the white sedan had come to a rest on its roof. The windows were blown out and the undercarriage tipped toward the pavement, obscene and exposed. There was no one else on the road and I drove another three or four miles with the growing disquiet of my thoughts. *Is that an old car, abandoned and rusting in the ditch? Is this a recent wreck? Could there be people in there still?* Shades of the Irish Hills, and a woman dying in a field, flashed before me and I had to turn back, just to make sure. I slowed to a stop where the rusty undercarriage rested on the lip of the ditch, brambles curling into the vacant wheel wells. Yellow foam upholstery lay in disintegrating piles, nesting material for small creatures. The tires were gone, stripped long ago. I felt like an idiot, one with an overactive imagination, but I had to go back, just to make sure; that wrecked car would have haunted me otherwise.

Past Estacada the rural roads ended and the multilane traffic of Portland began. After days of sharing the road with few other vehicles, the trucks, noise, and speed of Highway 205 was disconcerting and the exit ramp to center city could not have been more welcome. The hostel was on the corner of Eighteenth and Gilsan streets, a lovely turn-of-the-century building with polished wood floors, high ceilings, and a boy with a beautiful Eurasian face behind the front desk. I checked in, threw my pack on a top bunk in the women's dormitory, and napped for an hour before walking downtown to send a travel update to my family, explore the city parks, and look around what was rumored to be America's most livable city.

The library was cool and shaded, with still air and hushed voices drifting across marble floors, but after sending a few e-mails out, I left it for the waterfront park, where teenagers gyrated in the sun, dancing through the last hours of the city's annual Rose Festival. The smell of sweat, beer, and sun-baked concrete filled the air. The stalls of a farmers' market, filled with jewelry and fancy trinkets, clustered close to the river and a band belted out classic Southern rock under a tent. I listened to "Wild Thing" played at volume before walking back to the hostel, a little bemused and a little lonely in the unfamiliar excess stimuli of urban sounds, city streets, and parks crowded with strangers.

From the pay phone in the basement stairwell I called Dave. His voice was pleasant, measured, and, as always, noncommittal.

"Hey." I could hear the clicking of his computer keyboard in the background and knew that I had interrupted him while he was programming. "How're you doin'?" This was not the greeting of a man who was busily stuffing a suitcase to come and meet me in Oregon as we had discussed weeks ago. He had a Ph.D. in aerospace engineering, he could read a map, a calendar, and a flight schedule, and I had too much pride to badger him into making travel plans to come and see me. He had known roughly where I was since the day I left him, the direction that I was heading, and how long I would be in Oregon. He wasn't coming, had never intended to. I was livid.

"I'm leaving Oregon tomorrow, Dave. Why don't we cut the crap? You're not coming, are you?" His response was devastatingly casual and he said precisely the wrong thing.

"I hadn't really thought about it. It takes a couple of weeks to get good plane fares. I'll look at the maps." Whether it was intentional or not, I knew that he was lying. He would never look at the maps, would never book a flight. The pathetic reality of his indifference toward our romance finally hit home. I could think of nothing to say and my anger burned instantly to ashes. I ended the conversation quickly, trying to salvage my feelings and, for some reason, his.

"Well, maybe you'll come out as I head back," I suggested. There was no sarcasm, only sadness. He told me that he thought this was a fine idea and to keep him posted about where I was, but I knew that we would never meet on the road. This was my trip, my adventure, and I finally understood that he had no interest in sharing it. I hung up the phone, rested my forehead against the wall, thought about my unreciprocated love, his cowardice, and, whether he meant it to be so or not, his unkindness in not telling me directly what his lack of action explained so very clearly. Perhaps he had been trying not to hurt me as he equivocated. Perhaps he thought that eventually he wouldn't have to tell me that he didn't love me, and that he never would. Perhaps he thought he wouldn't have to say difficult things, that I would just see it. Well, I saw it then, clearly. Anger began to crawl up my spine, tightening and curling between my shoulder blades in a vicious knot. I called him back. The phone rang only once before he picked up.

"You know something, Dave? You may not have thought about it, but I have. I've thought a lot about it. And you know what I think now? I think that I don't want you to come out to meet me. At all. Here or anywhere else. I don't need this. I'll see you when I get back to New Jersey. Maybe." I hung up the phone with a crash before he had a chance to respond.

I still was fumbling with my calling card and wallet, fingers suddenly grown large and clumsy, when a slight but powerful-looking man with closely cropped hair came down the stairs. He stopped and looked at me.

"Are you all right?"

"No, I'm not. It was . . ."—I jabbed an angry finger at the receiver, unsure of what to say—". . . a difficult phone call. But," I said, my eyes beginning to fill with embarrassing tears, "in about ten minutes I'm going to forget all about this and I'm going to be just fine." There was conviction in my voice, and I stormed up the stairs and out onto the street, but it took me more than ten minutes to collect myself. For the better part of an hour I cried in a coffee shop, sniffling miserably, squeezed into a corner out of the line of sight of staff and customers. Dave and every petty thing he had ever said pinged from one part of my cranium to another. Couldn't he have just told me how he felt, or in this case, didn't feel? Goddamn him to hell for not saying what was difficult yet true. How stupid and how oblivious I had been to fill the void of his silence with my own feelings. Soft Celtic ribbons of music flowed from the stereo, milk frothed, and the low hum of conversations that I was too self-absorbed to eavesdrop upon rose and fell. I listened instead to the sound of the muscles constricting in my chest, tearing fibers one from the other in a location that felt like it just might surround my heart.

My breathing was still ragged, but when I felt like I could walk the streets without tears, I went up to the grocery store on Eighteenth Street and bought a bottle of wine and a package of Marlboros. There wasn't a soul I knew in that lovely, friendly, suddenly empty city, and I felt horrifically alone. Jumpy, nervous energy crackled through to my fingertips and I was ready to do anything, preferably something dangerous and precipitous, just to fill the vortex of raw emotion with something tangible. I shook a cigarette from the pack and fumbled with a lighter. *Options. What are my options?* I could move to Oregon, today, declare myself free of the East Coast, of Dave. I could pick up a boy in the hostel. I could run, north into the mountains of Canada or south to the openness and solitude of the desert. Motion mattered, not direction. What could I find that would root me back in this moment? What could I search out that would make me feel real and in control of my own life, of my own feelings? I found Lucy, sat on the curb with my feet tucked under the shadow of her exhaust system, leaned against the slope of her tarp, and breathed in a couple of choking drags trying to decide what to do, where to run. I kicked off my boots, rubbed my toes in the rain-gutter sand among the bits of twigs, a chewing-gum wrapper, and a cigarette butt that was not my own, while scraping bits of melted asphalt off Lucy's chrome with fingernails that were already shredded. *Fuck it. And fuck him. I'm probably better off alone anyway. Apparently too damn difficult to get along with and too damn difficult to let go. That spineless sonofabitch.* My anger turned to sadness and back again to anger. I smoked the last of my cigarette, crushed it into the pavement, pulled my boots back on, and stamped back to the hostel to see about finding a glass for my wine. Hostel rules prohibited alcohol in the building but there was a park almost directly across the street.

The kitchen was empty. An empty jelly jar would function as a glass and, holding one, I turned from the cupboard and came face to face with the man from the phone.

"Feeling better?" He grinned broadly and nodded at the bottle.

"I'm getting there. Would you like some? I can offer you half a bottle and a seat in the park." He accepted, I took another jelly jar from the shelf, and we headed for the park, where we sat, bare toes in the grass.

Mitch was a sweet, angst-ridden, gay physical therapist who was in the midst of making the brave relocation to Portland. He knew no one there and was staying in the hostel until he found himself a suitable apartment that would double as an office and workspace as he set up his business again. People like Mitch impress me greatly. It's one thing to tumbleweed all over the continent in a grand circular adventure with the realization that home lies at the eventual end, it's quite another to pack everything in the back of a car and just go in search of a new life and a different reality. As the afternoon light stretched and softened toward evening, Mitch and I sat in the park and talked of space, of both the physical and emotional sort, of honesty, and of the need for love. We talked of the differences in how men and women express themselves, the need for open communication, and how difficult that can be, whether in gay or straight relationships. It is a human need to understand and to be understood, yet true communication between two people is often a patchy thing that comes in flashes and illuminations, or sometimes does not come at all.

That night I fell asleep over my journal and was grateful when one of the women in my dorm gently moved it out from under my arm, placed it atop my pack, and turned the lights out. The thoughtful kindness of strangers, when superimposed upon the casual cruelty of a lover, is such a bittersweet thing.

The heat of the night did not lend well to sleeping, and the morning hours were a little fuzzy-headed with the aftereffects of wine, but I did manage to repack, reload, and have coffee with the hostel crowd before pulling out at 8:30 A.M. Mitch hugged me in a spine-cracking squeeze and pressed a red glass button into my hand that read "The purpose of life is a life of purpose— Robert Byrne." He was still waving as I twisted the throttle and roared up Gilsan Street.

Across the Columbia River I drove only a few miles into Washington state before stopping in the town of Vancouver to get an oil change at the Harley dealership. It had been more than three thousand miles, much of it dusty Great Plains riding, since I had changed Lucy's filter and I was beginning to feel decidedly guilty about the blackening oil that coated the dipstick when I did a pre-ride mechanical check each morning. A. J., a tall mechanic with a booming laugh and a quick wrench, put Lucy up on the lift and began to work. He spent more time than was necessary, checking the brake fluids, the pressure and balance of my tires, the tension in the drivebelt, and tightening the screws that held my side-view mirrors in place. He unscrewed the transmission filler plug and peered into the crankcase with a small flashlight.

"It looks OK, but I'm gonna change your tranny fluid for you for free 'cause I admire your courage," he said. "Not too many women got the moxie to do what you do. You're my hero."

In the shop I bought a new faceshield for my helmet. Desert sand borne on blasting wind, as well as gravel tossed up from passing trucks, had pitted and scarred the plastic of my old one to the point where the scratches and dents fragmented the late afternoon sun into dazzling prisms of refracted light. Driving west at four o'clock in the afternoon with the shield down was like driving through a kaleidoscope: beautiful but blinding. The new one was so clear that it was like looking through a single pane of polished glass, and I left the dealership with A. J.'s warm handshake, sharpened sight, and Lucy chugging happily along on new oil and transmission fluid.

A. J., his extra effort, and his compliment had made my morning, but as I buckled my saddlebags at the local post office, the other public interpretation of what I was doing showed itself. A man wearing a T-shirt a bit too tight for his protruding stomach looked Lucy up and down,

"That's not yours, is it?" His small eyes scanned the parking lot, searching for the husband or boyfriend who should be driving. I could feel my jaw tighten.

"I don't see anyone else around, so it must be." I went back to my saddle-bags.

He looked at my yellow license plate. "You didn't drive all the way out here from New Jersey, did you?"

"I did." The final strap was buckled down.

"Kind of adventurous for a little girl like you."

I rotated on the balls of my feet, stood up, and fixed him with a cold stare. "I'm a full-grown woman."

As the weeks and then months passed, I should have gotten used to the comments about women and motorcycles, as well as other people's perceptions about what "girls on bikes" were supposedly capable—or not capable—of doing, but I never did. It happened every day, without exception, that someone at a gas station, a parking lot, a diner, or a stop sign would make a comment about how surprised, delighted, shocked, irritated, or inspired they were to see a woman traveling alone on a motorcycle. Sometimes I appreciated it. Comments like A. J.'s earlier that morning were an affirmation and would have meant the same thing and carried the same weight if the word "man" was substituted. I was fully aware that not many people of either gender had the time, the opportunity, or the inclination to do what I did, and if people noticed, appreciated, or commented on that fact, I was delighted to hear it. It was, however, the purely gender-related negative commentary, offered simply because I was "a girl," that raised my hackles. People will question men on motorcycles about the power and safety of the machines they ride, their destination and the distances they drive in a single day, and whether they travel with companions for safety or company, but no one, *ever*, will question the fundamental abilities of a man to ride a motorcycle. It happens all the time to women.

As the man walked away I pulled on my jacket and wrenched at the zipper, muttering castrating things better left unsaid. Torquing Lucy's throttle a little harder than necessary, I roared out of the post office parking lot toward the silent forests of the Cascade Range.

Route 503 wound its way into national timberlands and past the back slopes of Mount Saint Helens. Eight thousand snowcapped feet high, Mount Saint Helens had conical sides oddly truncated and soot-capped from the explosion that had blown the peak off twenty years before. I remembered the mason jar full of powdery yellowish gray ash that my sixth-grade science teacher had brought to Massachusetts shortly after the eruption, and I looked forward to seeing the crater from where it had come. Halfway between the last gas station in Yale and the next one in Randle, however, I realized that I did not have enough gas in Lucy's tank to take the forest service side road all the way to the crater overlook and still make it to the next town. I settled instead for sweeping views of the mountain from a variety of roadside turnouts.

It was a frustrating afternoon, and I wasn't exactly sure why. Part of it was that an emotional day and a hot restless night in Portland had left me irritable, weary, and longing for open, easy, and scenic roads that required little concentration. Unfortunately, the road through the Gifford Pinchot National Forest was slow, narrow, and contorted and twisted its way north through landscape scarred by heavy tree harvesting. Pinchot was a national forest but not a national park, and as such it could be, and was, used as a timber resource area. Weyerhaeuser operations, and logging generally, were a massive presence, and the twisted rubble of the clearcuts left me viscerally depressed and angry. Logging is an important and necessary industry, and God knows I've spent most of my life living in houses both constructed of, and heated by, wood, but there is something disturbing about the sight of obliteration where there were once old-growth timber tracts. I know that it is hypocrisy to live in wood-trussed homes and not understand that the timber comes from places like Pinchot, just as it is hypocrisy to eat steaks and not appreciate that meat comes from butchered animals, but I don't enjoy spending time in slashed timber zones or slaughterhouses. I twisted the throttle and Lucy rolled through the miles, her engine a constant, steady, and reassuring pulse of feeling amidst the visual discomfort of damaged landscape.

I was ready to stop by the time I turned north onto Route 169 toward Black Diamond, a town of two thousand people that owed its existence to the coal that has been dug from its hillsides since the 1880s. Nearby, there was a state park with a little tent symbol marked in my Rand McNally where I thought I would stay for the night, but I needed to stop in town first for dinner fixings. My humor did not improve in Black Diamond's grocery store. Weary, caked in dust, sweat, grease, and the red mud of clearcut soil that had eroded across the asphalt, I wandered the Safeway aisles with my leather slung over one arm and picked out some hummus, crackers, and a can of mandarin oranges. The security guard, a tall plainclothesman with a drooping mustache and a blue baseball cap, followed me none too discreetly as I made my selections. There was a ladies' room in the back of the store and I took the opportunity to run steaming water into the sink before heading for a campground that lacked plumbing. I was almost sure that had I stepped out of a minivan instead of off a Harley, and had I been dressed in Anne Klein rather than Wilson Leather, the violent hammering on the bathroom door as I took an extra minute to wash some of the grime from my face would not have occurred. Did he think I was going to stuff a can of oranges down my tank top? Just where would a Frisbee-sized container of hummus fit inside my green army pants? I emerged to find the man casually examining a rack of sunglasses near the ladies' room door.

"You can go in now if you'd like. It's free." He said nothing and silently followed me up to the cashier and out of the store, watching with arms folded as I put wallet and groceries into my saddlebags. Thoroughly out of sorts, and wallowing in self pity, I slouched out of town toward Kanaskat-Palmer State

Park and hopefully solitude. *A blasted landscape and suspicious unfriendly people who take me for a thief—I have driven five thousand miles on a motorcycle for this?*

Even in my disgusted mood, I had to admit that the campsite, tucked between the spreading roots of tall trees, and encircled with thimbleberry bushes, purple lupines, yellow buttercups, and bunches of tiny, white, star-shaped flowers, was lovely. I set up my tent and ate a few crackers.

"Hey, how're ya doing?" The voice came through the trees where, in the fading light, I could see the two large tents of the five men who were camped at the site next to mine. The voice was friendly, just an acknowledgment that I was their neighbor for the evening, but I was not in the mood to be sociable.

"Fine," I said. *Ah god, fuck off and leave me alone in my berry bushes,* was what I thought.

"Excellent. We're just coming off the mountain and have lots of beer if you want one later." Beer? Now that was a different story. I could be pleasant if a cold beer was the incentive.

Mike, the owner of the voice, worked at the University of North Carolina, Chapel Hill. He was pixieish with a red beard and twinkling blue eyes framed by fine wrinkles, carved by what I suspected was a combination of laughter and a life lived exploring the out-of-doors. His hair was a bit too long, with unruly curls at the back of his neck, and his voice filled with warmth and love when he spoke of a small daughter named Quinn whom he was teaching to climb.

An experiential educator at UNC, he had just finished leading a Rainier summit expedition, climbing with four other men, one of whom was his brother. They had finished their attempt earlier that day and two of them had summited, but not Mike, who had strained a knee in the approach and had chosen wisely, although with great disappointment, to sit out the day on the glacier as his brother and another friend took the peak. I spent the evening with their group, drinking a couple of Rainier Beers and laughing at the locker-room-been-out-on-the-mountain-and-lived-to-tell-about-it humor of these men. They were unshaven, glare burned, unshowered, and totally charming. Mike and his friends made no assumptions, never said a word about "girls on bikes," and did much to redeem the day.

IT WAS A SPECTACULAR MORNING, COOL and clear, a morning to breathe deeply and to taste the mountain air. It was a morning when my thoughts began to finally turn in earnest to the meeting that would take place later that afternoon.

Waiting over the border in Kaleden, British Columbia, a little better than a half-day's drive away, was my biological mother Gloria, her son Blair, and her mother Isabel. I had not met Isabel or Blair, but Gloria and I shared a five-year relationship so I was less nervous than I might otherwise have been as I fired up Lucy and headed north for Canada.

In the summer of 1969 my parents had adopted me through Canada's Children's Aid Society. Unlike the adoption facilitation offered by many other agencies, where files were commonly sealed or destroyed in the interest of protecting the privacy of adopted children, birth mothers, and adoptive families, the Children's Aid Society had developed a system of independent mutual registration that allowed birth mothers and the children that they had given up to contact one another as long as both parties, mother and child, wished this to happen, and as long as the child was over the age of eighteen. Gloria had registered when I was eighteen, but it had taken me an additional four years to do the same.

I have very few relatives in North America. My maternal grandparents were immigrants from Scandinavia who had only two children, my mother and my uncle. My father emigrated from Denmark to Canada as a young man and was the only one from his family ever to leave the Old Country. I visited my aunt and uncle and their one child for a few weeks in Ontario every summer, but my understanding and knowledge of my "relatives" was limited by distance. Eight hundred miles of highway separated my mother from her hometown, and we rarely traveled to Denmark to visit with my father's family. This is not to say that I lacked a family structure. Our family—my mother, father, and brother—has always been strong and intensely nuclear. We take care of one another, are fiercely loyal, and have an extended group of friends, mostly people like my parents, who were immigrants to America, who function as our "relatives" at family celebrations, graduations, and holidays.

Although it was something that was openly recognized, I never really thought about being adopted, never considered the possibility of contacting my biological mother, until I spent a year living and studying in Ireland while I was in university. Unable to afford a plane ticket home for Christmas, I traveled to Denmark to spend a few days with my father's family.

"My father's family" is how I thought of my Danish relations as I had met them only once, when I was seven years old. They were, of course, my family, too, but I did not know them in the same way that I knew my aunt, uncle, and cousin in Ontario, and I did not know them with the same level of intimacy as I knew our circle of family friends. This was neither deliberate nor dysfunctional; it was, rather, a matter of geography. Christmas dinner that year was at my uncle's house, and while there two things began to chew on my understanding of what "family" meant and how it was expressed. First, I did not speak Danish and, as a courtesy and an expression of welcome, the dinner conversation was conducted almost entirely in English. Second, there were fourteen people who sat around that dinner table: mothers and sons, fathers and daughters, cousins and aunts and uncles. One cousin had his father's height and large capable hands, another aunt had a straight spine and a merriment that was reflected in her daughter. Every single one of them shared some feature, some mannerism, some element of posture, with at least one other person at that table. Everyone except me.

That night as I lay in bed I did some hard thinking. These people were my family, I knew that, and that central fact was never in doubt. However, the questions that circled and nibbled around the periphery of that certainty were troublesome: *how* did I know that they were my family? There was neither language nor body type to connect me with any of the people who sang Christmas carols around the tree that night. We communicated because they could speak English and were kind enough to use it in their own homes so that I would understand what was being said. So what *exactly* was it that bound us together? And where were those other people, the ones with whom I did share physical characteristics or unintentional mannerisms?

I knew what made a family. I knew it through instinct and through what I had learned in my parents' home. Families are made through choice, not biology. They are created through love, commitment, communication, forgiveness, patience, understanding, and support, all freely shared. These elements are more important than ties of biology, or even language or culture. In the absence of those intangible and unscientific, yet critical, elements, even "natural" families will fracture. Our family is strong, transcends the occasional difficulties of multiculturalism and personality, and is sure of our unity because we have made that *choice* to be a family, have fostered those fundamental elements, and have made those commitments to one another.

Still, in the aftermath of Christmas dinner, and long after I had returned to America, the questions were still there: how exactly did I define my own family, and where were those *other* people, the ones to whom I was linked genetically? Two years later I decided to go looking for answers and registered with the Children's Aid Society.

The Society guided Gloria and me through a series of steps, including counseling and letters forwarded through the agency, which spelled out histories, hopes, and expectations for a future relationship. Each of us was given the opportunity to cease communication at any time, and home addresses and phone numbers were not released until both of us felt ready to meet. Following nearly a year of letters and a few months of phone calls, Gloria and I met at her home in Montreal in the winter of 1994.

Our initial meeting was dizzying, frightening, and enormously risky. The dominant North American view of a "family" does not include prescribed roles for birth mothers or adopted children or what their relationships toward one another might be. When an adopted child begins to explore the idea or possibility of meeting a birth parent, even the most seemingly simple questions, such as what is a family, what is a mother, what is a father, what does it mean to be a daughter, to be a son, are open for examination. In some ways this is an incredibly important series of questions for all parents and all children, adopted or not, to ask of themselves, but they are questions that can also be enormously disruptive and threatening to a traditional understanding of what it means to be a nuclear family.

Initially I thought it was fundamentally important to tell my parents that I was considering contacting my biological mother. I wanted to explain to them why I was doing this, what I was looking for, and, most importantly, what I was *not* looking for: another family. My father listened, understood, and encouraged me to continue, but my mother was indescribably hurt and angry that I would even consider such a thing. Although I tried to explain, she believed that my interest in contacting Gloria constituted a rejection of her as a parent. She thought that it was a negation of everything that she had ever given or sacrificed as a mother. None of this was true, but at the time, and as offended and indignant as she felt, she was unable to listen to or to hear what I was saying. I tried to understand her perspective and how threatened she felt, told her that I was sorry, and promised that I would never speak of it again. She's my mom and I would never deliberately hurt her. I never spoke of it again to my father either as I did not want to put him in the position of having to keep my secret: that the following year I contacted Gloria.

I kept my silence for five years. One day, home from graduate school on a visit, my mom and I sat in the sunshine of the driveway drinking coffee and talking about my brother and his wife, who were considering an overseas adoption, as well as my mom's best friend, who was now a grandmother thanks to the adoption of a little boy from Russia.

"Did you . . ." She stopped and put her coffee cup down on the driveway. "Did you ever follow through with contacting your biological mother?" I shifted lower into my chair and stared at the oak blossoms scattered across the asphalt.

I could feel the adrenaline pulse in my neck. It had been an ugly conversation the last time that we had spoken of this and I did not want to repeat the experience.

"I don't know what to say to you, Mom."

"No, no, it's all right. I've thought about it and I want to know now."

"I did. Four years ago."

"Did it go well?"

I nodded.

"What's she like?" My mother was smiling.

Reunion between a birth parent and child can be an affirming and loving experience, but it is always complex, rarely easy, and it is not necessarily something that every birth mother or adopted child can or should do. The decision concerning whether to attempt to establish a relationship is something that is highly subjective and entirely dependent upon the needs and expectations of the people immediately involved. Gloria and I were fortunate in that we wanted similar things from our relationship: a basic knowledge of one another, an understanding that things had turned out "all right" in both of our lives, and an ongoing friendship. Over the years we have gradually come to know one another and to establish a connection that has much of the intimacy that sisters might share, or perhaps bears similarity to the sort of relationship between an aunt and niece. Our bond is not quite as intense as mother and daughter, but it is very real and very strong and will last throughout our lifetimes.

It was a reality, but not a problem as I saw it, that Gloria had kept my birth a secret from her family for nearly thirty years. It was only recently that she had openly discussed with her parents and her sons that she had given birth to a daughter as a teenager. I cannot pretend to fully understand the reasons for her silence about my existence, but it mattered little. What was most important to me was our relationship with one another. Gloria, however, had decided that the time had come to introduce me to her family. My motorcycle trip, and the leg north through British Columbia, would coincide with her planned holiday to visit her mother and son. We would all meet in Kaleden.

. . .

In Monroe I left Route 203 and turned Lucy to the east following Route 2 up into the mountains. Here the Cascades formed an unlikely jumble where jagged black pinnacles shadowed the gentle green slope of the valley below. I climbed past the villages of Sultan, Start Up, and Gold Bar, crested Stevens Pass at four thousand feet, and dropped off the other side, following the glorious tumble of the foaming green Wenatchee River. Fire had burned through the high ridges between the Wenatchee and the Icicle Rivers in 1994, part of a series of blazes that consumed two hundred thousand acres of timber in a single summer, and the ranks of standing charred trees were in stark contrast to the cool slide of the water.

The river valley dropped and widened slightly where the Icicle and the Wenatchee came together. Leavenworth, a bizarre Bavarian theme town, sat just east of the confluence. In the 1960s, as the local timber industry exhausted itself, the Leavenworth Chamber of Commerce hit upon the "Project Alpine" idea and rebuilt and reinvented Leavenworth in a Bavarian-Swiss style. Tourists came by the thousands when alpenhorns replaced axes. Commercially, it was a wildly successful undertaking and over a million people come each year to stroll faux cobblestone sidewalks, listen to piped-in yodeling, and drink pricey espressos served by waiters in lederhosen and feathered caps. Even the local Dairy Queen and McDonald's were done up with peaked roofs, gingerbread trim, and alpine wall murals depicting placid cows munching their way through green pastures under glaciated mountains. But Leavenworth was surreal—uncomfortably so—and I only stayed long enough to fill Lucy's tank before following the river out of town.

Dropping down into the Columbia Valley, the temperature began to rise in ovenlike ways. The pavement became a liquid shimmer of intense reflected sunlight, and fifty miles an hour did nothing to disperse the additional molten waves of combustion heat rising from Lucy's engine. By the time I got to the banks of the Columbia River, and the intersection of Routes 2 and 97, it was over ninety-five degrees in the shade. On the road it was hotter.

What was misery for me was a blessing for the agricultural production of the region. The Columbia River Valley is fruit country, and apricots and cherries hung in huge drooping bunches from trees festooned with glittering red and silver Mylar paper that was supposed to keep the birds away. What looked like small paper bags encased fruit in some orchards and added to the ornamental effect of the trees.

The Lone Pine Fruit Stand was the only fruit stand that I have ever seen flying a black and orange Harley-Davidson flag. It stood on the west side of Route 97 headed north toward Chelan and seemed a natural choice for a place to stop, get out of the heat, buy some cherries, and be assured of welcome. I was still sensitive to what had happened in Black Diamond the evening before. Inside it was cool and clean, with refrigerated cases for the fruit and vegetables at one end of the building, and displays of small crafts, handmade soaps, and a juice bar counter at the other. On the wall was a crisp one-dollar bill, framed on the opening shift six days before. Jenny, the pretty, sandy-haired girl behind the counter, made me a fantastic fresh raspberry milkshake and I took it outside, under the shade of the front veranda, and waited for the noon intensity of the sun to dim. A pickup truck pulled up, the door opened, and a giant with blue-mirrored aviator glasses glinting above the underbrush of a thick brown beard dropped huge booted feet onto the dusty ground. This was Jim Walker, owner and manager of the stand, as well as close to six hundred acres of fruit orchards in the Columbia River Valley. A Harley fan, he was delighted to see my dusty Lucy parked out front and immediately came over to talk about bikes and traveling. Jim drove some sort of a ridiculously beautiful custom bike, which he kept polished to gleaming perfection and occasionally brought to shows. Lest he be confused with the class of people who owns expensive machines simply to show rather than ride, he quickly followed his description of chrome and airbrushed mirror paint with, "I do ride it lots, though, ten, twelve thousand miles a year." The conversation shifted from Harleys to fruit.

"What are those little bags hanging all over some of the trees?" It was an odd sight, and I was curious. Jim explained that those were fuji apple trees, the fruit destined for the luxury markets of Japan. The bags, several layers of them, protected the delicate white skin of the apples from insects and the sun. The apples ripened in their shaded, individually constructed shelters, until a day or two before harvesting, when the second-to-last bag was removed, leaving just a cellophane wrapper so that the apples could develop a slight pink blush before being hand-picked, boxed, shipped, and sold at twelve dollars a pound in Tokyo and Kobe. Most of the gross sales went to pay labor and middleman costs. Jim and his wife, Sue, had opened the fruit stand and juice bar in hopes of getting a bit more return on their product through direct retail than they got on wholesale. Jim sighed and scuffed one hobnailed boot through the dusty gravel.

"Used to be that if you had twenty acres of orchard you could make a good living, send your kids to college. Not any more." Falling fruit prices due to overseas competition and the efficiency of refrigerated high-speed transport had cut deeply into the profits of what used to be a highly lucrative business. At two in the afternoon Jim had to get back to his orchards and I needed to get back on the road. He dropped one great hand on my head in a fatherly pat as he stood up. "Now you be careful out there."

The river shone like polished blue glass through the pale motion of heat waves rising from the pavement. It was hot, very hot, and sweat crystallized in powdery white streaks up my jawline and into my hair. Climbing the valley in thirty-mile stretches, I stopped every forty minutes to pour something liquid from gas station refrigerators into my system. The cooling effect of bottles of V-8, Gatorade, and grapefruit juice seemed to evaporate almost instantly. Despite the uncomfortable riding conditions, it was impossible not to notice the different sort of beauty that emerged as 97 continued north, still following a riverbank, but leaving the deep roll of the Columbia for the shallow run of the Okanogan. The land was semi-arid, with strong slanting upthrusts of rock lining the valley that led to the Canadian border. Always there were the fruit orchards, but on the banks of a less bountiful river, the long, straight rows of carefully pruned trees were broken by great stretches of range acreage for cattle.

There was no line of traffic at the Canadian border and the crossing was a straightforward one. As I rolled into Osoyoos, British Columbia, I noticed in my side mirrors that a police car had pulled out of a parking lot near the customs station and was following closely. Too closely. Tired from the heat and with a backache coming on, I signaled well in advance for the benefit of the officer, and turned left into a liquor store parking lot to pick up a bottle of wine for Isabel in Kaleden. The patrol car turned right and parked in a lot across the street. Mirrored sunglasses winked and flashed through the cruiser's windshield. Annoyed, I jerked off my helmet and raked my fingers through stiffened hair. *Great, Deputy Dawg thinks he's going to bag himself a biker today.* I felt like giving the officer either a big friendly wave or my best Jersey middle finger salute but refrained from doing either. Inside the liquor store, the lady behind the counter helped me choose a deep ruby-colored cabernet, which came from the vineyards in Washington State, and which I hoped would lubricate any awkward reunion moments. She had a warm smile and kindly way that almost made up for the officer whom I knew was waiting outside. It is a sad thing when liquor store clerks do more to promote the friendliness and humane order of a town than do the police. With the wine wrapped in a paper bag and secured under the ratchet strapping of my pack, I pulled on my helmet and jacket and fired up Lucy. The constable, unsurprisingly, pulled onto the pavement behind me. He was no more than eight feet off my back wheel all the way to the town line, toward which I cruised at three kilometers under the speed limit. As I crossed into the next municipality he spun his wheel and U-turned back toward Osoyoos, his tires throwing up rooster tails of dust. What an ass. Osoyoos's finest must have very little to do if they can spend half an hour following a biker around town looking for the tiniest traffic infraction.

IT WAS ONLY TWENTY-FIVE MILES to Kaleden and all the shape-shifting meanings of those words—"family," "child," "parent," and "daughter"—that I had tried not to think about all day, that I had not thought seriously about since leaving New Jersey, came boiling back up. In the focus and intent watchfulness that driving a motorcycle requires I had lost myself, as well as all of my hesitations about first-time meetings with both my biological mother's and father's families, in each curve of the road. As nonchalant as I tried to be about the prospect of meeting Gloria's family in British Columbia, and later my biological father's—whose name also happened to be Dave—in Alberta, I was nervous. There was no need and no mental space to think about that nervousness in Iowa when the trip was new and I was still learning how to live on a motorcycle day after day. There was no incentive in Colorado, California, and Oregon, where altitude, challenging driving, and the sheer magnificence of the land kept my mind on what was immediate, to think about what that nervousness implied: was this something that I was prepared for? Did I fully understand what the long-term implications of meeting my biological family were? Did Gloria's and Dave's families really want to see me? Early in the trip, this day was always thousands of miles and many weeks away. I would think about it later, I told myself, but rolling north out of Osoyoos, later had become now. Gloria, her mother, and her son were waiting just up the road.

Isabel's house sat just below the crest of a grassy hill that overlooked the Okanogan Valley and its chain of lakes. I parked Lucy at the bottom of the driveway, next to the black metal mailbox painted with the street number that Gloria had given me. The early evening air was still and warm, and the silence, broken only by the raspy singing of grasshoppers, was palpable when I shut down the bike. I was exhausted and apprehensive and breathed deeply, summoning temporary energy and confidence great enough to swing my leg off Lucy's saddle and walk up the sloping driveway. The house was silent, the only motion the flash of glittering red and silver Mylar streamers that floated from the branches of a heavily laden cherry tree in Isabel's front yard. I opened the gate and walked slowly up the driveway. Halfway to the front door it opened. It was Gloria.

"Hey there!" I quickened my pace. It was good to see her and she looked relieved to see me.

"You're here! You're late!" She pulled me into her arms. As always she was elegant: slender, cool, and beautiful, her platinum hair pulled into a ponytail and her makeup flawless. Her toes, peeking out from Italian leather sandals, were painted with sparkling blue polish. One of the things that was clearly not passed down through genetic channels was a sense of fashion, style, and personal grooming. Where Gloria was always dressed in the latest designer creations, hair done and nails manicured, I maintained a wardrobe whose major supplier was the Salvation Army, rarely wore makeup, and was more comfortable in biker boots than high heels. Both my mom and Gloria agreed that I could and should "do more," and both referred to the way I dressed as "your refugee-waif look." That day in Kaleden was no exception; I was dusty, sweaty, tired, and in desperate need of a washing machine. Gloria, however, didn't seem to care. "Look at you! You look great! Look at those muscles! What have you been doing?"

I laughed. "Driving motorcycles. It does wonders for the upper body." An older woman and man came out of the house, Isabel and her husband, Joe, along with Gloria's twenty-one-year-old son, Blair. Isabel was tall, taller than either her daughter or me, slim, and had the same bright blue eyes that we all shared. She wore shorts and my gaze drifted down past her knees to ankles that Gloria had said were just like my own. Where Gloria had a fragile-looking bone structure with graceful wrists and ankles that were a hand-span around, Isabel and I had the solid legs and ankles of the highland women of western Scotland, from where Isabel's mother had emigrated early in the century. Isabel's eyes looked a little wet when she put her arms around me.

"We're so glad you're here. Welcome." She spoke close to my ear, softly, just like her daughter did when she was emotional. God forbid anyone should see you cry. This was something we all shared. Gloria spoke up.

"Karen, this is Blair, my oldest son." Blair shook my hand, a perfunctory squeeze, and crossed his arms over his chest. A little over six feet tall with sharp features, sloping shoulders, and a dark blond flattop perfectly gelled to stand on end, he looked nervous, more nervous than I.

"Hey, how you doin'?"

"I'm great, Blair. Really great, and glad to be here." He smiled, boyish with big teeth and a wide grin. Feet shuffling, his arms fell to his sides. Joe looked around.

"Where's your bike?"

"Down at the bottom of the drive. I wasn't sure where to park it so I left it there." Joe stepped back onto the white cement of a shaded carport and moved a lawn mower a few feet back.

"It's a Harley?" I nodded. "Well, you can pull it in here if you don't think that thing is going to leak oil all over my concrete." I laughed, assured him that it wouldn't, and walked back down the driveway to get Lucy.

We spent the evening sitting by the swimming pool, talking about travel, our schools and jobs, and what each of us would do as summer shifted to fall. Joe and Isabel were thinking of moving to a retirement community as the house had become too large for them to maintain with Joe's sometimes fragile health slowing him down a bit more each year. Blair would return to university in Edmonton, and Gloria was looking into the possibility of a new job. The sky deepened to a purple blue, the grill smoked with chicken and burgers, and the conversation flowed with no awkwardness or hesitation.

A friend who is also adopted had met his biological mother a few years before I met Gloria. "What was that like?" I asked him, expecting a story of soap-opera proportions and high drama, a story where long-lost ties begin to spontaneously reknit and tears, recriminations, and declarations of love or forgiveness or anger would be heightened and extreme. I expected a story with characters and emotions that I would not wish to have in my own well-defined personal and family life.

"Surprisingly casual," he said. If there is mutual permission for contact, if all of the people involved have had time to think through what a reunion might mean to them, both individually and within the context of their families, there is no drama, there are no declarations, and there is only "surprisingly casual" shared conversation and togetherness that sometimes, as the months and years pass, deepens into bonds of friendship, or even a sense of extended family.

For those few days in British Columbia, as I met Gloria's family, it was as if I was a distant cousin come to visit after a long absence. Part of this ease of introduction was that Gloria and I already shared a history and knew one another well. The disturbing elements of our early, scary, and awkward meetings were long past and we had a relationship that was comfortable, accepting, and open. In Kaleden, there were only occasional references to intimacies that must have once been very painful, and limited awkward moments as we brushed briefly against relationships that had yet to be established and defined.

Early one morning Isabel and I sat together in the living room. It was six A.M. and the rest of the house was still asleep.

"Isabel, when did Gloria tell you about me?" She handed me a fragile, white porcelain cup painted with purple violets, poured tea from a matching pot, and was silent for a long moment.

"You can call me Grandma if you're comfortable with that." I wasn't, but something in her eyes said that she wanted to hear that from me. In my immigrant family, we called my mom's mother Mummu, the Finnish endearment for "grandmother," and we called my dad's Farmor, Danish for the same. Calling Isabel "Grandma" would be a betrayal of neither woman, but there was a familiarity, an intimacy, in the word that I did not yet feel. However, for Isabel's kindness, for her acceptance of me, and for her love of Gloria, I would try to call her Grandma if that was what she needed to hear.

"OK."

"Gloria never told me, but I knew. Dave's parents also told me about you. Just after you were born, when Gloria was still in Ontario, they called. But Gloria never seemed to want to talk about it and I wanted to respect her wishes." Isabel handed me a spoon and the sugar in silence. Gloria had, of course, told me the particulars of my birth and the months that preceded it: an unplanned pregnancy and the lies she and Dave told their parents about their teenage plans to travel Canada during the summer of 1969. I was not aware, however, that Isabel actually knew about Gloria's pregnancy at the time, and I did not understand why mother and daughter, each knowing the reality, would never speak of it for almost three decades. Gloria had told me that she suspected that her mother knew, but that as one year turned into the next, as she married and had two sons, there seemed to be no time that was right to bring it up, no way to start the conversation. Perhaps it was enough that each knew, that each believed the other understood and accepted that knowledge. Perhaps there was no need to speak of it openly. They had finally talked about it only after Isabel's mother died in 1997. Gloria had sent me the obituary and a few photographs of my biological great-grandmother and let me know that she had decided to talk to Isabel, to finally lay out in the open that there was another woman who had the same bright blue eyes and the same solid bone structure in her wrists and ankles.

Blair and I walked downhill toward the lake through the heavy warm evening air. My head barely reached the level of his shoulder and he looked down at me, shortening his stride a little so that I wouldn't have to trot to keep up.

"This is weird," he said.

"Yup. This is weird." For Blair, the situation was particularly odd. After all, I had been raised with the knowledge that I was adopted and had had a lifetime to get used to the idea that I had a biological family out there, somewhere. Blair had just learned of my existence a few months before.

It had not been Gloria, unfortunately, who had told him that he had a biological half-sister. It had been his father. Gloria's ex-husband, in a fit of anger one evening, and in response to some irritating teenage behavior, had spit out the information about Gloria's secret and my existence. The story, hurled like a weapon in the middle of an argument, was an ugly recitation of what irresponsible conduct could lead to. The choices that Gloria had made in the summer of 1969 would be difficult to understand even in the gentlest and most exploratory of conversations, and Blair's father had done nothing to help him make sense of what he had been told. As a result, Blair was angry, but not at his father's betrayal; he was angry at his mother's silence.

"She should have told us herself. We had the right to know about you. What she did was wrong." We walked in silence for a hundred yards. The asphalt held the heat of the day and the scent of warm tar and newly mown grass filled the air. I felt sorry for him and tried, not overly successfully, to explain.

"This isn't about you, Blair; it isn't even about me. Your mom made decisions a long time ago, before she even knew your dad and before you were ever born, that she thought would be best for herself and for her child."

"She should have told us."

"Maybe she should have. I think she would have when she was ready, and she's ready now, but she wasn't then." Blair was a sensitive boy. His parents had divorced when he was still small, and, soon after, Gloria had moved to a different city to pursue her career. Parenting at long distance is difficult, and Blair and his brother missed the daily contact with their mother. The surprise revelation of another "lost" child was hard on him and it would take months, if not years, for him to begin to understand his mother's choices and what his relationship with me might become.

I stayed three days with Isabel, Joe, Gloria, and Blair and was grateful to have the opportunity to see them together, to get to know them as a family with all of its interwoven history and relationships, and to see where Gloria, whom I previously knew only as an individual, fit into the larger structure. I was also grateful for their welcome, their acceptance, and their willingness to talk about what had happened so many years before while focusing on what was really important: the future.

I LEFT KALEDEN AT 7 A.M. with a few tears all around. Isabel pulled me close and whispered, "We love you," into my ear and Gloria gave me a similar squeeze, dark glasses hiding her eyes, a silent shake in her shoulders betraying everything.

It was a clear, still morning, and the road curved slowly north along the western side of the chain of lakes held within the Okanogan Valley. The weather was changing, however, and as the morning lengthened it got colder and the wind took on a damp, raw edge that smelled of rain. Route 97 passed through Kamloops, rising into a valley where Douglas firs, hemlocks, and cedars grew in clustered patchy stands surrounded by hillocks of soft tawny grasses. On the dark ridges pushing toward the mountains to the west, the grass turned entirely to forest and trees rolled in unbroken waves to the horizon. On a ridge near Savona, I stopped at an overlook to admire the view: eighteen miles of silvery blue lake stretching all the way back to Kamloops. In the 1890s, before the railways, and finally the roads, came through, steamship paddleboats used to carry passengers and gold seekers north across those waters.

Near Walachin the first shower swept over me, spraying a veil of water that was more mist than rain, and I did not bother to put on wet-weather gear as I thought that I would be dry within the hour. I was wrong. What I did not know then was that, in leaving the Okanogan Valley, I had crossed over into the much wetter coastal zone during a summer when the interior of the continent baked and the coasts dissolved into clouds and rain that lasted for weeks. I would be wet for the two days that followed, and a long, damp month was ahead. The passing showers and the sunshine that interspersed them were lovely in their own mercurial way, however, and it was a heightened sensory experience to drive out from under black bilious clouds that dropped sheets of rain onto asphalt that steamed and smelled of wet tar, onto pavement that was largely dry and where the air exploded back into dazzling sunshine and warmth. The clouds moved in as the afternoon progressed, darkening and thickening as the wind picked up and the temperature dropped twenty degrees. The stretches of sunlight became less, and finally disappeared altogether. At Cache Creek I finished layering on every bit of dry clothing that I owned. Under my leather was a fleece jacket, a sweater, a long-sleeved shirt, and a tank top. A scarf was knotted around my throat and I wore winter gloves and polypropylene long underwear. I was almost, but not quite, warm.

Roughly paralleling the Frasier River, Route 97 burrows into the deep woods of British Columbia and was originally built as a stagecoach and post road in the later years of the last century. It brought fur traders, trappers, homesteaders, and, above all, gold seekers, north toward the timber, the land, and the gold fields of the Cariboo Mountains. Communities, as well as services in unincorporated townships, still bore names that marked their distance from Lillooet, the southern terminus of the original road. At 100 Mile House, as the showers turned to steady rain, I finally admitted that the precipitation was something I could no longer count on driving out from under within a few minutes, and I stopped to add the final layer of a rainsuit.

By Williams Lake I had driven more than three hundred miles through country that was gradually filling in with deep forests. The coffee that I drank in a gas station parking lot, my fourth of the day, was another jolt of energy and warmth, but it could not disperse the cold that had stiffened my hands and face, and I was beginning to feel tired and chemically hopped to the point of dizziness. I moved on through Soda Creek with the realization that I had to stop soon. It was raining in earnest, drenching precipitation that varied in intensity from blowing mist to pelting sheets of water hurtling across the road. My feet were soaked and shivers ran up my spine in body-shaking waves.

McCleese Lake, a community that was not much more than a gas station and a row of brown cottages, appeared out of the mist and rain. In the fading light of the early evening there was little indication where pavement ended and lake began; only the cottages marked the shoreline. A sign with a small camping symbol read CUISSON LAKE RESORT—6 MILES and pointed east up a side road. I took a right onto a paved surface that powered Lucy most of the way up a mountain, climbing in sharpening hairpin turns before dropping swiftly over a ridge. Four miles up another sign, this one pointing down what looked like a quagmire of a dirt track, indicated the way to Cuisson Lake. What to do? I went a little farther up the paved road, thinking of finding a flat place to camp, but the marshy verges, low-growing scrub, and thoughts of grizzly bears wandering around the otherwise deserted landscape made me turn back. I stopped at the entrance to the track, considering it again. Wide puddles of uncertain depth marked the first twenty feet, beyond which the road stretched back into the forest, a single lane of semi-liquid clay and saturated pine needles. Street motorcycles, especially heavily loaded ones, are not designed to go sliding through the mud on mountain roads. *This is lunacy. I'm going to drop Lucy into some slimy sinkhole full of muck and never be able to get out. Maybe I should just go back down to McCleese Lake.* There were those little cottages that I had seen fronting the lake, each with their own front porch, and one of them would probably be empty. I could stay dry, but at a price I suspected would eviscerate my budget for the week. As I sat on Lucy mulling over my options, a silver SUV drove up out of the dirt road. A woman in the passenger seat rolled down the window to stare at me in some wonder as I waved her to a stop.

"Is there camping by the lake?"

"Yes."

"How's the road?"

"Rough, but you'll be all right."

Against perfect judgment—the woman was, after all, assessing the road based on four-wheel-drive as well as four wheels—I took her advice and inched Lucy into the muck. Mostly gravel, with an inch or so of liquid mud covering the surface, the road held well, and aside from a couple of slippery moments as I inched around trench-sized potholes, moments that would have set me to sweating had I not been so cold, I made it to the lakeshore.

Cuisson Lake Resort was a collection of trailers and cleared camping spots nestled under cedar trees near the water, rented out by the day or the week. It was the sort of place where families came year after year, spreading themselves far enough apart for privacy but close enough so that the children, whom I could see dashing through the trees in brightly colored slickers, could play together. A proprietress named Maureen, bright blue eyes dancing with merriment above the Mexican blanket pattern of her heavy coat, showed me around the tent sites. I chose one in the midst of a grove of trees, a tiny clearing that looked a little more drained and dry than the rest. Under the shelter of Maureen's awning I filled in a registration slip and chatted about the weather with three other women who had gathered there. Where it had been hot and dry in Kaleden and the Okanogan Valley, the temperature inching past a hundred degrees just the day before, at Cuisson Lake on the other side of the Cariboo Mountains, it had been fifty degrees and horribly wet. One of the women stamped her feet, warming them inside heavy rubber boots that reached the knees of her damp blue jeans.

"I haven't been dry since last Thursday!" Despite the sogginess of the evening, and the week that preceded it, Maureen was indefatigably cheery. She loved her camper near the water and wanted to spend as much time there as possible during the summer but, in addition to managing the resort with her husband, she also juggled a second full-time job in the valley and was raising three children.

"And they're boys!" She shook her blonde curls and chuckled at this final difficulty. Talking about her children brought a maternal light to Maureen's eyes, and she looked at me critically for a long moment. I was soaked and filthy, no longer felt fully human, had started to visibly shake, and must generally have been a miserable sight. "You know what?" she said. "We have a little trailer that's just opened up. The Marshmallow."

"The Marshmallow?"

Maureen laughed. "Yes, we call it The Marshmallow, because it's tiny and pink. But it has heat and I'll give it to you for the same price as a campsite." She reached out and patted my arm. "I'd rather you were inside; the rain is supposed to just get worse tonight. You stay right there, the girls will mop it out, and we'll get you dry inside." I didn't have to be asked twice.

A half hour later, inside a seventies-era pink-and-white minitrailer small enough to be pulled behind a Volkswagen Beetle, I peeled off wet clothes and stood naked beside propane lamps that gave off heat along with a soft amber light. It was a huge relief to get out of the rain, the cold, and the rapidly lowering darkness of evening. A tent would have been survivable, the rain fly was watertight and my sleeping bag was dry, but this was an unexpected luxury and a much-appreciated kindness. Outside the wind pulled damply through the fir boughs and rain hammered on the roof. Loons were singing from the darkened waters of the lake as I curled up under the drying heat of a gas lamp in my gift trailer. The mercy of strangers is a miraculous thing.

It was still drizzling when I woke, but the night's heavy rain had ceased, leaving a landscape sodden and obscured by heavy drapes of mist rising like wraiths off the lake. Maureen came rushing out of her trailer, business card in hand, as I packed up Lucy.

"I'm so glad you were inside, it rained all night. I wouldn't have slept a wink if I knew you were out in that." I thanked her with genuine gratitude and promised to send other travelers in the direction of Cuisson Lake.

Back on 97, the valley was lush and the fields at roadside, where they weren't flooded into large ponds, gleamed in shades of pale jade lit by the anemic sun rising through thickening mist and rain. Log barns—hand-squared and chinked—dripped, solid and black in the far pastures. Culverts and bridges spanned rushing torrents of swirling brown water barbed with branches, small trees, and a drowned sheep.

I stopped in Kersley for a roadhouse breakfast and to call my parents. Driving in the rain always makes me a little lonely. In the restaurant I chatted with a solidly built woman with long, gray-streaked, braided hair. She wore a vivid turquoise sweatshirt with horses running across the front and crocheted a complicated lace pattern as she spoke. Her fingers moved rapidly, the lace forming like flowers growing on a trellis, but she never looked down at the complexity of her work. There was little talk but of the rain, forty-six millimeters of it yesterday, she said, steady and drenching the last couple of weeks. The current weather system was not expected to move out for another two days. Her neighbor had lost forty acres of hay to the weather in the past week; it sat sodden, unusable, rotting in the fields.

The rain had begun again and the run into Prince George was wet and cold. The town itself was a depressing destination: a grubby little crossroads city with lumber, pulpwood, and oil-refining industries at its heart, and a bridge of creosote-soaked timbers forming a blackened and slimy approach across the muddy churn of the Frasier River. Few towns are appealing in a downpour, but Prince George looked like a northern cesspool. It was, however, the intersecting point of Routes 97 and 16 and I needed to pick up 16 running west to get to Prince Rupert, where I would board a ferry for the Inside Passage and Alaska.

At an Esso station I stopped for gas, stepping off Lucy and onto feet that were almost totally numb from the cold. My left foot, engaged in shifting, had fared a little better than my right, but both needed motion and movement to restore the blood flow. The Esso was one of those combined gas and convenience plazas, the interior well lit and warm. The girl behind the counter smiled at me even though I left a dripping trail of muddy boot prints on her gleaming tiled floor. If Prince George had a redeeming element it was her.

Outside, I called Dave from the pay phone beneath the overhang. Driving in solitude through an obliterated landscape, my thoughts had turned inward. I had been angry and hurt when we last had spoken in Portland, and I wanted to talk with him again; actually talk this time, not to retract what I had said or to negate how misled and foolish I felt, but to speak honestly and openly, and maybe, just maybe, to sort things out. *Maybe he would tell me that he really did want to come out and see me. Maybe he had already booked a flight and was waiting for me to call so that we could arrange a meeting.* These were foolish thoughts, developed in the rain and the loneliness of a cold, wet day. When Dave picked up the phone he seemed neither glad nor sorry to hear my voice on the other end of the line. His usual indifference and equivocation was what came across. Yes, he wanted us to spend time together, but no, he thought it would be a bad idea if he came out. I did not understand. Why would he say that he wanted to see me and take no action to make it happen? Why should I have to back him into a corner to have him show even the slightest bit of interest or affection? Better questions were: why had I fallen in love with one who was clearly not interested, and why was I continually doing this to myself: making long-distance phone calls, trying to make it right, trying to understand, trying to give him every opportunity to feel something, anything, for me? It was demeaning, and I had no one but myself to blame.

"So where are we, Dave, what do you want?"

"I don't know." He sighed and was silent.

"You don't know? What does that mean?" A few tears slid down my nose and I tried to keep them out of my voice while attempting to find some understanding or to feel some closure. This could not continue.

He sighed again. "You can interpret 'I don't know' any way you want." There was nothing but dismissal in his voice and, after the better part of a year, as I stood in the rain in Prince George, I finally knew exactly how to interpret "I don't know." It was over. I hung up the phone, and for the first and only time out there alone on the road, let my composure completely slip. Crouching down, back to the wall, I leaned my forehead into the heels of my hands, felt every muscle in my ribcage constrict, and started to cry. Beyond my immediate sight there was only the rain, the pools of gas-slicked water, the haze over that ugly town, and the knowledge that someone I had loved did not have the courage to tell me that he did not, and would never, feel the same way. Misery. The solitude I valued so much was suddenly agonizing. I sat there for a few minutes, disconsolate, wretched, and wet. A native man came across the asphalt to use the phone. He looked at me and looked at Lucy.

"Sportster, huh?"

In momentary disbelief, I stared at him from where I slouched against the wall. How could he ask about a motorcycle when my face was streaked with dirt and tears? But maybe he was trying to be kind. Perhaps a question about the immediate, the obvious, the neutral, was the only thing a humane person could say when faced with another person's emotional wasteland. I could do nothing but nod. He smiled, stepped around me, and reached for the phone receiver. Gradually, out of sheer willpower to restore something that might look like poise and direction, I pulled myself together enough to get Lucy back on the road.

People always say that you cannot run from your problems. I have not found that to be entirely true. Especially with Lucy, and the intensity of focus required when negotiating two wheels through tight corners, problems are—at the very least—tucked away for a time. There they rest, back and out of immediate potential for damage, until the bike stops. With the cessation of motion they emerge again, but often with greater circumspection and objectivity.

The diminishment of pain was not immediate, however, and in my loneliness I talked to Lucy and to myself as we crested the rolling hills coming out of Prince George. In the low rumble of her engine, she seemed to respond. *Shhhhh . . . it doesn't matter. Let him go. Let's just disappear. There's nothing to regret except that he didn't love you as you loved him. I'll take care of you and you take care of me. We'll run together, far and fast, and everything will be all right. Lose this thing in the road.* I was crying again inside my helmet, big slow tears. I thought about stopping, just sitting and watching the dissolved landscape for a while, but the desire to get away from Prince George, away from the pay phone at the Esso, and away from Dave was stronger.

There's nothing like the emergence of the sun after days of rain to turn one's thoughts from despair to renewal. By Vanderhoof, the clouds were beginning to break, first with a tiny sliver of blue peeping between the gray masses, and then with full blasts of sunshine that lit and dried the asphalt. I drove from one patch of light to the next, feeling the gradual upward shift in temperature.

At a roadside pull-off under Sitka spruces, three gleaming Harleys with five riders, three men and two women, sat parked near a picnic table. I pulled over to eat some lunch and before I could get my helmet fully off, one of the men approached; three-day bearded and, like his friends, outfitted in gleaming and creaseless leathers, each set of chaps, jackets, bandanas, and beanie helmets emblazoned with the Harley-Davidson logo. They looked as if they had stepped off the dealership floor ten minutes before.

"How much rain did you get?" I removed my helmet, hung it with care on one mirror, took my earplugs out, and stared at him for a long moment. For some odd and perverse reason, looking at the mudless bikes just off the ferry from Seattle, at the women in their carefully applied coral pink and burgundy red lipsticks and their patches embroidered with roses twined into the Harley logo, I took grim pleasure in what I told him.

"Two days. Folks up in the Cariboo say it's not supposed to clear until Wednesday." For their sake I did hope that this assessment was pessimistic, but they were riding west, up and into challenging country and heavy weather. Their brand-new leathers would be pristine for about another hour. They were RUBs—Rich Urban Bikers—with the maximum of expensive gear, new bikes, and minimal experience. This was their first road trip, they said, and their plan was to ride into Jasper and then head south, down the Icefields Parkway and back to Seattle. I wished them luck and drier weather as they stepped onto their bikes, the women riding on the back, the straight pipes roaring. No one put in earplugs and no one put on rain gear. They would be considerably deafer and wetter by the end of the day.

I left my own rain gear on until Burns Lake, moving rapidly through the last few passing showers that dotted the route. At a Mr. Bagel I stopped and bought a thick frothed chai followed by a coffee chaser. Sitting on the porch outside the front entrance, I hoped that a double dose of caffeine and warmth, combined with the strengthening sunshine, would get me through the afternoon. I still felt drained and lonely and unsure of what the purpose of all of this was. What was I doing on the outskirts of a tiny town close to North of Nowhere? I sipped my chai, looked at my maps, and tried to figure out where I could stop and sleep.

EXHIBIT G: *Wayne*

Wayne pulled up on a purple BMW 1150 cross-purpose motorcycle with hard panniers. His wife and daughter were a few minutes behind, driving a green jeep. Once, twenty years before, he had set off on the same motorcycle trip to Alaska that he was about to repeat.

"I want to see what's changed," he said. "I hope it's not much . . . except the condition of the roads!" He sat down beside me, his wife's coffee and daughter's juice balanced on a cardboard tray on his knee, and motioned to where our bikes sat parked side by side. "We're so lucky, it's like living a dream!"

The green jeep pulled in and Wayne rose to greet his family. I stayed where I was and thought hard again about what my dreams had been when I started on the road to North of Nowhere: I had wanted to see the great spaces of the continent slowly roll past, I had wanted to meet the people of small-town America and Canada, I had wanted to spend some time alone, and I had wanted to meet my biological family. Sometimes the road was exhausting, wet, and lonely, but each day I was finding what it was that I sought. I was lucky, this was a dream, and Wayne was right.

. . .

According to my guidebook, Houston, British Columbia, was home to the largest fly-fishing rod in the world: a sixty-foot anodized aluminum pole complete with a nearly two-foot "fly" that stretched over Main Street. I had planned on staying in one of Houston's parks, which catered to the hundreds of fisherman who descended on the town each year in concert with the salmon run, until the man from the appliance shop next to the Mr. Bagel came over to talk after Wayne and his family had left. He suggested I drive past Houston to Tyhee Lake Provincial Park. It was beautiful there, he said, and less crowded.

The countryside coming into Tyhee was itself magnificent. In the late-afternoon sunshine, wet fields glittered and shimmered and the drying air danced and fractured into a polychrome of color and light. The ephemera of the landscape became solid and had a centering reality, however, when a huge doe suddenly emerged from the forest and ran toward the road. I hit the brakes, slowed rapidly, but she never stepped out, only stood with her tail raised for flight and watched with enormous liquid brown eyes as I passed.

Tyhee Lake was, as promised, a lovely spot. A green lawn spilled down from the tent sites to a small lake ringed with snowcapped peaks. It was cold and another rain shower was blowing in on the failing light, but I peeled down to my underwear and a tank top, and walked out from the pebbled beach to wash the last of the day's sadness from my limbs. The water flowed past as my arms sliced the surface in long, clean strokes. The road dirt of the day washed from my hair as I dove for the sandy bottom. Beneath the surface of the lake I could feel the ragged fibers of my mind and heart beginning to knit.

OLD HAZELTON IS A EUROPEAN RIVERBOAT community that was the
commercial hub of the Canadian northwest for half a century, until the rail-
roads arrived in 1914. An idle paddlewheel boat, dry-docked and silent, had
been preserved as a fish restaurant. The boiler from another ship stood rusting
in the park; naval machinery that was strangely incongruous amidst a planting
of dryland shrubs and graveled walks. The narrow streets were nearly deserted.
Despite the carefully preserved storefronts and the new library, Old Hazelton
had the feeling of community that had long since peaked, its best years sliding
down the river a century before.

The native communities that surrounded Old Hazelton were much more
vibrant. I visited the K'san Village, a center for indigenous arts and cultural
preservation, where native docents led groups of German tourists through a
recreated village. Lodges, one for each of the four main clans of the Gitxsan
Nation—wolf, fireweed, frog, and eagle—were fronted by heavily carved red
cedar totem poles that told the history of the clan in stacked figures that supported one another up the length of the pole. Atop one pole, a little apart,
stood the frock-coated and top-hatted figure of a nineteenth-century European.
The pole beneath him was blank of carving.

Fifteen miles from K'san, down a sometimes paved, sometimes graveled road, the village of Kispiox—"Hidden Place" in the language of the Gitxsan— stood at the confluence of the Skeena and Kispiox Rivers. In a corner park, away from the school and the small store that marked the center of the village, the totem poles of communities that no longer existed, and poles that had been moved for preservation and protection, had been collected to stand on an acre of soft green grass. The day was warm and sunny and only the sound of a chainsaw broke the stillness of the deserted park. I left Lucy at the far corner and went to walk among the totem poles. They were gorgeous, powerful, and a little eerie. Ranging in height from perhaps thirty to fifty feet, some were elaborately shaped: people and animals sitting one atop the other from base to pinnacle. Others were simple: the smooth shaft of the pole rising to support a single animal or bird. Two were inlaid with abalone shells that glowed in nacreous shades of purple, blue, and silver.

A broad-shouldered native man with a chainsaw stepped into view and slowly, methodically, began to demolish the swaying perimeter fence that surrounded the park. He moved from one upright to the next, sawing through the supports and pulling them from the earth, removing the interrupted view of the park, of the poles. Finished, he shut down the saw and walked with me through the stands of history carved into what were once mighty trees. We spoke a little of the weather.

"Such a beautiful day" I said. "So much nicer than these last few."

"Yes, in our language"—he swung his arm in a slow arc from the shoulder, palm up—"this is _____." The word was soft, had many syllables, and there was music flowing through the vowels. "Warmth, sunshine."

"And what do you call the opposite?" He hesitated, not sure of what I was asking. "Bad weather. What is it called in your language?"

"Oh." He said the same word as before, changing only the last syllable. "Snowing, raining." He paused. "But it's not really *bad* weather, because it's all . . . nature." We walked on, the sun on our backs, only the sound of grasshoppers breaking the silence. He motioned toward the wall of the mountains, black and capped with heavy white mantles, that rose in the distance. "The snow is leaving us late this year." Farther inland, in white communities, the discussion was also of the late snow, and of the early summer floods to come when the pack finally melted. People cursed the abnormally long, cold, wet spring and worried that the rising streams and rivers would further damage farms and roads as the meltwater came down from the peaks. The man mentioned none of this. The cycle of the seasons was given, nothing to rage against, nothing to judge, it just was. He spoke next of his family.

"My wife is Frog Clan. I am Wolf Clan." He explained that lineage was passed through the mother, that his sons and daughters would always be Frog Clan. When his daughters married they would keep their clan affiliation and would pass it on in turn to their daughters and sons. He talked of language and culture and what his life had been like as a boy. He told me about the Jesuit school that he had attended, closed now. "It was up on the ridge there." He pointed to a heavily timbered rise of land. "Priests lived there, too, but it wasn't like them residential schools. They never stopped us from speaking our own language." We stopped before an elaborately carved pole. A human figure crouched at its base, large tears flowing in cedar sadness down its face. "My grandmother told me about all of these, but you know, young man, in this ear, and out that one." He shook his head ruefully. "Oh, I been all over: Vancouver, Victoria, Prince Rupert, Prince George. A person forgets quick in places like that."

"But you remembered enough to want to come home?"

"Yes." His smile was sudden and joyful. "I belong here."

The road to Terrace runs at the foot of the Seven Sisters Mountains, a single strip of asphalt at the bottom of a deep valley. Black and vertical, elemental and jagged, the Sisters and the lower buttressed ridges that supported them were not mountains that invited even the idea of wandering. Further on, the Skeena River rushed swift and cold just past the edge of the pavement, the waters glacial green and cloudy with pulverized rock. Dark stands of Sitka spruce filed up the slopes until they found their way blocked by gravel slides or vertical expanses of dark stone. It was spectacular country, but not overly welcoming. The landscape was too immense, too dwarfing, too sharp and forbidding for a stranger, someone who did not belong there, to feel at peace. It was the sort of landscape that was less a backdrop than a watchful presence. It was the sort of landscape that left an ominous rumble in the psyche; a rumble that reminded the traveler to bring a full pack, ice axe, and crampons, and to be prepared for an assault—not a stroll—if they wished to walk into that pitiless place. There was a sense that although roads had been cut, rail lines laid, and small towns built, this was wilderness still, and always would be.

As I drew close to the coast the clouds thickened and lowered, tearing their underbellies on the sharp spikes of the peaks. Thirty miles from Prince Rupert, the salt-laden smell of the sea began to rise from gravel banks and the tangled snags of dead trees exposed by low tide. The river became broader and clearer, more tidal than glacial.

Prince Rupert bills itself as "The City of Rainbows," an overly romantic but damply appropriate moniker given the wet weather that often holds for days at a time. As morning mist turned to afternoon rain, I found a hot shower and bed at Pioneer Rooms. Close to where the fishing boats came in, it was a dim but clean boardinghouse, a little battered and frayed in its cheap furniture and yellowed linens, but run by a sweet-faced woman whose tenants included both long- and short-term boarders. Three young Japanese travelers made noodles in the common room and opened a can of octopus packed in black ink while a woman paced the halls upstairs in worn, fuzzy pink slippers, her hair covered in a nun's wimple created from a pillow slip held in place with a safety pin, her lips moving in silent prayer. In my room I unrolled the last clean thing from the bottom of my bag, a long black skirt, pulled it on, and walked with bare feet slipping inside boots down to the Laundromat to wash some of the grease, mud, and bugs of British Columbia from my clothes. Later I walked the shoreline streets down to Cow Bay, a boutique and restaurant enclave built for the tourists who came ashore with the ferry. At the "Cowpuccino's Coffee House," decorated in all things Holstein, I sat over postcards and a frothy latte, waiting out both the afternoon and the rain. It had been a hard run since before Prince George, and I was tired. The thought of not doing much of anything but watching the Inside Passage slip by ship rails for the next day and a half was enormously appealing.

. . .

Boarding would not begin until 8:30 A.M., but I wanted to find out the protocol for getting Lucy onto the boat and was at the docks by 7:30. Waiting by the roll-on deck, but separated slightly from the rows of motorhomes also preparing to board, I met Skip and June, a retired couple from Gainesville, Florida, who were doing much the same thing as I was, except from the vantage point of a 1995 custom Harley pulling a trailer that, among other amenities, contained a pop-up tent and an eight-inch-thick air mattress. Skip was a great bear of a man with thick arms and a wide grin. June was petite with copper-red hair and a ready laugh. They traveled often and widely on their bike, much to the chagrin of their friends and family, but loved almost every minute of it. We talked of the road, of weather, of the capabilities and repair record of our bikes, and compared notes on the exact place we had been when the rain had finally stopped two days before. We were nearly last aboard and the pursers squeezed us in between already loaded motorhomes in the interest of saving space. Eighteen-inch steel tie-down "buttons" rose two inches off the floor and we each chose one to angle the frame of our bikes above and dropped our kickstands to the side. I was lashing Lucy's frame to the button with ropes provided by the crew when the chief purser appeared to look things over, having already inspected Skip and June's bike.

"Where's the other helmet?" he asked.

"For whom?"

"Your partner."

"There isn't one. It's just me." He stared at me as this novel bit of information registered, watching as my hands moved between ropes and machinery. He laughed and shook his head.

"Later, when we get underway, why don't you come up to the bridge. I'll show you how to sail a ship and you can tell me something about your trip." This sounded like a fair trade and I agreed.

The Alaskan Marine Highway runs two ferry systems, one in the southwestern part of the state, serving the Kenai Peninsula and the Aleutian Islands, the other a long run that begins in Bellingham, Washington, and terminates in

Skagway, Alaska after sliding through the great natural beauty of the Inside Passage. Many of the small towns and cities, including the capital of Alaska, Juneau, were not accessible through the wilderness interior by road. Everything that went into or out of those communities had to be brought in by ferry or float plane.

The people on the ferry reflected the transportation-and-tourism realities of the region. Dozens of seniors, their tour buses parked on the lower decks, wandered the lounges and the cafeteria. A few pale-faced college students headed for cannery work in Ketchikan and Petersburg slouched near the windows of the front observation lounge. Bicyclists and hikers unrolled sleeping bags and stowed their backpacks under the heat lamps of the solarium on the top deck. Families from Passage communities watched as their children played on the clean gray carpet where the ferry naturalists would come and give short presentations on the geology and wildlife of the area.

A few hours from Prince Rupert, we docked in Ketchikan, and Skip, June, and I went on a ten-dollar bus tour. The first stop, downtown Ketchikan, was a vision of tourist hell, where fur bikinis and salmon sausage competed for window space below signs screaming advertisements for "Authentic Native" work. The big cruise ships stopped there, and tourism was the major economic engine for three short months of the year. Just outside of the city center the bus stopped again at the top of a salmon ladder. With the exception of bright pink fillets lying motionless on ice in a supermarket case, I had never seen salmon before, and I leaned far out over the railing to watch the determined fish making their final swim upstream. The long gray shapes waited in the eddies below the ladder, resting, gathering energy and oxygen, before leaping up the channeled waters of the creek.

From the ladder it was on to the village of Saxman, where Tlingit carvers sculpted totem poles from immense cedar logs. The carving studio was damp and cold, and mist-laden air rushed in from the sea through the open windows, mingling the scents of salt, fir trees, and freshly cut aromatic cedar. I shivered inside my leather jacket. Darald DeWitt, master carver, sat comfortably in a T-shirt, beads strung across his chest, a chisel toylike in his massive hand. Nude pink curls peeled from the logs onto the floor. Darald handed me one and I kept it, tucked into my wallet, until it fell to fragments months later. Out of the log before him, fiercely beautiful shapes were emerging: bear and raven. Later, the graphic designs of tooth and wing and claw would be emphasized in black and red paint.

Sailing north, the bizarre city of Juneau is the next stop after Petersburg. Juneau is home to thirty thousand people, cannot be reached by road, and has no room to expand because the vertical landscape that rises behind and around the immediate city limits forms avalanche shoots that would obliterate any new outward development. A historical oddity, Juneau was established in 1880 when wandering prospectors Joe Juneau and Richard Harris were shown where they might find gold by Tlingit Chief Kowee. It was only a matter of weeks before word leaked out that Juneau and Harris had struck it rich. The rush was on. Until the early 1940s, Juneau produced 90 percent of all the gold that came from Alaska. Thousands arrived looking for wealth, and some stayed, eventually establishing it as the capital city. Two state referendums in the last twenty years have proposed the shift of the capital to larger and more accessible Anchorage, but Alaskans chose to maintain the location of their governmental center, regardless of its isolation. Cynical commentators have suggested that, if nothing else, the geography of Juneau has effectively achieved what the body politic of most other states has not been able to do: contain the size of the government.

Back on the boat, and on the final leg of the journey up the Inside Passage, I met Dan Shain, a scientist and explorer from Rutgers University. In the strange twilight of an Alaskan midsummer night, we talked for a couple of hours about my trip and his research before getting off the ferry together in Skagway. Dan was in Alaska to study ice worms, mysterious creatures that lived on glaciers, ate red algae, and could survive only a degree or two above or below the freezing point. At five degrees centigrade their bodies would liquefy with heat; at minus five degrees they would freeze. The fragile creatures existed, burrowing down to where the temperature was a constant and comfortable zero, in some of the world's harshest climates and within tens of thousands of tons of shifting ancient ice. Dan pulled out electron microscopy photographs of his worms. Their leering saw-edged jaws and odd, dimpled heads, made massive by magnification, almost leaped from the black-and-white pages. They were horrible-looking things, but he was clearly fascinated with them. Dan planned to spend weeks in the far north on funding from *National Geographic*, clambering mostly alone on the roofs of some fifteen glaciers, avoiding crevasses and fissures caused by the summer melt, all to collect samples of worms that varied genetically from glacier to glacier. He thought that his research might ultimately have applications ranging from the preservation of tissue for organ transplant to the preservation of entire life systems for space travel, but mostly he thought that ice worms were "very cool things." Dan had a beard to match his voice, soft and brown, and when he spoke of his wife and year-old son waiting for him back in New Jersey, I wondered at the wisdom of his research methods. Scrambling solo over glaciers in remote wilderness areas, with little previous ice experience and no way to call for help, was not the most sensible thing I had ever heard of. I was, however, in no position to criticize the wisdom of anyone else's travel plans.

Dan's little car was parked at the front of the auto deck. When the ferry docked, he disembarked before me and was waiting at the top of the ramp when I gunned Lucy up the slope twenty minutes later. Two other men, Harleys packed, parked, and ready to be loaded onto the southbound ferry, were with him and I pulled in beside the three with a nod. The bikers looked tired, shoulders rounded and leaning on their bikes, but not ragged. Was it the late hour or the miles?

"Where'd you come from?" I asked.

"We're up from Texas," one said, straightening a little with pride. "Where'd you ride in from?"

"New Jersey." They looked at me and looked at Lucy.

"You rode a Sporty from New Jersey?" I nodded. The two men looked at one another.

"OK, you win." We laughed and walked a slow circle together around the bikes, talking of equipment and road conditions. One, dropping a hand onto his panniers for support, walked with a noticeable limp and the grimace of a new injury.

"What happened to you?"

"Started to slide. Road construction. Set my foot down. I wouldn't recommend it."

On a loose-surfaced road it could almost be expected that there would come a point—an intersection of gravel, dirt, or water—where the bike would start to slide. Hydroplaning or fishtailing on surfaces that were either unstable, slippery, or sheeted in water happened with cars, too, but on a motorcycle it was a particularly frightening experience. With only two wheels, if one—usually the rear—lost traction with the road surface, a sideways slide created an instant gut-churning feeling of loss of control. The rational way to correct a slide was by steering into it: shifting one's weight, but not necessarily turning the handlebars, and giving the throttle a "goose" to power the bike back into forward motion and straight-line control. However, slides always happened quickly, and sometimes instinct took precedence over rationality. In the Texan's case, as the back wheel moved out of the forward line, and the center of gravity shifted to one side and down as the bike started to lean, he panicked, thinking that he might fall. Instinctively, he locked up the brakes and dropped one foot to the road, trying to correct the sideways motion of his motorcycle with a booted thrust into the gravel. This was an excellent way to break an ankle or fracture a femur. Keeping one's feet on the pegs and steering through a slide was a much better way to get through it without getting hurt, but it took conscious discipline that wasn't always available when bike, road, and body all shifted unexpectedly and quickly. The Texan was lucky to still be walking, to still be driving, and I promised both myself and him that I would watch for the slippery bits in construction zones, of which he said there were many.

I followed Dan into town and we pulled into a campground. It was 2 A.M. and the sky was a soft golden gray, the subdued early glow of a northern sunrise that would turn pink within the hour. We set up our tents and crawled into our sleeping bags, but it was not a restful night. The train tracks fifty yards away, the coffee drunk right before disembarkation, and that strange, softly glowing sky kept me awake and restless. But I was there. Alaska.

I WOKE DAN AT 7:30 AND we packed up and headed to breakfast. Before I had a chance to stop him, he paid for both of our tent sites and managed to grab the breakfast check as well. Truth be told, I didn't feel like doing battle over it. I had enjoyed his company and appreciated the conversation, which lasted for more than my usual chance meeting of a minute or two. I talked to so many people each day: gas station attendants, waitresses, travelers, bikers, shop owners, retirees, people in parking lots and on sidewalks, people with whom I shared a place at a diner's lunch counter, and people curious enough about motorcycles to ask about mine, but I rarely conversed with anyone. Sunshine was, however, creeping down the mountain-shadowed streets of Skagway and, after finding the bottom of my third cup of coffee, I said good-bye to Dan and fired up Lucy. I was a little sorry, and suddenly a little lonely, as I left him sitting in the diner with his research notes, but I was headed over the mountains and he into them.

Any loneliness was quickly assuaged by Klondike Highway 2, which crosses the Coastal Range through White Pass, and connects Skagway with the Alcan Highway just south of Whitehorse in the Yukon Territory. White Pass had long been a funnel for those seeking the sea, or the interior, through the tangle of the mountains. Thousands had crossed on foot during the Yukon gold rush of 1898, dragging the ton of material and foodstuffs required by the Canadian government over the Chilkoot Trail, but until 1978 no permanent highway existed. If road-building was an art, the hundred-mile stretch of Highway 2 was a masterpiece. Long, slow curves climbed steadily, more than three thousand vertical feet from the sea level in Alaska, across the pass, and then tumbled two thousand feet back down into the Yukon. It was a cold, clear alpine morning and I rode, gaze shifting now right, now left, trying to concentrate on the road, look at the scenery and ignore the disturbing signs, "avalanche zone" and "do not stop." There was no traffic, I saw no other person, and the only evidence of the thousands that had gone over the pass before me was the abandoned remains of the silver ore sorter that last served the Venus Mines in 1910. The timbers and clapboard sidings leaned crazily, pearl gray and gradually splitting with years and weather. To the east, north, and south, the jumbled ridges of the mountains staggered and lurched, streaked with snow and gravel washes. The deep blue of the shadowed Pacific stretched like a bolt of raw silk below and to the west.

Lakes of different colors scattered across a rugged landscape of high tundra and lichen-painted stone. In shades of spring-fed blue or glacial green, and with water that was further pigmented by the mineral composition of the surrounding rock, the lakes sometimes merged one into the other in a tangle of colors ranging from golden yellow to green to sapphire. Tutshi Lake was the largest, and shone silver blue, the reflection of the vertiginous landscape mirrored in its face. This was the high country, with its predominance of rock, lakes that were liquid for only a few short months of the year, and flora that was scattered and stunted, growing no more than twelve inches tall from graveled roothold to wind-blasted leaf.

Reid was a hard-rock miner from Sudbury, Ontario. His family and mine were intertwined, in that generations of our men had gone down together into the shafts that pockmark the landscape around Sudbury to dig for nickel, copper, and trace metals like gold and silver. The men also had built hunting shacks and weekend cottages at the west end of a lake thirty miles from the smelters and slagheaps of their workdays. Reid's father had taken my mother waterskiing when she was a girl, and Reid himself was the teenager who pumped gasoline into the boat that brought my parents down the lake for a summer holiday the first year they were married. As a child I played with Reid's two nieces and we three little girls saw something heroic in him. He had a physical build that spoke plainly of what he did for a living: broad shoulders, strong legs, and hands that dwarfed the cans of soda and fruit ices he bought for us at the marina dock. Handsome, with a square jaw, curly black hair, and bright blue eyes, he was also a great fisherman and drove his outboard-powered boat faster than any other adult we knew. Best of all, Reid knew how to fly airplanes and had an orange and white Cessna that he kept in immaculate condition. He took us, all three squeezed into the backseat, soaring over the lake country of the near north. We swooped over old beaver ponds where the forest met shallow water, to look for moose and bear, dropped low over small lakes to find the shoals where the big bass might later wait for our baited hooks, and lifted out over Georgian Bay to see the enormous cruising boats of the wealthy where they docked at Killarney Harbor. He loved to fly and it took little childish wheedling for him to take us aloft.

In later years, no longer a child, my relationship with Reid changed and broadened. We became the sort of friends who saw each another only once a year for a few days during the summer, and when we were together it was if we had never been apart; the conversation was that easy and that natural. This was rare and wonderful, yet strange, because on the surface we had nothing in common. The difference in our ages, the geography of where we each lived, and our vastly different life experiences implied that we should rapidly run out of things to say to one another. But it was never so. We continued to fly together, sometimes setting down in remote lakes where we pulled huge bass from reed-choked shallows. Reid listened to my dreams of faraway places and told me his own plans for the future. Once he took me down into the mines, a mile deep, and showed me the tunnels and the darkness in which he worked each day.

Every year, for the past six, Reid had taken his holidays away from Sudbury and the mines, flying up to the far north, where he would rent a camper truck and spend a few weeks driving through the enormous landscape and almost endless daylight. Although he never said it, I always thought that his love of flight, of soaring, and of the huge open spaces of the Yukon and Alaska had something to do with finding the antithesis of the environment in which he worked each day. In the summer of 2000, his holiday and mine would intersect, and we had agreed to try and find each other in Whitehorse. Through e-mail, each knew on what day the other would arrive in town, but we had no specific plan for where and when to meet.

It was early afternoon when I began my hunt for Reid, searching for him at the floatplane base, the Whitehorse airport, and at the potlatch festival underway in the fields by the river. A potlatch is a feast, a celebration of plenty and giving, traditional to the native peoples of the northwest. The crowd was filled with men in plaid shirts and women dressed in soft deerskin with beadwork in their hair, but Reid was nowhere to be seen. Distracted by the spinning dances of children and the heartbeat drumming of music foreign to anything I had ever heard before, I stopped looking for Reid and for an hour just sat on the banks of the river, watching, listening.

I finally found him back in town. I turned the corner at the local Tim Horton's, headed for the tourist information center, and there he was: tall, a wide chest and smile, a crushing hug. As I had wandered Whitehorse, Reid had been making plans for us for the following day. An acquaintance, a pilot named Ronnie with a four-seater plane on floats, would take us flying over the Coastal Range. The weather forecast was for clear skies.

Ronnie showed up at the floatplane base at 10 A.M. holding his four-year-old daughter Rianna by the hand. While the men gassed up the plane and did the preflight check, Rianna and I amused ourselves by picking magenta fireweed and pale pink wild roses and dropping them one by one into the bluish-black waters of the Yukon. By 11 A.M. we were finally lifting into the air and soaring west out toward the ice-sheathed peaks of the St. Elias Range. As Rianna fell asleep, propped up against Reid's shoulder in the backseat, the country climbed quickly, out of the wide bands of forest toward the treeless slopes of the high tundra. We saw the flash of white chamois sheep, startled by the roar of the plane, bounding upward toward their craggy refuges. We flew over a flock of mountain goats and saw three caribou, two of which were stretched out on an ice field, asleep on their sides, seeking the cool of the surface while the third stood watch. In a canyon, we spotted a cow moose and her calf wading in a glacial stream. Ronnie's plane lifted over the passes and flew low over the permanently glaciated ice fields of the high peaks. The only hint of softness, where the high ridges turned cold and jagged, stone and ice unbroken by growth or greenery, was the shocking sapphire blue of a shallow glacial lake temporarily warmed to fluidity in the summer sun. The bottom was only more ice, however; no fish would ever swim there, and by October, if not sooner, the lake would thicken and freeze and disappear. Over the massive rampart of a vertical wall, Ronnie dropped the plane into a steep dive and hurtled into a closed canyon. I watched the striations of millions of years of rocky upthrust flash by a few meters from our wing tip. He wheeled low and hard, banking up and out to just clear the end wall as we emerged over a low pass. There are moments when you know with certainty that if there is one wrong move, one tiny error on the part of another, you will cease to exist. If the one who dares your life makes up for skill with brashness, the feelings that result are fear and horror and anger linked to short-breathed palpitations. With Ronnie, however, who had flown these passes hundreds of times, who flew like a madman as his tiny daughter slept in the seat behind him, I felt no fear, only resignation. Ronnie was in control and I was almost sure that he would not fly us into the face of a cliff.

On our way back to Whitehorse, as Reid settled into the white oblivion of engine noise and hundreds of acres of recently burned timber flashed carbon black beneath the plane, Ronnie casually propositioned me over the headphones. Would I be coming through Whitehorse on the way back from Alaska? Yes. Would Reid be traveling with me? No. Why not? We were just friends meeting for a few days and our roads would be different once we crossed the Alaskan border. Well, if I'd like to come and stay with him, I was welcome. If I needed money he could find me a job in the concrete operation he owned. The only complication was that it would be best to time my return for two weeks hence as his girlfriend would then be away. Reid told me later that Ronnie "did well with the ladies." This did not surprise me. He had the greenish gold eyes of a predator, hair a little long and curling where it brushed his collar, and the body and deeply tanned skin of one who has worked outside most of his life. In a more hedonistic moment I might have considered his offer, but no, not there, not then, not on that trip. Ronnie was looking for the rush of a summer fling, but I had that every day on the open road and didn't need to find it in the arms of a stranger.

That evening we cruised up the Yukon, the river flowing swift and strong through Miles Canyon, on a tugboat called *The Schwatka*. A century before, miners inclined toward the poetic thought that the foaming rapids that filled the gorge looked like equine manes, and named Whitehorse for the spectacle. The hurtling current remains but the rapids that gave the city its name are gone, drowned in the construction of the hydroelectric dam that created Schwatka Lake and filled Miles Canyon with an additional twenty vertical feet of water. The boat's heavy engine tugged and strained against the power of the current and the canyon widened into a cliff-ringed, roughly circular area, called Devil's Punchbowl. During the gold rush of 1898, the force of the uncontrolled Yukon swirling against the curved walls of the Punchbowl created rips and whirlpools that capsized the homemade boats of prospectors and pulled many men to their deaths. Some believed that beneath the churning water of the Punchbowl there was a tunnel that disappeared into the bowels of the earth. Unrecovered bodies, of which there were many, were thought to have been sucked down into that nameless oblivion. Now, with the Yukon twenty feet higher and twenty feet calmer, boys and young men leaped fearlessly from the cliffs into the water below. It was not, however, totally benign. I watched as the divers swam strongly for minutes to advance the few yards back to shore. Those deadly currents still boiled beneath the relative calmness of the surface.

It was a beautiful evening with soft, cool, moist air and gradually fading light that left a gold and purple luminosity hanging in the summer night sky. Past Miles Canyon, swallows dipped and swooped in and out of nests dug deep into the sand and clay bank of the river, searching for insects to feed their hatchlings and filling the air with the rustle of their wings and the tiny, sharp twitter of their speech.

23 | WHEN THE ROAD GETS ROUGH

MY CAMPSITE WAS SET AMONG A patch of wild rosebushes and after folding up my tent I sprawled out on the ground looking up at the brightening sky from underneath a scented cloud of delicate pink flowers. I picked one to press between the pages of my journal, vainly hoping that the fragrance caught within the five perfect petals would endure, and interrupted two black beetles making love inside the bloom.

Reid led as we left town and I stayed about fifty yards back from his camper so that I could see the full sweep of scenery. The road was lined with purple and yellow wildflowers, undulating meadows, and low-growth shrubs, which eventually shifted to tall spruce in the distance, and to far mountains ringing the horizon. It was a landscape just as open, wild, and uninhabited as northern British Columbia had been, but in the broad spaces of the Yukon there was less of a sense of claustrophobia than there had been in the labyrinth squeeze on the banks of the Skeena River.

The mountains of Kluane National Park, which spurred north from the St. Elias Range, rose high, patterned with snow and glaciers, a backdrop to the town of Haines Junction. The peaks were forbidding, rocky, and treeless; the shattered crags gripping shards of ice in strange contrast to the lush green of the summer forest below. We stopped for coffee at Madley's store and rolled across the street to get gas at the Shell station.

The boy behind the counter had red hair, clear pale skin, and a European accent that I couldn't quite place. I gave him a credit card and we waited for the approval to come through.

"Beautiful day," I said.

"Yeah, a bit warm."

I took mental stock. I was wearing four layers of clothing and was about to add long underwear. The frigid wind keening down from the glaciated peaks carried raw hints of winter in its teeth. We would be fortunate if the thermometer nudged above fifty-five degrees. "Warm?"

"Yup, a snowcat, 350ccs under me, single track, four feet of snow, minus fifteen degrees: *that* would be a beautiful day," he said.

"You prefer the winter then?"

"Yup . . . could last another couple of months as far as I'm concerned."

Reid was finishing a conversation with two men on Harleys when I returned to the pumps. They were complaining, he told me, of horrific road conditions past Haines Junction.

Every summer, as soon as the weather permitted, stretches of the Alcan Highway, hurriedly built in the early 1940s as a wartime haul road, were torn up to be widened and straightened. The section between the Donjek River, just past Kluane National Park, and the Alaskan border had been one of the most difficult sections of the highway to construct and remained one of the most challenging to repair and resurface. Underlain by permafrost and flooded by meandering glacial melt rivers and streams that fed hundreds of small swamps, lakes, and creeks, road building and repair through the area was at best dirty, hard, and mosquito-filled work.

Reid's face creased with concern. "They say it's bad, Karen, really awful, all torn up. What do you want to do?"

"Well, there's one road to Alaska, and we're on it. Guess we're going to drive through it. OK?"

"OK." Pulling out of Haines Junction, the road was fine; dry and smooth and spectacularly beautiful. The eight-thousand-foot mountains of Kluane

Park rose on one side, the topaz immensity of Kluane Lake lay on the other, and the serpentine road, undercut by gravel wash creeks, ran between. The lake shimmered under weak late-morning sunshine, filling the valley between the Kluane and Ruby Mountains with the pale silver of light refracted off opaque glacial water. We stopped for lunch and more gas at Destruction Bay, a tiny community that had earned its name when a freak storm had completely flattened the first village in 1952. I was filling Lucy's tank when two mud-encrusted and exhausted-looking Texans pulled in on Harleys.

"How's the construction?"

One shook his head silently. The other answered, "Lots of it."

"How many miles is it actually?"

"Twenty-four." He said the words slowly and deliberately, as if he had watched the odometer painfully tick off each tenth of a mile.

Foolishly optimistic in the haze of silver sunshine, I chirped, "Oh, is that all?" The Texan, tired and dirty, was silent and looked at me like a slow child who would soon discover harsh reality. I felt like an idiot.

As if the specter of chewed pavement and a roadbed composed mostly of sucking mud and gravel was not enough to worry about, shortly after we got back on the road, the RV driver behind me pulled into what would have been a passing position, had there been a passing lane on that narrow mountainous road. He blasted past four vehicles at sixty miles an hour, uphill and around a curve, with no possible sightline for what might have been coming the other way. *Bastard.* I let up on the throttle, waiting to see if he would make it, watching for the carnage, and preparing to lock up the brakes and slide toward the drainage ditch if another car or truck came the other way around the corner. He made it, the elephantine Winnebago moving back to the right on the far side of the curve, but along with relief came rage. Where the pavement is shared, what keeps most of us alive is a basic respect for relatively simple rules that have their genesis in consideration for the lives of others. If that man wanted to risk his own life, fine. If he died in a twisted wreck as a result of his own conscious choices, so be it. Unfortunately, one day the backside of a blind curve was not going to be empty when he attempted something similar, and it would be some hapless family of five in a minivan or some innocent teenager taking her date home who would pay the price for his arrogance and speed. What made his haste truly baffling was that in another twenty miles, his scramble would be reduced to a crawl in the major road construction that we all had to traverse.

Past Burwash Landing it began. I knew it would be bad when, waiting in line for the pilot car that would take a convoy of cars, pickups, RVs, eighteen-wheelers, and the odd motorcyclist through the single lane of the construction zone, the woman holding the slow/stop sign motioned me forward to join the rest of the bikers up front. She knew what I would learn in the next hour and a half: motorcyclists did not want to be behind any of the larger vehicles as they kicked up mud, dust, and loose rock in their slide through twenty-four miles of obliterated road surface.

Five other bikers waited at the top of the convoy talking, smoking, and looking for a weather report on a radio. All were men, all drove big-frame Harleys—Fat Boys, Springers, and an Electra Glide—and all were up from Pennsylvania. I hadn't met anyone this far north who had driven in from the East Coast on bikes and I was excited to see them. We introduced ourselves all around, I declined a cigarette, and we stood talking for a few minutes about what we had heard regarding the condition of the Alcan between there and the Alaskan border. "Hellish" was the word most frequently used and the only good thing that anyone could think of to say was that it hadn't rained much in the region for the past few days. At the very least the construction site might not be a quagmire. There was something odd about those bikers, however, they looked too . . . *clean* . . . and where was all their gear? None of the five bikes carried anything more than a single set of modestly sized saddlebags.

"Guys, where's your stuff?" I was genuinely impressed that they had managed to travel this lightly and hoped that they might be able to suggest ways that I could cut down on the bulky gear I carried. Not one of them seemed to be packing as much as an extra sweater. Now this was efficiency.

"Uh . . . well . . ." One of the tougher-looking men suddenly appeared sheepish. He rubbed the back of his hand across ten days of stubble. ". . . the girls came, too."

"The girls?"

"Yeah, our wives. They're in one of the motorhomes back there." He jerked a thumb toward the line of the convoy. "They carry all the gear and we get a shower at the end of the day." *Ah, I get it now.* This was not a bad deal; these men didn't even have to carry rain gear, and they could ride all day without having to worry about where to find spare parts, tools, or a dry place to sleep at night. From the women's perspective, if they did not drive bikes themselves, I could well imagine that taking turns piloting a motorhome, while still having a vacation with their husbands, would be far preferable to bouncing around on the passenger seat of a motorcycle all the way to Alaska and back from Pennsylvania. The flagger waved to us that the southbound convoy was coming through and that we should all saddle up. I turned to my new stubble-faced friend.

"You want to ride point?" The thought of leading five men on heavy bikes plus twenty or more other vehicles through the construction zone did not appeal to me. Riding point meant that the leader was responsible for finding a solid line through soft corners and for setting a pace that was safe for all concerned. It was always easier to watch and follow someone else's line and pace when going through such areas. Unlike many riders who learned to drive motorcycles as children, rocketing through sandpits and woods roads on dirt bikes, I had started driving relatively late, at sixteen, and had never learned to be comfortable riding gravel or soft surfaces.

"No, if you've gotten this far on your own we trust you to lead." The other four men nodded in agreement. *Ah shit.* Too embarrassed or too macho or too *something* to admit that I did not want to ride point, I pulled on my helmet, fired up Lucy, and grimly swung into the saddle. At the flagger's signal I moved out, feeling very much like a tugboat leading a line of tankers into treacherous waters.

It was awful. Pure hell. Some of the worst and messiest road construction I've ever seen. There was no pavement and only mud, gravel, potholes, slippery surfaces, and huge road-building machinery crawling in and out of the soft roadbed marked the twenty-four miles. Remembering the limping Texan at the ferry in Skagway, as Lucy's back tire fishtailed out from under me with disturbing regularity, I kept a single mantra running through my head: *feet up, keep your feet up, feet on the pegs, feet on the pegs. No broken legs needed today. Just ride it out, mile by mile.* I nearly lost it once, sliding uncontrollably through a foot-high ridge of soft earth that ended with eight inches of mud. At the last possible second, as Lucy heeled toward the ground, I goosed the throttle, powering the back wheel into line and straightening her slide. My jaw was sore from clenching my teeth and I was covered in mud by the time the zone finally came to an end. I tried not to think about the fact that I would have to ride the same section again on my way out of Alaska.

As the first solid stretches of pavement began again, I pulled over at a gas station, waved good-bye to the bikers from Pennsylvania, and waited for Reid, who was a mile or two back down the line of the convoy, to catch up. Eventually I saw his camper coming and pulled back onto the road again. The heavy construction, where the underlying roadbed had been excavated, was finished, but patchy surface repair, where frost heaves and potholes had been dug out and smoothed, but not repaved, continued for another hundred miles. "Caution Loose Gravel" signs marked the beginning of frequent two-hundred-yard stretches of dirt topped with lima bean–sized loose rock, which alternated with half-mile stretches of clear pavement. It was exhausting driving: downshifting and dropping speed as the gravel approached, the jolt of front shocks as Lucy dropped a few inches from the ragged edge of the pavement, steering through rising dust and loose rock, another jolt as the pavement began again, and acceleration through the solid section only to downshift once again as the next gravel patch approached. One hundred seventeen miles from Destruction Bay, ninety of it under construction, Beaver Creek was a welcome stop and much-needed rest.

EXHIBIT H: *Deferral*

A man wearing a Brooklyn T-shirt ambled across the packed gravel from a long, low row of motel rooms where he was repairing the vinyl siding.

"Where are you from?"

"New Jersey. Are you from New York?" I pointed to his shirt, assuming that it referred to one of the city's five boroughs.

"No, and the shirt's from Brooklyn, Cape Breton Island. I haven't been there either, but I want to go"—he motioned to Lucy—"on one of those." In his voice was longing, and the sort of tone that implied such a trip might never happen.

"It is possible."

What flashed in his eyes when he looked at Lucy faded and disappeared. "I know, but I have to stay here and run this place."

"That's what managers are for."

"One day." He nodded and turned to walk back to his work.

"Hey," I called after him, "don't wait too long."

He waved his hand over his shoulder. "Ah, I've got lots of time." The space grew between us and I spoke more to Lucy, more to myself, than to the man in the Brooklyn shirt.

"I hope so."

. . .

I was gassing up and Reid was inside the store searching for his usual can of ginger ale, when two Harley Dyna Glides pulled in. Both riders wore mud-encrusted full rainsuits and had the hunched, exhausted, filthy look that I was sure was mirrored in my own posture and visage. One of the riders pulled off a helmet. She was a woman. I crossed the parking lot at a jog. That summer I met, at least in passing, hundreds of men on motorcycles, some out for ten-mile rides, some out for ten thousand, but that lady in the parking lot of the 1202 Motor Inn in Beaver Creek was one of only four women I met who drove their own motorcycles. She was in her late fifties, had pale blue eyes, short spiked white hair, and graceful hands that were as grease-encrusted as my own. She and her husband had driven from upstate New York in the last two weeks and had gone to Anchorage via Dawson City and the Top of the World Highway. Apart from the Alcan, the Top of the World Highway was the only other road that joined Alaska with the Yukon. It had a reputation for fantastic scenery, but it was a hundred miles of unpaved dirt and it had, she told me, turned to slime when the rain began the week before. They had their bikes to twenty miles per hour the entire way, and hers had broken down with electrical problems halfway into it. Now, they were headed back down the

Alcan and would catch a ferry to Prince Rupert from Haines and then drive back toward New York, stopping in Calgary for the Stampede. There was great weariness in her face, voice, and manner. She did not look unhappy, just exhausted. It was the look of too many miles covered in too little time.

"How's the ferry?" she asked.

"Clean, dry, and a really good place to rest. The Passage is gorgeous, and you can just sit there in one of those forward lounges and watch the landscape slide by." She looked relieved. I wished them luck and safe travels and left them to go inside and join Reid.

Rested and feeling somewhat better, Reid and I drove on to the border. The crossing was straightforward and a few minutes later we were in Alaska. Across the border, the road was far less bruising than it had been in the Yukon. There was construction on the U.S. side, too, but the stretches of good pavement were longer and the parts that had been torn up were mostly underlain with packed reddish earth that provided good traction.

The last seventy-mile section of the day was through the northern reaches of the Tetlin National Wildlife Refuge, almost three-quarters of a million acres of low, rolling hill country dotted with hundreds of tiny lakes. The refuge had been established to protect the nesting territory of tens of thousands of ducks, trumpeter swans, loons, osprey, and bald eagles, as well as other kinds of wildlife species. Lit by the slant of the late evening sun, and as passing showers washed over the hills, the lines of the landscape turned to soft watercolor forms. In one pale green and amber valley a trumpeter swan floated on an onyx roadside lake, serene, beautiful, and completely undisturbed by the noise of Lucy's engine. Did he know that he was safe in Tetlin? We stopped at the Lakeview Campground, which was state run and had no fee, for the evening. Reid did the cooking as I looked on, exhausted, but I had to laugh. Reid's cooking was always tasty but he knew how to prepare exactly one dinner: fried steak, boiled potatoes, and some sort of vegetable. In all the years that I had known him, and with all the fish we had caught together, I had never seen him cook anything other than fried steak, boiled potatoes, and some kind of vegetable. More showers were forecast, and after dinner Reid offered me a comfortable padded bench in the camper. I slept warm, dry, dreamless, and physically spent.

24 | ALONE AGAIN

WE LEFT LAKEVIEW SOMETIME AROUND NINE, but later I couldn't seem to remember just when the day had started. My watch had begun to hang on my wrist unnoticed and unconsulted and I wondered if I shouldn't just put it away, bury it in my pack, and admit that my life was now a function of weather and daylight, of hunger and gas mileage, rather than time.

The Alcan between Tetlin and Tok was brilliant with purple fireweed springing up between the charred poles of fire-damaged trees. Skeins of mist rose from low marshy sinks, softening the blackened scars on the timber and highlighting the brilliance of the blooms. Aspen, cottonwood, willow, and spruce lined the road in places, untouched by the burn, and creating a variegated greenness undergirded by tiny colored explosions of wildflowers: indian paintbrushes, wild sweet peas, roses. The pavement was generally good after the misery of the day before and only one longitudinal frostheave crack, which I did not see until I was already upon it, sent me skipping. We stopped in Tok for gas, coffee, and a stroll around town before we parted. Reid was going north toward Fairbanks, and I was going south, headed for Anchorage and the Kenai.

Whether one comes to Alaska via the Top of the World Highway or up the Alcan, every traveler who enters or leaves the state by road has to pass through Tok. There is no other route. As a result, what has sprung up in a community of twelve hundred people, six blocks long and two blocks wide, is a hodgepodge of visitor services: gift shops, hotels, restaurants, and gas stations. Reid and I walked down Center Street, stopping into the All Alaska Gifts and Crafts shop, which had a grouping of two sadly impressive taxidermied wolves chasing down an equally pathetic stuffed Dall sheep. Bear leg traps were for sale; cruelty for only three hundred fifty dollars. The Burnt Paw gift and dogsledding shop was gentler on my greenhorn sensibilities. Three huskies from Susan Butcher's Iditarod racing lines watched passing tourists, their fuzzy noses emerging from doghouses within roomy fenced runs. Three tiny puppies, two black, and one with stripey golden brown fur, were for sale. They planted the soft pads of feet too wide for the rest of their bodies against the wire of the fence and licked my fingers with raspy pink tongues. I had the urge to tuck one inside my jacket and take him with me. Instead, Reid bought me a deer-bone zipper pull, with a black outlined wolf scrimshawed into it, as a souvenir of our time together.

After a bone-crunching hug and several admonitions to be careful, Reid swung his camper north onto the Alcan while I took Highway 1 south for Glennallen. It was twenty-five miles of glorious, flat, construction-free highway. Lucy galloped along at sixty miles an hour and I felt free, totally unencumbered and alone in the boggy, lake-filled, mountain-shadowed, deep green spruce country of Alaska.

The country flattened toward Glennallen, the run of the Copper River a brown swirl to my left. Heavy rains the week before, the same rains that had washed out a major bridge on the Richardson Highway, closing one of only two north-south roads in the state, had filled the water with the flotsam and soil of storm-driven erosion. At a lunch stop at a roadside pull-off I followed a little side trail down to the river. The flow was shallow and broad and fractured into splinters of silted rivulets, which smoothed large gray stones with the gentle abrasion of glacier-pulverized sand. I was squatting down to watch the water and was running my hands over the humped backs of the stones when I noticed tracks on the edge of the river. They ran in a line, a heart-shaped rear pad and four large front toes depressing the mud, each ending in the thrust of a claw.

Large and "doggish," the tracks were filling slowly with water, and clearly had been left just a few minutes before. A family pet? I doubted it. The traffic had been light to the point of nonexistent that morning and there was no one else at the roadside pull-off. A lone wolf? That was a better bet and the hairs on the back of my neck went up as, real or imagined, I scanned the bushes for the yellow eyes that I was now sure were watching. I half dreaded and half hoped that the wall of bramble and willow would part with a rustle and a totemic fantasy would become reality. The undergrowth was silent, however, and only the river and the low hum of tiny insects broke the silence as I stood, waited, and then slowly turned and began to pick my way back up the trail.

It was a hundred miles to Sheep Mountain Lodge, where I would spend the night in a youth hostel. The terrain and Highway 1 climbed together into the ridges as the temperature and weather descended, the views becoming evermore magnificent with the peaks of the Chugach Mountains rising to the left and the high slopes of the Talkeetna Mountains soaring to the right. Between passing rain showers that became more frequent as evening approached, I caught especially dramatic glimpses of the southern snowcapped mountains and the icy blue shimmer of the Tazlina and Nelchina Glaciers. Lucy's front wheel seemed to be keeping pace just under the edge of a front that I suspected was going to drop quite a lot of rain in the next several hours. In the last forty miles of the day, showers turned to steadily falling rain and an icy headwind began to tear at my jacket and gloves, forcing water past the Velcro closures at my wrists and neck. I did not stop at the Eureka Summit overlook to watch the rapidly disappearing view of the Chugach but instead hunched low over Lucy's tank and ran for shelter.

Wet, cold, and bone tired, I pulled into Sheep Mountain Lodge at a little after six. My hands, red, chapped, and tinged blue with the cold and wet, shook as I signed the registration slip. Anjanette, who owned and managed the lodge with her husband, Zack, stood behind the desk and smiled at me.

"You look as if you could do with a soak in our hot tub."

"Your what?" I wasn't sure I had heard her correctly.

"The hot tub. You'll warm right up in there." Clearly I had stumbled into Nirvana in the shape of a youth hostel.

The hot tub was, in fact, paradise. In a cedar-lined room I locked the door, took off all my clothes, slid in, and watched the clouds and mist sliding down the grassy slopes of the mountains through panoramic plate-glass windows. I could feel the warmth from the water creeping up my arms and legs like magma flowing through fissures in rock. Sometimes, at the end of a long, cold, wet ride, when hands lock in frozen claws around the throttle and every downshift becomes a conscious effort to break and move paralytic muscles in the hands, lower legs, and feet, reaching the immediate destination—getting off the bike, finding food and shelter—becomes an animalistic need. Vision narrows, the mind slows, and the body assumes whatever position or mechanized function will best achieve speed and the terminus of the day. In the intensity of that focus, there is a temporary loss of some of what it means to be human, weather and pain become tangible, and internal conversations about anything other than the immediate cease. Had Anjanette asked me for information more complex than my signature—where I was from, the place where I had started the day, the name of a friend—I do not think that I could have told her. Immersed in warm water, however, under a roof, and with the immediate prospect of dinner steps away, I could feel my brain starting to loosen along with the cold-seized muscles in my shoulders, and a sense of being human returning.

After dinner I took my journal and went to sit in the lodge's greenhouse. It was warm and leafy with the odor of damp potting soil, steam heat, and new growth. Beyond the glass, patches of sun were chased down the mountainside by pursuing showers. I sat with my chin resting in my hands, abandoned pens and notebook, and watched the spectacle of light and shadow. Well fed and dry, clean and warm, I was happy, and a little lonely. The play of light on the mountains and the living breath of the plants made me wish for someone to share the evening with. The lodge was filled with all kinds of people, but what I was missing was a companion, not company. Reid was gone, driving north for Fairbanks. It felt good to be on my own again, moving or still, silent or talking—if only to myself—just as I pleased, but I missed the gentle friendship and quiet togetherness that I had had for the past two days. I sat in the greenhouse alone until the dark sky and hammering rain finally overtook the last of the light.

BEYOND THE ROOF OF THE GREENHOUSE, the summits of the peaks were hidden in misty clouds, and light morning rain smudged the clarity of the panes. Magpies scampered across the lawn, flashing their black-and-white plumage, elegant and irreverent all in a moment. Over coffee and an enormous sourdough roll, I pulled a *National Geographic* off the shelf and read a 1901 quote from Henry Gannet, director of the U.S. Geological Survey: "If you are old, go by all means, but if you are young, stay away until you are older. The scenery of Alaska is so much grander than anything else of the kind that, once beheld, all scenery becomes flat and insipid. It is not well to dull one's capacity for such enjoyment by seeing the finest first."

As I finished breakfast, the mental debate began: rain gear or regular clothes? Even the final misty exhalations of a passed storm can soak through leather and put a chill into the body core that will last all day. Regular clothes or rain gear? Perhaps as I dropped lower, out of the "grander" mountains and toward Anchorage, I would also drop out of clouds, out of the rain. Shards of blue sky were already flashing in the rents of the woolen gray clouds. Those bits of azure decided it and I left my rain gear rolled up and packed away as I left Sheep Mountain Lodge.

The road toward Alaska's largest city and the sea gradually loses elevation, falling toward the Matanuska River. A glacier of the same name gleamed across the valley, a great shimmering pale blue snake sliding out of the mountains. A veil that was half fog and half cloud hung in a horizontal drape, sheltering the ice and bisecting the jagged peaks of the Chugach Mountains that rose behind it. The sun came out in fits and starts, and although my legs were wet to the knees with the spray coming off the road, the rest of my body was dry and almost warm.

Halfway to the valley the sunlight began to lance through rips in the clouds, and suddenly, an entire flare of light illuminated a bend in the road just ahead. It always amazes me, that first blast of sunshine and warmth, coming out of what may be hours or days in rain, darkness, and cold. There is something transcendent in it; a flash of heat and light, and a physical lifting of the heart in the chest with the first intake of warmer, drier air. I raced toward the pools of sunshine to catch them before they disappeared, slowing Lucy for a half second and coasting into the bright air, eyes wide and breath on the intake. The visual drama of the lifting front was there, too. The great crags of King Mountain— now cloaked, now exposed—tore the gossamer fibers of clouds that pulled themselves over the ragged shoulders of the peak to drifting shreds. Tendrils of fog, wispy as smoke, chased one another from treetop to outcrop, lifting and dropping on the upwelling of river breath and the light breeze climbing the valley. The river foamed and drummed at the foot of the mountain, icy blue and gray, here running with the clarity of glass, there opaque with bluish gray glacial flour, mottled and dappled in the warming morning.

After the openness of the road that stretched behind me toward the Yukon, the growing bustle of traffic and Alaskan commerce, a musk-ox farm, a reindeer operation, and roadside vegetable stands, which lined the pavement into the city, was disconcerting. The streets were busy with people and traffic, and the roadside air, heavy with the tangy smoked smell emanating from salmon-bake restaurants, invited a longer stay, but I was more interested in what lay ahead, down the Kenai Peninsula. I got through Anchorage and out the other side as rapidly as possible, stopping only to shed a layer of clothing and to fill Lucy's tank for the run down the Cook Inlet.

Volcanic peaks glittered icy platinum in the sunshine across the electric blue of the Cook Inlet and the tidal waters rushed out to sea in visible haste. The creamy beige of the exposed flats grew wider with each passing minute. It was a glorious landscape but a perilous one. My guidebook warned about walking down to the inviting flats where they sprawled empty, heating in the sun. The speed with which the tide ebbs and flows over the fine silt creates a particularly viscous sort of quicksand. People had been trapped there, would-be-rescuers unable to extricate their half-sunken bodies, as the drowning tide rolled in. I stayed high above the flats, stopping only to dangle my feet over the edges of the crumbling verge, eat cheese and crackers, and watch the danger-ous beauty of the landscape.

It was a slow ride down the Kenai through the greenery of alpine mead-ows strewn with wildflowers and rushing glacial streams, on twisting two-lane roads that lifted through heavily forested passes. I left Route 1 near the village of Moose Pass and continued south on Route 2 toward Resurrection Bay and Seward. The following day I wanted to visit the Sea Life Center, a research, animal rehabilitation, and education facility, which had been built partially with funds from Exxon following the disaster in Prince William Sound. I also only wanted to ride half the day. The road in from the Yukon had been bruis-ing, and I was tired.

Just outside of Seward the Exit Glacier squeezes between two low peaks in a fissured jumble of massive greenish slabs of ice streaked with bands of pul-verized rock. A river flowed from its base, and a gravel access road that curved uphill toward the mountains, toward the ice, had been built on its banks. The campground was filled by the time I arrived in the early evening but I wan-dered around anyway, ambling down the narrow trails, looking for a spot to illegally pitch my tent. A young couple, watching me walk the circumference of the campground twice, invited me to share their spot.

Jaime was pretty and petite. She had been an inner-city schoolteacher in the Southwest, but by late June of her second year in the classroom she had had enough of the gangs, the streets, the noise, and the poverty. She and her hus-band, Scott, had quit their jobs and were on an extended ramble through Canada and Alaska. They thought that one day they might go back to their old lives, their old professions, but for now they were delighted to be out exploring the north just as their whimsy took them each day. Also camping nearby, and quickly engaged in conversation, was Michael, a young environmental lawyer from Pennsylvania. He and I were dispatched to the river for ice to cool the beer that Jaime and Scott offered. We scrambled down the embankment to the gray-ish waters. Exit Glacier hung a mile upstream and from the tumble of the current we collected ice that was perhaps ten thousand years old.

Teenage girls, many of them native Alaskans with long black hair caught into roped braids, splashed and giggled at the edge of the river, dabbling their hands into the water to feel the icy chill. They were part of a Mormon youth group from Anchorage and were spending a few days camping in the mountains of the Kenai. Later that evening at the centralized shared cooking and eating spot, which also boasted a locked food closet to minimize the threat of grizzly bears wandering from campsite to campsite in search of ursine dinners, I met up with the same girls. They asked about Lucy, about New York and Washington, D.C., and told me about their lives. I had incorrectly assumed that they would be familiar with the backcountry wilderness that surrounded us, and I came to realize that, like any other group of teenagers born and raised in urban areas, they understood the world of the city: closely knit neighborhoods, shopping centers, cell phones, pop music, and public transportation. For most of them, this was their first trip into "the bush," as well as the first time they had slept in tents, and most couldn't wait to get back to Anchorage.

I returned to my tent, to Jaime, Scott, and Michael, and to the cold beer and a warm bottle of burgundy that Michael produced from the trunk of his car. It was a slow wonderful evening and we stayed up late, wrapped in jackets against the cold night air, talking until the sky began to darken and a few pale stars emerged over the glacier.

EXHIBIT I: *The Frontiersman*

The Resurrect Art Coffee House Gallery in Seward had a name that said it all: strong coffees and teas and beautiful pottery and jewelry work all housed within the structure of a rebuilt Lutheran church. High gothic arched windows let in quantities of misty light, illuminating the simple dark trusses and wide-planed floorboards. I stood in line chatting with a contractor who was buying coffees for his crew.

"Alaska's changed," he said. "Used to be all dirt roads running out to Kenai. People've changed, too. Used to be you come out here, do whatever you want. It's not like that anymore." In the last twenty years, cruise ships, planes, and paved roads had made the north more accessible to outsiders. I thought about places like Juneau and Ketchikan, where the frontier was clearly gone, the streets lined with boutiques selling canned salmon and fur products to the thousands who disembarked from the immense cruise ships for shopping and mini-excursions.

"Is it the tourist industry? Is that what's changing things?"

"No. It's not that. The population is growing. I read somewhere that the average Alaskan—a person who lives here—has been here ten years or less. It's just getting citified." We reached the counter. The woman behind it turned to get me a foaming hot chai.

"Wait," he said, slapping another five-dollar bill on the counter, "I want to pay for that." It was sweet and totally unexpected. He shook my hand, wished me good luck, and walked out the door, an uncitified and genteel man.

. . . .

The tanks at the Seward Sea Life Center were multistoried structures that allowed visitors and scientists to watch what went on both above and below the surface of the water. "Woody," a massive golden sea lion, undulated past glass walls two stories high. Slow and ungainly on land, he was grace and power in the water, back flippers and rolling body creating an aquarian dance of lithe elegance. A pulse of front flippers, a slight cant of the head, and he torpedoed toward the "fish cannons" that propelled dead herrings into the cloudy green sea water, while researchers tracked his movements and feeding patterns. In other tanks, as some tufted puffins rested on rocky ledges, others "flew" beneath the surface, wings spread and pumping in space reversed: air had become water. Pollock, trout, and salmon cruised inside transparent walls. Rockfish and octopus squeezed themselves under outcrops of constructed reefs. There was a "touching pool" for young scientists to come and handle the brightly colored starfish and the crustaceans, which scampered from one hiding place to another in the attempt to escape tiny hands.

Leaving the Sea Life Center and Seward, which was rapidly disappearing in the thick fog rolling in from the sea, I took the road once again up through Moose Pass to the Soldatna turnoff. Posted signs on Route 1 promised nine miles of construction and delivered eight of washboard-slick clay and gravel. I counted every half-mile, Lucy's odometer slowly ticking over, and hated every sideways slide and every mud-filled, fathomless pothole.

From Soldatna to Ninilchik the highway was wide, relatively straight, and anxiously fast. It wasn't just the RVs barreling along at seventy miles an hour that I found unnerving. Just outside of Soldatna, standing by the side of the road and calmly ripping vegetation from the highway verge, was the largest cow moose I had ever seen. Twelve hundred pounds if she was an ounce, she had dinner-plate–sized feet and stood at least six feet tall at the shoulder. For everyone's sake, I hoped that she had the sense to stay where she was. I wouldn't know who to bet on if it came down to a collision between that moose and an average pickup truck or a small RV, but I think my odds would be on the moose.

It was late afternoon when I pulled into the hostel in Ninilchik, a log home built on the lip of a narrow valley where the Ninilchik River flowed with serpentine undulations. Frank was the hostel manager, and as the doors did not officially open until 5 P.M., he sent me off to do a little local exploring; past the hostel down to where a dirt side road crossed the river a few miles away.

"The fish weir," Frank said. "The kings are running, now that's something to see." It was. Just south of the bridge, steel grates had been dropped across the river so that biologists could count the population, and also weigh and examine a few individual fish, as the king salmon made their way to spawning places upstream. I pulled Lucy to the edge of the road, flipped up my visor, and stared at the water. Huge red fish by the hundreds were massed before the weir, alternately thrashing and resting in the yard-deep water. They were, on average, thirty inches long; great-headed and hook-beaked fish that flung themselves against the metal gates in fruitless, yet unceasing, attempts to continue their swim upstream. Downstream hundreds more waited, fins cresting sleek and shining from the shallow water. Many had deep, whitish lacerations and scars on their backs where gulls, sitting on rocks, had pecked at them as they swam by. I sat on the weir watching the spectacle until the afternoon shadows grew long across the writhing backs of the king salmon.

Back at the hostel I settled in for the evening with Dan and Mary Kate, a father-daughter pair from Minnesota out touring on a Honda Gold Wing, and Grant and Todd, two friends originally from Kansas, who had both settled in the Seattle area. Todd was a big man, with a ready laugh and a prematurely white beard. He had been an EMT for years and ran a company that provided medical support services to movie crews. Recently married for the first time, he was clearly and delightfully besotted with his wife, who waited for him at home. Grant was tall, slender, with a runner's body and a smile that spread unevenly across his face when he laughed, which was often. Also a family man, he had married a fellow airline pilot. The two friends were in Ninilchik to fish the salmon run. Grant, as a pilot for Alaskan Air, held a license that allowed him to go dipnetting for fish, a privilege generally reserved for Alaskan residents. From what I had seen that afternoon at the weir, they would have no problem catching their limit.

A shower felt good and I crawled into a bunk bed in the women's dormitory, having decided that I would take the following day off and go wander around Homer, only a few miles down the road. The last few days I had felt chronically tired and my lower back was starting to hurt. I needed a break.

The hostel's "food cache," groceries abandoned or donated by previous guests, was better than most. For breakfast I rustled up scavenged pancakes and coffee and sat chatting with Grant and Todd, who were as excited as ten-year-olds headed for the creek with bamboo poles on the last day of school. The men left and by 9:30 I was out of the hostel, too, rolling toward a much needed session at the Laundromat. While my clothes sloshed in muddy water, I stood in my rainsuit and called my sister-in-law from a pay phone outside. We didn't talk about anything of importance and I had no real reason to call, it was just that sometimes—tired, dirty, and alone—I needed to hear news of domesticity, local weather, how long it had taken my brother to mow the lawn last weekend, what had happened that day at work, and when they would take their summer holidays. I needed to know that I was still anchored to my family no matter how far away I was.

Back inside, as I rolled my two extra pairs of socks into compact balls and folded my one extra T-shirt into a fraying square, the Laundromat owner passed around a plate of home-smoked fish. He had a barter arrangement with a local man, he told me, laundry service for smoked salmon. Firm and moist, lightly salted, and with the flavor of wood smoke throughout, it was so good that I asked if I could have another piece. He handed me two whole fillets in a Ziploc bag.

"For the road," he said.

I turned Lucy toward Homer, following Route 1 and the lower coastline of the Cook Inlet. The snowcapped peaks of the Aleutian Range were visible across the water, flaring with bright white light as ripped clouds released occasional torrents of sunshine between the purple black masses building over the sea. Out on the Homer Spit, I parked Lucy in a gravel lot and walked back into town, stopping first at the memorial to those lost at sea. It was positioned to draw one's eyes down the inlet, past English Bay, toward the open ocean, and reminded the visitor that every year some who go down to the sea do not return. The ocean both feeds and consumes those who ply its waters as fishermen, supply-boat skippers, and mail carriers.

The gray boards of the wooden sidewalk echoed hollowly under my boots, as well as under the footfalls of several hundred other people, and I walked feeling a little dazed by the unaccustomed bustle of tourism and commerce, the unexpected jolt of a stranger's shoulder against my own, the colors and signs and noise of merchandise, restaurants, and music. Fishing charters sailing out of Kachemak Bay advertised their services along the boardwalk to land-based RV captains, as well as to those who fancied themselves watermen and who had traveled to Homer specifically to reel in the teeming halibut and salmon. There were trinket shops and art galleries, most with a temporary seasonal look, selling everything from two-dollar hemp bracelets to thousand-dollar carved ivory and scrimshaw. A pair of beautifully beaded sealskin moccasins caught my eye, but the price tag was larger than I could afford. I left the shops and walked down to the beach, where I sat cross-legged on the shore and watched the play of the receding tide on the rocks. Flat-surfaced ovoid stones that fit comfortably into the palm of my hand paved the shore in shades of charcoal and brown. Bits of green sea glass flashed in the foam and I watched three bald eagles feeding, two tearing at some sort of flesh near the water's edge and one flapping along the shoreline with a silver herring in its talons. Out in the water a sleek brown head, eyes shining huge and black, emerged. The harbor seal swam at the surface for a few minutes and then dived beneath the waves again.

Late in the afternoon, after accomplishing some practical shopping—mink oil for my boots and gloves, a thick wool hat bought for a dollar from the Salvation Army, and a bottle of Pepsi with a pocket flask of rum to go with it—I turned back toward Ninilchik. It had been a slow, restful day, my back had stopped hurting, and some of the body weariness I had felt since the northern Yukon was gone. I felt ready to head for Denali the following morning.

Half an hour after I rolled back into Ninilchik for another night at the hostel, Grant and Todd appeared, returning from an enormously successful day of dipnetting. As Todd wanted to spend the following day deep-sea fishing for halibut with a charter boat, Grant asked if I wouldn't consider staying to come salmon fishing with him. I had strong suspicions that he was looking more for someone to run the small motor on his inflatable Metzer than he was for a true fishing buddy, but how often do such invitations come along? I had no schedule and no one to please but myself, so I said yes and put off packing my gear.

GRANT'S CAR REEKED OF PUTREFYING FISH, the upholstery smelled like something out of a cat food factory, and I was quite sure that the rental agency was not going to make a profit on the contract. It was strange to be inside an enclosed vehicle and I rolled the window down as we drove to Grant's secret river fishing spot, both to air out the odor of yesterday's salmon and to feel the breeze on my face. The wind was damp, blowing in from the sea, bringing with it shreds of the rain and mist that hid the commercial fishing vessels anchored just offshore.

It was a hundred-yard walk to where the gray sand banks sloped down to meet the water. We inflated the baffles in the orange Metzer boat and lugged it, a two-horsepower motor, two large nets, and a huge cooler through tufted grass and deep, soft sand. My arms were aching and the ropes were beginning to cut red welts into my hands even before the water came into view, but I wasn't about to call for a rest when we were this close to tens of thousands of salmon.

Dipnetting is not the most challenging of fishing methods, but it is decidedly exciting. All one need do is sink a net into the water—any good-quality landing net will do, although those laced with green or black string are preferable—and wait until a salmon swims in. With the fish running in the thousands this doesn't take long. Sitting on the gunnels of the Metzer, we made short passes up the river at midstream and rode the current back down. The first pass we caught nothing. On the second Grant pulled in a coho salmon weighing perhaps eight pounds. On the third, as Grant ran the motor, I sank my net into the current and waited, peering into the silted water. Less than five minutes later a fish swam into the back of my net with surprising strength, rocking my shoulder and arm back and down. I pulled the net up and though the water as Grant had shown me, angling the mouth toward the surface so that the fish could not escape.

"I've got one! I've got one!"

"Slowly," Grant said. He was laughing at my excitement. "Pull him in slowly."

The salmon rolled and struggled, the mercury flash of its belly gleaming silvery white as it fought the interlaced strings. This was not the sort of fishing I was used to: sitting motionless on placid lakes where I pulled bass, already tired after being reeled through sixty feet of water, into a wide, stable aluminum boat. The Metzer was small, my knees almost touched Grant's as we perched on either side of the boat, and landing a big struggling fish while negotiating nets, motors, and the chop of an Alaskan river was not as simple as I had thought it would be.

Finally over the gunnels, my salmon flopped and thrashed, further tangling itself in the net. The mucus that coated its skin, easing its glide through icy water, covered my hands in a slimy glaze and getting a good grip took some doing. Eventually, I managed to work my fingers into its gills, thumb in one side and fingers in the other, and pull it free of the net. Grant opened the lid of the cooler and I stuffed the big fish in, locking the lid as the salmon thrashed a few final times. Flushed and giggling, I started untangling my net.

"That was great!"

"It's better than sex, isn't it?" Grant was grinning broadly.

"Almost . . ." I laughed. "Not quite, but almost."

The first two catches set the pattern for the day and usually on each pass up the river we alternately landed another seven- to ten-pound fish, although in the end Grant caught a few more than I did. We made a good team. As

Grant's net rocked back with the force of an ensnared salmon, I would reach for the motor and keep the boat steady as he landed it. As he slid up his gunnel to extract the fish from the net I slid down mine, counterbalancing the boat as the current of the river swirled around us. When I pulled a fish from the net, Grant, with a practiced flip of the wrist, would fling open the cooler as I dropped another coho onto the growing pile inside. We only missed the rhythm once as I landed the day's largest salmon. She was ten-plus pounds of wriggling slippery silver and as Grant opened the cooler the fish gave a mighty lurch. Her tail hit me full in the face, snapping my head back with the force of a slap that spread slime from chin to forehead. From the fish's perspective I probably richly deserved it. I hung on grimly, shouting at Grant who was nearly incapacitated with laughter, "Oh my God! That's disgusting! Open the fucking cooler!" Still giggling, he helped me stuff the fish, curling its tail fin to make it fit, into the cooler. I wiped the mucus from my face. It was everywhere: in my hair, up my nose, through my eyebrows. Grant was unsuccessful at stifling his merriment.

We fished until the cooler was full of salmon and then beached on the southern bank, where the gravel and rock made for firmer footing, to fillet them. The upended cooler made an impromptu gutting table, and as I held the head of the fish through the gills and lifted the fins, Grant carved large boneless slabs of firm pinkish-orange flesh with clean sweeps of his slender knife. I slid the fillets into plastic Ziploc bags while Grant, with a neat flipping motion of his right hand, scooped the fish guts from the cooler top and tossed them backward, past his right hip and into the river. I didn't pay much attention to the landing point of the heads and entrails until I heard a *thwap* very unlike the previous sounds of fish heads hitting the water, as well as a muttered curse. A sinewy man in his fifties, hair greased back and a crumpled cigarette hanging from the left side of his mouth, was staring at us. His hard hawkish face was deeply tanned, and he wore black rubber boots and a ragged sweater covered by a knee-length blue mackintosh. In his left hand he held a rod and reel and with his right he slapped at the slimy river of fish intestines that was sliding down the back of his jacket. There was silence as he turned and took one step up the bank. Grant said nothing, correctly assuming that he was about to get punched in the nose. Bursting into a volley of apologies—"Terribly sorry, didn't see you, how awful, please forgive us"—I stepped between the men. The man stopped, nodded, and turned wordlessly back to the river. After that I watched carefully where Grant's fish guts were landing.

We finished with the first batch and returned to the river. The number of people on the shore had gradually increased throughout the day and there were a couple of other small boats that also fished the middle course of current. A gentle camaraderie and conversations in both Russian and English played between boats and those standing on the banks. There were too many fish for competition or envy. The mist turned to rain and Grant and I hunkered down under the brims of our ball caps, told stories of home and family, and fished until we caught our limit: twenty-five coho salmon. By 3 P.M. we had gutted the last one, deflated the boat, and lugged a cooler filled with a hundred pounds of fillets back to the car. We were tired, wet, cold, hungry, and totally delighted with the day.

That evening Grant and I put together the fixings for a huge salmon bake while Todd, *bless him*, gathered everyone's slimy and odiferous fishing clothes and took them down to the Laundromat. One fillet was enough for all three of us, as well as a recently arrived British bicyclist, and came from my enormous, feisty, prize salmon. While Grant covered it in brown sugar and lemon juice, and the kitchen slowly filled with the aroma of baking fish and a hash of fried potatoes, onions, and bacon, I opened a can of corn and stirred a box of brownie mix for dessert.

Betty, a missionary lady on vacation from the native communities where she worked to spread the gospel, shared the kitchen with us. She was a tiny woman with silver spectacles, and quick, birdlike hands. I have strong negative opinions about missionaries doing "God's work" in communities that have their own traditional belief systems, but in the warmth of the kitchen and in the kindness of her eyes, I left the topic alone. The other guest at the hostel that night was Doug. Like me, he had arrived via motorcycle, a BMW R1150GS cross-purpose machine that had a reputation for being able to survive just about anything that the pavement, or the lack thereof, could deliver. For the last eight years and 180,000 miles, Doug had been alone on the road, riding all over Central and North America. He spoke of his travels in a stream of consciousness, in the way that people do who have been by themselves for far too long. *Would I be like this at the end of my trip? God, I hope not.* He reminded me of solo backpackers coming out of the woods and into town after weeks of rough trail and little companionship, or of the physically infirm elderly who leave their homes only rarely and whose children never come to visit. He was a little crazy. Not dangerous, just "off." Perhaps he knew this and knew that it was time to go home. He said that he had come to Alaska to ride one final road before going back to Washington state to settle down. He had come to ride the Dalton Highway, the haul road from Fairbanks to the oil station at Deadhorse on Prudhoe Bay. It is the northernmost road on the continent.

I had considered driving the Dalton myself but was leaning against it as it was rumored to be nearly five hundred miles of unpaved hell with no gas and dubious road conditions made more exciting by transport trucks going inhumanly fast. Any thought I had of doing the run disappeared completely with Doug's commentary. Here was a man who had happily run ill-repaired roads all over Guatemala and El Salvador but who, when he talked about the Dalton, spoke of it as "one of the worst roads I've ever seen." Part of the problem was that Alyeska Pipeline Service Company, the consortium of seven oil companies that managed and maintained the pipeline as well as the road that paralleled it, was in the midst of a heavy construction project on the northern reaches of the highway. With the recent rainy spell, that section had become a quagmire of deep mud underlain by permafrost and punctuated by extruding boulders. By the time he reached Deadhorse, Doug was so shaken and battered that he had looked into putting his bike on a transport truck to avoid having to drive it back to Fairbanks. The fee was five dollars per mile and there were no tie-down straps for the bike. He would have been impoverished, and his equipment shaken to bits by the time he got back down below the Arctic Circle, so he picked his way back slowly, carrying extra gas every mile of the haul road return to Fairbanks, and swore never to do it again. My Lucy had come as far as Alaska but I did not think that she would survive such a run and I decided then and there not to attempt it.

After dinner, while Todd washed dishes, Grant and I sat out on the back porch watching the sunset glow fade from the sky. Pink and orange and gold swirled in the undersides of the mist and gathering rainclouds as the sun finally slipped below the horizon. The wind had dropped into silence when the dogs started to bark upstairs. From the deep woods on the other side of the river I heard something screaming. Horrible and eerie, the great wrenching wails came from behind the thick green wall of the forest beyond. It was the sound of someone in great pain. Todd came out to listen.

"Well, it's either someone being torn apart by a grizzly, or a lost cub," he said. "Either way we're not going down there." Frank, the hostel owner, appeared on the porch, listening.

"Bear cub," he said, "calling for his mother." We scanned the valley through the rain with an assortment of Frank's binoculars. The crying had stopped. On the far side of the river something brown—something huge and brown—was moving. She stepped out of the low shrubs and dropped down to the river, a mother grizzly with three cubs trailing her. A massive creature, she walked slowly to the bank, sat back on her haunches, watched the flow of the water, watched the bounty of the giant king salmon still fighting their way upstream. She dropped into the shallows and walked thirty yards upriver, her enormous head swinging slowly from side to side as she scanned the bottom. Suddenly, her right paw lashed out and down into the water with effortless speed, and she flipped a three-foot king salmon onto the bank. The fish in her jaws, and the little ones trailing behind her, she slid into a thicket of small trees and brush and disappeared.

"SO WHAT ARE YOU GOING TO do today?" Betty sat on the edge of her bunk watching me pack my things. I grinned.

"Well, I'm going to go get wet." That was the expectation, the plan, and the reality as, with the exception of two fifteen minute hiatuses, it poured rain all day. Grant and Todd were loading their things into the rental car when I came out to strap my bags back onto Lucy. The doors were open and I could smell the fishy upholstery from fifteen feet away. We said good-bye and both men wrapped me in crushing bear hugs.

"Come out and see us," Todd said. "We're old fishing buddies now."

"Next year, same time, same place," Grant added.

For the first time in two days Lucy was fully packed and, despite the miserable weather, I rode out into the mist and the rain feeling good, feeling strong. After two days of rest my back had stopped hurting and the low, reassuring throb of Lucy's engine reminded me all over again about a love for motorcycles and the kind of travel—visceral, sensual, experiential—that they make possible. The precipitation fluctuated from cottony mist that obscured everything more than ten feet off my front tire, to sheeting rain, to drenching heavy spray that seemed to lift off the pavement as much as it fell upon it. The wind drummed across the dissolved landscape, biting cold at fifty-five degrees. My feet were wet by Soldatna, by Coopers Landing capillary action had pulled the damp from my gloves and boots up my arms and legs, and a hundred miles from my morning start I was totally drenched and freezing. The Tesoro gas station plaza in Girdwood was as good a place as any to thaw out and drip partially dry for a few minutes.

It was warm and dry inside the convenience store and I stood just to the left of the front counter breathing in the greasy smell of overcooked hot dogs. My right hand curled around a paper coffee cup, red, rain-wrinkled fingers temporarily warming. As I shifted my weight from one foot to the other, forcing blood back down into chilled extremities, tiny streams of water oozed through my bootlaces and a gradually expanding puddle formed on the floor around my feet. Outside, the plaza hosted a steady caravan of motorhomes. While the men pumped a hundred dollars or more of fuel into vehicles that averaged eight miles to the gallon, the women came inside, fluffing out carefully coifed hair. I watched as they made their way to the ladies' room. One of the men, gold card in hand, came in to stand in the short line before the cash register. His idle perusal of the key chains, cigarette lighters, maps, and motor oil racks came to a halt as his eyes reached me. He stared. Granted, I must have been a sight. The collar of my battered leather jacket peeked up from under the roll neck of a duck yellow raincoat and bright purple men's rain pants covered my legs in baggy folds to the ankles. I thought about the ladies in the restroom and ruefully assumed that salmon fishing and blowing rain had not done wonderful things for my cosmetic appearance. The man had a stern face and an upright carriage that looked like it might have been learned in the military. His brown eyes narrowed as he peered at me from behind silver-rimmed glasses. Tanned legs, thin but muscular, dropped below the pressed creases of his Bermuda shorts to black socks and sandals. I smiled at the man—him and his socks—thinking of my own father's similarly disastrous fashion choices.

"I saw your bike outside." His tone was more aggressive than friendly and the smile dropped from my face. "It has New Jersey plates."

"Yes, it does."

His eyes narrowed and his voice became loud and challenging. "Do you mean to tell me that you rode that bike all the way from New Jersey?"

Conversation at the counter stopped and the cashier and other customers were silent, staring at us.

"Yes."

He considered me for a long moment. "Are you on drugs?"

I laughed. "No." A skeptical eyebrow raised itself above the right lens of his glasses. I took a long swallow of coffee. "However, on days like this"—I motioned to the rain buffeting solidly against the plate glass, sheets of water coming in directly off the Cook Inlet— "I really think they might be helpful."

There was silence and then a giggle from the grinning cashier. Ultimately the man gave an amused snort and told me that he and his wife were from Pennsylvania and were, like me, spending the summer on the road. He asked about Lucy, how I chose my route, where I put my tent at night, and when I expected to return back East. His wife reemerged from the ladies' room, the gas bill was paid, and he moved toward the exit. Nearly at the door he stopped and turned back to me.

"What a great trip . . . I envy you."

The rain continued and began to pool in puddles that spanned the road. One hydroplane was enough to remind me of the danger of speed through deep water and I slowed down, pulling over occasionally if a car or two collected behind me. Traffic was light, however; no one likes driving in a monsoon, and I had the Parks Highway north of Anchorage mostly to myself.

There was a youth hostel in Talkeetna, a hundred twenty miles up the Parks, toward which I was headed for the night. A former mining village, presently a staging area for climbers preparing to challenge Mt. McKinley in Denali National Park, Talkeetna was a good place to stop, not only because I intended to visit at least a part of Denali the next day, but also because the thought of putting up a tent in the dropping temperature and continuing deluge was not appealing.

Three nights under a roof, I am getting soft.

Late in the afternoon, at the tourist information center on the access road to Talkeetna, I pulled into a parking lot paved in egg-sized gravel. It was a struggle to find a place where I was able to put Lucy's kickstand down, lean her into it, and be sure that the loose rock would not give way under the weight of five hundred pounds of machinery. Soaked, extremities numbed by the cold and the wet, tired, and covered in mud, I was irrationally irritated when a silver-gilt Jeep Grand Cherokee pulled into the parking lot and stopped easily near the front door. The driver's side door opened and a man about my age stepped out, clean, dry, and wearing an expensively embroidered sweatshirt from a local glacier flight-seeing company. *Some people have it easy,* I thought viciously to myself. *How dare he even nod politely? I've earned my trip to Alaska mile by bruising mile, and here's this pampered jerk waltzing in like he's on the Grand Tour of Europe. I'm looking for shelter and he's probably concerned about visibility for his next hundred-dollar-an-hour flying tour of the backcountry.* Foul tempered for no good reason except the weather and the day's long miles, I was determined to be crusty, aloof, a Lonesome Traveler above the petty tourism concerns of this . . . this *yuppie.*

The woman behind the desk was helping two loud German ladies figure out their revised sightseeing schedule given the weather. By loud, I do not mean rude, I mean only that they compensated for lack of grammatical proficiency and vocabulary with volume. I stood to the side, dripping muddy water onto the blond hardwood floor and watching The Yuppie collect brochures for guided salmon fishing excursions. He looked at me and I glared back as he began to close the space between us in a slow amble. He was tall and a bit thick around the neck and waist. A few freckles scattered across his pale face, and his light reddish brown hair was well cut and combed. I turned and looked pointedly out the window.

"Kinda wet out there," he said over my right shoulder. There was no escape.

No shit, really? was what I thought. "Yes, it is," was what I snarled in response. I instantly felt ashamed of the tone that emerged. He was just trying to be civil and I was behaving horribly. So he was clean and rich, did this make him an evil person?

I sighed and tried what I hoped was a more friendly tone. "Where are you from?" It was the standard traveler's question. My voice sounded weary and I tried to keep the savage note out of it. Wherever it was that he was from, I was sure he had flown up here, warm and dry, to pick up his fancy rental SUV. He had that well-fed, rather impractical, investment banker or lawyer look to him that I had gotten so used to seeing on the streets of Princeton over the course of the last two years.

"New Jersey."

I nearly choked and looked at him again, this time more critically. *Dear God, please let it not be so.* The clean trousers and expensive new sneakers were beginning to look horribly familiar. The silver-gilt SUV parked outside, the glacier flight-seeing trips. Where else could he be from? Here was a man whose fancy car alarm I had set off with sonic blasts from my straight pipes not so many months ago, I was sure of it. I breathed deeply and forged ahead, looking for the suicide thrust. "Really? Me too. Which town?"

"Princeton." He smiled, sure that I would recognize the name.

With the exception of the park road that lances into the interior of Denali, Talkeetna is as geographically far away from Princeton as one can get on paved surfaces and still be on the North American continent. It is at least five thousand miles as the crow flies between western Alaska and central New Jersey. The route I had chosen, through the tiniest of towns and on the twistiest of roads, was longer than that and had evolved in part to put an end note on my time in the rarified, sterile, uncomfortably wealthy, and safe world of the Ivory Tower generally and Princeton particularly. Yet, here it was. Princeton, New Jersey, had trailed me all the way to Talkeetna, Alaska.

All my ambivalence about my university experience bubbled to where I hoped it was concealed just beneath the surface. I was forever and eternally grateful for the scholarship and the opportunities that the university and my department had afforded me, and if I had to roll back the clock to that final spring I spent with the Peace Corps, if I had to make a decision again about which graduate program to attend, I think I might well make the same choice. However, at that time, still living and working in the Balkans, I made my choice sight unseen and did not realize the level of conservatism and academic insularity within the Princeton program that was supposed to train people for careers in public service. I wanted to learn how to save the world; I learned statistics instead. I wanted to learn about how to speak the truth and have it heard; instead I learned about "political capital" and "framing." For a public policy school, we were noticeably heavy on the "policy" element—the more regression analysis and quantitative economics and econometrics the better— and noticeably light on the "public" part of things. Issues of social justice, equity, service, or even ethics were rarely, if ever, discussed in a classroom set- ting. The dean of my department had been an inarticulate economist who had a tendency to fall asleep during public presentations and had once introduced the secretary general of the United Nations, after an embarrassing pause as he considered the man's name, as "Coffee Ann-ann." I had several wonderful pro- fessors and a few horrendous ones, one of whom publicly referred to me as "that bitch." I had brilliant classmates, most much brighter than I, many of whom went into domestic or international public service with the govern- ment, foundations, and nonprofit organizations. There were others, however, who did what the curriculum of our department largely trained us to do: they marched off to be the investment bankers and the consultants who would maximize the private profit margins and "spin" the public image of corporate interests.

In the conventional sense I "did well" at Princeton—although my grasp of statistics and economics left a lot to be desired—but I'm sure that I never really "fit" there, either culturally or socially. Whether walking past the pricey empo- ria of Nassau Street or standing before the neo-gothic collegiate architecture of the university quadrangles, there was a palpable sense of entitlement, a pro- jection of the inherent value of wealth and display, and the insularity of a narrow society that believed implicitly what we were all explicitly told: that we were "special," that we were "the best and the brightest." It made me uncomfortable. I wondered about the costs of functionality, of success, within such a world. Would what was real, what was true, and what I had come there to learn be lost in the parade of Princeton's conspicuous consumption, lost in the blather of cocktail parties, academic functions, and skewed curricular values?

Despite my ambivalence about my point of origin, Colin, as The Yuppie introduced himself, was delighted with the news that I had just finished my degree there. He was a genuinely nice man and was pleased to meet someone from home this far from Nassau Street. Indeed, he did live on Nassau Street and he was, in fact, an investment banker in New York. He asked a lot of questions about my trip. He asked what I would do when I returned. He asked for my phone number. I didn't have one and told him so. An address? No, not that either. Apart from the warehouse in Trenton where my few belongings were stored, my home was presently loaded onto Lucy. Colin gave me his telephone number and asked me to call when I returned as he wanted to know that I had made it home safely and also wanted to take me out to dinner. He was trying to be kind, I felt guilty for my evil thoughts about Princeton yuppies, and I promised to call him sometime in early September. The German ladies left and Colin moved forward to inquire about flight-seeing and visibility.

Glass cases filled with fragile beadwork jewelry stood in open ranks around the floor of the information center. The slender floral lace chains, created from brightly variegated beads, were marvelous and lay next to ropes twisted thick with, but made delicate by, the thousands of tiny hand-strung bits of glass used to create them. There were earrings and broaches, bracelets and hairpieces, some of them set with larger handmade glass and ceramic beads, but their hallmark was the intricate building of tiny glass bead upon tiny glass bead. The artist was Sheila, the woman who stood behind the tourist information desk.

Sheila was tall and had a mane of kinked black hair that fell down her back. A striking woman with a direct voice and a ready laugh, she was not conventionally beautiful, but she had a presence that made you look at her more than twice. Her jewelry had won prizes but the arts and the tourist industry were relatively new experiences for her. For fourteen years she had worked on a crab boat in the Bering Strait.

What I was doing was nothing compared to how Sheila had lived her life. Crab fishing in the Bering Strait is, according to OSHA, the most dangerous profession in the country. Crabbers ply their trade on wintry seas that can shift from calm to thirty-foot swells within a matter of hours. Alaskan crab, as any supermarket shopper knows, is expensive, but its greatest cost lies in the loss of the men and women who harvest waters only a few degrees above freezing. The reward for crabbers can be tens of thousands of dollars grossed in a few short weeks, but the money is hard earned on a weather-lashed winter ocean. Fourteen-hour shifts of backbreaking labor operating the tons of equipment, which swing over shifting, heaving, ice-slicked decks in subzero temperatures, are typical. The fatality rate for a crabber in the Bering Sea is three times that of commercial fishermen anywhere else, and four and a half times that of the average long-haul truck driver. One percent of the crabbers who ship out from Alaskan docks each year do not return, and of those who do come back, hundreds are maimed for life. Fourteen years was a long time for anyone to work, to survive, a crab-boat existence. I was impressed.

Sheila sent me to the youth hostel, ten miles up the spur access toward Talkeetna. The road was dirt, more mud than solid ground after several days of rain. With evening approaching, I decided to forgo sightseeing until the morning and headed straight for shelter.

A young woman named Heather owned, managed, and lived at the hostel. Among other things, Heather was an amateur "musher," engaged in building a sled-dog team. Twelve little houses were spaced throughout her fenced-in backyard, and from each the furry nose of a dog emerged. The dogs watched me, nostrils twitching, as I climbed the back steps, but not one of them moved. More sensible than I, they knew enough to stay under a roof when the weather was as foul as it had been that day. Two other dogs, a huge golden Lab who was not part of Heather's racing team, and a lean, muscled husky who was, met me inside. Like Susan Butcher, Heather rotated most of her dogs into the house from time to time so that they would bond with her.

In the evening, Heather, the dogs, two other women from Toronto, and I ranged ourselves over the couch and the floor and watched *The English Patient* together. One of the Toronto women was knitting a woolen hat in forest shades of green and brown. The click of her needles, the warmth of that house, and all of us women sitting together to watch a romance of love and war was wonderful, safe, and soothing. I was sitting on the floor with my back against the couch when the yellow Lab curled up at my knees and rested his giant head on my thigh. His tail thumped twice on the carpet, his eyes closed, and he was asleep within minutes, my hand stroking his ears. The husky settled onto the couch behind me, nuzzled my ear, rested his nose on one of my shoulders, and draped a long-limbed paw over the other. I breathed in the scent of wet fur and peaceful breathing. Heather stared at me.

"I've never seen them do that before. Are all dogs like this with you?" I admitted that most were. I am not Dr. Dolittle, but I do seem to share some affinity with four-legged, tail-wagging creatures. If only I did as well with my own species.

It was still raining, fat drops of water splashing through the drenching mist, but the radio said that it was due to stop in the afternoon. Hope for better weather was floating, albeit with water wings. I thought that a later start would get me a better chance at seeing Denali, although the mountain was notoriously shrouded in July. I puttered around the hostel until 8:30, writing in my journal and listening to Heather's eclectic collection of CDs, before hunkering down under a heavy sweater and the hood of my rain jacket to walk into town for breakfast. There was a shortcut through the graveyard near the climbers' memorial.

Talkeetna is the staging point for many successful and a few tragic expeditions each year. With a summit height of 20,320 feet, Denali rises a total of eighteen thousand feet from base to summit. It is the largest mountain in the world. Mount Everest, and a few other peaks in the Himalayas, are higher in absolute elevation, but even Everest rises only eleven thousand feet to its summit from its base on the Plateau of Tibet. Although most of the twelve hundred climbers who annually launched summit attempts did so in June, when the weather was clearer and the glaciers firmer, Denali often claimed a mortal tithe. Some of the bodies were recovered, but many—climbers who had fallen into crevasses or plummeted thousands of feet from ridges—were never found. Denali was a mountain that demanded expertise and claimed the inexperienced, or the simply unlucky. In Talkeetna's graveyard, nineteen-year-old neophytes on their first major expedition were memorialized beside world-class climbers. One stone read, "His grave—the South Buttress. His Spirit—Free." Another, "To the Summit!" I wondered if, at that final moment when the crevasse opened or the avalanche let go, they counted the cost? Or, was the magnificence of the mountain, of the journey, worth everything? Yeats came to mind: ". . . The years to come seemed waste of breath, a waste of breath the years behind, in balance with this life, this death . . ." I thought of Dan, the ice worm explorer from the ferry, out alone on the southern glaciers, and said a short prayer for his safety.

The Roadhouse Café smelled of baking sourdough, frying eggs, and hash. From my perch on a wooden stool I had a scone and coffee strong enough to stand a spoon in, wrote postcards, and stared through the window at the saturated landscape. The rain fell unabated. By midmorning there was no sense in delaying any longer so I squished my way back to Lucy, loaded her up, said good-bye to the women, one of whom handed me the hat that she had knitted the evening before, and set off into the rain toward Denali.

One hundred fifty miles later, in Cantwell, the last town before the park entrance, my hands and feet were once again soaked and freezing to the point that I had to pull over to let them warm up. It was painful when they got that cold, and it made driving difficult. Just standing on feet that are numb and forcing blood back into them sends hundreds of tiny bolts of fiery pain up the ankles all the way to the knees. As for my hands, they simply ached. I felt eighty years old, catastrophically arthritic, and genuinely miserable as I shoved my throbbing hands under my arms and walked with a clenched jaw, forward and backward, until the pain became less. It was moments like that when I almost wished I had a bigger bike: something with a fairing to block the wind on my lower arms and legs, something with heated grips, something with hot-air vents right by my feet, something with a plug-in unit for an electric vest, a stereo, an automatic reverse, a gas gauge, a CD player, and built-in luggage. I had mocked them, those huge wraparound machines like the Honda Gold Wing or the Harley Electra Glide—*if you want to drive a bike, drive a bike, not a compact car*—but at moments like that there was nothing I wanted more than a cumbersome, ugly, gas-guzzling, luxurious motorcycle.

Twenty-five miles later, in the parking lot near Denali's visitor's center, I was packing my rain jacket back into a saddlebag, hoping that it would be for the last time that day, when a rental RV pulled into the space beside me. A man in his early sixties with fawn-suede oxford shoes stepped from behind the wheel.

"Are you driving that thing?" I was too tired for clever responses or the espousal of the feminist cause.

"Yes."

"Well, at least you've got good weather for it!" I looked at him, the new ball cap, the wrinkle-free sweatshirt, the creased trousers.

"It's been raining for the last three days." The precipitation had stopped twenty minutes ago and in the shadow of Denali it was cold. Had this man noticed any of this inside his RV?

"Oh . . . well, yes. But it's not raining now!" I nodded and gave him a half-smile.

The center was a swarm of people, alive with tennis-shoed grandmothers and booted backpackers looking at alarming displays about the importance of following bear precautions in the backcountry. It is a worthwhile thing to remember that in the far north humans are not at the top of the food chain. A few days later word would filter out of Denali about a backpacker, sleeping in his tent in a designated campspot, killed by a grizzly looking for food in a nearby trash-dumping area. With every campsite booked months in advance, I opted only for the fourteen-mile drive into the park, the farthest distance that was possible to go on one's own. Only park buses took people farther into the interior. That short loop, however, gave hints of what could be seen if one had more time to disappear into the backcountry for a week or more. The sun, in the rapidly changing weather patterns that marked the Alaskan summer, was fully out. Light sparked tiny rainbows in the water droplet prisms held in the grasses of high alpine meadows. An enormous caribou grazed at roadside. His antler rack, covered in the brown velvet of new growth, spread in crowned tiers four feet above his head.

Tired by the time I left the park late in the afternoon, I drove only another thirty miles up the Parks Highway toward Fairbanks before stopping at a riverside campground. The bank where I set up my tent was shaded and cushioned by the needles of tall fir trees that filled the evening air with the damp scent of wood and pine pitch. I put on my last pair of dry socks and hung the others to dry from my handlebars. It was a small thing, but after so much rain it felt good to have dry feet and to know, judging by the sky and the lack of tactile humidity hanging in the air, that there was the prospect of a clear day to follow. The light softened and I sat watching the gentle rush of water flowing over gravel and silt, while the sky changed from rose to orange to the deep, glowing indigo blue of a clear night in an Alaskan summer.

THE SKY SHIFTED FROM MOTHER-OF-PEARL PALE to abalone blue as I rode toward Fairbanks. There were no houses, no side roads, only the rippling green crests of the forest receding back into the wilderness. There was no traffic and I saw only one other person, a native man standing alone by the side of the road somewhere near Anderson. He was handsome, arrestingly so, with an angular face, coppery skin, and a slim upright bearing. His blue-black hair was held back from his forehead with a red cloth band. At least ten miles from the nearest settlement, he was not hitchhiking or walking. He simply stood, looking at the sky, on the side of the road. What did he see in that clear sky, that open country, that empty road?

In Fairbanks, I stopped at the Harley dealership to buy souvenir T-shirts. Picnic tables, arranged outside under the shade of a striped awning, provided a natural place for bikers to meet and gossip while their machines were being serviced and I joined the small gathering.

Tim was from Georgia. Over six feet tall, he was bungee-cord thin with a soft voice and a ponytail knotted every inch from neck to waist with black elastics. He and a friend had just driven their bikes up the Dalton Highway to the Arctic Circle. My heart leapt. *Maybe I should reconsider the drive to Prudhoe Bay.*

"How was it?"

"Not good. Bike broke down and we were lucky that some boys with a pickup gave us a ride back to town." I thought back to the horror stories Doug told in Ninilchik. The evidence was piling up that this was not a good thing to do on a motorcycle. I stuffed my new T-shirts into my pack and drove a few blocks down the street to mail them from the post office.

I was in the parking lot when a man approached me.

"Is that a Harley?" His speech was slurred and he was a little unsteady on his feet. In his thirties, with a strong frame and dark hair falling across his forehead, he might have been handsome had the rheuminess of alcohol not been in his eyes and too-slack mouth.

"Yes."

"You're pretty. Where are you going?" He was standing too close to me and I knew from the tone of his words that I was about to have a very bad day if the conversation continued. Years of solitary traveling and living in countries and neighborhoods where one had good reason to be watchful have fine-tuned my sense of self-preservation. There's a horrible vibration, an energy of violence, that is sometimes palpable when an individual too physically close is about to act. It comes with a visceral pulse, a sharpening of vision, and a sense that things are about to go badly awry. I had learned, the hard way, to listen to my intuition and to the blood in my neck when it started to pound.

Intuition will not always save you from a bad situation. Once I was searched by military policemen at 3 A.M. on a train in Serbia as I traveled from Hungary to Macedonia. While one man held a machine pistol to my head, another ran his hands over my body and under my clothes, and a third disappeared with my passport. Without my papers, I had become a non-person, and as the first two men pulled me off the train and steered me toward a drainage ditch beside the tracks with a gun against my spine, I was sure that I was about to be raped and almost as certain that they would put a bullet in the back of my skull when it was over. The only thing that saved me that night was the third soldier coming out of the guard booth with my confiscated passport. He stood and watched as his commander put it back into my sweating hand and then pushed me back toward the train. Other times intuition is more helpful;

a sixth sense that someone is walking too closely behind, a casual conversation where questioning becomes intimate or interrogatory, an uncomfortable closing of personal space. All of these things and more are cues that I had learned over the years to listen for, and react to, before situations spiraled out of control.

I looked around the parking lot and the surrounding buildings, scanning for options, or at least witnesses. The lot was full of cars and pickup trucks but empty of people. The slow-moving line in the post office would not be sending anyone out through the glass doors soon. I stepped around Lucy's front forks, putting her frame between the two of us.

"Take me for a ride." It was a demand, not a request. I demurred, trying not to escalate things.

"You wouldn't fit. Look. My bags are on the passenger seat."

"Sexy motorcycle girl, I'm coming with you." He stepped toward me and dropped one hand on Lucy's seat. I stepped back another foot, keeping my weight forward, and shifted inside my jacket. There was a switchblade in my inside left breast pocket, bought on the Bulgarian black market after a particularly ugly incident in the fall of 1997 when local thugs had kicked in the door of my apartment. I knew how to use it but also knew not to pull it out unless I fully intended to bury it in his carotid artery. I looked at the man carefully. Under the drape of close-fitting black jeans and white T-shirt, there was no outline of a weapon, concealed or otherwise. Unless he carried a boot knife, something that I doubted he was sober enough to reach for quickly, he was unarmed.

I stepped forward and stared directly into his eyes. "Get your fucking hands off my motorcycle and get the fuck away from me. You fuck with me and I *guarantee* you will fuck with every biker between here and Whitehorse." My vocabulary becomes somewhat limited in moments of stress, but what I said did seem to get through to his saturated brain. He stepped back.

The threat of backup from the rest of the steel-horse brotherhood was vague but real. In that small northern city he had probably seen enough bikers coming through, if only to visit the sole dealership for several hundred miles, to know that we can be a fairly clannish bunch. If I needed them, I knew that Georgia Tim, and anyone else sitting at the tables just up the street, would help without question or restraint. He retreated a few steps and turned.

"Bitch. I'll see you later." It was an empty threat. Men like that, fortified by a fifth of God knows what and running off some power fantasy, either drink themselves to obliteration in a couple of hours or sober up enough to remember their own weaknesses. It's the ones who seek victims when they are sober, or the ones packing weapons, who are dangerous, and that man was neither. I knew he wouldn't come looking for me.

Late that afternoon, having crossed the Chena River to walk the galleries of the University of Alaska Museum, thoughts of the Dalton Highway, the Arctic Circle, and Prudhoe Bay kept reemerging, refusing to settle into the oblivion of negative decision. Should Fairbanks be my turnaround city, or just a stop on the way to the Arctic Ocean? Was I ready to decide that Fairbanks was the end, was as far as I wanted to go, and that it was indeed time to turn around and go home? If I left immediately for the Dalton I could make it to the campground at the Yukon River Bridge before the evening got too late. What to do? At the Wolf Run Café I bought myself a double mocha and a little more time to think. Two women shared the patio with me. Their four-wheel drive truck, thick yellowish brown mud caked to the tops of the window frames, sat parked in the gravel lot beyond.

"Where've you been?" I asked.

"Prudhoe Bay and the Dalton Highway." This was almost too good to be true.

"What do you think about taking a motorcycle up there?"

The woman's clear blue eyes raked over me. She shook her head. "I think no, definitely not."

Her friend, a little more circumspect, hedged. "Well . . . you've come this far, you'll probably be fine."

At the end of a conversation about mudholes, potholes, loose gravel, and thundering transport trucks I decided, no, definitely not. This was a bad idea entirely. But twenty minutes later, driving back toward the city center, Lucy humming low and powerful beneath me, I changed my mind. I was going. At a Kmart I walked the aisles until I found a three-dollar plastic Tupperware jug that would hold the several gallons of extra gas I would need crossing the tundra where there were no communities, no gas stations, a road that would probably pound my bike into scrap metal, and no one to ask for help if I needed it. I stood in line waiting to pay for my jug thinking, *This is stupid. Fundamentally idiotic. Why am I even considering this? What am I looking for: a photo opportunity beside the* WELCOME TO THE ARCTIC CIRCLE *sign? A panoramic shot of the oil rigs at Prudhoe Bay? What am I trying to prove, and to whom?* My hubris was about to take a huge chunk out of my ass. I *hated* driving gravel, absolutely despised it, so why was I planning to subject myself to an extra four hundred miles of it? Just what was I looking for? Scenery? The variety and beauty of landscapes and vistas between Princeton, New Jersey, and Fairbanks, Alaska, had been astonishing, and all indications were that in the seven thousand miles of return riding, there would be more than enough fantastic things to see. Was this some Mallory-esque fantasy: drive the Dalton because it's there? There were hundreds of roads to drive on my way back to the East Coast and thousands that I would never be able to. Choices had to be made and costs had to be considered; it was not possible to do and see everything. It was time to turn around and head, albeit indirectly, for home. I walked back to the housewares department and, firmly and finally, put the jug and any lingering thoughts of the Dalton back on the shelf.

In celebration of sensible decision making, I booked myself into Grandma Shirley's Hostel, which was rumored to be the best hostel north of Anchorage.

Grandma Shirley and her home, part of which she had converted into a guest house for low-budget travelers, matched. With light flooding in through huge windows and a smile that lit her entire face, the house and its mistress exuded welcome and sunshine. Truth be told, Shirley did not look like much of a grandmother. She had the expected white hair, clipped into soft waves that framed her face, but she was radiant with the vigor and enthusiasm of a woman half her age and twice her stature.

"Come right in! You can park your bike out here by the picnic table. Yes dear, that's right, take off your shoes. Less dirt in the house. How wonderful. I've never seen a woman motorcycle touring by herself. We get lots of men, but you, you're the first! Come right in!" She bustled about, slippered feet lithe on the stairs, showing me the sun-filled bunkroom, the showers, the kitchen, and the lounge. "Let us know if you need anything, we're right downstairs!" A finger-wiggling wave over her shoulder and she was gone. There were ten other people at the hostel that night, including a couple from Maine driving an expedition-style British Land Rover. They had traveled from southern Maine to Fairbanks and were now headed south toward the Pan American Highway and Tierra del Fuego. Originally they had planned to take their Rover all the way up to Prudhoe Bay but, somewhere past the Arctic Circle, they discovered a hole in their radiator and decided to turn around before a small problem became a large one. They seemed tired and didn't talk to one another much. I wondered if long days on the road, jammed into a not overly comfortable Rover, were bringing them together or highlighting their differences.

A young man named Steven Vajda was also booked into Shirley's. He was thin, not emaciated, but he seemed to be built mostly of sinew and muscle. Tanned skin stretched tightly over the planes of his face, the tendons in his legs and arms were corded and visible, and I would have been surprised if he carried more than 4 or 5 percent body fat on his frame. He wore long, tattered shorts, a sun-bleached T-shirt, and his hair appeared to have been cut without the aid of a mirror, using either a jackknife or kitchen scissors. All this stood to reason as he had bicycled from San Francisco to Grandma Shirley's Hostel over the course of the previous two months. He had pedaled the entire three thousand miles, except for the stretch between Whitehorse and Circle—a village that marks the end of the Steese Highway. For that leg he had loaded his bicycle into a canoe and paddled and floated his way down the Yukon River for a week. Steven was an adventurer.

Strangely, Fairbanks had a reputation for great Greek and Thai restaurants. Steven and I decided to splurge on dinner as we had both decided that afternoon that Fairbanks was the pivot point of our journeys. Although there was no hiding the holes, the frays, and the embedded chain and engine grease, we cleaned up as much as possible. I left my helmet behind and we rode into town on Lucy, shouting and laughing over the roar of her engine and the whistle of wind in our ears. The Greek place was closed so we went to the Thai and ate huge plates of pad thai noodles and chicken swimming in gorgeous saffron cream sauce, all of it washed down with lemongrass tea. We talked of adventure, the people we had met, and the flow and balance of the road beneath two wheels. His mouth stuffed with noodles, Steven exhorted the benefits of a fifty-mile day on a bicycle.

"I take three days to travel the same road you do in three hours, but I *know* that road better than you ever will." He was right of course. My miles racked up in the thousands as his did in the hundreds. I felt the sweep of a continent and marked time with mountain ranges and coastlines spread across four different time zones, but the tiny wildflowers, the exhalation of lakeshore breezes, the hidden berry patches, and the shape of individual leaves that marked Steven's day were a blur in mine.

The road had taught us a few shared things, however: patience and a willingness to listen to the melody line of the miles singing whatever song they would; an acceptance of what each day brought, accompanied by very little forethought of what was to come on the morrow; and peace and self-awareness, a feeling that one's skin fit well over one's back and shoulders and that the voices that spoke inside one's helmet were genuine, as they emerged from the silence of solitude rather than the chatter of society.

The teapot was empty and we drove back to Shirley's under the corona of a midnight sun, as close to the Arctic Circle as either of us would get. At least on that trip.

LEAVING FAIRBANKS FOR DELTA JUNCTION AND the northernmost leg of the Alcan Highway, it was cool enough to be cold at fifty miles per hour and dense, cloaking mist settled into the creek banks and depressions that marked the low roll of the land. The sun slowly burned into brightness and broad bands of emerald grass emerged, edging the blue-green forest. On a hillside power line cut, a cow moose grazed, two calves beside her. I pulled over to watch them. Although the babies were nearly four feet tall at the shoulders, they looked tiny, almost fragile, beside the massive frame of their mother. Awkward on long, slender legs, they tottered on the slope, bumping their shoulders against the cow's knees, searching for temporary stability, like any child just finding its feet. The trio nibbled their way across the cut and disappeared into the woods.

Outside of Richardson I stopped again for a roadhouse breakfast: a piece of coconut cream pie that stood a full eight inches above the plate. The woman behind the bar was slim and strong looking. In her late forties, she had work-hardened fingers bound by a wedding ring and spoke with a voice that carried the rasp of late nights and too many cigarettes, one of which burned in the ashtray near my coffee. The news blared on the television.

"You're traveling alone?" she asked.

"I am."

"You're a gutsy lady." She took a long drag on her cigarette and blew the smoke toward the ceiling. "I'd like to do what you're doing, but wouldn't by myself." I thought about the couple with the Land Rover in Fairbanks and the silence, not entirely comfortable, that existed between them.

"No," I said. "It's the people who travel together, and who have to compromise, who are the gutsy ones. Me, I do exactly as I please." She stared through the smoke of her cigarette for a long moment, nodded, and crushed it out.

The Alaska Range rose out of the mist, blanketed by forest, the underlying crags peeking through rents in the tree cover, glowing pewter through the green firs. The pavement was open, smooth, and flowing. Past Port Alcan, which straddles the Canadian border, the road construction began again and I slowed down, reminding myself to keep my feet on the pegs, relax, and just ride it through, mile by mile. As much as I loathed driving through zones where solid surfaces had been eradicated, there was no sense in raging against what was beyond one's control. The mud, gravel, ditches, and heavy equipment that made up Alcan roadwork was not meant to be enjoyed, it was meant to be accepted and survived.

EXHIBIT J: *Where the Heart Beats Slowly*

On the veranda of the 1202 Roadhouse, a slim young man from Winnipeg, nineteen or twenty years old, was sweeping and straightening deck chairs.

"For two summers I've come here," he said. "I need the money for college."

"But why here? Surely there are jobs closer to home?" He turned to scan the horizon. Low-growing scrub, brush, and bog melted upward toward the high country of the Wrangell and St. Elias Ranges. Light lancing between a tangle of black-bellied storm clouds had turned the landscape into a calico of green, rust, gold, and deep lavender.

"I dunno. I like it up here." I looked into the slow stare of his eyes. Peace and belonging shone there. One day soon, perhaps at the end of the summer following his last year of university, he would not be going back to Winnipeg. In the northern Yukon he had found that rare thing: a place where he belonged.

. . .

Rain was never very far away and just after the village of Koidern I drove into a few westward-moving misting showers. The glow of yellow sunshine slanted toward the east and the light and moisture intermingled. As if a huge hand had smeared a palate across the sky, three full spectrums of prismatic light arced across my left shoulder and dropped to the road ahead. For a couple of miles I drove, watching the rainbow as it seemed to follow me, one colored pool of light that marked its end always ahead, the other always behind. I pulled Lucy to the side of the highway and just sat, watching the rainbow shift and grow, the colors alternately fading and intensifying. I lack the words, and perhaps the grace, to explain it well, but there was humming, a singing or vibration in the air, as if the spectrums of light and water had a life force all their own. I had heard this music only once before, a decade past, sitting on the edge of a cliff on Ireland's Achill Island, and looking west over the long roll of the Atlantic Ocean. A storm sweeping in off the sea had also dropped a rainbow, and then a second. The bands of light widened and brightened as they came closer and then suddenly the color swept over my rocky perch and the singing began. Maybe it is always there, the vibration of woven light, but it just takes some fantastic display of the power and the beauty of the natural world for one to begin to listen to it. I took my helmet off to hear the song of the rainbow, watched the spectacle of color, and felt my chest contract and the tears begin; for the sheer beauty of that moment, for the privilege of being there.

It was a gorgeous afternoon and evening, the mountains spare and lovely above, the valleys lush and green below. Showers chased sun and reversed their game. I traveled beneath it all, running south and east, inscribing a concave sweep through the southwestern quadrant of the Yukon. Finally through the worst of the construction, I was gassing up at the Kluane Wilderness Village for the final few miles of the day, heading toward a campground at

Destruction Bay, when I noticed that the surrounding air had begun to darken. It was only 8 P.M., too early in those latitudes for evening to have arrived, and I stepped around the corner of the small filling station to look up into the high ridges of the St. Elias Mountains. Sulfur-edged black thunder-heads were boiling over the exposed and rocky parapets thousands of feet above and sheets of rain were dropping in heavy veils that obscured the high ridges. The storms were gathering and I watched them begin their sweep from the high country down toward Kluane Lake and Destruction Bay. Thunder rumbled in the distance and flashes of lightning illuminated the atmosphere in garish, slashing, yellow-blue incandescence. All of a sudden, the tiny rental cabins next to the gas station looked like a much better option than driving into the teeth of a violent thunderstorm and setting up a tent on an exposed lakeshore.

There was more rain in the early grayish light, but it was diminishing, much lighter than the torrents that had swept through the village hours before. Lucy's engine, as always, turned over with a low rumble as soon as I pressed the electric start and we rolled out onto the Alcan as the last of the rain fell. The bare, mineralized slopes of Sheep Mountain glowed copper red and sulfur yellow, and gravel-bedded streams channeled the snowmelt from thousands of feet above toward the topaz waters of Kluane Lake. With the wet road, new snow on the peaks, and winds howling down the slopes of the mountains, it was a dramatic ride; primal and bleakly beautiful, yet bitterly cold and damp. Ninety miles later, pulling into Haines Junction for coffee, chocolate, and gas, I stepped off Lucy, half frozen and feeling much less than half human. It was incredible how physically draining prolonged cold could be. I could ride ninety miles in a single shot on a clear warm day and never feel a hint of weariness. That same ninety miles, in the teeth of a freezing wind that chewed the sensation out of hands and feet, was an exercise in agony and exhaustion.

The air warmed as the topography dropped, and the clouds began to clear near Whitehorse. A spirit house cemetery stood just north of the highway near the village of Champagne; rows of miniature cottages, each painted green and white, which were said to hold the prized belongings of the deceased. Although burial is now the most common form of interment, until the arrival of Russian and European missionaries at the beginning of the nineteenth century, the people of the far northwest cremated their dead and interred the ashes, along with their possessions, within the spirit houses. Although the religions of the West had changed the local culture forever, the spirit houses remained. I only slowed long enough to read the sign on the low graveyard fence: "This cemetery is not a tourist attraction. Please respect our privacy as we respect yours."

At Johnson's Crossing, eighty miles south of Whitehorse, I stopped in front of a small store to stretch and admire the elegant span of the green steel bridge crossing the Teslin River. Nearly two thousand feet long, it was built high enough so that steamships, which brought all external materiel to the town of Teslin until the Alcan was finished in 1942, could clear the underside of the bridge. As I turned to slide back into Lucy's saddle, I noticed a pay phone on the wall of the store, stopped short, thought for a minute, and called Dave. We hadn't spoken since that horrible afternoon in the rain of Prince George and there had been no e-mail communication from him either. My anger was gone, I had no hopes or thoughts of reconciliation, but I did want to hear his voice. Once, before we were lovers, we had been friends. He picked up the phone on the first ring and seemed surprised and glad to hear from me. We were a few minutes into the conversation when he paused.

"I miss you," he said.

"Do you?"

"Yes."

"Well, I stopped missing you a while back." It was not my intention to be cruel, but it was true that I had begun an intentional process to seal my heart to him somewhere in northwestern British Columbia. He was silent for a moment.

"Probably about five thousand miles ago?"

"About that." I was unwilling to dismiss him completely; maybe the friendship was still there for the saving. "But I think about you still. I'll catch you on the flip side of this, Dave. We'll get together when I get back." I did plan to go see him when I returned to New Jersey, but I had shed the skin of whatever was left of our romantic relationship. There were no regrets save that I should have seen the obvious sooner than I did. I put down the phone and for a blissful change felt steady and collected. I did not want to be with someone, either physically or emotionally, just because that person was lonely. I wanted more, and deserved better, than that.

It was another forty miles to the Teslin Lake Campground. I set up my tent and sat on top of a picnic table, boots resting on the bench, eating peanut butter and crackers and watching the surface of the lake change from deep blue to burnished silver. Forty-five minutes later Dan, the Gold Wing rider from Minnesota who had been touring Alaska with his daughter when I had met them in Ninilchik, rolled in, his motorcycle purring so low as to be almost silent.

"Well, well, well, look who's here!" he chortled. It was good to have some company, a well-met friend of the road showing up once again. Mary Kate had flown home from Anchorage, not because she was tired of traveling with her dad, but because she had exhausted her vacation time and had to get back to work. Dan was on his own again and enjoying a different sort of traveling: that of a solitary rider.

I woke to the explosive screech of a raven standing just outside my tent's screen door, croaking his raspy voice almost directly into my ear. Sitting bolt upright and coming groggily to my senses, I watched as the sadistic feathered beast hopped from tent site to camper to pickup truck, systematically waking the entire population. On the roof of a parked van he hopped up and down, stamping his sharp-clawed feet and tuning his croaking up a decibel to make sure that the people inside were fully awake. Clearly he was encouraging us all to pack up early and leave behind whatever goodies and trash that he might like for breakfast. I heard Dan shift and snort inside his tent. "What the *hell* kind of alarm clock is that?"

I laughed and began stuffing my sleeping bag into its sack. I wasn't going to be getting back to sleep so I thought that I might as well pack up and stomp my way out into the chilly morning. Dan, still making displeased noises, apparently had the same thought because within minutes he was dressed and shuffling between tent and motorcycle. Muttering crossly to himself, he disappeared with a roll of toilet paper in hand—one could never be sure of the availability or quality of paper in campground outhouses—and returned a few minutes later looking positively disgruntled. A little smile was, however, lurking wryly around the corners of his mouth. He marched past me, his words lingering in the chill air in puffs of frozen crystal vapor. "The *only* good thing about waiting in line to use the outhouse is that when you do get in there the seat is a *little* warmer."

Dan was still packing up when I pulled out and we agreed to meet in Swift River for breakfast. Teslin, the first stop for morning fuel, was smaller than I expected: a scattering of modest houses and a single gas station–roadhouse combination. I was sorry to be traveling through too early to see the George Johnson Museum. Mr. Johnson was a local Tlingit man with a passion for photography. After the Gold Rushes ended, and before the Alcan Highway was cut through northern British Columbia, Johnson had photographed both the traditional ways of his people and the changes that had come with the introduction of modern technology—hunting rifles, for example. The arrival of the highway in 1942 was ruinous for the Tlingit. Contractors and soldiers brought with them the alcohol and diseases that decimated both the traditional culture and the population of the local people. It is said that Johnson stopped photographing his neighbors in the mid-1940s because he could not bear to record their destruction. It is a sad irony that the highway, which brought devastation to Mr. Johnson's people, also brought him fame for his beautiful images of a vanished way of life.

I pulled into Swift River, a little cold and damp from the droplets of water kicked up off the wet road by Lucy's tires and the mist rising off the lakes and rivers. The roadhouse was a small space with four battered blue-and-white Formica tabletops flanking a central wood stove. Greasy and not particularly clean, it was the type of place where one could find massive breakfasts that were best ordered well done. Four men, all of whom looked like they might be related to the short-order cook, leaned on their elbows from barstools fronting the counter and grill. Like the cook, two wore yellowed and spotted tank tops, which exposed their aging, yet muscular, arms. Each had a grease-edged ball cap and one, who walked with the slow hitched gait of a former rodeo rider, sported a silver-gilt belt buckle that could have been used to plate a large sandwich. Another biker sat hunched and miserable in the corner. Blue jeans and a thin sweatshirt had done little to protect him from the cold. His hands were wrapped around a huge cup of coffee and I asked the cook for one like it. Dan showed up as I was halfway into my first mug and we ordered Denver omelet sandwiches. What must have been three eggs, along with ham and peppers and cheese, all spilling out over the edges of two pieces of wheat toast, arrived minutes later along with a fresh boiling splash of strong coffee. We talked and laughed. Dan told me stories of his years of motorcycle touring and how, although he missed his family, it was always hard for him to come back home, leave the road, and garage the bike. We finished our breakfasts. I was riding a bit faster than Dan, holding an easy fifty-five on that section of smooth roads, so he wrapped me in a huge hug and we said our good-byes in front of the roadhouse.

The run into Watson Lake was lovely, flanked by more river and lakeshore vistas, deep green forest, and the gradual climb of the land toward the Continental Divide. Watson Lake is the home of the Signpost Forest. In 1942 Carl Lindley, a homesick soldier assigned to the military construction crew that built the Alcan, pounded a sign into the ground there, pointing the way to Danville, Illinois. Over the years, the men and women who worked on the highway, and increasingly the tourists passing through, have added their signs. They are nailed to stripped lodgepole pine trunks set up in "groves" by the town of Watson Lake, and form a vertical patchwork of municipal memorabilia. Many of the individual signs had clearly been "borrowed." Sharing a pole with one from Hamburg, Germany, another from Marion, Iowa, and a third from Harvey Station, New Brunswick, a crisp green-and-white highway overpass sign pointed the way to El Paso, New Mexico. As delightfully quirky as the forest was, and no doubt as uplifting to the local economy as it is, the entire construct was more than a little bizarre. Small kiosks had mushroomed on the edge of the forest, where vendors sold pre-finished shingles of wood, indelible markers, and painting supplies. People wandered through the groves in that otherwise nondescript town of just under two thousand people, hammering their placards up to mark their presence, their passing. There already were more than forty-two thousand signs posted; how many more would be added in that single summer? I left no sign of my own, preferring to drift through Watson Lake unnoticed and unrecorded.

THE CYCLIST WAS A SOLIDLY MUSCLED diminutive woman in her early forties with salt-and-pepper hair, lively eyes, and a quick smile. She was traveling to Calgary from Inuvik, a town in the Northwest Territories at the very end of the Dempster Highway. Inuvik was more than a thousand miles from where we met on the eastern embankment of the bridge that crosses the Hyland River, and she had at least another thousand miles to pedal before reaching Calgary. It was an epic ride through reindeer and bear country; she'd already crossed two major mountain ranges, and the Rockies still lay before her. I was deeply impressed. I ask her why she chose this type of travel.

"I love the North," she said, looking at the roll of mountains in the distance, "and I wanted to see it. This time of year there's twenty-two hours of daylight up there." She asked me about Lucy and whether motorcycles could be driven in the winter.

"No, New Jersey winters, you know; too much ice and too little snow."

"Do you have a car, too?" She seemed surprised when I nodded my head.

"Yes, I am a gasoline junkie." Looking at her sleek, lightly loaded, and petroleum-free bicycle I felt the guilt of a resource wastrel. An RV whooshed by, top-heavy, swaying, and speeding, too fast and too close. We both stepped off the edge of the pavement and looked after the RV with annoyance. She shook her head.

"It's amazing. People go on holiday to slow down and get away from it all, then they take it all with them and drive eighty miles an hour." She put on her helmet, settled back into the seat of her bicycle, and pedaled up the hill, legs pistoning, a cheery wave to say good-bye.

Perched on top of the embankment, I watched the river splashing over the rounded backs of bullfrog-sized stones, ate my lunch, and spent a few minutes really *noticing* what was around me. The low hum of grasshoppers chafing their musical legs rose from tall grasses interlaced with low-growing wild strawberry bushes. I picked the tiny red fruits, crushed the sweetness and the seeds in my mouth and lay back to watch the slow, circling dance of three pale yellow butterflies. The voice of Steven, my bicyclist dinner companion in Whitehorse, was in my ears: *I take three days to travel the same road that you do in three hours, but I know that road better than you ever will.* Like the RV, I, too, was rocketing along, blowing through thousands of miles. Over the previous six weeks I had seen the grandeur of forests, the tracery of coastlines, and the ramparts of great mountain ranges but I had to admit that, save for the occasional roadside stop, I was missing most of the roadside microcosms. Queen Anne's lace nodded on slender green stems, great filigreed heads bowing above the yellow primroses tucked in at their roots. Below, the slow gurgle of the river sang in time with the insects and I felt myself grow drowsy. How much we each missed, but how much we could each see in our different modes of travel, my bicycle acquaintances and I. I got the grand sweep of the continent, they got the intimate examination of a section of the same. Which mode was right? Which was better? I did not know and it did not matter. There was no absolute, each wanderer must find their own way.

Dipping south through the small community of Fireside, two roadside characteristics caught my attention: the scars of a forest fire and more black bears than I had ever seen before. In 1982, a fire, the second largest in British Columbian history, burned through four hundred thousand acres of timber. Nearly twenty years later the forest had yet to reclaim the hills. The landscape had a scorched and abandoned look to it; the blackened stumps of pine broke through scrubby underbrush with the obscenity of compound fractures. The low growth and berry bushes that sprang up after the fire were, however, prime habitat for black bears and, on average, I saw one every five miles between Fireside and the Liard River. They came to the roadside to look for carrion, someone told me later, listening for the sound of vehicles and hoping that an unwary deer or goat would step into the path of an RV doing eighty. There were enough bears, loitering by the side of the road, to indicate they had some success in this. One youngish bruin, perhaps last season's cub, sat on a small rise just above the pavement watching passing vehicles, watching me. With his pale, creamed-coffee nose, deep black coat, fuzzy-cupped ears rising above a broad forehead, and wide paws planted solidly below bulging shoulders and haunches, he was a beautiful animal. There was no traffic and I slowed, just wanting to look at him for another second or two. But as we regarded one another, he rose from his haunches and began to trot down toward the road, angling his approach to where our paths would intersect should I continue at ten miles per hour. I hit the throttle.

Everyone I met who had traveled the Alcan Highway told me that I absolutely must stop and soak at Liard Hot Springs. I pulled over for the evening to find that the provincial campground at the entrance to the springs was filled, but that a privately run campground across the street, Trapper John's, still had spaces available. I booked a spot, pitched my tent, changed into shorts and a sports bra, and headed into the woods for a soak.

Flora and fauna unique to northern Canada thrive in the moisture and heat at Liard. According to posted signs, the perpetual warmth of the springs supports more than two hundred forest plants, including fourteen orchid species that survive in British Columbia only because of the geothermal activity. Swimming between the hummocks of mosses and grasses, in the vaporous water that bubbled out of the earth at over one hundred degrees, were tiny, almost translucent fish.

The springs feed into two pools, the first a half mile back into the forest and reached by boardwalks built across hundred-yard stretches of spongy, sulfurous, steaming mats of wetland vegetation. The second pool is a quarter mile farther. The first pool, "Alpha," was clear and slightly sulfurous, twenty feet long and four feet deep in most places. It varied in temperature from gently soothing to move-right-along-before-you-parboil, depending on the part of the pool in which one sat. Despite the packed campground at the entrance, there were only twelve other people floating silently or talking quietly near the edges. I slid into the water, kneeled on the black and gray pebbles that covered the bottom, and felt the heat sink into my tired muscles. I stretched my neck, let my face fall to the surface, breathed the water's mineral steam, and watched my silver rings turn black. I kept my silence and distance from the other bathers and communicated only with the hot water as it gently eased the weariness from my back and the dust from my skin. A half hour later, with fingers and toes already soft and wrinkled, I ambled up the boardwalk, past a smoking waterfall, and into the steaming woods to the "Beta" pool. Beta was an opaque robin's-egg blue, with a mud bottom that sloped away to swimming depth and thick mats of bright green moss and algae ringing the edge. A few small mats of root and moss had detached from the banks and drifted across the surface, emerald islands in a sea of improbable blue. Although Beta was larger, fewer people were there, only five including me. No one spoke, and except for the occasional sharp twitter of a bird and the hissing bubble of a hidden spring, the silence was total. With the heavy greenery of the forest and the humid silence closing into my ears, I sank into the water, floated on my back, and let my legs drop into the cooler depths as fingers of warm water massaged my shoulders. Paradise. At Beta, I kept one eye open, however, scanning the trees that grew right to the edge of the pool. I had heard that a couple of years before, a sow black bear, perhaps thinking that a woman swimming in Beta was a threat to her nearby cubs, had pulled the bather from the water and killed her. It was a thought that blew to hell any possibility of complete relaxation.

Nearly an hour later, feeling vaguely drugged, I made my way slowly back to Trapper John's. A couple from Alberta had pulled their motorcycles up next to Lucy and had pitched a tent not too far from mine. The woman was only the second I had met who was driving her own bike and I was delighted when they asked me to join them for a beer near their small campfire, which smoked just enough to keep the clouds of hovering mosquitoes at bay. We laughed about the small hazards of motorcycle travel: the bugs, mud, and grime that inevitably coat the skin, and chance encounters with the back ends of bumblebees at fifty miles an hour. Although both were in their late forties, they were new to motorcycling. They spoke of their children's surprise and nervousness when they announced that they had decided to learn how to ride in the interest of acquiring a new skill and traveling together. I thought that the ability to shock and amaze one's teenage offspring was a tremendously positive indicator, both of them as individuals and of their parenting skills. We talked for an hour and I crawled into my tent, exhausted and content: the road, the soak in the springs, and the beer conspiring toward oblivion in minutes.

I knelt in the dirt twenty feet from the gas pumps, near the small towing and repair shop at Trapper John's. The girl working the pumps, glossy brown curls rioting down from where she had unsuccessfully attempted to tuck them under her hat, had given me free rein in the shop to take whatever tools and drainage pans I needed to change my oil and filter. The reciprocal part of the bargain was that I bought all my replacement oil from her shop. It took me just a few minutes to unclamp the drainage hose, unscrew the filter, let the thick black oil slide into the bucket, install the replacement filter, and put the whole system back together again. I have always done the basic maintenance on my bike myself, but as the minutes passed and I pulled what is an extremely simple lubrication system apart and put it back together, I felt more and more like a one-woman carnival sideshow. Had it been a man crouching there in front of a garage, tools laid out on a drop cloth with motorcycle parts beside him, he wouldn't have gotten a second glance. But a woman was different, and people stared. A man in his mid-seventies got out of his RV to stand beside me as I fitted the new filter. I ran a slick of oil around the rubber seal, screwed the piece on, reclamped the drainage hose, and filled the oil reservoir with clean fluid. The man watched all of this in fascinated silence from a few feet away. Finished, I looked up at him and smiled.

"That's it. All done!"

He nodded, clearly unsure of what to say, began to turn on his heel, and then turned back. "Ahhh . . . now you have a good, safe trip, little girl."

"Thank you."

He walked away, shaking his head. His wife waited inside their RV. I was glad to wipe down my borrowed tools, return them to their places in the shop, and cease being a spectacle.

31 | TEN THOUSAND MILES AND MORE

THE PAVEMENT NARROWED AND SNAKED THROUGH passes and gorges, negotiating the labyrinth of a mountain stronghold only recently penetrated by the transport system of a modern continent. Although the Muncho Lake section was perhaps one of the most beautiful on the Alcan, it had also been one of the most difficult to build. In 1942, engineers had blasted the road, yard by yard, into the rocky slopes, hauling the rubble away with horse-drawn sledges. Lucy leaned and swayed into the corners. Nearly ten thousand miles into our journey, we were now less separate entities—rider and machine—than a single moving being. It was fantasy, but sometimes she seemed to correct for frost heaves in the pavement, for the tightening lean of an accelerating curve, before I consciously realized it. Riding had become as natural as walking or breathing.

Although lower and more rounded than those of the coastal ranges, the peaks of Muncho and Stone Mountain Provincial Parks had the same wildly spectacular northern beauty. The heights were bare, seven thousand vertical feet of exposed red and gray rock, with sharp buttresses and massive fins gentled only by the cascades of gravel slides. Stone sheep, cousins of bighorn sheep, were everywhere. Hundreds of delicate hooves stepped lightly between boulders and found footholds on the narrowest of crags. The rams had huge ridged undercurling horns that framed strong, heavily browed foreheads and deep-set chocolate eyes. The ewes were slightly smaller, and the kids had the baby cuteness of gangly legs, long-lashed fuzzy faces, and perked ears. Many were on the slopes and a few were by the side of the road, nibbling the sparse, coarse vegetation. I slowed my speed to twenty-five but the kids stayed close by their mothers; all the sheep seemed to know enough to stay out of the road, and I had seen no roadkill carcasses. I throttled up to thirty-five. Minutes later, however, coming around a blind corner, a small herd suddenly appeared in the middle of the pavement.

It was one of those surreal moments when time slows and the duration of things that happen in milliseconds stretches unnaturally long. A woman had stepped out of an RV that was pulled to the side, but not off the road, and was walking toward the sheep with a camera, snapping pictures and effectively herding them directly onto the pavement and into oncoming traffic. There was no way to stop and I knew that just behind me, on the other side of that blind corner, a Jeep following a few hundred yards back was about to rocket into the turn. With both the front and rear brakes engaged, I skidded hard toward the left as the sheep scattered to the right. I saw the woman, in her pink sweatshirt and white sneakers, crouching with her camera. Realizing what she had done, she covered her mouth with her left hand, turned her shoulder, and waited for the impact. I narrowly missed three of the St. Bernard–sized animals and flashed a glance in my side mirror as I heard the squeal of Jeep tires locking up on the pavement. They had missed the rest. The indignity and relief of almost, but not quite, getting killed in a combination of sheep and tourist ignorance struck me as funny, and a slightly hysterical giggle fogged the inside of my face shield. It would have made for one of the more interesting obituaries that my hometown newspaper would ever carry: "Local woman killed with herd of herbivores." The adrenaline rush left me nauseated, however, and I had to stop at the next roadside pull-off to breathe and let the shaking in my hands subside. In the silence that followed the flip of the engine kill-switch, my ragged inhalations seemed loud and I could hear the hammering of blood in my ears. There was no point in going back to confront the woman in the pink sweatshirt. I had seen in her posture and in her hand, lifted to cover what might have been a scream, that she knew she had done an incredibly stupid and thoughtless thing and had created a situation where people, as well as the animals that she appreciated enough to want to photograph, might have been badly hurt or killed. I had seen the fear in her eyes. She would remember.

The Alcan climbed up and out of the Toad River valley toward Summit Lake, the last liquid jewel set into the crown of the Stone Mountain range. Mount Saint George rose from the lakeshore to just over seven thousand feet, every crag, crack, and fissure visible in the pellucid air and reflected in the still, black water. The ubiquitous stone sheep were joined by caribou, singles and pairs, that grazed at roadside, their shaggy necks extended and ears pricked for the sound of approaching vehicles. Granite turned to greenery where tall stands of aspen and white fir emerged as the southern entrance to Stone Mountain Provincial Park approached. The highway was broad and empty, climbing the Tetsa River Valley in wide sweeping turns.

In Steamboat, a town that was not much more than a café on a hilltop, I stopped for lunch, climbed up on a picnic table, and sat cross-legged, looking back at the fantastic view of ridge upon ridge of barren mountains, the crags just barely softened in the slight humidity of the day. Native peoples had lived there for thousands of years, but what must early European explorers, or even the men who cut the Alcan through this territory in 1942, have thought of that vista of barren peaks? The stony ridges looked like a barricade, an imposing, impenetrable fortress, and it was impossible from the Steamboat ridge to judge the possibilities for entry between those walls and towers. It was a vast and starkly forbidding landscape.

An older couple had also pulled off the road to admire the view. They walked in silence, hand in hand, toward the far end of the picnic area where the ground fell sharply away. At the edge, they stopped and he put his arm around her shoulders, drew her toward him, and she rested her head on the slope of his chest. Sitting there atop my picnic table with my solitary lunch of sardines and crackers, I suddenly felt very lonely. Where was my road companion? While the great benefits of solo travel include mental space for sustained thought and reflection, as well as interaction with strangers in ways that are muted when one has a companion, one of its great drawbacks is the absence of what that couple in the picnic area had: sharing. The view before them was one that they could breathe in together and it was an experience to be held in their collective memory. Northern British Columbia was something they could talk about, appreciate with one another immediately, or save for reexamination weeks, months, or years hence. "Do you remember that ridge just outside of Muncho Lake? Do you remember how beautiful it was?" I could, of course, save the same memory of the same view, tuck it away in my jewelry box of recollection, padlocked and preserved by the journals I kept, but it wasn't the same. I focused on the view, adjusted my range of sight from the couple in the foreground to the stone-clad ridges beyond, and tried to bring the power and beauty of the mountains back to the immediate in the interest of obliterating at least a part of the tightness in my chest.

The road descended and countryside began to flatten out. With the drop in elevation the heat began to rise, but it was still a perfect riding day: eighty degrees and windless, light traffic and bright sunshine. Road construction began again, but through Fort Nelson it was a matter of a few gravel patches; small tears in the ribbon of pavement that were only wide enough to slow Lucy briefly from an easy galloping pace of sixty miles an hour. I had been warned, however, about heavy road rebuilding in the area, and thirty miles south of town I came upon the hallmark of a badly torn stretch: a line of transport trucks, parked and waiting for the oncoming traffic to pass through the construction zone before they proceeded.

The road crewman, a boy with a stop/slow sign and a badly sunburned face, told me that it would be a twenty-minute wait, and that what lay ahead was fifteen miles of newly laid chip rock. Coated with oil and compressed into the bed below by the weight of either rollers or passing semis, chip rock— before it settled—could create a pall of dust eight to twelve feet high that boiled off the road with each passing vehicle. Construction crews would only allow traffic to move in one direction at a time because visibility was so poor in the midst of the swirling dust that two-way traffic was sure to result in head-on collisions.

For enclosed cars and trucks, new chip rock and the dust that it created was manageable. The worst one got was dirty paneling slightly nicked by flying rocks. For motorcyclists, however, it was like driving through an eighteenth-century Welsh coal mine after a shaft blast: the dust was blinding and clogged every orifice, biological or mechanical. For improved visibility it was best to leapfrog the line to the front of the convoys. Behind the pilot car, the dust was still horrific, but at least one could set the pace and not run the risk of connecting with accurately named chip rocks flying backward off the double treads of eighteen-wheelers at upward of thirty-five miles an hour.

At the front of the convoy, I pulled off my helmet and chatted with the truckers who were engaged in resigned grousing about the time that they lost on the road every day due to the construction. Some made the round-trip run over this patch twice daily, losing as much as two hours as they waited for their turns to convoy through. They recognized, however, the need for the work and no one complained too loudly about having the chance to get out of their cabs and stand around talking and smoking. I asked about the dust ahead.

"It's thick," one driver told me. "They laid the chip rock a week ago and are waiting for the traffic to pack it before they come in to finish and seal the job." It was a windless day and the dust would hang over the road.

The boy with the sign told us that the oncoming convoy was on its way. The truckers shook my hand and wished me good luck as they climbed into their rigs. I closed the vents on my helmet and zipped my jacket up to the throat. The pilot car swung into position, taillights and high beams on. This was not a good sign. The big rigs engaged their gears behind me and we pulled out onto a surface that was happily more stable than I expected. The road base was relatively well packed from the combined tons of the transport trucks of the past week, and although a very shallow gravel top layer made the slow pace of the pilot car necessary, it was manageable. However, as promised, the dust was horrendous. What had been a thin pall of yellow powder in the air as we entered the zone rapidly became dense, billowing drifts. Visibility decreased to forty feet, then twenty, and I kept my eyes locked on the taillights of the pilot car in front of me, and on the patch of gravel immediately before Lucy's front tire. There was no edge to the road that I could see, no center dividing line, and the landscape of green trees and mountains that had been my constant companion for the past many weeks disappeared entirely. From time to time I flashed a glance at my odometer and rode the fifteen miles one mile at a time with the tiny encouragement of the numbers flipping over. The truckers stayed back, vague shapes in the dust, which I appreciated. If I lost control in deep gravel or started to slide in the occasional mudhole, from where they sat in their rigs, somewhat above the ground level dust that swirled around me, they would have time to react. Five miles passed, then ten, then fifteen. The dust began to lift to the thin pall that marked the terminus of the section, and I could see the road crew worker, her sign with the "slow" side held toward us, and the northbound convoy behind her. On firm pavement again, I gave a thumbs-up to the pilot car driver and twisted the throttle, blowing into the sunshine and the wind at seventy, then eighty miles an hour, trying to blast off some of the yellow powder. A few miles past the zone, with dust still coating my faceshield, I pulled over. I was caked in the stuff. Fine as talcum, it was in the creases of my jacket, between laces of my boots, and behind my ears. There was no visible indigo in my jeans and the corner of my pale gray cardigan, which had been peeking unnoticed out from under my jacket, was a muddy yellowish color. The jacket and the cardigan came off and I was attempting to shake them out when the first of the truckers came roaring by. One by one, grinning broadly as they sat clean and dust free inside their filthy rigs, they gave me a blast of their air horns and a friendly wave as they passed. After wiping down my helmet, both inside and out, with a blue bandana that came away ochre colored, and failing miserably to do much about the condition of my clothes, I continued south into the clear afternoon air.

EXHIBIT K: *On Walkabout*

One of the more decrepit automobiles I had seen on the Alcan was crawling up a long slope at forty miles an hour. It was a shade of blue that was not quite green and the color seemed to be peeling off along with large chunks of rust. The driver's side window was down and as I passed I could see a tanned elbow resting on the doorframe.

A few miles later the same jalopy coasted to a stop at the same pull-off where I was chewing a few dried apricots.

"G'day then."

"Hey. How're you doing?"

"Managing. About forty-five miles an hour. Anything faster and the radiator overheats and there are these alarming rattling noises." Glenn was a young Englishman with a slight Australian accent covering his clipped London speech. "Here." He handed me a toffee and I passed him my bag of apricots. He had bought his car in Anchorage the month before and was driving, very slowly, to California.

"Will it make it?" I asked. Up close the car looked like it was afflicted with a bad case of mange and I cast a critical eye over a frame that seemed about to give way and drop through its shocks to its axles.

He shrugged. "It's made it this far." It was a good point and I was in no position to offer advice about the wisdom of any particular mode of transportation. "It doesn't really matter," he continued. "I've lots of time, I'm on walkabout for a year." He grinned. "Maybe three." Glenn was a traveler, a wanderer, at peace with the world and with himself. Whether he got to California next month or next year was irrelevant.

. . .

The setting sun stretched the shadows and burnished the land with all the warm shades of old metal: tarnished silver rivers, oxidized-copper forested hills, and air that glowed with bronze and gold. I pulled into Pink Mountain, population ninety-nine, and home, according to a roadside billboard, of Darryl Mills, a champion bullrider. The fireweed was said to bloom brightly there in early summer, inspiring the town name, although others said that it was a native red-barked willow that made the hillsides glow with a pinkish color in the late fall twilight. Regardless, it was a softly beautiful area and even though I saw neither bullriders nor red willows nor blooming fireweed, I did find a campsite bedded with soft needles on the crest of a low ridge.

A hot shower in the campground bathhouse smelled of iron and sulfur and I stood for long minutes with the mineralized water running down my tired shoulders and back, letting the last of the road dust and weariness wash down the drain before stepping back into filthy clothes and returning to my campsite. A Louisiana couple riding double on a rebuilt chopper—her long auburn hair and his beard caked with the saffron dust of Fort Nelson—pulled into a spot next to mine. They looked exhausted and after a few acerbic comments on the condition of the road, they walked wordlessly toward the showers. I returned to Lucy, checked her belt for imbedded gravel, wiped down her windshield and mirrors, and glanced at the odometer. I had passed the ten thousand-mile mark. The campground store sold beer, and I bought a single can and drank it in my tent in celebration.

IN A CAFÉ IN WONOWON, FORTY miles south of Pink Mountain, I asked a man about the fifteen-foot billboards I had seen that morning: DANGER! POISON GAS! NO STOPPING!

"Oh, it's something about the cyanide gas that escapes sometimes when they pull the oil up." He twisted his ball cap a little tighter onto his head and ran the back of one hand up a stubbled cheek. "We don't worry about it though, it doesn't happen very often." This was not reassuring but as it turned out, poison gas was not the real danger of the morning.

The Alcan Highway cuts through the heart of Fort St. John. Although slightly wider in town than on the outskirts, it is still a single lane going in each direction with narrow gravel shoulders and a deep ditch on either side. At 8:30 in the morning, driving on the left side of the southbound lane, there was little warning and less time to react when a blue pickup truck, driven by a boy of no more than seventeen, forced past me on the left at probably double the speed limit. I edged toward the other side of the lane as his bumper barely cleared my front foot peg, but there was nowhere to go; his friend and racing companion was coming by on the right, one set of tires on the pavement, one set churning through the gravel on the shoulder. For a heartbreak moment, as the boys jockeyed for position and an oncoming eighteen-wheeler appeared in the distance, I was sandwiched between two half-ton pickup trucks. There was no point in locking up the brakes, it would have done nothing but slide me one way or the other, into the side, or under the wheels, of a truck, from which there were now three to choose. A single clear thought flashed without panic, anger, or avoidance into my consciousness: *I am going to die.* The only thing to do was to release torque on the throttle, let the forward momentum decrease with deceleration, and hope the boys got past and away from me as quickly as possible. They did, one pulling in behind the other, a corrugated steel bumper narrowly missing my front wheel. The oncoming truck passed and both darted across the opposite lane and into the parking lots that fronted a shopping center. There they raced and circled one another like overgrown, metal-clad, and deadly puppies.

In the aftermath there was none of the adrenaline rush or nausea that usually follows a near miss. There was only cold, clear anger. Just as the woman snapping pictures and driving sheep across the pavement at Muncho Lake had highlighted, the unfortunate reality was that I could be as solid and careful a driver as humanly possible and still not survive. After driving motorcycles tens of thousands of miles over the course of fifteen years, I was not cocky about my own abilities—such an attitude is ultimately fatal for even the most seasoned of bikers—but I was experienced enough not to make terminal errors. The primary danger of the road, leaving aside darting animals or freakish forces of nature, lay in the stupidity and carelessness of people who thought of nothing but their own entertainment, gratification, or of getting from one place to another as rapidly as possible. It was those people who were going to get me killed.

Dawson Creek is fifteen hundred miles from Fairbanks and is, depending on the way one views it, either the beginning or the end of the Alcan Highway. For me it was the end. On the southern outskirts of town I stopped to buy more crackers, sardines, cheese, and canned vegetables in a large, modern store with gleaming floors and piped-in music filtering through the aisles. There were so many smells: green vegetables, bread and cookies baking, bunches of tulips held in buckets of water, the cardboard and plastic wrap of packages, the detergent used on the floor. There were so many colors: red bell peppers, pink salmon lying on ice, piles of green limes, the graphic designs of soda cans, the pale hues of shampoo bottles. The music drifted over everything in a pastel blanket of sound. It was fascinating and overwhelming. I remembered what Charlie had told me back in Nevada—*Your senses return out here*—and wandered a few extra aisles just to sniff and to see and to hum along with wordless orchestrated music that two months ago I would have found intensely annoying. I like music, all kinds, and occasionally found myself stopping into diners and cafés not only for a cup of afternoon coffee, but to drop a couple of quarters into a jukebox in the interest of changing the tunes that ran through my head much of the day in counterpoint to the backbeat of Lucy's engine. Even supermarket music would do. Near the deli case, in front of a display of canned peas, I hummed the erased parts of John Denver, Whitney Houston, and Dan Fogelberg, remembering the melody lines to sing again later.

I left Dawson Creek and headed southeast on Highways 2 and 43 through Pouce Coupe, Tupper, and Beaverlodge. The landscape began to flatten under the expanding sky of the high prairie. In the lee of the Rocky Mountains, and still too far west for exposure to the unchecked winds that sweep the central prairies, there was a gentle, sheltered feel to the land.

Grande Prairie was the beginning of the Big Horn Highway and the last stop for fuel before the road turned south and ran through hundreds of miles of forest toward the foothills of the Rockies.

EXHIBIT L: *The Lessons of Pain*

The gas station attendant was a pretty girl with a softly curved face and light brown hair pulled back in a ponytail. She was also badly cut and bruised. A nasty healing slash slanted across her forehead, her right eye was a third covered by a clot of purplish-black blood, there were abrasions on her chin, wrists, and elbows, and large green and purple contusions spread over her exposed forearms and across one side of her face.

"What happened to you?"

She gave a short, not quite bitter laugh. "My boyfriend and I were driving go-carts at the track. We were racing and I lost it, rolled, and went through a barbed wire fence." I nodded and avoided saying anything critical. I was sure that she had heard enough of that sort of thing already.

"You're all right?"

"Oh yeah. It looks a lot worse than it is. It doesn't even hurt anymore." She was young, tough, and would heal—as I had healed at her age—with a greater respect for machinery, speed, and control. Lessons learned with that kind of pain are rarely forgotten.

. . .

I filled up with 96 octane and hoped that the hills ahead were not too steep and that the wind would remain light. The next opportunity for gas was Grande Cache, one hundred twenty miles away. I could do one hundred thirty miles fully loaded but that gauge was for rolling, not mountainous, terrain and did not account for blasting side or headwinds.

The top sixty miles of the Big Horn were not particularly interesting. The country was flat, the road straight, and timber companies had been through some time in the last few years to clearcut wide swathes of forest. Many of the strips had been replanted with new trees that grew in military ranks, their fuzzy piney tops about three feet high, the child soldiers of corporate paper production. The lower sixty miles were better, although harder on the gas mileage, as the foothills began. The road lifted and arched, cresting ridges that flowed one into the other, rolling toward the rock wall of the central range in the distance. As the land washed the mountains, the peaks poured down weather in response. Even before the thick black clouds begin to gather in earnest I could smell the rain: a heavy tincture of wood mulch, water, and sulfur that spoke wordlessly of storms descending from altitude. It was no surprise when the first fat drop exploded off my faceshield, and I rode into Grande Cache as brief showers chased blue shadows into the gold of late afternoon sunshine.

Grande Cache is a small community set high on a plateau, strangely beautiful with its tangle of recently abandoned mining architecture, narrow gauge rail lines, coal houses, and chutes, crawling up the hillside. The Smokey River Coal Company, which took its name from the river that runs in the valley below, dominated the industry of Grande Cache from 1901 to the spring of 2000 with the extraction of coal from both open pit and "room and pillar" mines. In contrast to the dark decaying infrastructure, the meadows that surrounded the mine buildings glowed emerald, flashing to brilliance with fleeting and shifting illumination. The valley was surreal in the refraction of light escaping at odd angles through the thunderheads, and the river was shrouded in the haze of passing showers and warm mist rising off the water into the relatively cooler air. Black seams gleamed where the road had been blasted through hillsides, and a shaft, a gaping hole eight feet in diameter, pocked the face of one cut twenty feet above the pavement; a tunnel of darkness leading to nowhere. The pavement was wet but the rain had temporarily ceased and I flipped up my faceshield and slowed. There were no other vehicles on the road, and I did not want to rush through that strange beauty where nature met industry, light met darkness, and rock met mist.

There was movement at the verge just ahead and to the right of the road and I was slowing Lucy further when a wolf stepped out onto the pavement, trotting on slim legs toward the other side. She stopped, not quite to the edge, slender and poised, her coat a mélange of grays and browns. Her ears were alert and forward, standing erect over golden brown eyes that stared directly into mine. She was the size of a large husky, although a little more delicate across the chest and in the bone structure of her face, and one of the most magnificent creatures that I have ever seen. There was something in her stare. It may have been fantasy at the end of a long day of riding, coming into that strange and lovely place, but I could have sworn that there was an understanding that passed between the two of us. We were the same, moving in our solitude through that valley where wilderness and human endeavor came together. I nodded my head to her, she dropped her nose a fraction—*was it in return or just the sniff that precedes flight?*—and then she was gone, totemic, strange, and splendid.

33 | AND WE ARE *HOMO SAPIENS?*

WHITE-THROATED SPARROWS WERE SINGING WHEN I woke to lifting clouds and early morning peeks of sunshine. They have the sweetest voices of all the northern summer birds and I lay in the warmth of my sleeping bag for a few minutes, my hat pulled down over my eyes against the light and the chill, just to hear their solo: one lifted soprano note, followed by three or four altos.

The roads were drying when I left Grande Cache and I ran the remaining eighty-five miles of the Big Horn Highway before breakfast, dancing through the corners and climbing the low ridges, as the Rocky Mountains became larger and clearer in the distance. In the wind a cool morning became a cold day and my hands were beginning to spasm and seize as I rolled into Hinton. The first fifteen minutes of my first Tim Horton's experience since Whitehorse was spent in the ladies' room, running warm water over aching fingers and cursing my own stupidity for not pulling over to put on cold-weather gloves.

Route 16 west out of Hinton rose gradually in banked curves toward the wall of the mountains. A flash of movement to the right caught my eye as a full-grown doe bounded off an embankment, running toward the pavement. She was elegance in motion and I saw the smooth slide of her muscles beneath the sheen of her pale coat, and her eyes wide and intent on the opposite side of the road. A fraction of a second was enough to know that we would arrive at the same point at the same moment if she continued her speed and trajectory. I hit the brakes while she, for a single sharp intake of breath, hesitated and lurched forward again before veering away from the pavement at the last possible second. *Oh Christ, too close, too damn close.* My sternum vibrated with the pulse of a hammering heart. *Don't sweat it,* I mumbled, breathing deeply and resuming speed, *this kind of shit keeps you sharp, keeps you alive. Just keep watching, keep alert.*

With a two-day, ten-dollar entrance fee at the Jasper National Park boundary, I crossed into the midst of spectacular mountain scenery. Enormous rock fins rose out of the earth, great sailfish cresting out of the seas of the valley floors. The mountains lifted their spines, breaching the fragility of the green forest that frothed at the base of soaring ridges. The music began. Breezes became notes in the air and gusts began the hum of melody that is rarely absent in those places where the land stretches toward the sky. The mountains make a sort of pipe organ. Each peak a register of notes, each crag a pipe, a million pipes, a thousand registers, each with its own top and bottom tones: some deep and booming, others a tiny delicate whistle that one must stop breathing to hear. This is the music of the mountains.

Shallow lakes dotted the high valleys just at roadside. Some were black as fractured obsidian with malachite green algae framing their edges. Others were the opaque blue-gray of glacial meltwater. A huge elk, with velvet-covered branching antlers, grazed at roadside. I slowed but didn't stop. Four other vehicles, including two RVs, had already pulled over and their occupants were busy adjusting lenses and setting up the perfect souvenir photograph, much closer to a thousand-pound, sharp-hoofed, and dagger-horned animal than I would have been comfortable with.

There was a sign just outside of Jasper, NEXT SERVICES 153 KMS, and although my gas tank was only a third depleted, I thought it best to stop and top it off. Another biker was at the gas station. Peter was an enormous Australian in his late forties who had stopped playing competition rugby only two years before. Steel-gray, windblown hair brushed his shoulders, small gold hoop earrings were in both lobes, and his eyes were rheumy from too much wind and, as I later found out from his stories, too much whiskey. He had taken his bike apart in Sydney, crated and shipped it to Los Angeles, and then flew to California six weeks later to collect and reassemble the machine that he admitted was his pride and joy. Two months of riding were to follow, if the money didn't run out first, and he planned on spending his final week of motorcycling in North America at the grand carnival that is the annual biker rally at Sturgis, South Dakota. That year marked the sixtieth anniversary of the rally, and as it was the year 2000—millennial even for bikers—it was expected to be a huge affair. We gassed up and Peter bought me coffee in the small restaurant that was a part of the service station. After five weeks on the road, I do not think that he had made peace with the silence. He told story after story, chain lighting the next off the tail of the previous: of weather, of chance acquaintances, of singing at the top of his voice as the miles rolled by, of bottles drunk on the beach, and of waking up dreadfully hungover with little clear notion of even which country he was in. I didn't get a word in edgewise, but he needed to talk, and I was happy to listen.

Outside, other motorcyclists were beginning to collect. South of Jasper the Icefields Parkway stretches to Banff, justifiably famous for its scenic grandeur and consummate engineering. Considered to be one of the best motorcycle roads on the continent, the parkway was a popular weekend run for all sorts of bikers. Finishing our coffee, Peter and I walked outside to talk to the group that had just arrived: six friends, four men and two women, all riding in from Calgary to do the parkway before heading south for the border and the Sturgis rally. They'd been out only one day, their late-model bikes were polished to a high gloss, they wore spotless leathers, and nearly everything was imprinted with the Harley-Davidson logo. Only the men were driving. They heard our stories in brief: Peter's travels from Australia, mine from New Jersey.

"How long have you been riding together?" one man asked. His thinning hair was partially covered by a carefully knotted Harley print bandana and he wore a leather vest held together by chains over an immaculate white T-shirt.

"We're not. We just met. Here, at the pumps," said Peter.

"You're not alone, are you?" one of the women asked, lips pursed disapprovingly.

"Yes."

"Oh, I could never do that!"

"Yes, you could. It's not hard. It's just one day after the next." Peter saw what was happening and grinned wickedly.

"I travel alone, too!" His voice was loud and his Queensland drawl broad. There were silent nods all around. He was a man. It was expected.

They were a decent, friendly group of people, overly image conscious perhaps, but there was nothing reprehensible about any of them. Given that, I was surprised at how I felt as we stood talking. Old and ugly feelings—derision, judgment, and disdain—were rising as I stared at their shiny expensive bikes and listened to them clucking at my "gutsy" but "risky" behavior.

Years before I had backpacked a thousand miles of the Appalachian Trail, walking from Georgia to Maryland in a two-month session in the woods. Although I walked alone most days I knew the other long-distance hikers who were in my general vicinity and who kept roughly the same pace that I did, averaging fifteen to twenty miles a day. Sometimes, coming through campgrounds that were close to the road or weaving our way through the state parks systems, we would meet "dayhikers," or "weekenders," as we somewhat scornfully referred to them. There was a sense that we created for ourselves that we were somehow "serious," professional and tough in what we did day in and day out. Those other people, those clean suburbanites with their new boots, their showers, and their soft beds at the end of the day, they were somehow dilettantes. They carried light daypacks, we noted, left the woods at sundown, and were less deserving of the achievements given by the mountains. It was all bullshit. We were not better, stronger, or more worthy of the mountains, having spent weeks instead of hours in their shadows and upon their shoulders. The us-them divide that we created based on how heavy our packs were, how filthy and ragged we became, and how long we stayed in the mountains before going into town to resupply was only an attempt to make heroic what was simply a rather unconventional lifestyle. In hindsight, I realized that there were other more positive, less exclusionary ways to do this. What really mattered was whether we all, distance hikers or dayhikers, enjoyed our time in the woods for as long as we were there. So what, years later, was generating this feeling of scorn that I felt for those clean and polished bikers? Was it because I was tired and getting ragged? Was it because my bike was a bit older and had a few more miles and dents on it than theirs did? Was it constantly having to defend that I was a woman and that I drove alone that made me look with contempt at those carefully dressed ladies who rode behind their husbands, appropriately matching leather accessories holding back their hair? I didn't like the feeling, it was ugly and petty, and I buried it rapidly. *What is really important here? Is it miles, clean or frayed clothes, polished or battered paint jobs? No.* What was important was they were out enjoying the road, enjoying their bikes, and showing the world in the best way they knew how much they loved what they were doing. After twenty minutes of conversation we all saddled up with the promise to try to meet at a bar called the Broken Spoke in Sturgis a few weeks hence. Peter shook my hand, and with a pirate wink headed north on Route 93 as I headed south.

There was a narrowing of pavement twenty miles south of Jasper, where two lanes of southbound traffic became one so that each vehicle could stop at a ranger checkpoint to have their park pass examined. At the merge, a speeding minivan passed me on the inside, the driver nearly clipping my front forks as he dodged in front of me. He had succeeded in getting one car length ahead and had nearly wiped me out in the process. It was the third time in as many days that I had nearly been run off the road due to other people's lunatic behavior, and my last shred of composure disappeared. I didn't care if the driver was six-foot-three, drunk, and had a backseat full of crowbar-wielding friends. I didn't care if he hadn't "seen" me. I didn't care if he was rushing to be by his wife's side as she delivered their first child. Anger at inconsideration gave way to rage. I pulled around the left side of the van where it had stopped to wait for the single car ahead of it to drive through the checkpoint and hammered a black-gloved fist on the driver's side window. *Bang. Bang. Bang.* The glass shuddered.

"What the *fuck* is wrong with you?!" I screamed the words through the glass. A wide-eyed face looked back at me. The man was in his late thirties, with a short black beard covering a weak chin and a seat belt deeply creasing his stomach and chest. The wife, a similarly soft-faced woman, cowered away from the confrontation on her husband's side of the car, her ears and shoulders shrinking together as she cringed against her door. In the backseat two children, an older girl of perhaps ten and a little boy of maybe six, stared at me with slack mouths. The driver did not roll down the window and did not answer my question. This was understandable considering the circumstances. Not only is there really no appropriate response to "What the fuck is wrong with you?" but I was completely beyond any semblance of rationality. He probably thought that if he rolled down the window to say anything to me that I would grab him by the throat. He was right. "It means *that* much to you to get there first that you have to cut me off to do it? Are you out of your *fucking* mind?" The car in front of us pulled ahead and through the checkpoint. The driver was still staring wordlessly at me, eyes momentarily flickering to the open space and clear road in front of him, unsure of what to do. "Well go ahead, *asshole.*" I slammed my fist one more time against the window, rotated my wrist, and pressed the back of my hand, middle finger raised, against the glass. The tires squealed and the minivan went through in a cloud of rubberized smoke.

Generally, confronting people in cars or trucks while driving a motorcycle is not a good idea. Sheer mass and quantity of reinforced steel is always in their favor. But this man, in concert with the incidents of the previous two days, had pushed me past the point of caring. Rage is, however, not a good road companion and I clearly needed to get off the pavement for a while, both for my own safety and for that of the people I was beginning to feel the need to beat senseless with a torque wrench. I took the narrow, windy, potholed, and just barely paved access road toward Mount Edith Cavell and the youth hostel at its base. My guidebook listed the hostel as "rustic" as it had no electricity. I hoped this also meant that there would be a lack of minivan-driving tourists.

The hostel was closed when I pulled into the gravel and packed-dirt driveway, but a sign said that it would reopen for new guests at 5 P.M. It was a small cluster of buildings: a simple house and office for the manager and two bunkhouses, one for men the other for women, with a communal kitchen and common living-room area between them. An outhouse was set well apart from a water pump at the far end of the parking lot. I found a chair and a small table on the deserted back porch and ate crackers and a tin of smoked mussels for lunch. Breathing in the cool mountain air, I felt the morning's anger dissipate, clarity return, and a deep weariness settle in. It was time to stop driving for the day and to spend the afternoon walking through the meadows and between the small lakes that lay at the feet of the great peaks. It was time to look for a little peace in stillness.

The Angel Glacier is an extrusion of ice that waterfalls hundreds of feet down from a saddle linking a buttress and the main peak of Mount Edith Cavell. A thousand feet above the valley the iceflow spreads horizontally across the ridge and up the slope of the mountain, forming the "wings" of the angel. The "body" hangs below; not quite vertical, fragmenting and temporarily suspended, thousands of tons of green- and gray-tinged ice hovering above a strangely lovely curry-yellow lake. A smaller, lower glacier blankets the southern end of the valley, moaning an irregular hollow song as it calves into the opaque water. The Angel shifts and sighs its own dirge from above. The frozen masses are celestial in form, the winged ice luminous with crystal and trapped sunshine, but they are also deadly storehouses of avalanches, given the combined forces of gravity and the natural weakening processes of the summer melt.

A popular area with dayhikers and tourists, and easily accessible from the road and the parking lot below, all of the trails that approached the Angel and the lake were heavily posted with warnings in several languages about the dangers of hiking on or beneath the glacier. I stopped a moment to read them before walking to the far side of the lake, where I spent much of that afternoon morbidly watching what looked like an advertisement for Darwinian selection.

It was a warm day and I ran my hands over ice-polished stones in the shallows of the clouded water, listening to the distant groan and creak of ice. From the Angel above, rivulets of water ran down the exposed face of the rock into the snowfield that lay between the lake and the face of the mountain. I watched incredulously as a family of five, three children and two adults, climbed onto the snowfield and began the traverse of perhaps a quarter mile of open space directly under the body of the glacier. Halfway across, the reverberation of what sounded like cannon shot, but what was actually an avalanche letting go on the Angel's left wing, filled the air. A dull rumble preceded the fall of rock and ice, and thousands of pounds of rubble cascaded off the edge of the glacier with the roar of artillery. Mother and Father took off at a dead run, outpacing their children and leaving them behind. Had the avalanche not been interrupted by a high horizontal ledge, regardless of the parents' speed and sense of self-preservation all five would have been buried in the fall. There was a horror-movie quality to watching the little family group slow to a walk and continue their amble across the snowfield. The movie became truly surreal when a group of Japanese tourists followed them, stopping only when they reached the point directly below where the avalanche had let go. They stopped, sat down on a jumble of large boulders, and looked up expectantly.

Sometimes I think that most people have become so far separated from the natural world, inside the protection of their homes, cars, and fire department–staffed communities, that they forget that the forces of nature are real, uncontrollable, and can be deadly. The power of the wilderness, its weather patterns, climate zones, and animal inhabitants, has become sanitized and pacified through the postcard windows of our television sets, movie screens, and glossy coffee-table books of pretty photographs framed by quotes from Thoreau, Emerson, Muir, or Hillary. How else can one explain the tourists that are gored or mauled every year as they attempt to get close to wild buffalo, or bears, for a candid photo opportunity? How else can one explain otherwise intelligent people who climb into the mountains on a summer day, lightly clad, unprepared, and headed for the peaks only to die of hypothermia and exposure when the altitude and the weather change? What were those Japanese tourists, climbing underneath the fall of a hanging glacier, thinking when they had just witnessed the reality of an avalanche? What were they waiting for as they looked up at the tons of ice above the heads of their children, their spouses, their friends?

In the late afternoon light I walked back to the hostel, appreciating the slower perusal of the brightly colored individual wildflowers that tended to turn into a spangled blur at fifty miles an hour. Orangey-red indian paint-brushes nodded their heads on shaggy stems, huge golden dandelions echoed the bright sun above, and the soft tiers of fuchsia fireweed bloomed their brilliance just back from the road's edge. Beyond, in the valleys where dark stands of firs and pale green meadows shared space, small black lakes gleamed with a mirror finish, reflecting the few white puffy clouds that sailed across the deep blue sky.

That evening, after finishing the few chores that would pay for my night's stay, I perched on a tree stump in front of the hostel, looking down the fall of the Tonquin Valley toward the towering rock wall of The Ramparts. The looming slope of Mount Edith Cavell rose above the valley to the left in snow-laden horizontal ridges tapering to a bare pyramidal summit. The clouds were starting to build and collect in the western distance. They clenched in violet-edged fists and occasionally let slim shafts of light from the setting sun through their fingers to bounce off the crags of the mountains. Where the rays struck, the snow glowed pink and gold with the odd flash of refracted illumination. The colors in the rock deepened as the angle of the light decreased: deep grays, greens, thin veins of burgundy. The music had begun again, the sonata of a single instrument played by the sun. I stayed to listen, and to watch, until the light faded to darkness.

THE JAPANESE WOMAN WHO HAD ARRIVED at the hostel late the previous evening talked with me as we loaded up in preparation for the day ahead. It was an extraordinary conversation for a number of reasons, among them that her own motorcycle stood parked beside mine. She traveled solo and was tiny to the point of fragility. Although she was an inch or two taller than my five foot three, I probably outweighed her by twenty pounds. Her glossy black hair was cut in an ear-skimming bob that framed a delicate, almost elfin, face. Dark designer jeans encased her slim legs and a Hermès silk scarf of beautiful color and pattern was knotted around her throat. Our conversation was limited as her English vocabulary was probably not more than one hundred words, and my Japanese was nonexistent, but what she told me, through single words, chopped phrases, and pointed references to the map spread across my gas tank, impressed me greatly. Her name, as close to the pronunciation that I can approximate, was Kisiael. She was a university student in her home country and had flown to Alberta six weeks earlier than the English course, which she was planning to take in Edmonton, would begin. Carrying two duffel bags and a selection of bungee cords, she had walked into the Edmonton Honda dealership, bought a single piston four-stroke 250cc Savage, bungeed her bags to the frame, and taken off into the Canadian wilderness for a month of solitary riding.

On any machine this took guts, but on the one she had it took more than that. Her bike was tiny, almost toylike, when parked beside the heavy steel contrast of Lucy's frame. It was new certainly, and Honda had a fine reputation for mechanical solidity, but where people often questioned the power and small size of the bike I rode, at 1200ccs Lucy had nearly five times the power and was half again as heavy as the Savage. However, Kisiael told me that for her this was a big bike; at home she was used to driving the 125ccs. In three weeks of riding in Canada she had had only one problem: one of her duffel bags, lacking a rigid frame, had collapsed onto a superheated exhaust pipe. The pipe had melted through the fabric of her bag as well as through the case of her brand-new microthin laptop computer on which she had intended to take travel notes and do her school work.

"Very bad, Karen. Very bad. Computer no work." She chuckled a little as she showed me the melted and twisted backing of a sophisticated piece of electronic equipment. I doubted whether product warranties would cover a situation such as that.

Kisiael was an amazing individual. Her English was minimal; she had no previous experience with traveling in North America; she knew little of the people, the culture, or the customs of Canada; and she drove a bike that was much better known for its urban agility than its long-haul capacity. Yet she did what few people attempt: a solitary multiweek trip through some of the highest and most demanding paved-road motorcycling that the continent had to offer. Through eighteen U.S. states, four Canadian provinces, fifteen thousand miles of riding, and close to three months on the road, I never met anyone like her. Her curiosity, humor, love of the road and of motorcycles, as well as sheer bravery inspired me for the rest of the trip and beyond.

Heavy clouds were beginning to build over the Icefields Parkway as Lucy rumbled and climbed with the curve and slope of the pavement. It began to rain steadily and despite stopping to put on a rainsuit, I was drenched within fifty miles. By the time I passed the lower glaciated reaches of the Columbia

Icefield, the rain was sliding in sheets across the road on the back of a howling wind. Route 93 bent and twisted upward, passing what I assumed were spectacular overlooks, but which were now views to nothing but wooly banks of moisture generating clouds with a sense of yawning space beneath them. High on the central ridge, surrounded by barren sweeps of gravel and ice, the temperature fell and it would have been bitterly cold even without the precipitation. Northbound RVs and tour buses blasted by, sending up sheets of water to join those already on the downward trajectory, and as the visibility decreased, I knew that the Parkway was no place to linger. As the day progressed into afternoon it was only going to get wetter, colder, and more dangerous to be above the treeline, wedged between the Athabasca and the Columbia Glaciers, and sharing space on a contorting road with vehicles much larger than Lucy. By the time I passed the Icefields Center I had lowered my head, hunkered in behind the partial shelter of a moderately paced motorhome, and was taking the ride mile by mile. On a better day I would have liked to stop at the center, to have learned more about the glaciers that continued to sculpt those peaks, but as it was I thought it best to use the brightest hours of the day to get through the weather, south and down off the ridge. The Parkway eventually began to drop in a series of switchback turns to Saskatchewan Crossing. The pavement bed was cut directly into the rock faces and the descent reminded me of that coming off the Continental Divide on Route 82 into Aspen a month back, except that that ride had been in the sunshine. The rain waterfalled off the rock cuts, cascading down the faces, blowing in icy veils off the summits, and pouring directly onto the asphalt in gushing downspouts. It was challenging driving with tight turns, water-sheeted pavement, and side-blasting wind. I started to shiver. Shivering was not an entirely negative thing as the spasms, running across my shoulders and down my arms, broke some of the road condition–induced muscle tension. It also forced me to take the deep breaths that would both still some of the more violent tremors and center my thoughts on the immediate road rather than the horror of the weather.

Thoroughly wet, shaking with the cold, and beginning to feel the physical exhaustion of several hours of tough driving, I was relieved to see the gas station plaza at Saskatchewan Crossing. I parked Lucy with a grateful pat on her gas tank, pulled my helmet off, and looked at the sky. Was it possible that the rain was a bit lighter and the sky was a slightly paler shade of churning gray? I went inside the restaurant and spent twenty minutes in the ladies' room with my hands under hot running water, slowly thawing out. Marginally warmer, I bought a steaming coffee and a bowl of chili and sat away from the windows, hoping that when I next looked out the view would be different.

The interior din was that of the rushing tourists, the bleep of cash registers, and the rodent squeaks of plastic lids being fitted onto styrofoam coffee cups. Tour buses pulled in and disgorged thirty to fifty people in a burp. They quick-stepped from their enclosed environments on wheels to the enclosed environment of the station. Toilets flushed, the hot-air hand dryers added their tinny voices to the din, candy bars and coffee were purchased, and the people hustled back onto their buses to be whisked away. *Was this their mountain touring holiday? Did they ever get off their buses and into the weather and wind?* I hoped so. Thoughts like this, though not quite charitable, were a perverse necessity to keep moving through weather that was truly foul. There had to be a belief in the value of experiencing "reality," no matter how ugly and rain-driven it was. Why else would any relatively sane person get back on a motorcycle to ride through unambiguously disgusting weather? I tossed my empty chili bowl into the garbage and almost gladly stepped outside into diminished wind and rain.

The rain finally stopped as I drove out through the foothills of the mountains, leaving Route 93 for Alberta Highway 11 east. The long slow corners of 11 bent in a great arc, east and slightly south, giving downward sloping views of small lakes and huge peaks; Mounts Loudon and Michener standing off the main ridge in solitary grandeur. Highway 11 was the road that would take me to an appointment that had been anticipated for decades and planned for months: a meeting with my biological father, Dave, and his family at their home in Innisfail. The first prickle of nervousness ran up my spine as I followed it east, running with the failing light toward the Canadian prairies. It was getting late, it had been a hard day, and I was ready to find a place to camp, to rest, and to mentally prepare for the following day.

An eleven-year-old girl and her father, whom I had spoken with at the gas pumps back at Saskatchewan Crossing, had told me that all the campgrounds within forty miles of the parkway were booked solid. Their information unfortunately proved correct; it was, after all, the height of the summer season, and I drove fifty miles before I saw a campground sign not hung with an additional "full" placard. By Crescent Creek Campground I was more than tired, and although the provincial park sign by the side of the access road warned of four miles of unimproved gravel ahead and suggested "pass at your own risk," I was willing to try it and hoped fervently that there was a clear spot at the end of the road where I could pitch my little tent and collapse for the night.

Crescent Creek is named for the waterfall that spills over the edge of a new moon–shaped parapet into a pool of turquoise froth. Just past the falls, the road turned left, paralleling the upstream creek, deeply shaded by fir trees. I had had about enough challenges for the day and was not delighted to see that the road crossed a wide intersecting stream at the bottom of a sloping gully by means of what looked like concrete railroad ties half buried in the stream bed. The campground was on the other side. I kicked Lucy into neutral and got off to look at the crossing. Green algae grew in patches on the concrete and the water was deep enough to come a third of the way up my tires. It was going to be wet and slippery, but I was too tired to drive back to the road and begin looking for another spot to spend the night. A steady pace was what was called for; too slow and there would be no momentum to get up the incline of the other bank, too fast and I would lose traction on the algae. I stepped back from the stream and watched the headlong rush of water toward the falls. There was a lot of rain shedding from the mountains and I wondered what the flow would look like in the morning. Would it be passable? *The hell with it, tomorrow will take care of itself.* I stomped Lucy's shift back into first gear, gunned her across the stream, up the bank, and into the campground beyond.

Stan and Sarah were the campground "hosts." Hired by the Albertan and British Columbian governments, they were one of the many delightful pairs of retired couples who were happy to spend their summers living out of their RVs in park areas where they managed the paperwork, fee collection, and general welcome wagon activities. Stan settled me into a campsite marked by a picnic table, a sheltering grove of firs, and a gravel pad for Lucy. "There you are," he said, "nice and quiet. Why don't you get set up and come down and tell us about your adventures?" The light was fading, most of the clothes I owned were soaked from the deluge of the Icefields Parkway, and I hadn't eaten anything since Saskatchewan Crossing. We agreed that perhaps a morning chat would be better. Stan got back into his pickup truck, reversed a few feet, and then stopped. "Oh, one more thing. Walter might come to visit you. He likes young ladies, but he's harmless."

"Walter?"

"A juvenile elk. He wanders through quite often, just to sniff around. But he doesn't bother anyone."

I was too tired to care about baby elk, or anything else that did not involve immediate food and shelter, so I thanked Stan for the warning, draped my clothes over Lucy's handlebars and luggage, set up my tent, shook out a mercifully dry sleeping bag, ate some peanut butter and crackers, and crawled into bed. Oblivion was immediate.

At 5 A.M. I woke with a start, fully awake and listening hard. There was something large, something not human, moving outside the tent. A footfall close to the fabric wall sent tiny reverberations up through the tent floor. It sounded more like the fall of a hoof than it did the stamp of a soft padded paw with large claws attached so I carefully unzipped the screen and fly of the tent, wiggled forward on my stomach, stuck my head out, and looked directly into the large brown eyes of an elk. So this was Walter. He had been snuffling at the fabric of my door, head lowered, front hooves slightly apart, and as such we were nearly nose to nose as I emerged. He was a gorgeous animal, already large, standing more than four feet at the shoulders. Nubbins of first-year antlers sheathed in brown velvet poked up between his large erect ears, and his deep brown, almost black, nose quivered as he sniffed at me, backing away.

Stan and Sarah were up and talking to another camper as I strolled down the road to make good on my promise to come and chat with them for a few minutes. Sarah saw me first and greeted me with bright eyes and a wide smile.

"There she is!" She turned to her guest. "She's the one I was telling you about, the girl on the motorcycle."

"Mornin', Sarah. Hey, Stan. Guess what, Walter came to visit this morning."

"He does like the young ladies." Stan shook his gray head and chuckled. "It must be the perfume or the shampoo."

I laughed. "I'm not really sure about that. I haven't seen perfume in a couple of months and my last shower was three days ago."

An hour later I waved good-bye to Stan and Sarah. They were inside their RV fixing breakfast as I crossed the stream and made my way back to the road to begin the ride toward Innisfail, and Dave.

THE ROAD TO INNISFAIL HAD ACTUALLY begun months before I saddled up Lucy and drove west, out of Princeton, out of one life and into another. Meeting my biological father, Dave, and his family began with a single phone call to the Calgary dispatch office of the Royal Canadian Mounted Police. Four thousand miles from where I sat chewing the ends of my fingers, a policewoman took what must have seemed a very strange message. She phoned Dave on his office extension.

"A woman called claiming to be your biological daughter," she said.

"Give me her number."

"She said . . ."

"Give me her goddamn number."

Four months later, I sat in the cool of his kitchen on a hot Alberta summer day, and Dave told me that he had been waiting for that call. Waiting three decades. "I knew you would call," he said, "hoped that you would, but I was afraid that you wouldn't."

In the spring of 2000 Dave was fifty years old. He was a constable, had been married twenty-three years, and had three daughters who ranged in age from sixteen to twenty. None of his girls was aware of my existence. I was thirty-one and a graduate student finishing my final semester of a master's degree program. In late March I made that phone call and did what I had sworn I would never do: invade the life of a man, a family, who had not given me direct permission to do so. But I had no other choice.

There was a tumor lodged in the musculature of my chest. It was small, soft, a slight convexity of the skin just to the left of my sternum, but growing rapidly. Like so many other women do, I stupidly tried to ignore what was happening. I was active, healthy, about to start a new job in a new city, and planning a motorcycle trip that would take me to Alaska for the summer. There had to be another explanation for the protrusion just above my heart. I played soccer in a men's league, the game was fast and rough, and occasionally I took hard body blows. *A subdermal hematoma, that's what this is,* I told myself, *nothing more.* I was too young, I thought, for the obvious to be true. It wasn't logically possible and it wasn't the right time for this to happen. *It will go away; next week it will be gone.* Next week came and it was still there, just a little larger. My boyfriend finally noticed what I did not want to see. One morning in early light he moved the hair off my shoulder and ran two fingers gently from my collarbone to sternum.

"What's that?"

"It's nothing." His eyes narrowed. His mother had died of breast and lung cancer a few years before and he knew denial when he heard it. A half hour later he sat, livid and finally silent, as I called the campus health clinic. That afternoon, a nurse and two doctors later, an oncologist asked me for a cancer-related family medical history. I didn't have one. I had been adopted as an infant and knew nothing of the health of my biological mother, or father, or of their respective families.

"You need to think about making some phone calls," the doctor told me. Her voice was low, gentle. "This is probably nothing but it would be helpful to have as much information as possible."

. . .

Dave was little more than a boy in the summer of 1968, a promising baseball player with an athletic scholarship to a college in the Seattle area, when his girlfriend, Gloria, became pregnant. Gloria, a fragile-looking eighteen-year-old with clear blue eyes and a will that belied her stature, was both unable and unwilling to tell her conservative Scotch Protestant family and alcoholic father about her pregnancy. Ethically opposed to having an abortion, she suggested to Dave that they do what seemed the simplest thing: leave town. He agreed. They told their parents that they were going to explore Canada together, a few months of an on-the-road education before they returned to British Columbia, to universities, to traditional futures. He would play baseball and go to school and she would enroll in secretarial college. It was all lies. The truth was that they needed to buy a little more time; time to decide on their relationship, time to decide if they could build a future together, and time to decide if they could be parents to an unplanned child.

They drove to northwestern Ontario, to Sudbury, a city where there was work: hard-rock mining a mile beneath the surface for Dave, and a job in a Sears paint department for Gloria. They had a tiny walk-up apartment, bills, no family, few friends, and as the months went by and Gloria's slim waist grew thick, a relationship that fractured as their arguments became more frequent. The fighting was constant, over everything and nothing, and eventually he left to go back to British Columbia, back to take the certainty of the baseball scholarship over the unknown of a difficult relationship and a baby that was coming soon. Gloria was six months pregnant and stayed on alone, refusing visits, too proud, too stubborn, and too ashamed to admit to her family that being in Ontario was anything other than an experiment with independence. Dave came back once to try and work things through. He loved Gloria and thought that they could make a life and a family together, that if they just talked enough they could make it work. They couldn't. A few weeks later he was gone again, this time with the final realization that, whatever their relationship had been, there was nothing left to salvage. However, the question of the child, Gloria's child, Dave's child, still loomed large.

. . .

"Is this going to be OK, Dave, are you sure?" I asked. "Because it doesn't have to happen right now."

"Oh no, it's fine. Everybody wants to meet you. They're all excited you're coming."

I had phoned a final time from a gas station in Nordegg to let him know that I was on my way. He thought it would take me an hour and a half to get to Innisfail, maybe a little more, and he would be waiting. I hung up the receiver. The gas station yard, a quarter acre patch of dirt, was occupied by two men, one of whom was tinkering under the hood of a broken-down Jeep caked in mud that was inches thick on the frame and in the wheel wells. As the man working on the V-6 cursed and dropped wrenches past the engine block and onto the tacky ground below, the other sat, feet on the dashboard, rolling and lighting a joint as thick as my pinkie finger. He sat back, inhaled deeply, and watched as I stepped out of the booth.

"Here." He held the joint toward me, his single word wreathed in smoky exhalation and the easy camaraderie of the road. He looked at me with a sleepy grin, scanning my wild hair, battered leather, and filthy hands through half-closed eyes. "You want some?" I considered the joint for a moment. My heart was pounding with the conclusiveness of the phone call and I could feel the dull beat of blood in my neck and ears. The appointment was final. I was about to meet half my biological family, including three half sisters, one of whom would not be entirely pleased to see me walk through the door of her home. Perhaps a hit would do me good. Then again, I was driving a motorcycle and going to visit a man who just happened to be a police officer.

"Thanks man, but the bike. You know."

He nodded slowly. "That's cool."

I fired up Lucy and slowly drove back out onto the highway. Eighty miles later, in the town of Caroline, I stopped. As a guest I couldn't arrive empty-handed; my mom had taught me that. I pulled over at the liquor store and went in for a bottle of wine. Red? White? My dad liked the French cabernets and some of the Australian shirazes. What did Dave like?

On the outskirts of Dickson I stopped one more time. A quick glance into one of Lucy's side mirrors confirmed what I already knew: filthy roped hair, a dirt-streaked face, and clothes that hadn't been washed in two thousand miles of hard riding. A stop at a campground that advertised both showers and washing machines was just what was needed. There was no way that the engine grease stains were ever going to come out of my trousers, but I told myself that I should make the effort to look relatively well put together. I would be late, but I thought that clean clothes and shampooed hair might give me some much-needed confidence. *And where was my mascara and eye pencil?* I hadn't seen them in weeks but I knew they were somewhere in the bottom of my pack. I dug until I found the cosmetics, but ended up not attempting the eyeliner. As it was I nearly blinded myself in long-unpracticed mascara application.

The shower, a dollar for ten minutes, washed away most of the dirt but none of the fear. Beginning to panic, I tried to remember how easy it had always been when I spoke with Dave over the phone. His voice was a smooth baritone, pitched a little higher than what I imagined a police officer would sound like, and I knew that he wanted to see me. I had called several times between New Jersey and Nordegg, to let him know where I was and that I was safe and well, and each time I offered him the opportunity to back out if a meeting was going to be too difficult for his family or for himself. What I was also offering was the chance for him to save me from my own cowardice. As much as I wanted to meet Dave and his family, I was afraid. What if his daughters were resentful and hurt by my presence, by my very existence? I already knew that Jenn, the eldest, had deep concerns about her place in the family, now that this stranger, this older sister who wasn't a sister, was coming into their lives. Was she still the oldest? Was she still her daddy's first girl? What did his wife really think about me, the illegitimate evidence that he had once loved another woman? Would we find things to talk about? Would the silences be awkward? What would happen if they did not like me, if they felt like I was an intruder, if they did not want to see me again? Even more problematic, what would happen if we all grew to trust and respect one another and wanted to continue this relationship? What would that relationship be? I already had a family to whom I was intensely loyal. I was a daughter and a sister to other people in other places. I couldn't be a daughter in both families. Or could I?

There were no answers to be found in advance and other basic questions also loomed. What did I want to know, and what could I do about, the cancers that ran like black threads through the fabric of Dave's family? Regardless of what our emotional relationships would eventually be, we all shared a common genetic heritage.

The timing of my arrival in Innisfail was in some ways fortuitous; the majority of the immediate family would be there, staying at Dave's house. His one surviving sister and her husband, as well as their closest family friends, had arrived a few days before. They were coming in from all over British Columbia and Alberta, coming mostly for a vacation and a visit. But there was also a funeral.

She was six when she died, this latest victim, a tiny girl with an obscenity of a tumor that wrapped around the back of her brain and sent tendrils into her spinal column. It was inoperable, and they buried her the day after I arrived. Three years before it had been Dave's sister. Marianne had been a woman with a personality as vibrant as the paints she mixed for her surrealist canvases. She traveled widely and had great passions for life, art, and creative living. In a horrible display of prescience, the year before she was diagnosed with the breast cancer that eventually took her life at the age of forty, she painted a canvas that foretold what was to come. The central figure was a woman, nude and forced onto her back by a swarm of nightmarish creatures that writhed across her abdomen and up over her breasts, teeth bared for the jugular. The title of the painting was written in careful pink script that followed the border: "We'll See How Brave You Are."

When they cut the tumor from my chest I lay on my back, naked from the waist up, fully awake, and listening to my surgeon discuss with her assistant whether she should rent that house on the shore for two thousand dollars a week or go with something more affordable in the mountains. My father had taught me to be stoic, but bravery was not something I could readily muster, and a few tears slipped, thankfully unnoticed, into my hair and ears. The smell of burnt flesh hung in the air as seeping blood vessels were cauterized, and the growth was pulled from the lips of the incision. It was a yellowish lobed thing held in a fine web of the bright red capillaries that had fed it. Ultimately it proved to be nonmalignant. As my surgeon removed the stitches a week later she told me that she expected not to see me again, but to watch for this sort of thing in the future. She reminded me that with a family history like mine, strange growths, nonmalignant or otherwise, should be dealt with aggressively.

The irony of it all was that I was ultimately grateful for the threat of cancer that had opened the doors to Dave and his family. In the months between the first phone call from my dorm room and the last phone call from Nordegg, I had learned that his family was delighted that I had contacted them, that they did want to see me, and that the real tragedy would have been if I had never come looking for information.

. . .

Dave telephoned Gloria a few weeks before she had her baby. In their time apart, both had done some serious thinking about love, life, and their unborn child, and each had come to a very different conclusion. Gloria had spoken with the Children's Aid Society and was proceeding with her plans to give the baby up for adoption. She recognized her position: young, unmarried, without the support or knowledge of her family, lacking in education and marketable skills, and too inexperienced to properly care for a child in the ways that she believed children should be raised. Her personal goals and aspirations had also yet to be realized and she felt that she was not ready to become a mother in all of the ways that were unrelated to biology. She did her research and knew that the Aid Society's screening process for adoptive parents was exhaustive. They would find the sort of family and stability for her child that she felt she could not provide herself. For his part, Dave had spoken to his parents, confessed that Gloria was carrying his child, and that he had realized something deep within himself: he wanted to be a man, a father, and wanted to raise his child. His parents agreed to help him. He and the baby would come back to British Columbia, and if Gloria wished, she would come, too. Together they would raise the child that, despite the social stigma of illegitimacy, he still wanted as his own. Over the phone the two discussed their very different visions for the future. Gloria refused to have any part in Dave's plan.

Moreover, she refused to surrender her baby to it. Dave's father, as well as her own, had struggled with alcohol abuse for many years. Although neither man was violent, both were emotionally distant and could be viciously cruel in how they verbally expressed themselves to their families. Dave had faith that things would be different for his baby; he was confident that he did not have the same issues with alcohol that his father did. He also believed that as his father aged, he was coming to terms with his addiction and would be a much better grandfather than he had been a father. For Gloria, even the possibility of her child growing up with the paternal relationship that she herself had endured was anathema. They argued; Gloria was adamant and hung up the phone. When the dial tone cleared Dave called a lawyer.

I was born in April of 1969, and instead of going back to British Columbia with Dave or to a new adoptive family, I was in foster care for four months until the family courts made their final ruling regarding the adoption. As the unmarried father of an illegitimate child, Dave had no rights under Canadian law of the time to make a decision regarding my future. In August an Ontario woman, who had married a Danish immigrant, adopted me and shortly thereafter our entire family moved south of the border permanently, to Massachusetts, where I spent my childhood.

Gloria stayed on in Sudbury, with too little money and too much pride to go home. Finally, her family called in late August and offered to send her a bus ticket and help her enroll in secretarial college, if only she would come back to British Columbia. She did.

Dave, emotionally ravaged by what he saw as the loss of his child, did much to try to destroy himself. Although he did go to Seattle and attempted to play baseball for the college that still wanted him enough to have deferred his scholarship for a year, his heart wasn't in it. Within months he had given up the game, dropped out, and become a drinker and brawler. There were several nights when he tried to convince a Marine recruiter to send him to Vietnam. Young men of many nationalities had been coming back from Southeast Asia in body bags for years and he thought that perhaps the U.S. military might not say no to an inebriated Canadian who really wanted to go. Fortunately they did.

Five years later, Gloria admitted to the man who would become her husband that she had given birth to a daughter, but for twenty-five years she never discussed it with her family. Dave's family knew, as did the woman who eventually became his wife, and they grieved with him, but there was nothing that they could do but wait for a phone call that might or might not come.

. . .

Innisfail was small and quiet, a prairie town with a clear-day view of the Rockies ninety miles to the west, and I had no trouble following the simple directions that Dave had given me over the phone that morning. Fewer than seven thousand people lived clustered around a short main street with a few shops and a couple of restaurants. The town was girded by the industry that employed most of those who were not wheat farmers in the region: a couple of meatpacking plants, a Ralston-Purina factory, and several light-manufacturing operations. I had driven eleven thousand miles to get to Innisfail—agricultural and blue collar, unpretentious and thoroughly unnoticeable—and the knots in my stomach and the dryness in my mouth told me I should just keep driving. Instead I pulled onto Dave's street and scanned the mailboxes for his number.

The house was surprisingly normal. I'm not sure what I expected, but there it was on a corner lot in a quiet subdivision. Like the homes that surrounded it, the architecture was unremarkable: two stories, a peaked roof, bluish gray exterior paint, a large second-story deck built up on pressure-treated six by sixes, a fenced yard, and a detached garage. Opposite the garage, on the far side of the street, I dropped my kickstand and rested Lucy slightly uphill, her front wheel angled toward the house. I didn't feel like I should pull into their driveway, into their garage, into their lives. Not yet. After one more deep breath, I cut the engine, pulled off my helmet, and unzipped my jacket to the waist. With neither the rush of the wind nor the altitude of the mountains, the prairie heat was instantaneous and enveloping. I pulled the key from the ignition and looked at the house again. A man stood under the shadow of the open garage door, watching me.

"Where have you been? You're late. I was worried." He was smiling broadly. "Another five minutes and I was about to call the patrol to see if there had been an accident." He sounded very much like a father berating his daughter for not calling to tell him where she was.

I swung off the bike and moved toward the garage, apologizing, explaining the wine, the shower, the laundry, and then just stopped in the middle of the street to look at him. So this was my biological father. His hair was thick and prematurely silver. A bristling mustache dominated the lower third of his face, not quite obscuring his grin. He still had the powerful shoulders of the ball player that he had once been and the stocky physique of a man whose lifestyle and profession kept him in good physical shape. He wore a T-shirt, long shorts, and had the bare feet of a man who had just come running down the stairs without thinking to put shoes on. Under dark eyebrows his brown eyes were piercing, quizzical, and reflected at least a little of my own nervousness.

I stood in the sunshine as his eyes raked over me. I had Gloria's light brown hair and clear blue eyes and although my stature was small, I had the strong athletic build of his other daughters.

"Just like the rest of them, not very big." He paused a moment and we stood there looking at one another for a few seconds. "I don't know what to say . . ."

I walked toward him.

"Hi," I said. "It's been a long time." I reached to put my arms around his neck but he stepped forward first and caught me in a crushing embrace.

His voice was low, almost lost in the tangle of my hair. "It's been a very long time."

Later that afternoon Dave and I walked together, out past the golf course and the edge of town, on paths that followed fields and skirted the road grades, the rhythm of our strides filling any gaps or awkwardness in conversation. There were few enough of those. Strange as it was, we picked up some sort of friendship, a thread that bound us together, as if it had always been there, waiting. Perhaps it had. We talked mostly about his family, his work, and how these two central parts of his life had developed. Dave and Colleen had met the year after he returned from Seattle, and he had proposed less than a month after their first date.

Dave joined the Royal Canadian Mounted Police on his second attempt and in doing so realized a dream that had been his since boyhood. The work wasn't always easy and it was rarely routine but he felt the importance of what he did each day. A week before I arrived, he had been on call when a tornado touched down in the Pine Lake Campground twenty miles north of Innisfail. There were six hundred camping and motorhome sites there, most of them occupied, when the twister blew through, tumbling and crushing cars like tinfoil and blowing apart the fragile walls of motorhomes. One hundred forty people were injured and twelve people, including a two-year-old child, died. Dave was called in to pull bodies from the wreckage and to search for the missing. He told me of his shock, of his initial disbelief at the suddenness and the totality of the destruction, and of the sadness that still lingered. The traffic deaths that he saw in the normal course of patrolling the highways, brutal as they sometimes were, were more understandable to him than a freak act of nature that spun people hundreds of feet into the middle of a churning lake that had been placid only an hour before. He looked at me, surprised, I think, by the recitation of his own emotions.

"I couldn't tell the girls," he said. "They don't need to hear all that. Maybe they wouldn't understand. But you, you've seen things like that, haven't you?" I nodded, thinking of the half-dozen former war zones. "You understand." I did, not only those elements of his life that dovetailed with my own experiences, but I understood him on a more basic level. I understood him through instinct rather than experience, through intuition rather than evidence. It was, again, the thread that connected us.

People sometimes ask me if I was ever bitter about being given up for adoption, if I felt discarded or thrown away, if I held a tiny corner of rage for the people who had given me life, but not a home. I never did. My parents built the reality of a family with the children that they had adopted using all of the tools that are critical in any successful family: love, loyalty, patience, acceptance, and I never questioned what the concept of a family was as I had one almost from the very beginning. Parental love was never lacking. It was never verbally expressed in our staunchly Scandinavian household, but it was demonstrated in a myriad of ways. My parents are not perfect, and our relationship has not always been smooth, but considering how much they wanted to adopt children, and how hard they tried to give my brother and me what they believed was a proper upbringing, I intuitively understood that the converse part of that arrangement—that of giving up a child—must be an agonizing decision for those who have to make it. Rather than anger, when I thought about my birth parents I always felt a sense of sadness, not for myself, but for them.

Dave told me about Gloria, the flashfire of their romance, the volatility, the passion, and the destructiveness of their togetherness. He shook his head. "There was a time that I would have done anything for that girl." I believed him.

We walked back to the house in the afternoon heat. In the cool of the kitchen, Dave handed me a beer and we sat at the table talking until the girls arrived home. I was nervous when I heard their feet running up the stairs to the deck and kitchen door and suddenly it all felt strange again. Who were these girls? Half sisters? New acquaintances? Lindsay was first. She was a pretty sixteen-year-old, her father's baby, and a two-in-the-morning worry. All teenage fashion and long-limbed attitude, she walked with a spring in her step that matched the insouciance in her eyes. Melissa was next, the middle daughter, nineteen years old, friendly, smiling, outwardly calm, and with a riot of short, spiked hair that spoke of personality that might not always be as placid as her outward demeanor suggested. They shook my hand, poured ice-filled drinks, and dropped laughing into kitchen chairs. "Ohmigod, you're really here! How weird is this? How long can you stay? No, it has to be longer than that!" Jenn, twenty-one, blonde ponytail just brushing the back of her sunburned neck, arrived last, tired and dusty from a long day spent cutting grass for the municipality. She eyed me warily, clearly not as pleased to see me as her sisters. She pulled off her shoes and dropped into a kitchen chair as far away from me as she could get.

"Hi."

"Hi, Jenn."

"You're here."

"I am."

"How long are you staying?" She wasn't rude, not cold, just cautious, suspicious, and I could well understand why she might feel unenthusiastic about my presence in her kitchen. Moments later, as she got up to head for the shower, she announced that she would be spending the evening with her boyfriend and not to expect her back until late. Dave frowned and I stepped in before he could say anything.

"It's OK, Jenn, you and I can talk later."

She stared at me. "OK." She turned and left the kitchen without a backward look. She just needed a little time to sort things through, she needed to see for herself that I was no threat to her, or to the way her family operated. I watched her go and smiled at Dave.

"It's all right."

Colleen, Dave's wife, was on her way up the stairs and I stood up as she came in the door. She looked at my extended hand, walked past it, and wrapped me in a teary hug.

"Oh, we're so glad to see you." Her arms tightened and she rocked me back and forth like a little girl.

It was a marvelous couple of days, overwhelming and intense. Dave's sister Brenda and her husband, Mack, arrived from British Columbia, and I spent long hours sitting on the porch in the evening dusk, a beer in hand, as Brenda, Colleen, Dave, and various combinations of the girls tried to tell me thirty years and more of family history in three days. Brenda especially saw in me shades of her sister Marianne and talked with a cathartic intensity about Marianne's life, her travels, her art, and her final year. Brenda had been Marianne's caregiver in those awful, and strangely beautiful, final months when she had helped her sister die, telling her every loving thing that she ever wanted to say, and trying to hold on to her for as long as possible. She spoke of the drugs, the pain, Marianne's friends; both those who stayed to help and those who couldn't bear to watch the damage that the cancer eventually wrought. Dave sat in his chair, leaning against the rail of the deck, listening, silent, his eyes lit with pain. I knew that Brenda spoke of Marianne as much for herself as for me. In my restlessness, my motorcycle wandering, my solitude, and independence, Brenda saw her dead sister, and for moments, looking at me and talking of her, Marianne might have been alive again.

In those evening conversations, Marianne became real to me, too, and this was both joyful and frightening. Who knows if, how, and where temperament, interests, and proclivities are fused into the genetic code? If it were true, that Marianne and I shared something of the same spirit and the same curiosity for experiencing life, the other question that had to be asked was: what else was hardwired into the genetic code that I shared with Marianne? Was that my fate, too, to burn with intensity as a young woman and then ultimately to lose everything to a horror of disease? Brenda said that I reminded her of her sister and I carry her words today with celebration and dread.

For me, those long evenings were necessary but they had a surreal quality that took me months to sort through. I am sorting through them still. It was like coming upon an alternate reality, and I thought a lot about the "what ifs" of my childhood, of my parents, of my own family vis-à-vis theirs. If Dave and Gloria had made slightly different choices all those years ago, the family stories and present realities that they explained to me on those summer evenings might have been mine, and all of my experiences, from childhood to adulthood, that I had had in my own family's embrace, might not have existed. I love my own family absolutely and unconditionally and would never "trade" them for Dave and Colleen and their daughters, even if such a thing were either possible or desirable, but I thought that if things had been different, that if somehow I had grown up in their household instead of my own, I might very well have been happy there, too, but for different reasons. Oddly, and perhaps appropriately, it was Jenn who brought these two realities together.

On my second evening in Innisfail, Jenn sat with me at the kitchen table and asked what I thought of her town and her family. I told her as honestly as I was able to what I had seen and heard, and how much I valued the openness, candor, and welcome of her family. She was quiet for a moment and then asked, "And what about your family? Do you have brothers and sisters? What are your parents like?" I told her about Massachusetts, my older brother, and how we were alien to one another as teenagers but how we were now finding more common ground as adults. I told her about my parents, how much I loved the relationship that I shared with my father and how he and I were so alike in our interests, values, and career choices. Jenn and all of her sisters had trained in figure skating since they were small and the things that they could do—jumps, spins, and complicated designs on the ice—were completely beyond me. She giggled as I admitted that I could barely skate backward without hurting myself. Later that afternoon, I put Jenn up on the back of Lucy and we drove through town. She wrapped her arms around my waist, laughed into the wind, and when we came back to the house, driving smoothly into the garage, she told her dad that she wanted a motorcycle.

It would be all right.

Melissa came in at 5 A.M. to hug me good-bye. She had to be on the golf course for work at her usual early hour. At 6 A.M., unable to sleep anymore, I switched on the bedside alarm clock and listened to the local pop radio station, thinking about the incongruity of leaving when I felt that I had just arrived.

By 7 A.M. I was packed and loaded. Breakfast was unusually quiet. From time to time I would catch the eye of Colleen or Dave and realize I had been staring at them, or they at me. I think that each of us hoped that this would not be the last meeting, but at the same time wondered, what if it was? There is a lot of road between Alberta and New Jersey, and a lot of emotional space between the family that they are and the family that I would be returning to.

Breakfast finished, we trooped outside, took pictures in the backyard, and speculated on the day that lay ahead for both them and me. There was a tightness in the smiles that emerged when those final photographs were developed and everybody was trying to hide the fact that they were crying. They were a warm, open, and demonstrative family; something that I liked very much, and something that my own family was not. Colleen held me in her arms. "You come back soon," she said, and I promised that I would try and work something out for Canadian Thanksgiving. Lindsay hugged me and ran back inside the house so that she wouldn't have to see me leave, and Jenn crushed me fiercely before stepping away. Dave walked with me out to Lucy and wrapped me in a long hug. "I'm really glad you came." It was a simple statement and everything that needed to be said.

I pulled out of Innisfail through fields of bright yellow rapeseed, and hayfields vivid green with the new growth that would be the second cutting at the end of the summer. A few slow tears slipped down the inside of my helmet and I wondered if it was possible to live in two lives, and in two families in tandem. For the family I had just left standing in their Innisfail backyard, I wondered how they were feeling at that moment. They had made it clear that they considered me a daughter in their household. What did they feel as a daughter, just returned, rode away into the clear morning sunshine toward the western mountains?

PREOCCUPIED WITH THOUGHTS OF THE PREVIOUS three days, I noticed little about the towns I passed through as I retraced my route back into the mountains. The flow of the land was endlessly fascinating, however, and I watched as fields interspaced with woods gradually gave way to deep stands of forest. Streams flowed out of the rising wall of the mountains, so clear that, unless marked by bridges and culverts, they were unrecognizable as water. The breeze picked up, bright and blustery, filled with sunshine and gusts that exhaled short bursts of sound and pressure as they moved past my helmet. In the long chute of a valley leading into Saskatchewan Crossing the wind gradually intensified to a blasting howl, broken only by the force of Lucy's windshield, as it funneled over and across the open expanse of Abraham Lake.

Jumbled peaks and massive glaciers overhung Route 93 running south, painting the pavement in broad bands of light and shadow a half mile or more across. Occasionally, as light refracted off a glacier, there was a greenish tinge to the air and a fishbowl feel to the landscape. Lucy flew through the curves, leaning into the light, swift and strong with the energy of solid steel and liquid motion.

Just north of Banff I turned right, onto the spur road for Lake Louise and the Victoria Glacier. One of the things that I had resolved to do in the course of my trip was to drink tea at the Chateau Lake Louise, a grand 1920s-era Canadian Pacific hotel. I didn't care how much it cost, it was the principle of the thing, a *Breakfast at Tiffany's* fantasy, and I wanted to be Audrey Hepburn for half an hour. I parked Lucy in one of the dusty visitors' lots two hundred yards downhill from the chateau and walked up a curving drive lined with carefully trimmed hedges and elaborate flower beds, toward the hotel. The chateau's east wall rose at the top of the slope, flanked by turrets and cut by regular rows of windows: a silvery castle on the shores of a glittering lake. A man wearing pale gray and green lederhosen and a soft peaked hat with flowers tucked into the band stood in front of the massive doors playing an alpenhorn. His deep sonorous notes flowed over the lawns to meet the tourists walking up from the parking lots, as well as to greet the guests who left their keys with the valets and their luggage with the bellhops. The lobby had thick, plush carpeting, an inlaid marble floor, heavy dark furniture, and a concierge wearing a better suit than most New York executives. Three young ladies, bridesmaids from some elegant wedding, swanned around the lobby and sitting areas, carelessly dangling large ribbon-wrapped bouquets of deep red and pale pink roses from manicured fingertips, their burgundy and gray chiffon gowns swirling on the floor behind them. All as expected. I spent a few minutes wandering the ground floor, looking for the most suitably glamorous place for my tea and found four options: a dining room done in hues of cream and gold, a café-style restaurant, a bar with deep leather chairs and an impressive array of single malts, and a coffee shop. What I also found were polished windows too small to let the vista of the lake and the glacier really enter, but through which came hints of the staggering beauty beyond. The heavy carpets, drapes, chandeliers, gilded mirrors, and carved wood were suddenly close and oppressive. The hell with the fantasy and the carefully constructed indoor spaces, I was going outside. With my five-dollar moccachino and a three-dollar slab of banana bread—one corner dipped in dark chocolate—I went to sit on a concrete bench placed between the shaped balsam hedges that edged the lake. The far view of the Victoria Glacier was wonderful; a bastion of ice overhanging the clear turquoise of Lake Louise, which sparkled blue and white and gold in the hot midday sun.

The postcards and calendar pictures of the Lake Louise valley, which I had seen before leaving New Jersey and on which I had based my Audrey Hepburn fantasy, showed the chateau in its wooded setting: silent, beautiful, and seemingly far from civilization. It appeared to be a wealthy mountain monastery where a decent Sapphire gin and tonic could be had in the evening, or a slightly less-turreted version of Germany's Neuschwanstein castle transported to the Canadian Rockies. The near-view reality was not quite as I had imagined, however. The lakeshore paths were strips of asphalt clogged with tourists of all shapes and ethnicities trying to capture in a few photographs the beauty of the lake, the glacier, and the construction of the hotel behind them, with the inclusion of as many assorted relatives as possible. At the end of one of the paved paths was a boathouse, a charming cottage jammed with people lining up to rent watercraft at twenty-nine dollars an hour. Paddleboats and canoes bumped against one another, clustered on the near shore. With a huge lake to explore, the boats stayed close to one another and to the boathouse, tight as a group of goslings. My fantasy pictures never showed people, jostling overpriced rental canoes, dusty parking lots, busloads of tourists, or unhappy teenagers being dragged down paved pathways by parents doggedly committed to seeing the sights. I did not begrudge the other tourists for their numbers and their posing. After all I had come to see the same things that they had and we were all voyeurs of luxury in an extraordinary setting. However, the reality of Lake Louise was much more that of an amusement park than that of a cloistered world apart, and I did begrudge the ruin of my Holly Golightly fantasy.

A warm day was turning hot as I took the 93 bypass skirting Banff. Banff was rumored to be a gorgeous alpine town, but I had had enough of sightseeing and civilization for the day and was enjoying the open road, the rush of wind, and the mountains slowly lumbering past. Falling off the western ridges, 93 slid deeper into British Columbia in long, slow, westward turns through Kootenay National Park, following the Kootenay River gorge in deserted splendor. Signs tempted hiking at places like "Marble Canyon" and "The Paint

Pots" but at lower elevations the heat became even more intense and I drove on, riding the cooling breeze of Lucy's motion down an empty road.

Away from the wheeled congestion of the Icefields Parkway, my road company was largely of the four-legged sort. A cow moose raised a dripping muzzle from a drainage ditch, but never stopped her slow horizontal mastication of the green water plants that dangled from her mouth, and an hour later a coyote tripped across the road on slender legs and delicate feet. He stepped lightly as if the pavement was warm on his pads while his slim face and large ears turned toward Lucy's engine.

The late afternoon sun was hot on my back and helmet as I pulled into Radium Hot Springs. Like Lake Louise or Liard Hot Springs, Radium was another famous spa and resort and I had originally thought to stop and swim in the pools. With no calendar shots or postcards to shape my view of what Radium would be like, I had imagined it as something akin to the wooded natural beauty of Liard. There would be shade and sun, narrow walks and paths, cool waterfalls, hot pools, and steaming glens set back in the forest. I would park Lucy in the shade for a couple of hours while I swam and soaked. Unfortunately, it took only a few roadside moments to realize that Radium had been developed in ways that Liard had not, and I hoped never would be.

It had been eighty years since the construction of the Radium Hot Springs Lodge, another grand resort hotel, had sealed the fate of the springs and had begun the process that has cemented over whatever natural beauty there might once have been. If there was still a wooded glen standing among the clusters of condominiums and hotels that crawled up the sides of the narrow valley, I never saw it. Where naturally radioactive springs had once bubbled out of the rock and into the forest, tiled and concrete artificial pools, dug just below the level of the road, baked in the white heat of the day behind fenced, gated, and monitored paid entrances. People wedged themselves into the swimming areas by the hundreds. I kept rolling.

The heat had risen to where the rippling waves were palpable, coming off the road and out of the slow stroke of Lucy's V-twin. I stopped frequently for long swigs of water from the bottle I kept jammed between my T-bag and camping gear, and I wished for the thousandth time that I were not so para-noid about taking off a layer or two of protective gear in the blistering heat. I took another long gulp of water, unzipped my jacket to the waist, and headed for the border.

Waiting in line at the inspection station, I had only two cars ahead of me; but as Lucy coasted to a stop and the movement of air was reduced to nothing, the minutes of motionlessness stretched unnaturally long. Sweat ran down my torso, soaking my tank top and the waistband of my trousers. Roosville, British Columbia, felt like one of the lower levels of hell.

In the nine times that I checked through the U.S.–Canada border I never had a problem at customs. I had met many bikers, of the long-hair, tattooed, male sort, who had had their gear stripped from their bikes piece by piece as customs officers, looking for narcotics and concealed weapons, went through everything and even peered up exhaust systems with flashlights. Although slightly road worn and ragged, being a woman helped me as I did not fit the "profile" that often resulted in lengthy stops at the border for other two-wheeled travelers. The tone of the encounter with the officer in the guard booth at Roosville was, therefore, somewhat of a surprise. She was a slim, hard-faced woman with bleached hair and dark eyeliner. Severely plucked eye-brows lowered over a sharp nose as she ran my license plate through her com-puter. Her voice was curt and brittle, and all of the usual questions with none of the pleasantries followed. She had the look of someone who was going to enjoy taking me apart and I was sure that my luck with courteous officials and speedy crossings was about to change.

"Are you carrying any firearms, narcotics, or tobacco products?"

"No ma'am."

"Let me repeat, do you have any firearms or narcotics?" I could see her writing out the slip that would allow another officer to strip my bike. It was going to be an ugly afternoon.

"No ma'am."

"Where are you from?"

"New Jersey."

"Where are you going?"

"Back to New Jersey."

"How long have you been in Canada?"

"About three weeks."

"Where have you been?"

"The Yukon, Alberta, and B.C." She paused, stopped writing, and looked at me for a long moment. Her face softened.

"You're a long way from home." A smile played around the corners of her mouth and she nodded her head in amused understanding of how long this journey had already been and what was still to come.

"Yes ma'am, I am."

"Drive safely." She waved me through and, a bit puzzled at her shift in attitude, I crossed the border into Montana.

Eureka was the first town and I stopped for gas and groceries and drank an entire bottle of iced tea while reading the cover story of the *Montanan Standard*. It seemed that Sonny Barger and the rest of the Hell's Angels were having their annual gathering and vacation outing in Missoula that week, and police presence was expected to be heavy. *Aha, I get it now.* Did the officer at the border think I was some sort of an outrider for the Angels, on my way to hook up with the gang in Missoula? It explained her initial frostiness. The newspaper's front-page picture was of Barger. He was photographed with three fingers closing the hole in his throat, a memento of cancer surgery, so that he could speak to the reporter. At his side was one of his lieutenants, a massive, black leather–clad man with a goatee and a spill of dark auburn curls that fell well past his shoulders. Although there was little to admire about the criminal activities of the Hell's Angels, I did have to laugh at Barger's quote, given in response to a clearly nervous reporter's question about the expected behavior of the Angels in Montana: "We're just like your neighbors, only better looking."

The store clerk and I spoke briefly about the heat. The thermometer had pushed past one hundred degrees, and fires were crawling through the forests of Montana and southern British Columbia. It was the worst fire year in decades, and nearly nine hundred thousand acres of Montana and forty thousand acres of British Columbia would burn before the summer was finished. "The bush is tinder dry," he said. "One spark and she's gonna go up." I could see the unfortunate truth in his assertion as I rolled south out of Eureka. No fire had burned through the underbrush in a generation or more and the piled snags and detritus of the undergrowth were optimal tinder for a lightning strike or a single carelessly discarded cigarette. Should the Eureka valley ever begin to burn, with the fuel stockpile and the soaring temperatures, it would rapidly become a firestorm version of hell. I ran Lucy hard, up and out of the valley, seeking the higher elevation and the coolness that I knew I would find in the upper reaches of Glacier National Park. I was also running to make the park entrance before the sun started to slip. I had been told that the Going to the Sun Highway was one of the most beautiful roads in America, a sight especially glorious from the saddle of a motorcycle, and I wanted to be there by the late afternoon as the angles of light began to change. The country got higher and more rugged as I followed Route 93 south and east to Whitefish and turned left with the intersection of Montana Route 2 at Columbia Falls. The heat was still intense, but marginally less as the tiniest of alpine breezes began to shift the heavy, stagnant air.

Near the park's western boundary, a pipe spring spilled out of a rock cut near the end of a gravel pull-off. Slowing Lucy to a stop in a patch of shade, I stripped off my jacket, walked past a curious family of four getting back into a car that had all the windows rolled up, and dropped my head and neck under the continuous flow of water coming out of the pipe. The shock of the icy liquid nearly dropped me to my knees but I stood, letting it soak through my hair and wash the caked sweat from my jawline and neck.

I had just rinsed my bandana and knotted it, still dripping, around my throat when another biker pulled up on an old, but obviously well-loved and repaired chopped Harley. He was whippet thin with a battered black leather vest, filthy jeans, and tangled chestnut brown hair pulled back in a single elastic. Dunking his head, much the same way as I had, he came up sputtering.

"Whoo-whee, that feels good!" He shook his head like a dog coming out of a lake. "Hot one isn't it?"

"You got that right."

"You going into the park?"

"Uh-huh. I hear good things about the Highway."

"It's a great road. I come up here and ride it four, maybe five times a year. Don't never get tired of it neither. Here, I got something for you." He handed me a slip of paper that looked like a grocery receipt. It was an entrance fee proof of payment for Glacier National Park for the thirtieth of July 2000. "It's good all day, so you won't have to pay at the gate."

This small subterfuge was an example of three of the things I liked about the biker subculture. Neither of us was trying to cheat the U.S. Park Service, which probably needed all the funds it could get considering the Bush Jr. administration that looked like it would be coming in following the November election. We were, rather, thumbing our collective noses at car culture. It is an irksome thing to most bikers, myself included, that tolls and fees that apply to cars are hardly ever lowered for the motorcycle-driving public. It is rare when the base "vehicle fee" differentiates between four and two wheels even though we motorcyclists take up less space, get at least three times the gas mileage of an average SUV, generally drive more cautiously, and never throw cans or bottles out open windows.

The second thing we were doing in that small exchange was bending "the rules" just far enough to feel the glee of circumventing "the establishment," whatever that might be. Contrary to popular belief, the majority of bikers live within the limits of the law and are functioning and contributing members of their communities, as well as of the greater society. Bikers work for a living and for the maintenance of their machines—although not necessarily in that order—they pay their taxes, and most live at fixed addresses and are kind to their spouses. There is, without a doubt, the "one-percenter" subculture consisting of individuals who are social renegades in the criminal sense. These are the people who came to the general public's attention after a 1947 biker rally in Hollister, California, turned into a drunken riot. In the aftermath, a well-publicized photograph, which some claim was staged, showed a young man surrounded by crushed beer cans sitting with his feet propped up on the handlebars of his motorcycle. The image was assumed to be emblematic of bikers and their culture, and politicians of the time labeled those involved in the Hollister riot, most of whom were World War Two veterans recently returned from the Pacific Theater, as "vicious scum" and "the lowest form of human animals." In response, the American Motorcycle Association issued a statement claiming that 99 percent of motorcyclists were law-abiding citizens. In the public discussion that followed, those bikers who were *not* law-abiding citizens took the moniker "one-percenters" for themselves. Fifty years later, the vast majority of bikers still lead lives respectful of the legal code, but I do think that most are attracted, at least in part, by the perception and the potential reality of "freedom," in either the spatial or psychological sense, that driving a motorcycle creates. Clutching out with your left hand and accelerating by twisting your right is still an atypical thing to do in North America, where most people over the age of sixteen drive automobiles not motorcycles. Step across the saddle of a bike and you instantly become an outlier: something a little unique, something a little dangerous, and something a little more free than is normally allowed. What boy has not been told, "Don't drive those things, they're dangerous!" What girl, since the subject of girls driving their own motorcycles is still mostly a nonsubject, has not been told, "Don't go out with boys who drive motorcycles. They're dangerous!" Is it the boy who is dangerous? Or the bike? And so it goes. Those who actually do reject these narrow social conventions about what one must and must not do pertaining to two-wheeled transport often find themselves seeking other minor ways to flout "the system." The roadside exchange of an entrance-fee receipt was a small, silly thing, but it was a nod toward operating outside the norms of expected behavior.

The last thing that was happening at that roadside spring was that which I valued most of all: in that tiny slip, which saved me all of five dollars, was an explicit expression of solidarity. Motorcycles are a great leveler of humanity and an enormous point of connection between people who take them, and their riding, seriously. You may have a thirty-five-thousand-dollar custom machine straight off the dealership floor, and I may have a six-hundred-dollar fourth-hand clunker with a suicide clutch and three gears out of five that actually work, but we are both out in the same wind and the same weather. Both of us are going to get hit with splattering bugs and have to watch for the same ignorant parent chauffeuring their kids to piano lessons who just doesn't "see" us as they make that left turn across our lane. We are all going to see the beauty of the landscape, to inhale its scents, and to experience the lift and drop of the road from a very different perspective than those within enclosed vehicles do. Regardless of race, class, gender, creed, language, or sexual orientation, regardless of whether we talk for five minutes or spend an evening over burgers and beer, and regardless of whether or not we ever see one another again, we are going to have common ground. We are bikers. At a gas station I have never seen anyone step from a car, turn to a stranger getting out of another car, and say, "Hey, you drive one of those, too? Isn't it great? How's it running? How's the road ahead?" This happens all the time between motorcyclists. Motorcyclists are a vast and fractured family, with different priorities, prejudices, agendas, foci, and abilities, but they are a family nonetheless. I never asked the name of my biker-brother at the pull-off and he never asked mine, but he had a kind word for me, and did what he could to make my life just a little easier, even if it was only to hand me a park entrance receipt.

Glacier is a rigging of peaks that spans the border of two countries, linking a U.S. state and a Canadian province. Rising from ten-mile-long, four-hundred-foot deep Lake McDonald, which marks the western boundary of the park, the Going to the Sun Highway roughly bisects Glacier on an east–west access. It is a magnificent road, one of the top five that I traveled that summer. The pavement twists, climbing in long, rising grades up the sides of mountains that sail across the landscape like stone-prowed ships churning through an ocean of deep green forest. Bare top-spars of ridges crest thousands of feet above the treeline, lifting their stark rigging of glaciers into the clear air. The ice drapes in thick, gleaming, blue-white sheets off the heights, and grinds its way back down into the elevated depths of the high valleys. The road climbs through it all, a breathless two lanes that occasionally knifes through a projecting flying jib of golden stone. Low boulder-built walls gird some of the turns that swing above particularly precipitous drops, but for the most part the road is what it appears to be: a serpentine route that climbs with little pretension of absolute security, up to sixty-seven-hundred-foot Logan Pass. The Going to the Sun Highway is not a thruway for those with vertigo problems or for those who want rapid travel.

At Logan Pass, where low-growing indian paintbrushes blazed orange among yellow columbines and purple asters, and bear grass lent vertical elements in puffed spears of white, I stopped to admire the microcosm of the flowers and the macrocosm of the ringing peaks. Near an overlook I saw a flash of moving white fur and spent long minutes watching a small herd of mountain goats. Two animals were nestled, legs folded beneath them, in the deep green prickly softness of stunted juniper, while four others bounded along the crags above, nibbling at grasses and making impossible leaps from one rocky hoofhold to another. Nearer, only a few feet from my boots, a marmot rustled and snuffled through the undergrowth, her coat all the dusty shades of grays and browns that helped her blend into the rocky landscape.

The eastern road down from the pass was less steep and less dramatic in comparison to the enormous vistas on the western side, but it was still a spectacularly beautiful route. At the Weeping Wall, a fractured stream spilled off the top of a black rock face, cascading and shredding into a moving veil of running water and mist. The slanting rays of the setting sun turned the airborne droplets into liquid prisms and sheathed the wall in a shimmering blanket of rainbows. The pavement arced and fell to Saint Mary Lake, and the eastern approach to the park. A bow-shaped body of stream, glacial melt, and spring-fed water, Saint Mary is held within the clenched bare hands of the surrounding jagged mountains. At the Wild Goose Island overlook I stopped to eat a nectarine and watch the sun slide behind the looming peaks. The lake was silver, just stirred to luminescence by a light breeze shifting over the water. Near the center a small island with four huge fir trees was silhouetted black as the last rays of the sun streamed past it. The ringing peaks blazed a final brilliant obeisance to the day as mercury, amber, bloodred, and ochre light flowed down the ridges, erupting from the slopes in rivers of color, as if the pressured and glacier-scarred upthrust of land had suddenly become volcanic. The music of the mountains filled the huge space between water and sky and the enclosing ridges seemed to bounce echoes of light and sound from clifftop to carapace and back again. After all the miles, all the beauty, and all the fantastic spectacle of sea and land that I had seen over the course of those past many weeks, what was laid before me at Wild Goose Island overlook made me weep.

EXHIBIT M: *Appreciation*

I was still sitting on the edge of the overlook, watching the last liquid-silver shimmer of the reflected day, when a heavyset man in his forties came puffing up the hillside, walking the path that rose from the water's edge. He nodded a quiet hello and sat some distance away. His breathing gradually slowed and then there was silence. When he spoke he kept his eyes on the lake.

"Twenty-two years ago I worked here in the park and spent a summer in a cabin on that shore. Sometimes I think I would give anything to be there again." It was joy, not loss, that was in his voice. I heard no regret in those few words, only appreciation for what lay before us now and what he had been lucky enough to experience as a young man. How fortunate we are when we can understand and value what it is that we have in a given moment, and what an additional gift it is when we can carry that understanding and those values with us as we travel through life.

. . .

37 | ALWAYS THE SUPREMACY OF THE NATURAL

BEYOND THE IMMEDIATE SHADE OF FRONT porches or pine boughs, the air was thick, heavy, hot, and still. With temperatures forecast for more than one hundred degrees, and fires consuming thousands of acres of Montanan forest every day, what was usually a cool and beautiful state had become an ashy, overheated furnace. The television news reported that forest fires were spreading east and south, and clouds of hazy smoke, blowing in from the western horizon, were visible as I rolled out of Browning. As I had no interest in getting caught behind a line of flames, it was time to run, south for the Wyoming border and Yellowstone, staying at least a jump or two in front of the smoke, more than that ahead of the fires. Intense lightning storms were also forecast for the late afternoon and evening and I wanted to get through and out of the high, open rangeland and down toward the shelter of the Absaroka Mountains before the day stretched too late.

The country between the Two Medicine and Sun Rivers expanded into an immense grass landscape; huge and open, yellowish green in the haze-coated air, a stark contrast from the previous few days' ride through wooded and enclosed mountain spaces. There were no trees, rock cuts, or mountain ridges to impede or segment the vistas from the tops of the undulating hills, and the view from the crown of each lift in the prairie encompassed an unfettered line of sight to where the anemic blue sky met the horizon and leached into the white burn of a summer day. Lucy sang an open song as I shifted through her top gears, and we skimmed over the hills exposed, alone, and wonderfully free. It was so easy to edge the pace higher and higher. I hadn't seen a police officer in days. Perhaps they were all in Missoula hanging out with the Angels? At a long sloping stretch I ran Lucy up to sixty, then seventy, eighty, and ninety miles an hour. She was a powerful machine for her size: we hit ninety-five miles an hour, and could easily have flown faster. Wide-eyed mule deer watched a few yards from the pavement, ears lifted long and alert above their delicate faces, as I whistled by. Occasionally a flash of white painted metal glittered at roadside. The state of Montana had placed as many small white crosses as there had been deaths at the sites of highway wrecks. The memorials were an attempt to remember the dead, but even more so to remind the living of the fatal consequences of excessive speed and inattention. After a few miles of earthbound flight I slowed Lucy to an easy seventy-mile-an-hour pace, thinking of my own reaction time, the speed of bounding mule deer, and the small white crosses beside the road.

Route 89 through Dupuyer, Miller Colony, and Choteau was scenic and well maintained. Away from the usual tourist routes, the lack of cars and RVs on the gently curving rural roads of Montana was noticeable. When I did spot a vehicle, usually from miles away, it was invariably a pickup truck or the occasional Jeep. In fact, the greatest concentration of car parts I saw in northwestern Montana was in a marvelous roadside sculpture. Two Plains Indians sat on horseback near Choteau. They were made entirely of recycled bits of Chevys and Fords, with fifties-era shades of turquoise, bottle green, pale pink, and bright red, creating the war bonnet hues of the figures and the palomino dapple of their steel horses.

After passing what must be one of the world's flattest golf courses, all eighteen holes on one level surface, and the oddity of two Bactrian camels grazing in a roadside corral, I stopped in Fairfield for gas and a cup of strong black coffee. A man, who later introduced himself as Sam, was propped up against the station wall using the pay phone when I emerged from the store.

He was medium-sized and had eyes the same color as his sun-browned skin. A beer gut pear-shaped what would otherwise have been a symmetrical figure and tattoos marched up both arms. A greasy hat was jammed down over graying hair and both his jeans and T-shirt, from which the arms had been torn off, were well ventilated and none too clean. But Sam was polite and genteel in a small-town way and had a grin that lit up his face when he smiled. As I stuffed an extra granola bar and a pack of chewing gum into my saddlebags he asked what would become the standard question for the next few days: "Are you going to Sturgis?"

"I'm not sure. I hadn't planned on it especially," I said, "but since I'll be in the neighborhood, I just might." The rally was due to begin in South Dakota on Monday of the following week and bikers were already starting to cross the country by the thousands. Locations where people collect in numbers are not generally my favorite places to be, but I was beginning to think that it might be fun to go and see what happened when a few hundred thousand bikers got together. There was also some practicality in detouring toward the rally; after twelve thousand miles my treads were starting to wear thin. "I could also use another set of tires and I hear you can get them for a reasonable price there." Sam nodded and asked the other standard question.

"So where're ya from?"

"New Jersey."

"Holy shit. New Jersey did you say?"

I nodded.

"That's a goddamn long way away."

"It is." I did not tell him about the Alaska leg of the trip but spent a moment remembering what a goddamn long way away that had been, too. Sam looked at me thoughtfully. Did he see weariness in my face or hear it in my voice?

"You just remember that you're doin' somethin' that ninety-nine percent of them people where you're from would like to do but never will." Too few people pursue their dreams, and it was something to keep in mind when the miles, the heat, the solitude, and the road stretched long.

Past Fairfield and Vaughn, I dropped farther south and east on 89 and did a short stint on Interstate 15 through Great Falls. Great Falls had the first plastic strip-mall nightmare that I had driven through in quite a while: golden arches, chicken dinners, four lanes, all you can eat, drive through, lube-while-you-wait, on-sale-now. It was all horribly familiar and I hadn't missed it. On the outskirts of town, just past Malmstrom Airforce Base, it was a relief to turn south once again, back onto Routes 87 and 89, where mass-produced civilization, such as it was, ended and the deteriorating pavement led out into the desertion of the grasslands. Between Belt and Livingston, 89 was a secondary strip of asphalt that the big-rig trucks, many hauling raw timber, used as an access route to Interstates 15 and 90. The surface was split and patched, and mirrored every contour and frost heave of the land below. Grass grew right to the edge of the deeply rutted hard surface as if the pavement had been rolled out directly onto the prairie. I dropped my speed, took the corners a little more carefully, and pulled aside for the log trucks that rode too close to my luggage rack. I was not annoyed with the truck drivers and their tailgating hints in the same way I had been with retirees in motorhomes who had done the same thing on other roads. They were professionals doing a job, trying to make time, weight load, and distance, and they had priority. I was on vacation and did not have a schedule that necessitated my arrival anywhere in the immediate future. I let them pass with a wave.

Past Armington, 89 brought me down into the Lewis and Clark National Forest, into a former mining district, through a winding tree-shaded valley, and onto a road that was just above the roll of the Bell River. Was it the greenness that, after several hundred miles of gold parched grassland, made it seem especially beautiful there? Was it the shelter of the tress after the spaciousness and the exposure of the rangeland that made the valley feel intimate and protected?

Monarch was an old river town where false-fronted buildings, signs slightly askew, stood next to homes with sloping verandas and broken gates. The windows were dusty, the paint faded, and the last house at either end of the single street was sliding toward ruin. The little town was empty and silent and, with the exception of an old red Ford pickup, which bounced its way across the hardened mud ruts where Monarch's main street ended, deserted. I stopped for gas at a single pump of nameless brand and numberless octane in front of a decaying combination roadhouse and grocery. I was running low on fuel, so I said a short prayer to the gods of clean gas and filled my tank. No attendant came out as I screwed the cap back on, so I went inside looking for someone to give my three dollars to. The bar had a high ceiling and little light. Two old men sat in the gloom at opposite ends of the counter, silent and staring fixedly at their beers. They might have been carved in wax. Through the bar was a small room that served as the grocery and I found a woman with pale purple circles of weariness beneath her eyes behind the cash register. She nodded silently, took my money without checking to see whether I had pumped three dollars or thirty, and shut the register drawer with a soft metallic slide. There was something eerie about Monarch that I had trouble placing as I drove away from the roadhouse and down the gravel access road that also served as the main street of the village. Was it just the heat and lethargy of the day that made the old men silent and the woman at the cash register listless? Were all the dogs under their porches, sleeping invisible and silent in the only bits of cool dirt they could find? Or had I stumbled into a place that was drawing its last municipal breath? Monarch, and the people who lived there, seemed to be dying, and in dying it felt like they were resigned to the thought that their village had run the course of its history.

Past Neihart, narrow gauge rail tracks slipped, abandoned and twisted, down the side of the embankment toward the road, closely followed by the chutes that had once fed crushed ore into the vanished trains. In an old graveyard, lichen-blackened stones tilted at crazy angles, pushed to the side by eagerly sprouting young spruces. Who knows how many tens of thousands of trees were cut to provide men with access to the metal that they sought beneath the woodland floor. Now, in a sort of natural justice, the graveyards were gradually being reclaimed by the forest, which encroached over the bones of the men who had once cut it down. The played-out mining villages of the Lewis and Clark Forest reminded me of Austin, Nevada, where the silver had finally run out, and along with it the lifeblood of the town.

I left the valley and the trees when I crossed up and over the last low ridge of the Little Belt Mountains and reentered the rangeland, the heat, and rising wind. The humidity was building in the thick white air and if the ambient temperature was less than ninety-eight degrees I would have been surprised. The grass looked parched, withered, and yellow, and there was a sulfurous edge to the breeze that was just beginning to stir. A storm was coming, not for a couple of hours yet, but it was coming. I could smell it. Exhaustion and dehydration had settled in, along with a pounding headache, a sore back, and a beastly case of the PMS blues, and I needed a place to rest for an hour or two. I pushed through to White Sulphur Springs, thinking to hole up in the library, catch up on e-mail correspondence, and possibly find air-conditioning.

At 3:30 I was at the library. It was new, the blue-gray paint on the front door unfaded by the sun, and the entryway half fronted in thick modern greenish glass blocks. A wood sign on the door read LIBRARIES—AN INDISPENSABLE RESOURCE. A paper note was taped just above the door latch: HAD AN APPT. BACK BY 4:30. CLOSED. I sighed. *A library would indeed have been an indispensable resource today.* I drove Lucy slowly back up a yellowed hill to the outskirts of town and parked in the dusty lot beside the Truck Stop Café. After the third refill the waitress gave up on pouring water and instead left an entire pitcher on my table. I finished it, along with a piece of peach pie and two mugs of strong black coffee. A dollar's worth of quarters bought me seven songs on the jukebox and I settled back in my booth to eavesdrop on snatches of conversation; mostly about the heat, the haze, and the fires consuming the forests and grasslands of Montana at a horrific and seemingly unstoppable pace.

"Them fires are bad, but people sure do make money off'n them."

"'Cept for the loggers, who don't get to cut the trees."

The clock was edging past 4:30 when I drove back to the library. The air was choking. Thick, heavy, hot gusts of wind blew out of the west as if some enormous dragon lay there exhaling, breathing the fires that covered the land and the heat that filled the air. The library was open, blessedly air-conditioned, and staffed by ladies who could not have been kinder. I loved those small-town libraries, with their few rooms of books, a table or two of computers, and no appointment needed to access the Internet. There, no one peered over one's shoulder watching for access of "forbidden" Internet sites. I could well imagine that in towns like White Sulphur Springs, where everyone knew, or was related to, everyone else, no one would dream of viewing pornography at the public library; one's spouse or parents would surely hear of it by the end of the day. I caught up on the news from my parents, who were at their cottage in northwestern Ontario, where I looked forward to meeting them in a few weeks. The trout were biting, they wrote, and the lake was cool.

Beyond the green windows the sky was taking on an unnatural hue of late evening. Saying good-bye to the librarians, I stepped outside and was instantly caught in a blast of wind saturated with fat raindrops. I scurried back inside as seconds later the downpour and thunderstorm began in earnest. The rain and pea-sized hail came down in a deluge of water and sound while fluorescent lightning lit the storm from within, strobing the rain to momentary stillness in a field of violet illumination. Too furious and sudden to last long, the rain slowed within twenty minutes and the hail ceased as the popcorn thunderhead rolled east. The air still felt heavy but the storm had washed twenty degrees from the stifling air.

The dragon began to breathe again before I left the gas station in White Sulphur Springs, sending tendrils of superheated dry air through the cooled and misted aftermath of the storm. The rain, which had seemed so plentiful, disappeared into the gullies and the grasses, and before I was twenty miles outside of town, the road was again bone dry as it cut across the golden prairie. I passed abandoned farmhouses with clapboards that matched those of the similarly silent and empty grange and schoolhouses—weathered to silver in the sun and wind of that starkly beautiful land. The towns were minuscule: Ringling, Wilsall, and the largest, with just under three hundred souls in residence, Clyde Park. The heat was once again oppressive. I looked with burning eyes at a billboard outside of Wilsall's single roadside bar: STOP IN FOR A COLD ONE. It was an oasis image, and I wished that pouring a frosty beer down my throat was a possibility. I thought back to the boy with the joint in Nordegg. *Thanks man, but the bike. You know.*

In the southern distance the ridges of Gallatin National Forest and the Beartooth Wilderness, foothills to the Absarokas and Grand Tetons, appeared out of the haze. The slanting light of the early evening shot orange rays through heavy air and colored the hillsides with the faded shades of sun-bleached watercolors. Just outside Livingston I branched off 89 and took the parallel but smaller Route 540, a gorgeous twisty little southbound road that ran next to the Yellowstone River through Paradise Valley.

Paradise Valley was an aptly named place, where gold and pale green fields ran all the way to the encircling tall-timbered softwood slopes, and villages of stone and wood, bearing more resemblance to sixteenth-century central England than twenty-first-century western America, clustered under massive shade trees. There wasn't much time for bucolic musings however, as the daylight was sliding into blackness and lightning bolts were beginning to ricochet off the valley walls. I passed through the village of Pine Creek and twisted Lucy's throttle a little harder, leaning into the curves and running for a campground near the village of Pray. With a spot for my tent found in the last slips of purple and green light, I hammered the stakes into the ground as the first drops of rain began to fall.

THE YELLOWSTONE RIVER FLOWS CLEAR WITH the slightest hint of golden yellow in its pools as it slips over rounded boulders washed smooth and speckled with all the colors of quails' eggs. I pulled over just to watch the flash and shift of color under water and thought of a high school English class and a Gerard Manley Hopkins poem about the divine glory of "dappled things . . . all things counter, original, spare, and strange."

On the eastern side of the river, 540 followed the bank like a hand sliding down a body, every curve touched, every bend caressed. There is something about narrow roads that follow riverbanks that is magical; land flows with water and the traveler joins the tumult. There is charm, a beauty, a natural joy, in these small byways built on the water's edge. They might as well be deer paths or beaver routes when what is narrow and manmade bends to the pattern of the river without overhanging, changing, or overshadowing its course.

Gardiner was the last town before the Yellowstone Park boundary and I stopped for breakfast at the Brown Bear Café. Outside, motorcycles were parked in gleaming blocks of five to ten bikes, angled one next to the other, as their riders stopped in town for last-minute film, sunblock, or breakfast before heading into the park. I ate alone, at a table on the southern wall; thick oatmeal drowned in milk and heaped with sliced bananas, toast, and a truly great cup of coffee. More than a few of the restaurant's tables had filled with bikers tucking into enormous platters of pancakes, eggs, and hash browns. Most of them wore the standard summertime uniform: blue jeans, black boots, and a black T-shirt from a Harley dealership, usually at point of origin. I, too, was wearing my dealership tee, this one from Fairbanks. It wasn't so much the fashion, it was just that after days of obscene heat, my other two shirts were caked in sweat and road dust. One of the men at a table of five, all wearing the Uniform, all with a three-day scruff of stubble, nodded to me as I walked past him on my way to the cash register. In his late thirties, broadly built, and close to six feet tall, he was the smallest of the five.

"You drive a scoot?"

"Yes. Do you?" His friends laughed.

"Yours is the Sporty outside?"

"The red one with the bags." I pointed out Lucy and we compared bikes. The men were driving bigger machines, Fatboys and Heritage Softtails, and had less gear as they stayed in hotels rather than tents.

"Where are you from?"

"New Jersey." One of the men, looking at me with new interest, broke in. "Wait. I've heard about you! We met this guy who told us all about you; a girl on a Sporty traveling alone who's been all over Alaska and parts of Canada. Is that you?" I laughed. They must have run into Dan, my Gold Wing friend from Ninilchik, whom I had last seen over breakfast in Swift River, somewhere on his ride back to Minnesota.

"That's me."

"Awesome! Can I get a picture with you?" For five minutes I felt like a diminutive rock star as huge men draped burly arms over my shoulders. After individual photos and a group shot, I left them to finish breakfast as I headed into the park.

Another blistering day was on tap. There is no helmet law in Wyoming and, as I planned to spend the entire day in Yellowstone, driving slow, well-maintained park roads and stopping frequently to sightsee, I broke my cardinal rule and stripped off my jacket, lashing it and my helmet to the T-bag.

Wraparound mirrored sunglasses cut some of the white heat glare, as did the ball cap jammed down over my head, ponytail fed through the back to anchor it in place. I kept my gloves on to cut the vibration and to keep Lucy's grips from becoming slippery with sweat, but my arms were naked and exposed. It was liberating to feel the direct beat of sun and wind on bare skin, to be free of thick leather and the enclosed space of a helmet, and I drove slowly toward Mammoth Hot Springs, passing a small herd of elk grazing on the lawn of a park service building and a large herd of humans at the tourist information center.

The Springs were a magnificent wedding cake of white calcium carbonate ledges streaked with mineralized icing and veiled in low mists of boiling sulfurous water. Bands of lemon yellow, burnt orange, and burgundy red cascaded with the water down the sides of the formation, decorating the superstructure with harlequin colors. The park had built a twisting maze of boardwalks and small observation platforms between the major formations, and I was leaning on the railing overlooking shallow boiling pools of blue, orange, and pale green water when the man next to me spoke.

"Fantastic, isn't it?" I turned and came face to face with a strikingly handsome man whom I had noticed in the parking lot above a few minutes before. His thick black hair, cropped short and swept back from high cheekbones, crowned the gold skin and almond-shaped eyes of his Eurasian face. He and his traveling companions were Jehovah's Witnesses, he said, and had driven from their homes in Los Angeles to preach in South Dakota. A sightseeing stop in Yellowstone broke up the long trip back to California. Despite the fact that one of my half brothers is a Mormon and is enthusiastically looking forward to evangelizing somewhere in French West Africa, I do not like missionary activity generally. Living in Eastern Europe, a region of profound and ancient religious traditions, it always struck me as odd, and rather offensive, to hear young Mormon men, boys really, straight out of Salt Lake, with their pressed white shirts, narrow ties, and crew cuts, speak of "bringing God" to the people of Bulgaria. God, of both the mono- and polytheistic varieties, had been on the shores of the Black Sea and throughout the Balkans for millennia. The man I met by the Springs was kind and friendly, however. It is my own bias, my own standoffish neurosis, that tells me that all people of faith and "mission" must want to speak endlessly about their concept of God and salvation. This is simply not true. We spoke instead of the vast differences of culture within our one nation. He told me that South Dakota had a pace, friendliness, and rural peace that he, as a Southern Californian urbanite, was entirely unfamiliar with. And the space—the visible circumference of the horizon, the dearth of human population, the shapes rising within the land—it was to city eyes, used to the deliberate construction of architecture, an amazing thing.

At Old Faithful I parked Lucy next to an elephantine group of motorhomes and walked around the complex, stopping at the post office to mail my Alaska books home and pay my credit card bill. The main lodge was air-conditioned and packed with sunburned white people, the skin of exposed legs and arms glowing red below khaki shorts and golf shirts. "Moose tracks" ice cream, a vanilla concoction shot through with chocolate-covered almonds and peanut butter cups, eaten with a nectarine for desert, was lunch. *Fruit made it healthy, right?* I slathered on more sunblock before stepping outside and drank almost a quart of water. It was heat and sun management, but there was no way to fully cope with the inferno outdoors. Under my tan and the collected road dust, my skin was burning to a deep red.

The Old Faithful viewing area was a neatly constructed park reached by flagstone walks and tended plantings: a carved circle surrounded by grandstands and wheelchair-accessible paved paths. At 3:50 P.M., as promised by the clocks on the wall inside the tourist center, Old Faithful erupted with a whoosh in the center of a raked gravel plaza, watched by several hundred people, myself among them. The plume of steaming water rose forty feet into the air, and people oohed and ahhed and snapped photographs that would sit in shoeboxes for decades to come, but there was something produced, something staged, about the whole thing. Even though the geyser's given name implied its regularity, there was something weird about geothermal activity and the explosion of boiling water through a pore in the earth, which was clocked, scheduled, announced, and surrounded by grandstands. It was demented, but in a place like Yellowstone, where the figure-eight pattern of road that nearly every tourist drives has been resurfaced, boardwalked, and signposted within an inch of what remains of its natural life, I wished for a geyser that would do what geysers are supposed to do: spurt up with horrifying and unexpected force, the eruption of an unquiet earth spewing water, boulders, and caustic minerals in all directions. *What was wrong with me? Had I been in the far north, away from people and packaging, long enough that the solitude and the splendor was turning me into some sort of civilization cynic?* I hoped not, but at the same time, I wondered why that which was once beautiful and wild necessarily needed to be twisted and controlled into accessibility and predictability. The irony was, as much as I had loved my ice cream lunch in that gorgeous place, I hated the infrastructure that made it possible.

Artist's Point overlooks a mineralized chasm cut by the Yellowstone River and is flanked by fantastic rocky pinnacles and mushroomed shapes sculpted by wind and water and ice. The slipping colors of a Salvador Dali painting flowed through the crumbling stone to a foaming emerald waterfall that spilled into the river below. The fading light of the day, splintered by an incoming storm, lit the canyon in patches, illuminating here a gnarled pine stretching out over the gorge, there a boulder washed in ochre yellow and grayish green, teetering on the edge of oblivion. In the air, deep growls, like the sounds of distant artillery, rumbled and intensified. Flashes of yellow-green light in the upper reaches of the canyon heralded what was going to be a violent thunderstorm. It was time to get down off Artist's Point and under cover, if only in a tent.

At Canyon Creek Campground I pulled in to find that there were no sites available. The ladies behind the reception desk were very kind, however, and between referencing a computer reservation system and telephoning all over the park they found a single free tentsite, twenty-six miles away at Madison Campground. Outside the large plate-glass windows, the sky was an ominous purple green. I thanked the ladies for their help, took my reservation slip, headed out the door at a trot, and throttled Lucy hard into the rising wind, running to try to beat the storm.

I do not know why I continue to attempt to outrun weather systems on my motorcycle. It is a futile endeavor, especially with storms blowing in on a collision course. Leaving Canyon Creek I was already under the boiling lip of the system but I sprinted west, toward its heart, thinking that I might just get to shelter before it let go. I was wrong. The road that bisects Yellowstone National Park goes up and over a low set of hills and I was halfway up the eastern side when the first grasshopper-sized raindrops exploded off my faceshield. *Here it comes.* Sheet lightning lit the air through a wave of rain that rolled down the road and crested over me like the sea. I dropped my speed to thirty. I clearly had lost any opportunity to stay dry so I thought that I might as well just putter along at a rate where I trusted the visibility. *Wham!* The dull rumble of distant thunder had become sharply distinct ringing explosions of sound and pressure, and the dispersed flash of heat lightning had become sizzling blue-white bolts, vivid against the plum of the sky. *Ah fuck, I'm going to get fried.* There was nowhere to go. The shoulders of the road dropped in gravel softness to drainage ditches and I couldn't pull far enough off to the side of the pavement that I wouldn't worry about Lucy getting crushed by a hurtling RV. What strange priorities one has at moments like that. *Ping. Ping.* Bean-sized bits of ice bounced off my jacket and burned painfully into the exposed skin of my neck and wrists with the force of fired bbs. *Hail. Ah yes, this is great. Is there anything else? How 'bout a tornado to round things out? Go ahead, bring it on.* I spoke the words into the rising wind but thankfully was not answered by a funnel cloud. As furious and as rapidly as the storm came on, it was gone, roaring eastward in a passion of sound, ice, and exploding light. Hail pellets, heaped together in strange summer snowbanks, melted rapidly. I crested the ridge and dropped toward the western valley and Madison Campground. The pavement, superheated in the blistering sun of the day, turned the pooled rain to temporary wraiths of steam and mist. They rose over a valley perpetually seething and smoking with the forces of the earth's internal storms.

THE MORNINGS THAT FOLLOW VIOLENT EVENING storms always seem especially clear. The previous day's tempests had lifted the choking heaviness from the air, brought lower temperatures, and introduced a transparency to the atmosphere that had not been present for the better part of a week. Feeling awake and alive and breathing the scent of rain-damp forest, I bundled into all the dry layers that I could pull out of my pack, checked out of Madison, shifted Lucy into gear, and rolled out onto the pavement. I passed Beryl Springs, a bright blue paint pot of clear water blowing steam into the cold morning air, slowed enough to hear the soft hiss of escaping steam, and scanned the surrounding landscape of deep green firs reaching toward a sky that was shifting from early-morning pale to deeper blue by the moment. It was going to be a beautiful day.

Near Yellowstone's eastern exit I pulled over to photograph a Japanese garden that had formed, without human help, in a downward-slanted ravine. In the narrow canyon, a rivulet of a stream splashed and tumbled between sandstone spires, which twisted upward, framing gnarled junipers. At the other end of the pull-off a biker with an immaculate green Electra Glide crouched near his front wheel adjusting the footbrake with an equally gleaming wrench. It is one of the understood codes of the motorcycling community that if you see a biker who looks like he or she is having mechanical difficulties, you pull over and ask if you can help. Prevalent stereotypes are such that people in cars will rarely, if ever, stop to help a biker parked on the shoulder of the road. However, before I even started walking toward him, I knew that the man didn't need my help. He had a look of control and capability about him, expressed in the practiced fluid rotation of his wrist on the wrench, but there are times when code should be followed.

"Problems?"

"Nope. Loose foot brake."

He was tall. Even as he crouched I guessed that he stood about six feet, maybe a little more. A beaded belt fed through the loops of his spotless blue jeans and a pressed denim shirt hung across broad, square shoulders. The shirt was buttoned to the neck and wrists, but as he worked and one cuff rose, I saw the band of heavy tattooing that encircled his lower arm. It was the terminal edge of an elaborate design and I guessed that his arms, if not his entire torso, were gloved in ink. His hair was short, almost a military cut, chestnut brown interspersed with iron gray, and a neatly clipped beard skimmed his lower face. He was handsome and would have been more so had his face not been completely smashed at some point during his life. His nose slipped slightly to one side; the bones and cartilage that supported it lacked the usual linear regularity beneath deeply scarred skin. His eyes didn't set quite right either: his occipital bones looked as if they had been badly broken, and one eye swung just a few degrees to a right-of-center focus as he looked at me. He had the face of a man who had gone down in a bar brawl that had started with fists and finished with boots. Whomever had rebuilt his nose and eye sockets had done a good job, however. The scars, although numerous, were threads of white on his tanned skin. He wasn't disfigured in a horrific way, and the pain of the past that I sensed as I looked at him was not that of the present.

"You riding all alone?" he asked.

"Yes." He raised one eyebrow in quiet surprise but said nothing.

"Are you riding all alone, too?" Although I heard this question every single day, I don't think that he had ever been asked it before. He looked at me in silence for a moment and chuckled.

"Yes."

He finished with the foot brake and carefully wiped his wrench on a bandana before replacing it in the hard luggage of his motorcycle. He returned with a fliptop box of Marlboros, shook a cigarette out, and offered it to me.

"Thanks, no, but go right ahead." He lit one, inhaled slowly, and said nothing.

"Where are you going?" I asked. He was as careful and considered with his words as he was with his bike, tools, and dress, and he spoke briefly about a long loop up through the Dakotas. His wife lived out there, he said, and he thought he would spend about two weeks on the road. I told him that I was heading out through the Dakotas, too, but through Sturgis to have a look at the rally—he shook his head in amusement at this—and then on to Minnesota.

"Which road are you taking?"

"From here? Through Silver Gate, out 296 to Cody," I said.

"You should go ride the Bear Tooth." The Bear Tooth Highway, also known as Route 212, ran north, back into Montana.

"Really? Why?"

He stubbed the cigarette out in the gravel. "I've ridden everywhere. Upstate New York, Dakota, everywhere, but that road is the best I've ever seen." He looked me full in the face, his shifting eye focusing and slipping and focusing again. "It's got curves, overlooks, everything." His stare told me what his words did not. I stopped questioning and rode.

The Bear Tooth swung left past Silver Gate and climbed newly paved long switchbacks to Bear Tooth Pass, which towered nearly eleven thousand feet above the valleys and lesser mountains below. Smooth and well graded, the curves were so well designed that, despite the gain in elevation, I didn't lose speed on the corners. I had the highway largely to myself, and from golden roadside meadows only pikas and marmots watched Lucy pass, tiny fists raised to their chests as they stood tall on their hind legs to see over the dwarf grasses to the pavement beyond. The view from Bear Tooth Pass was incredible. High tundra cushioned ice-fractured rock, and the wind blew cold.

The valleys were full of jumbled peaks, as if mountains had been gathered from other places and dropped in great handfuls into the yawning void. The land glowed burgundy red, maroon, and violet, and the chasms below were softened by the haze of humidity and heat that could not be felt at altitude. Small shallow lakes, some sheltered by diminutive twisted conifers, shone a glassy iridescent blue among the jade-colored mosses, grasses, and occasional shrub. At lower elevations, fir trees could reach full stature—fifty feet or more—in forty years. At the top of the pass, where the wind howled and where travel was abandoned to the grip of winter six months a year, it might taken four centuries for a fir trees to reach its full stunted height of less than four feet.

At Beartooth Lake I followed a long gravel road to the water's edge and ate cheese and crackers on the grass, watching the reflection of a bright, mineral-banded, mesa-topped mountain in the unquiet waters. The sun felt good on my shoulders and, propping my rolled leather under my neck, I lay back for the better part of an hour inhaling the wildflower-scented mountain air and watching the occasional car or RV pull down the long access drive to look at the water. One truck stopped and parked. An old man, dressed only in a black Speedo swimsuit, swim goggles, and flip-flops, still-powerful muscles rippling under wrinkled mahogany skin, stepped from the passenger side. A younger man, fully dressed, walked with him and dropped a hand in the water as they reached the edge.

"Oooh-whee, that's cold! You sure you want to do this?" The old man smiled, nodded, kicked off his flip-flops, and waded in without hesitation. When the water crested his thighs he dove and swam with strong, sure strokes, silver droplets splashing in his wake, the length of the lake and back. I wondered what ritual I was viewing. Did a son or daughter come once a year to watch him swim in the reflection of the colored mountain? Another biker pulled up on a white Harley Softtail, parked, and levered his rangy frame down to where he was sitting in the grass, far enough away so that I could maintain my silence and privacy if I wanted to, but near enough to open a conversation if I chose. I said hello.

Jerry had a big, toothy smile and a cowboy's stride. He and two friends had ridden up from Texas with a plan to see the Tetons, Yellowstone, the Buffalo Bill Historic Center in Cody, and the hot springs in Thermopolis. After accomplishing the first two, Jerry's friends decided to get a little fishing in on the side. More of a biker than a fisherman—Jerry had a kind of nervous boyish energy that precluded patient silence in the shadows of a trout stream—he had decided to ride rather than fish and had left his friends wading somewhere in the Yellowstone River. We shared road stories for an hour and Jerry told me that he and his friends had already checked in to a nearby campground. If I was looking for a place to pitch a tent that night I could squeeze in with them. I thanked him but said that I would be well past their campground and through Red Lodge, Montana, before night fell. We said good-bye and I saddled up, leaving him sprawled on the grass, staring over the pointed toes of his boots at the lake and the mountain beyond.

I dropped down into Red Lodge and rising heat on long switchbacks cut into the southeastern wall of a valley before following the leap of 212 to the northwestern wall of the same. My front brakes had been squeaking slightly for the past few days and although they were functioning perfectly, I stopped in at the Harley dealership to have them checked out. The grades were too steep and the miles too long to have to wonder about whether my brakes would perform if I really needed them.

The dealership in Red Lodge was a classic Harley-in-the-summertime gathering spot for bikers. An orange-and-white striped tent had been erected in the parking lot, and bikers sat at picnic tables telling lies and truths about their machines and their journeys. The mechanic, Joe, a delightful man with lower arms that would have given Popeye a reason to look twice, checked my brakes.

"Nope. They're fine. They just collect dust when the riding is hard and start to squeak a little. It'll go away when you get onto cleaner roads. You been riding through dusty country recently?" I thought of the heat, the smoke, and the dust that I had been sweating my way through since Southern British Columbia.

"Yes. I guess I have."

A truck, pulling a trailer with two immaculate Harleys, rolled to a stop in the street as we talked. A woman jumped down from the passenger side, pulling the hem of her pristine white shorts a half-inch lower over long, tanned legs as she walked toward us. She wore a blue-and-white boat-neck T-shirt, had wrists draped in gold bracelets, and looked as if she had just stepped from an Ann Taylor catalog.

"OK!" she said. "We're ready to go! We'll see you in Sturgis!" She turned and looked critically at Lucy. Large blue eyes under bottle-blonde curls swiveled toward me. "You might want to give that thing a little wash." With a crimson-nailed, cheery wave to Joe, who gave her the most strained of smiles, she hopped back into the truck.

"That bitch. 'Scuse my language," said Joe. "You ride, you get grit. Them people don't ride if they think they'll get one bug or one raindrop. Spend more time polishing than they do on the road."

Lucy wasn't the only one who needed a wash. My clothes were filthy with dust, dried sweat, and my personal share of squished bugs. I found a Laundromat on the outskirts of town and sat in shorts and a sports bra reading old *Ladies Home Journal* magazines until my clothes were vaguely clean and mostly dry. A stop at the grocery store, gas station, and library followed. The lengthening evening did not bring much of a temperature drop, and as I loaded up Lucy I considered my options: take the Route 308 valley road to Belfry, gamble that there would be private campgrounds along the way as there were no public ones marked on the map, and drop down into Cody on Route 72 the next day. Or, go back up over the Bear Tooth, camp at one of the several areas that I had seen that afternoon, and ride the Chief Joseph Highway in the morning. In the south the mountains massed high and cool, their slopes shimmering in the deepening colors of the slipping sunshine, while the Belfry valley stretched long and hot to the east. There was not much of a choice to be made and I powered Lucy back up the Bear Tooth, thinking as I drove higher and deeper into the mountains that this was a road that I could ride again and again without ever wearying of the panoramas that opened at every corner. The man tightening the foot brake on his Electra Glide that morning had been right.

The sun was dropping as I crested the pass, and as one "full" sign after another marked the entrance to the campgrounds, I realized that tourists more timely than I had gotten up the Bear Tooth first. With so much open space, and many sheltering copses of trees, I considered just pulling over and pitching my tent wherever I might find a flat spot. There was, however, one problem. The Absaroka Mountains were grizzly bear territory, and I was far from sure that I wanted to establish solitary squatting rights with motorcycle saddlebags loaded with groceries. *What to do?* The thought came in a flash: *Find Jerry.* I rolled back to Beartooth Lake and cruised the loops of campsites until I found the white Softtail.

"Hey Jerry. You got space for one more?" There were three small tents already set up in a clearing that fronted a small stream and opened to a meadow beyond.

"Always. I'm glad you came back."

We squeezed the fourth tent in and built a fire. Jerry, listening to no protestation, settled me into his single folding chair and perched himself on a log. As the light faded we sat talking about the unrolling of life and pavement, about the beauty of chance, and the difficulty of choices. Jerry, divorced years ago in a bitter proceeding, was in a new relationship with a woman whom he loved and respected. They had been together a couple of years and she had started hinting strongly about getting married. The thought of marriage, of contractual permanence, made him nervous, but he lacked the objectivity to know whether he was uncomfortable because he did not think that they could spend a lifetime together or because previous experience had shown him that the promise of forever could go horribly awry. Part of the reason he had wanted to come on this trip, he said, and part of the reason that he had opted not to go fishing with his buddies that afternoon, was that he needed time, silence, and distance to think about the woman he loved and the shape of their possible future together. Jerry talked on, looking for clarity, as the fire burned to coals.

In the meadow there was motion. I caught it out of the corner of my eye in the instant before Jerry raised his finger to his lips. I turned slowly to see a yearling mule deer walking—three steps and then a halt to sniff the air and waggle her large ears—down the streambed. Jerry rose noiselessly from his log perch and moved, without the sound of the smallest snapping twig, through the woods, upwind of the deer. The cowboy's stride suddenly became the graceful motion of a hunter and I wondered how many times he had done this: tracked and circled an animal, getting closer for a kill, or just watching as we were that night. On the balls of his feet, and moving only when the deer moved, it was a dance between man and animal, elegant and fascinating. He came within five feet of the deer. One lunge and he could have touched her butterscotch flank. Instead he slipped back into the shelter of the trees and the young mule deer proceeded down the meadow unmolested.

An hour and a half later Bob and David showed up, striding big and bearish between the tents, empty-handed but with tales of a highly successful catch-and-release day. Jerry made thick cowboy coffee in an enamel pot resting on the burning logs and we drank it bemoaning the lack of a whiskey chaser. When it was time to go to bed, the four of us collected all our food and toiletries into a sleeping bag stuff sack, which that night functioned as a communal bear bag. The smallest and lightest of our crew, I swung myself up into the low branches of a pine and scrambled another twenty feet upward through densely growing twigs, to hang it from a slender limb. There were scratches to be had on the descent through the dark tree but they were well worth a night free from the worry of foraging bears.

The meadow beyond our clearing glowed a soft green in the growing light of early morning, and each blade of grass and sheaf of meadow wheat was topped by rainbow-edged water droplets. Jerry lit a slow fire with damp wood and put another pot of coffee on. As we packed up, each cramming sleeping bags into stuff sacks and rolling tents, I talked with Bob. He was a stumpy little man with a garden-gnome white beard and impaired hearing that made loud conversation a necessity. I asked about his wife and teased him a little about abandoning the womenfolk for a ramble with the boys. He told me about a few family outings, rafting down rivers and visiting national parks, but said that on the motorcycle trips he took with his friends, he was glad that women didn't come.

"It changes things. You have to watch what you say." He slammed the lid of his hard luggage case down with a bang. "And there's always, *always*, things like bathroom issues." He said this with surety, I took it as chauvinism. We had talked long past sunset the night before, telling jokes and stories and sharing our lives. Had my presence "changed" things? Did he feel like his bastion of quality masculine time had been intruded upon? Nobody at our campsite was riding sidesaddle and I expected treatment no different than any other man. Bob went to brush his teeth under the hand pump in the center of the campground and in the quiet I thought again about what he had said. He was right. Gender dynamics—platonic or sexual, friendly or antagonistic—did alter the way men and women spoke to one another, whether the conversation happened in isolation or in a group setting. After the most innocuous ten-minute conversation with a man, didn't I, too, often recognize a change in how I might otherwise behave or feel had I been alone or only in the presence of other women? How many times had I become self-conscious about my black-rimmed fingernails, wild hair, and whether or not I had had a shower in the past week if I was talking to a man? When I spoke with women some of these concerns emerged, also especially in the contrasts between them and me, but I never felt like I needed to prove or preserve my femininity as I sometimes did with men. For Bob, Jerry, and David, perhaps on these long rides together, they, too, could cease trying to prove or preserve their masculinity, perhaps they could cease worrying about what they thought the women of their families "needed," and perhaps they could just be themselves.

We saddled up and headed out of the campground, rolling down the gravel access road to where it intersected with the main. A few miles farther, the Chief Joseph Highway looped down from its juncture with the Bear Tooth through sage green foothills in long banked curves leading to the dusty ochre and yellow valleys beyond. It was a rapid drop, in part because of the good road surface and the quality of the engineering, in part because the Texans held a fast pace: seventy miles an hour carving into the corners, and running faster on the straights. We rode in staggered formation so that each bike would have the entire width of the pavement to work the corners. I rode fourth, hanging back sometimes to watch the three ahead of me with admiration. Those men knew how to ride. As the road flattened we picked up speed, seventy-five and then eighty miles an hour. Jerry was just ahead of me and I watched in fascination and dread as he leaned back and shifted his boots to rest—and steer—on the handlebars of his Softtail. Baseball cap jammed down over his head, he clasped his hands behind his neck, shifting his shoulders as if stretching. He drove like that for a couple of miles, as if settled into a favorite recliner, feet up and watching the country roll by him like some expansive theater production. It was, however, an armchair doing eighty miles an hour, and I was glad when he shifted back to a more conventional riding stance.

Halfway to Cody a deep gorge slashed the earth, opening the bottom of a valley in a ragged tear, and we pulled off to stand on the edge and feel the upwelling of cold, damp air from the river below. Jerry gave me one of the two pennies that he dug out of his jeans pocket, and with a private wish to speed them on their way, we let them drop together, hundreds of feet into the chasm.

As a woman traveling with Texans, I soon realized that it was impossible to pay for anything. The penny dropped into the gorge was just the start of it. David bought me breakfast in Cody, where we stopped to wolf down huge platters of hash browns, eggs and salsa, bacon, and pancakes, and Bob insisted on paying for my ticket to the Buffalo Bill Historical Center. The museum was enormous and we only saw a fraction of it. It was like some wing of the Smithsonian moved west, echoing the culture, technology, and artistry of the land past the Mississippi. Guns by the thousands, from tiny pearl-handled ladies' pistols to elaborately inlaid sixteenth-century rampart guns eight feet long, filled gallery after gallery, arranged in parallel floor-to-ceiling racks or mounted in great peacock-tail fans of firepower. Another series of rooms held long-dead specimen wolves, coyotes, and grizzlies, which reared up in front of plaques listing the date and place where they had been "harvested." Flooded with sunshine from tall windows overlooking an atrium garden, the Whitney Gallery of Western Art was my favorite wing of the Center. The sinews of Remington and Russell bronze horses flexed and pulled under the painted gazes of cowboys and Indians. N. C. Wyeth's work splashed brilliant colors and high-plains drama across the walls. Audubon prints showed the tiniest details of prowling cinnamon bears and birds on the wing. The paintings of Joseph Henry Sharp were especially beautiful, with their native subjects and realistic treatment of clear western light.

Hours later, visually overloaded by a morning spent looking at thousands of artifacts and hundreds of pieces of art, the four of us stood in the parking lot to say our good-byes. The men were headed south toward Thermopolis and I was eastbound for the Big Horn Mountains and Sheridan. David and Bob shook my hand and clapped me on the shoulder.

"Be careful."

"I will."

Jerry wrapped his arms around me. He was so tall that the top of my head barely reached his shoulder.

"Enjoy your life."

"I will. I hope you find what you're looking for, Jer. Ride safe."

"I will."

We fired up our bikes, swung into the saddles and went our separate ways. Heading northeast through Powell and Byron, into the hundred-degree heat of a Wyoming summer day, I keenly felt the clear white solitude of the road and missed the company of the Texans for many miles.

There was a scorching quality to the air, undiminished by the slant of the early evening light, as I rolled through the Big Horn Mountains. Near Ranchester the wind picked up and the fifteen-mile Interstate 90 run into Sheridan was accompanied by blasting gusts of superheated air. The dragon was awake again. Exhausted, dehydrated, and unsure of possibilities for camping and water past the city, I took the advice of the boy at the gas station and headed for the city park.

Camping was generously free on the soft carpet of grass that bordered Big Goose Creek, although a sign made it clear that two nights was the limit of Sheridan's hospitality. The problem with free facilities, however, is that they tend to draw a roadside menagerie of people who, myself included, were a cross section of the nation's wanderers, vagrants, and social oddities. A tax-dodging motorhome dweller, who claimed that "The Government" had recently confiscated several of his computers on a hacking investigation, was parked next to Lucy. A woman dressed in homemade jailhouse stripes, complete with pillbox cap, walked from campsite to campsite, collecting signatures on a petition that she hoped would set her dog free from the onus of Sheridan's leash law. Her enormous German shepherd, similarly decked out in a black-and-white striped bib with a black bowtie, grinned peacefully from the end of his tether. Two men in their late twenties with pressed cotton-poly dress shirts and precisely clipped hair set the small, hard suitcases of salesmen of a different era on the grass some yards away from my tent. They were talking about Jesus to an injured backpacker named Scott, who was staying in the park only until his twisted ankle healed enough that he could walk back into the Big Horn Mountains. The evangelists told me that they had no particular geographical plan for proselytizing, or funds to support the same, they simply got on the road one day in southern Louisiana and set out to experience the Christian kindness of strangers and to renew America's faith in the Lord. Declining an offer to discuss the miracles at Calvary, I zipped the screen door of my tent closed as the light faded to an orange glow over Sheridan. At 11 P.M. the dialogue between the two men, punctuated by the flipping of Bible pages and an occasional grunt from Scott, finally ended. Darkness and sleep fell across the campground.

The Ucross Valley had gently beautiful low hills that lifted just above the meanderings of the Clear and Powder Rivers. Towering cottonwoods, thousands of dusty green leaves turning dry sunshine to dappled moist shade, lined the drives that led to ranch houses set well back from the road. The communities were tiny: Ucross, Clearmont, Leiter, and Spotted Horse, each marked only by a cluster of houses at a crossroads. More noticeable were fields of purple clover so densely planted that the blossoms, their heavy heads nodding in the light breeze, completely obscured the talcum green of the leaves beneath.

After a short run on Interstate 90 out of Gillette, I turned at Pine Haven and headed north, toward Carlile and Devils Tower on Routes 14 and 24. The river-watered valleys were gone and the land was dry and red, scrubby and deserted. On the horizon, looming over low hills, Devils Tower rose nearly thirteen hundred feet in vertical, deep-fissured magnificence: a hardened magma core, all that is left of a volcano that never erupted some sixty million years ago. Native peoples have their own explanation for the formation. They say that many years ago, seven small girls were chased by a bear and, with the animal closing fast, they climbed atop a great rock and prayed to be saved. Just as the bear reached the girls, the rock lifted them into the air. In frustrated futility the bear dragged its claws down the sides of the rising monolith as the girls were elevated to safety, as well as to immortality. They became the Pleiades, or the Seven Sisters, constellation; shining stars set into the heavens through the mercy of the Great Spirit.

A group of bikers rolled in as I paused at a pull-off to photograph the Tower. Sturgis was less than half a day's drive away and the roads were beginning to fill with giddy motorcyclists anticipating the party and camaraderie that waited for them just over the border of South Dakota. The group that pulled in next to me was a raucous and happy bunch of New Zealanders, who stopped in a swirl of dust, shouted obscenities, and laughter. I was feeling a little tired and quiet, thinking of bears and stars and the faith of children in distress, and was not really in tune with the festival atmosphere that was beginning to build. I had to admire, however, the adventurousness and dedication of those eight men who had come halfway around the world to experience the largest of the American bike rallies. I took a group picture for them with the tower in the background.

"We'll see you again at Sturgis!" one man called as he saddled up. "I'll buy you a beer!"

"No, I will!" said his friend. Eight promises of beers later, they were gone in a roar of straight pipes, with only a curl of red dust on the road to mark their passing.

Route 24 skimmed the northern edge of the Black Hills National Forest before dropping toward the Wyoming border. There was some road construction, five miles of packed red earth that brought mostly motorcycle traffic to a staggered halt at a makeshift stoplight. We waited ten minutes before the oncoming line of traffic appeared. A couple on an Electra Glide just in front of me complained loudly to another rider about the long wait, how awful the roads were, and what an endless stretch of hell the piece ahead would be. I thought of Destruction Bay and the Yukon. Five miles of smooth, packed dirt was hell?

At Spearfish, just inside the South Dakota state line, I merged into the flashing steel rumble of big bikes and long-haul truckers on Interstate 90 and did the last fifteen miles into Sturgis at speed. Although the official start of the rally was not for another three days, from the bike traffic on the road, all of it headed toward one town of five thousand people, I was beginning to understand that waltzing into any campground in the immediate vicinity and finding a scrap of grass on which to pitch my tent was not going to be an easy matter. The biggest biker party on the planet had already begun.

THE HEART OF STURGIS RESTS BETWEEN two parallel streets, Lazelle and Main, that are densely populated for half a mile before the concentration of bungalow homes and small businesses thins toward farm fields. I drove into town on Lazelle, fascinated by the display of bike-related paraphernalia, products, and services that were already either fully operational or in the bustling process of being set up. Towering over a gas station was a billboard-sized television display screen, "Sturgis Cam." For the next ten days running, TV cameras would capture, display, and transmit pictures of the street party that was just beginning. Dunlop Tires marked its venue with an enormous inflated blue-and-yellow tire, and I pulled in to ask about getting a new set for Lucy put on the following morning. Although tire purchase and mounting was done on a first-come-first-serve basis, the manager had a clipboard with several pages of names of people who were expected to show up for tires the next day.

"Come early," he said, "before 8 A.M. if you don't want to wait in line for hours." I left my name, told him I'd be back in the morning, and pulled Lucy across the street to fill up.

"Hey baby!" At the gas station a bearded man on the other side of the plaza flashed a hand-lettered sign. It said SHOW ME YOUR TITS. I gave him the iciest of stares, replaced the pump nozzle, and screwed the gas cap back on the tank. He seemed flustered, unnerved by my silence, as if he were trying out his sign for the first time and hadn't gotten quite the reaction he had hoped for. "Hey. Sorry," he said. "I didn't mean nothin' by that." He didn't, either. I was just tired from the road and not in the mood for the burlesque propositions. The rally is South Dakota's answer to Louisiana's Mardi Gras; a ten-day carnival and bacchanalia of motorcycles, beer, music, tattoos, racing, men dressed in leather—lots of it—and women dressed in as little as possible. Municipal regulations make it a fineable offense, seventy-five dollars to be paid on the spot, if a woman exposes her nipples in public, but anything short of total feminine nudity is both tolerated by the police and encouraged by the bikers.

The culture of the modern Sturgis rally, a rally that the local Chamber of Commerce encourages to grow larger each year because of the revenues it brings in, is a mixture of artifice and authenticity. What started in 1938 with two hundred invitees arriving for time-track drag racing and off-road hill climbing has become a much wider festival of consumerism, posturing, and role playing, which centers only loosely on serious motorcycling. Most of the "bikers" that go to Sturgis—the men at least—do know how to drive motorcycles, although many choose to trailer their bikes to South Dakota behind pickup trucks or motorhomes. It is only a small subset of the modern rally participants, however, who comprise the hard-core and traditional sectors of biker society: the people who have never owned a car, the gangs, the racers, the bike mechanics and detailers, the long-distance riders who drive several thousand dusty miles to get to a rather remote corner of America.

The bikers of Sturgis are predominantly middle-class, white Americans: teachers, plumbers, construction contractors, computer programmers, telemarketers, nurses, and retired military. Most have jobs, homes, church affiliations, families, and responsibilities that they spend fifty weeks a year taking care of. For a few hedonistic days in August however, they can become different people, they can play the parts of renegades, they can be every B-movie concept of what a biker is.

EXHIBIT N: *Pas de Deux*

In real life he's an electrician and she's a bank teller. They have three kids, a fellowship at the Pentecostal church, dinner at her mother-in-law's every Thursday night, and a circle of respectable friends. A temporary dimensional shift occurs as soon as they roll across the Wyoming border and into South Dakota, as surely as if they had crossed into another universe, an alternate life. In Sturgis, he's a hard-partying, unshaven man with a wallet chain and a leather vest that exposes a bicep ringed by a tribal band tattoo. An unfiltered cigarette dangles from his lower lip as he blasts his straight pipes down Main Street. She's on the back of the bike: hot pants and high-heeled sandals, a dog collar, a leather bra, and a Marlon Brando cap slanting down above heavily made-up eyes. For a few days there is no mortgage, no Monday-morning punchcard, no watching eyes of small-town America. There is no PTA meeting, no Little League coaching, no ballet or trumpet lessons for the kids. There is only sweat and heat and beer and music and bikes and the raw sexuality of every bad-biker image that one could construct. It is a fantasy, a ten-day Halloween Ball, an alternative experimentation with a rebel life that the vast majority of people will never experience in reality. This is Sturgis, South Dakota, at rally time.

. . .

I had heard estimates that by the time I rolled into South Dakota early Friday evening, there were already one hundred thousand bikers in the immediate vicinity of Sturgis. By midweek of the official rally there would be more than four hundred thousand. Where was I going to sleep? Lashing my helmet to my pack I cruised Lucy slowly down Lazelle, bareheaded and looking at the throngs of people on the sidewalks, the pavilions, the advertisements, and the tents selling motorcycle accessories of every description. There was music, loud classic rock—Zeppelin and Creedence and Allman and Skynyrd—coming from a number of venues, and the smell of burgers and beer spilled on asphalt was in the air. I was at the end of the half-mile strip that marked the town's central core, and a hundred yards into the mowed and flower bed–lined residential district, when a boy, perhaps twelve years old, stepped off the sidewalk and into the street. He carried a sign, CAMP HERE. I pulled over rapidly, braking Lucy to a stop less than a foot from his sneakers. He didn't flinch or step back.

"Hey there. I'm looking for a place to set up a tent. Have you got one?"

He stared at me, suddenly shy. "Not me, at my grandma's house."

"OK. Does your grandma live near here?" He pointed wordlessly to a modest blue frame house on the corner of the next side street. It was set back from the road by two huge oaks that shaded the lawn and framed a wide front porch.

"How much does your grandma want for people to set up a tent?" The boy shrugged and dropped his chin. Clearly I was his first client. "OK, let's go ask her." I pulled Lucy into the side street, and together the boy and I walked into the kitchen of the house. Grandma, it turned out, had died the winter before, but the boy's mother and little brother now shared the house with an assortment of aunties and cousins whom I never quite sorted out. The mother, Lani, was like her sisters, a strong-shouldered woman with glossy black hair that fell nearly to her waist. Her youngest, Donovan, age seven, watched me from behind her left hip, his eyes huge with interest.

"You can pick your spot outside, anywhere you like," she said. "There's no hot water right now, the heater's broken, but the coffee will be on in the morning and the bathroom is here, through that door." Camping fees had not been mentioned and I wanted to clear this detail up. I had heard that even tent spots could become pricey when several hundred thousand bikers came to town. "Well we've never done this before." She said, "How does ten dollars sound?" That sounded more than reasonable to me. I handed over twenty dollars for the two nights that I expected to stay and headed out the kitchen door. Donovan was still watching with curious eyes. I stopped and turned.

"Do you want to help me find a place for my tent?" He nodded silently. We chose the grass-carpeted depression on the lee of the house where the gas meter and door to the basement were located. Donovan said nothing but watched with great interest as I pulled my tent from its bag. With absolute seriousness he helped connect the tent poles and handed them to me one by one. Finally he spoke.

"This is my grandma's house."

"I know. Your mommy told me. It's a beautiful house."

"She went to heaven."

I stopped what I was doing. "Do you miss her?"

"Yes. But I'll see her when I die." To be seven years old, and so sure of the great mystery of death, must be a comforting thing. With tent up and sleeping bag unrolled and airing, I stuck my head back inside the kitchen, met another cousin, and let them know that I was heading into town to get some dinner and would be back in the evening. Donovan waited for me by the door.

"No, Donovan, you stay with us. Karen will be back later," Lani said. "Oh, what time did you say you were getting up tomorrow?" I explained about the tires and that I would have to leave the house about seven. "The door will be unlocked. C'mon right in, get some coffee, and wash up before you go."

It was still hot as I walked the few blocks into town. Wearing no makeup, dressed in a tank top, loose army-green trousers, and boots, I was modestly attired by the standards that applied to women in Sturgis. It was, however, a very male environment and the comments began immediately.

"Hey baby, lookin' good."

"You want a ride somewheres?"

"Can I take your picture? Come sit on my bike." It was all harmless. By "male environment" I do not mean "dangerous environment," it was just that the ratio of men to women was severely skewed in the direction of the men and most of the women present had arrived with a boyfriend or husband. That made us single-looking types, even the slightly raggedy ones like me, a hot commodity.

"Nice arms! Do you lift?" The man was beside me at the Broken Spoke Bar as I stepped forward to claim my Corona.

"No."

"Well, how come you're so . . ." He stepped back from the bar and flexed into a mock bodybuilder's pose.

"I drive motorcycles. A lot." I flashed him a smile, turned, and walked deeper into the crowded bar. Eight to twelve hours on the bike, all day, every day, constantly adjusting my body and a five-hundred-pound piece of machinery to the cant and lift of the road, had tightened and strengthened my upper body. There wasn't much bulk but there was certainly muscle, moving noticeably under brown skin.

There have been times in my life when my body has been a source of embarrassment. When I was growing up, my mother discouraged fashion magazines in our house. She referred to them as "that trash" and understood that the images they presented of malnourished perfection were neither healthy nor realistic. However, like most young girls, I thought that those perfect women in the pictures were what I was supposed to grow up to look like. It never happened and never will. My body is built for endurance rather than grace. I have a light step but my gait has the loose hip swing of a cowboy, not a fashion model. Always small, I watched most of my girlfriends mature and develop those magazine breasts and hips, while I retained my boyish linearity. Too short to be considered "willowy," my brother summed up what I believed for years: that I was a big-eyed runt. People told me that I was pretty, but the beauty icons of the early eighties were Bo Derek, Christie Brinkley, and Farrah Fawcett. The popular girls in my school resembled them: they had breasts by the age of fifteen and were tall and blonde. I looked nothing like any of those women, so I dismissed the compliments as empty, cut my hair, and focused on studies and athletics. As a teenager, I was painfully shy with any boy in whom I had the slightest romantic interest. Once, fourteen years old and walking home from a soccer practice late in the afternoon, I met a boy hitchhiking back to his home in the next town. He was friendly, funny, and vaguely familiar, and as a car pulled over to pick him up he waved and shouted, "See you in school." The next Monday, dressed in the pleated gray flannel skirt and red knee socks my mother had chosen for me, I saw him again and realized who he was: the senior captain of the boys' wrestling team. In a maroon and gold letterman's jacket that made him look even larger and more manly than he was, his face lit up when he saw me and he left a group of his friends to come across the hall and speak to me. "Hi. The girl from the road! How ya doin'?" I was mortified. This handsome boy, this *senior*, this wrestling captain was talking to *me*. I could think of nothing to say, and as the color climbed from my neck into my cheeks, and his friends started to snicker, I turned and scurried wordlessly down the hall.

Four years later I stopped scurrying. I moved out of my parents' home at eighteen and waited tables, pumped gas, and cleaned offices to pay rent and save money for a solo backpacking trip. Long days at the restaurant and midnight shifts at the gas station taught me how to talk to all kinds of people, how to deal with all kinds of men, and that there was more than one kind of physical beauty. In the years that followed I learned that the attractiveness that actually matters, for both women and men, has more to do with confidence, intelligence, and what a friend of mine calls "presence" than it does with what is in glossy magazines.

The Broken Spoke, the largest bar in Sturgis, is a sprawling place with both indoor and what might be called "patio" seating. The patio has a central corral—a split-rail fenced, fifteen-by-fifteen-foot area for "events"—and further consists of a large yard paved in crushed gravel and surrounded by ten-foot chain link. Picnic tables arranged by the fencing provided perfect street viewing, and I found a seat and a beer and watched the parade of bikers coming into town for the evening. The police presence, both state and local, was noticeable but not intrusive. Both plainclothed and uniformed, they were serious about their jobs, however. In front of the Spoke, in the space of only half an hour, one bike illegally parked in a fire lane was towed, and a woman was pulled over for not signaling before changing lanes. All of this was accompanied by the hooting and derogatory comments of the bikers behind the fence. The ticket for not signaling aroused some unusually creative discourse.

"Ah fuck, man, loosen up!" The speaker turned to us. "That pig's got a billy-club so far up his ass it's tickling his tonsils." Loud vocal critique was also reserved for passing women who were either alone or with smallish companions.

"Whoo-whee! Look at that! Hey baby, can I give you a ride . . . on my face?" It was obscene, harmless, and very funny. My beer finished, I turned down four offers for a new one and walked up to Main Street to have a look at the downtown.

Main Street was closed to auto traffic for the length of its eight blocks. Motorcycles by the thousands were parked in angled rows: a row next to each curb and a double row along the centerline of the street. Bike traffic flowed, in a catwalk display of polished machinery, slowly cruising up one side and down the other, custom chrome tailpipes splayed, rear suspensions widened and lowered for fat wheels, and airbrushed gas tanks displaying artwork of eagles and Indians and naked women.

I scrambled to a perch atop a concrete barrier to watch the spectacle of steel and people. A girl in her midteens walked by with friends. Her skin was pale, as if she had not been out in the South Dakota sun all summer, and she walked with a coltish gait. Her green "apron" shirt was held together across her slim shoulder blades and waist with two ties, ties that fully exposed the tattoo that completely covered her back. A rendering of a demon's face was centered on her spinal column. It leered a one-eyed menace in black ink in an image that clashed viscerally, almost pornographically, with the girl's childish demeanor. The visage was half flayed, the muscles and tendons drawn exposed and obscene, the eye bulging from its socket as if pressured from within. It was shocking, horrifying, and a masterpiece of a tattooist's art. The woman sitting beside me on the barrier was watching the girl, too. She turned to me. "Now that's going to look lovely with an open-back wedding dress, don't you think?"

A tall African-American woman appeared at the end of the block and walked the street between the single and double row of parked motorcycles, the click of her stiletto heels lost in the roar of straight pipes. Startlingly beautiful, she had high cheekbones, short natural hair, and deep brown skin set off by white leather pants and a matching bustier. She moved through the sea of Caucasian faces with her head high, holding herself like a queen. Here was a woman with presence. I was not the only one who stared.

Back at the Broken Spoke, the music was loud and the packed bar smelled of beer, sweat, and leather. Out on the patio, while some patrons watched the mechanical-bullriders who occupied the central corral, others clustered around an upended cottonwood tree stump where nails pounded straight into the wood with a single blow would earn the participant a dollar. It was midnight, most people had been drinking since twilight, and neither the bullriders nor the nailpounders were having much success.

Creeping barefoot through the back door at 6:30 in the morning, trying not to disturb the quiet of the house, I realized just as my toes touched the kitchen linoleum that there was no need for stealth. Lani stood before the oven, a tray of muffins in her mitted hands. On the stovetop two enormous cauldrons of water bubbled.

"For your bath," she said, nodding toward the pots. "There's lots of cold water, just run it on top of the hot until the temperature's right. Pour yourself a cup of coffee, I'll get this in the tub." I was flabbergasted. Muffins, coffee, a hot bath, early morning cheeriness, and a soft lawn? I had clearly stumbled upon great-hearted people and camping paradise. In the tub I soaped my hair, rinsing what seemed to be a great deal of sand down the drain, before returning to the kitchen for a banana nut muffin, a cup of strong black coffee, and an early-morning chat with Lani about what it meant to be a woman alone.

Lani had divorced her husband some years before, after tolerating his physical abuse for much too long as she attempted to keep some version of a two-parent household together. Her own bruises and broken bones were negotiable, but when he started to hit the children she finally reacted. The police arrived with a restraining order at the same time that they removed him from the house, and Lani filed divorce proceedings the following month. It baffles me that any man would lift a hand against his wife and children, and although I intellectually understand the reasons why some women erroneously feel that they must tolerate physical abuse by their partners, it saddens me to know that lovely, strong, and capable women like Lani live with oppression and fear for years until they decide that an unacceptable level of violence against their children or themselves has been breached. For too many women, that level is set too high and they don't live long enough to find out what a peaceful and independent life would be. Thankfully Lani had.

At 7:40, I was third in line at Dunlop. The mechanics in the single bay, where two motorcycles at a time were fitted with balanced tires, worked rapidly and I was cruising back down Main Street within the hour. I wanted to test Lucy's new tires and took a short cruise toward the western outskirts of town, driving an "S" pattern to remove the factory sheen from the treads. Within three quarters of a mile I was past the last house and following Route 34 through the fields. I pulled over to U-turn back toward town on an upward-sloping gravel access to a pasture. The parade of incoming bikers had started and the roar of straight pipes filled the air. At the top of the slope, at the apex of a slow turn on two inches of crushed rock, a particularly loud blast caught my attention and I looked down at Route 34 for a critical half second, lost the momentum of the turn and tilted Lucy past the point of recoverable lean. Gravity took over and there was nothing to do but get out of the way as she dropped onto her left side with the sickening grinding sound of metal on rock. I rolled out of the way, into splashed gasoline and dust, instantly obliterating the positive results of the morning's bath.

Just like the time that I lost my balance in Colorado, there was not even a scratch or dent to mark her fall, but dropping Lucy on the outskirts of Sturgis, as bikers went by in the hundreds, was devastating to my pride. More importantly, it nearly caused an accident as three bikers locked up the brakes on their own machines in their attempt to stop, turn around, and come help me. I already had Lucy back up on her kickstand and was checking her over when my three would-be knights errant roared up the gravel drive. All were truly beautiful men in their late twenties or early thirties, cut-off T-shirts exposing heavily muscled, tanned, and tattooed arms. This was awful. Was it too much to ask that the people who witnessed my humiliation should be kindly grandfatherly types? Was it strictly necessary that the men who viewed my weakest moment as a motorcyclist look as if they had stepped directly from a Chippendale's calendar? At that moment I fervently hoped that the fuel-saturated earth would open and swallow me whole. It did not.

"Are you all right?"

"Fine, just damaged my pride."

"We saw you go down and thought you might need help." I could feel the scarlet of my face. I felt like an idiot. I was an idiot. I babbled some nonsensical explanation about slow turns, gravel, and distractions, thanked them for pulling over, swung a dusty leg over the saddle, and got the hell out of there as rapidly as possible. Dropping a motorcycle at Sturgis is the equivalent of the springboard diver who does a belly flop at the Olympics or the professional ballroom dancer who steps on her own dress and lands in a most ungraceful heap in front of the judges. Humiliation.

Slinking back to Grandma's lawn I found that the three bikers who had set up their tents next to mine the night before were packing up for a 150-mile day-trip loop of the Black Hills and the Needles Highway. They invited me to come along, but I explained that I had been on the road a long time and needed a day off. They nodded, understanding. The men pulled out, headed for the scenery of the Black Hills as I, camera in hand, walked back into town for the scenery of Main Street.

The raw consumerism of Sturgis was shocking. Before I left New Jersey I knew that the rally was about motorcycles and had a fair idea, from magazine pictures of Viking-helmeted bikers and women in barely-there bikinis, that people-watching would be a big part of the experience, but I was unprepared for the sheer volume of merchandise that was displayed and sold as part of the event. Anything related to motorcycles and biker culture, real or imagined, was for sale. Sidewalk artists airbrushed flags, wolves, and eagles onto the backs of leather jackets. Women with heavy-needle sewing machines altered the length of leather chaps and attached rally patches to jackets. Everything from beer steins to Zippo lighters to bandanas to jewelry had "Sturgis Rally 2000" or "Harley-Davidson" splashed across it. T-shirts took the lion's share of the cash and hundreds of rally designs heaped the tables. There were also the statement shirts: "Sure You Can Trust the Government . . . Just Ask an Indian," "Bikers Are Tired of Dying for Americans' Right to Drive Like Assholes," and "I Remember When Motorcycles Were Dangerous and Sex Was Safe." "If you can read this the bitch fell off" was a big seller, as was the ladies'-sized companions, "I'm the bitch" or "That's Ms. Bitch to You." More empowering was "I Ain't Your Fuckin' Baby," but this was balanced by the shirt sold next to it: "So You're a Feminist? . . . How Cute." "Silly Yuppie, Trailers Are for Boats," "Die Yuppie Scum," and "I Rode My Bike to Trailer Week" shirts commented on the pickup- and motorhome-based crowd, while others shirts were simply crude, raucous, and funny: "I'm Hung Like Einstein and Smart as a Horse" was my personal favorite.

A curbside table of glittering wallet and boot chains, pins, and jewelry caught my eye. Leaning over it, examining the selection of Zippo lighters embossed with stylized grim reapers, was a broad-shouldered man with hair greased back into a short ponytail that didn't quite control his black ringlets. A Hell's Angels jacket exposed his heavily tattooed neck and hands, but what really caught my attention was the rocker patch stitched below the distinctive winged death's head that was the Hell's Angels' symbol. It read "Chatham, Massachusetts Chapter." I knew Chatham and had been there many times. It was an old seaside community, once a fishing village, but was now populated mostly by wealthy retirees. The Angels had a chapter there? Where did they base, the yacht club?

Moving through the heavy oak and peat smell of new leather, I stopped to look at a table full of patches and chose one with an embroidered eagle and a narrow arcing rocker that read "Sturgis 2000" for my jacket. At the next table two women were looking over the selection of leather wallets, helped by a nervous salesman. The women were tall, in their late thirties, layered in gold jewelry, and had the corded shoulders and tight waists that spoke of years of aerobics classes. Matching tight white jeans stretched over their slim hips and the brunette wore a bikini top made of strategically placed, silver-painted scallop shells. The blonde's scallop shells were painted gold. I watched as the salesman hovered, answering questions and trying to look somewhere else, anywhere else, than at those shells. The women, noticing his discomfort, made a point of leaning over the table, reaching for merchandise close to his jeans, and adjusting their shell bikinis with long manicured fingers. It was wicked provocation and terribly funny to watch. A voice interrupted my bemused thoughts.

"What's a nice girl like you doing in a mean place like this?" He was taller than I and had an amused sparkle in his brown eyes. I laughed.

"That is *not* the most creative line I've ever heard."

"All right, all right. I'm a little out of practice, but you're very pretty, and I couldn't think up anything better to say before you walked away." We talked for a couple of minutes and Dale, as he introduced himself, invited me to dinner. I demurred, claiming not to know what my plans were for the evening, but actually not wanting to commit to a meeting with a stranger.

"OK," he said, "tell you what. I'll be at the Spoke at six, meet me there and I'll take you to dinner, if you want."

"OK." He shook my hand, turned, and disappeared into the crowd.

I spent the rest of the day wandering the shops and boutiques, contemplating the wisdom of a belly-button pierce as I lacked the courage for a tattoo, and shooting a few pictures. How could one not pull out a camera when there was so much material? Two men rode by on Electra Glides, inflatable love dolls flapping pink plastic limbs from their positions bungee-corded to the backseats, while a third rider followed with a huge stuffed gorilla riding pinion. A highly polished red-and-black Dyna Glide cruised east on Main Street pulling a trailer that carried a matching red-and-black coffin. Another bike pulled a cart displaying an eight-foot wooden cross. In the tolerance of the biker subculture, Vietnam veterans often find the honor, inclusion, and respect denied them by the greater American society, and POW-MIA flags flew beside the Stars and Stripes on many bikes, whipping in the wind on miniature flagpoles attached to luggage racks.

Tired, I returned to my tent for a long, late afternoon nap under the rustle of the giant oaks in Lani's yard. I lay on top of my sleeping bag thinking about the giant party that was about to begin and how much I wanted, just for one night, to stop—to stop being careful, stop being cautious, to drink, dance, pull the pins out of my hair, laugh, flirt, and to, *just once,* not be concerned with always watching, with always being in control. It was not possible to do this alone, however. What I needed was a friend. An escort.

I splashed my face with water, brushed my hair up into a clip to hold it off my neck in the last heat of the day, and made an attempt with eyeliner and mascara. The results looked a little strange—dark and startling. Digging through the bottom of my pack I found a pair of earrings, small silver suns that my brother and sister-in-law had given me years before, and spent a few minutes easing them through lobes unused to wearing jewelry. My wardrobe was at best limited, so I pulled on a mostly clean tank top and newly mink-oiled boots. My trouser hems were frayed and the waist hung low, as the intense heat of the previous two weeks had stripped another couple of pounds off my frame. Looking in the mirror I thought that the effect was perhaps a little road-worn and ratty, but it just might be acceptable in the low light of a bar or dance floor. I walked toward town trying to put a sway rather than a swing in my walk.

Back at the Broken Spoke, I bought a beer and stepped into the shadows near the wall, where I could watch and size up the possibilities at the bar. It is a mercenary thing to pick up a man for purely selfish reasons, but by my calculations it was still early enough in the evening that if the man in question decided that he wasn't enjoying himself in my company he could make other plans and I would head for home. There was one: young, handsome . . . and doing shots of hard liquor one after the other. Not good. He'd be obliterated and useless by 11 P.M. Another: huge and bearded, lots of tattoos, and well over six feet tall. Probably a big teddy bear of a man, but too intimidating to consider dealing with if the night got long and he got aggressive. What about that one? No, too slender, not enough muscle to take me where I wanted to go. I'll admit it was callous, a supermarket approach better suited to choosing tomatoes than choosing a companion. I knew, however, the body type and behavior that I was looking for and was hedging my bets that I could find someone with whom I could relax and really enjoy the party on this, my last night in Sturgis. A man stepped toward the bar: powerfully built but not more than five foot ten, a tight black T-shirt, thick brown hair, mustache, and the obligatory stubble. It was Dale, the man who had offered to buy me dinner earlier in the day. There was a wallet chain at the hip of his blue jeans, and he wore biker boots, but he had no visible tattoos. No wedding ring glinted from his left hand, which didn't necessarily mean anything. I watched him long enough from the shadows to be sure that no girlfriend, or other woman met on the street, was on her way back from the ladies' room to join him. He caught the attention of the bartender and ordered an O'Doul's. Perfect. He might ultimately turn out to be a jerk, but at least he wasn't going to be an alcoholically enhanced jerk. I walked to the ladies' room, poured my beer down the sink to the last few sips, and made my way back to the bar through the crush of mostly male bodies.

"Hey baby, are you here alone? Wait, stop and talk to me for a minute. You want a ride on my bike?"

"No. Sorry, I'm meeting someone. Thanks, I have my own." I pushed my way through to the bar with a smile.

I wiggled in beside Dale and his O'Doul's, and put my nearly empty bottle on the counter, hoping the bartender would take a couple minutes to notice.

"Can I get that for you?" He had a soft voice.

"No, thanks, but maybe the next one." Dale laughed. It was a calculated game of glances, positioning, amusing short stories, and casual flirtation and I was a little out of practice as it was over a year since I had been out on a date with a new man.

Dale was, like me, immersing himself in Sturgis for the first time. He and his wife had divorced two years before and, in a fit of personal postmarital therapy, he had bought himself a black 1998 Fat Boy and reclaimed something that he had loved as a teenager: the open road. His life was mostly work and family; he had two little boys whom he adored and who kept him in Colorado Springs most of the year, but he had taken this week to drive out to South Dakota to see the grand spectacle that he had been reading about for years.

We walked up to Main Street and Dale bought me my dinner of choice: an Indian taco—fry bread smothered in ground beef, salsa, cheese, tomatoes, and lettuce—all of it washed down with a lemonade, and we found a perch on the curb to watch the evening parade. I basked in the unfamiliar feeling of having someone there to point things out to and to talk with, someone with a different perspective, someone who noticed the things that I did not. We went to see the show bikes: fantasy machines modified to the point where driving them might be unwise, so glossy were the elaborate paint jobs, and so stretched were the front fork configurations. At the tent venue sponsored by Camel, impossibly siliconed women, dressed in the ensemble common to women bartenders in Sturgis—chaps, G-string, and matching bra—sold beer and handed out free cigarettes. A band played cover songs, loud and raucous, to an appreciative crowd. Dale slipped his hand into mine and pulled me up to dance.

Cheap Trick was playing a concert at the Buffalo Chip, a sprawling campground on the outskirts of town that was privately owned and therefore closed to police scrutiny unless the partying reached riot proportions. We walked out to Dale's Fat Boy and for the first time in a very long time, I swung up on the back of another's bike and let him drive. Neither of us wore helmets and the soft warm air blew my hair, released from its clips, back past my shoulders and out into the wind. It was one of those star-blown evenings where the distinction between air and skin is difficult to determine and the thought of dissolving into the blackness of the night becomes a reality. Dale's thighs were solid against the press of my knees and I could feel the pull of tendon and muscle as he shifted and accelerated into the unmarked velvet of the road. I wrapped my arms around his torso, my left hand low across the right side of his rib cage while the fingers of my right hand splayed across his chest. There is something intimate and sexual about riding on the back of a motorcycle. It is a surrender of sorts, a ceding of control, an acceptance of vulnerability, and an understanding that the one with a hand on the throttle controls speed, motion, direction, and destination.

There is some control, however, that a passenger has over the driver, too, or at least a form of communication where spoken words are lost on the wind. While the driver presumably has to keep his or her hands—at least one—firmly on the grips, the passenger's hands are free to roam. Dale was a construction contractor and had a body that spoke wordlessly of long days on the job site. The steady rise of his breathing brought the soft ridges of his pectorals into my right hand, his abdominals into my left. I resisted the temptation to slide my hands over his torso to feel where laterals met obliques, pectorals met shoulders met biceps and triceps. The man did, after all, have to drive a motorcycle.

We pulled into the Buffalo Chip Campground to the sound of Cheap Trick moving into the final set of the evening. Dale parked the bike, bought me a ticket, and with a light hand on my lower back, guided me through the crowd to a spot near the stage. A huge video screen towered above us, alternately showing the band and the screaming crowd. Girls perched on their boyfriends' shoulders and pulled their shirts up and off when the camera panned the throng. Nobody seemed to be wearing a bra. Motorcycles were parked throughout the crowd and, at the end of each song, along with the applause, shouts, and whistles, the roar of straight pipes matched and exceeded the blare of twelve-foot speakers as bikers voiced their approval with their machines. Dale stood behind me in the crush, his arms around my waist. The music raged, a physical pulse reverberating in my ears and down my spinal column. Dale kissed my neck, gently turned me around, ran his fingers into my wind-tangled hair, and kissed me full on the mouth. I wrapped my arms around his neck and stepped into the circle of his arms for a long moment. Eventually he released me, another song blasted from the stage, and two men standing beside us struck up a conversation with Dale. One of the men looked me up and down with the casual appraisal usually reserved for stockyards and I was glad for Dale's arm tightening around my waist.

"Are you going to enter the wet T-shirt contest? They're having the preliminaries after the show."

I pulled the front of my tank top out, glanced quickly down the front of my small bust, and laughed. "No. I don't think I'm . . . umm . . . *qualified* for that sort of competition." There were masculine protestations all around but there was no way in hell that I was getting up on that stage. The conversation turned tack.

"Where did you two ride in from?"

"Colorado."

"New Jersey." They looked at us, confused. Dale clarified.

"We met here. Tonight."

One clapped Dale on the shoulder. "You lucky fucker."

Five women took the stage following the final encore. At the end of the week, and after several preliminary rounds, a wet T-shirt title, "Miss Buffalo Chip 2000," would be awarded along with a thousand-dollar cash prize. The only rule was that the competitors had to be at least eighteen. The women wore identical white men's undershirts and, one by one as a bump-and-grind soundtrack began, they stood in front of a biker who had paid fifty dollars for the honor, as he poured half a gallon of water over their shoulders and breasts. The judging consisted of the loudness and duration of crowd applause, and the revving of bikes, as each woman spent two minutes gyrating on stage. In the end an enthusiastic, although slightly embarrassed, dark-haired and pink-cheeked novice took first place, beating out the other women who had the glassy-eyed direct stares and practiced moves of professional dancers. The contest over, the crowd started to drift away, back toward a parking lot filled with pickup trucks and motorcycles, or to the tents that could just barely be seen beyond the ring of floodlit space surrounding the stage. Dale and I drove slowly back to town.

At midnight Main Street was still packed and we wandered hand in hand through the crowd, stopping in tattoo parlors and talking about a design that Dale was thinking about for his shoulder; something that included a banner with his two sons' names on it. In the easy companionship of strangers attracted to one another, he told me little of his history and I told him almost none of mine. The past was not relevant to the present and the future only came up once when Dale stopped walking, swung me into his arms, and kissed me in the middle of the street.

"I'd love to see you again but it would never work and I know that."

"Why?" I teased. "Just because we live two thousand miles apart? Would that be a problem?"

"No." He was suddenly serious. "Look at what you've done, who you are. Look at you; you're beautiful, smart. I listen to the words you use and know that you would get tired of me." I felt as if someone had kicked me in the gut. Here was this decent, kind, sexy man telling me that because I had a fancy education, because my vocabulary was different from what he heard on the job site every day, that somehow I wouldn't find him interesting or attractive. His skills were different from mine, that was true, but he could do things that I could never dream of. He was a builder, a craftsman, and a parent. The things he thought about and accomplished each day were real and measurable, in the square feet of new homes and in the love of his sons. What did I do? Nothing that could be seen. I worked in ideas, wrote proposals, and designed projects that someone else would actually implement. I built nothing and did nothing that was tangible. No child looked to me for inspiration or support, no home waited for me when I returned. I even lacked the courage to settle into one place, to plant roots. Get tired of him? How can you get tired of someone who has everything, who does everything, that you do not? I explained these things to Dale, but I do not know if he believed me. In the end it didn't matter, we had no past and there would be no future, whatever the reasons. What we did have was a single, wonderful evening together.

At two in the morning Dale walked me back to my tent on Lani's lawn. We lay on the embankment, looking up at the stars, curled up in one another's arms, relaxing as time and conversation broadened and physical space closed.

"Come back to my hotel," he said, "or let me stay here with you. I want to wake up with you in my arms."

"No. I can't." He told me that we would be good together and I knew that he was right. There was no lasciviousness and I felt no shame in admitting that I wanted to experience the closeness, the sexuality, that fired between us. I told him that I wanted to feel his hands on my body, and twisting through my hair, and to wake up in a tangle of limbs, but that I still had to say no. I had spent the last two months alone and would ride east through the Badlands tomorrow, solitary as always, while he started his trip south and west to Colorado. I trusted him implicitly and had ridden on the back of his bike to wherever he wanted to take me, but somehow I felt that if I gave Dale that last bit of vulnerability that I would somehow come unglued, that every last barrier that I had built to stay strong and self-sufficient on the road would come crashing down, and that I would be afraid, emotionally rather than physically, to be alone again. Who would ride with me then? There was no one. Fine human being and gentleman that he was, Dale listened, said that he understood, held me a while longer while the stars swirled above us, kissed me gently, and left.

Later, sleepless in my tent, I cursed the choices I made: choices that kept me independent and free, but that exacted the huge price of loneliness.

With not much sleep, and probably too much alcohol, I woke up feeling more than a little wobbly. Steadiness returned with a couple cups of Lani's coffee and several large glasses of water. Donovan came out to help me pull up my tent stakes, stuff my sleeping bag, and watched silently as I loaded Lucy to leave.

"Why do you have to go?" We had spent just a few hours together over the last two days. He had told me stories and I had chosen pictures for him to color from books filled with monsters and superheroes.

"I have to go home, Donovan, my mom is waiting for me." He nodded silently and pulled a carefully colored Superman picture from his pocket.

"Here, I made this for you." I wrapped him in a big hug, kissed the top of his little-boy summer wiffle haircut, and put the picture between the pages of my journal. Lani came out to say good-bye and told me to make sure that if I ever came back to the rally, to come and stay with them, that I was always welcome, and that they would always make room for me. I told her that I would and meant it.

. . .

Route 14 ran west out of town and into the Black Hills. Along with hundreds of other bikers, I rolled past the casinos and through the historic gun-slinging quaintness of Deadwood before dropping south on Route 385 through lands that the Sioux held sacred.

The Black Hills were named for the thick stands of pine trees that appeared as dark rises from the bright gold sweep of the prairie. It is lush territory, still heavily forested, and dotted with small lakes held by the gentle slopes of the terrain. The Black Hills had been the traditional hunting, worship, and burial grounds of the Sioux and other tribes, for millennia before the devastating arrival of the Europeans. In 1868, the U.S. government signed a treaty with the Sioux that ensured them eternal tenure to the Black Hills, and to the rest of South Dakota west of the Missouri River. Unfortunately, mineralized green, pink, and yellow gold was discovered in the Black Hills in the mid-1870s, the treaty was revoked, and the Sioux, those who survived, were driven out. Today the Sioux occupy only a small fraction of the land west of the Missouri and live mostly on nine reservations in South Dakota. The four largest are Standing Rock, Cheyenne River, Pine Ridge, and Rosebud. The latter two have become synonyms for poverty and disenfranchisement, have unemployment rates in excess of 80 percent, and median family incomes that hover around twenty-five hundred dollars per year. On the Sioux reservations of South Dakota, life expectancies are that of developing-nation standards: twenty-five years less than the American national average.

Driving a motorcycle while hungover does detract from the typical joy of the experience. The rise and fall of the hills, usually such an extraordinary feeling, inspired nothing but nausea. Having eaten nothing but greasy street food washed down mostly with beer for the past two days, and with little but coffee to keep me going after a sleepless night, by the time I dropped over the crest of the last hill before the Pactola Reservoir I was feeling truly ill. I pulled over to walk around for a few minutes, breathe air that hadn't come through the plastic vents of a helmet, rehydrate with yet another half-liter bottle of water, my third of the morning, and eat a granola bar. With a few carbohydrates, fluid, and a shoreline walk, I felt a little better and fired up Lucy for the run down to Mount Rushmore.

Despite the obvious skill and tremendous effort that went into carving the sixty-foot visages of Washington, Lincoln, Jefferson, and Roosevelt into the face of a mountain, I have always thought that that particular monument in that particular place was a poor reflection of the arrogance of a conquering people. I understood that the political leaders of the latter part of the nineteenth century had wished to celebrate the growing power of a new nation, but why did it have to be in South Dakota, and on sacred native land, where so much blood had been spilled and where the promises of a great government, exemplified by the faces of the four men carved into a white granite cliff, had been so cynically and casually broken? It seemed to me that having such a tribute in the Black Hills did little to exalt the men, or the governmental systems, that it was intended to honor. A few miles away another monument, fifty years in the making and perhaps another century in the completion, was rising. Begun in 1948 by Korczak Ziolkowski in response to a request from Chief Henry Standing Bear of the Lakota Sioux, the monument to the warrior Crazy Horse, along with the attendant planned museum and university, will be a more place-appropriate tribute to the heritage and culture of the Black Hills.

Where Route 44 looped through the town of Scenic, distinctive pastel-colored rock formations pushed up from the grasses and the green of the prairie. The spires, escarpments, and ledges of the Badlands rose in the distance as the temperature climbed with the midday sun. I stopped in Interior, traded leather and helmet for a ball cap, glasses, and tank top, and drove the park loop, Route 240, as it doubled back from 44.

My guidebook, quoting the writings of General Alfred Sully, described the Badlands as "hell with the fires out," but I thought that they looked more like the bones of mountains, skeletonized of any shred of epidermal greenery or softening arterial pulse of mountain stream. In the formations one could read the passage of sixty million years of sedimentary buildup: layer upon layer of weather-carved rose, ochre, green, gold, and white stone that was eroding back into the prairie with every rainstorm, wind gust, and winter shard of splitting ice. The weather had left both sharp and soft contours behind it. Great finned clavicles of ridges towered above gently sloping, buttressed ribs. Bony-fingered white pinnacles pointed toward the merciless heat pouring from the August sky while sloping, rounded, low, cranial curves held the colors of the land. The hues of the Badlands were soft at midday, and the shadows hid deep in the crevices, but I found it necessary to drive slowly, ignoring the heat rising off Lucy, rising off the road, and take time to wonder at each new shape that appeared with the turning pavement, each new shade that glowed, muted but still noticeable, in the white spotlight of the day.

THE COFFEE IN STEPHEN, SOUTH DAKOTA, was cheap, black, and piping hot. Breakfast was on the bench outside the concrete-floored combination general store and gas station: a cellophane package of Fig Newtons and a view to the morning sun brightening the sunflower fields beyond. A gleaming white pickup truck pulled in off Route 47 and an older farmer stepped from the cab. His hands were huge, his eyes kind and curious.

"Where're you goin'?"

"Minnesota."

"Where're you comin' from?"

"Montana." Unless directly questioned, I had stopped telling people where I had been riding. Mostly I chose a state or two behind and a state or two ahead and let casual inquirers believe that these were the parameters of my trip. If I told the whole truth most people didn't know what to say, and they often looked at me as if I was either lying or some sort of freakish oddity.

"Not much to see 'round here."

"Everyone says that, 'flat, nothing to see.' But I like it. The Plains have a beauty all their own." He nodded slowly, eyes narrowed in thought. All his life he had lived near Stephen, he said, growing wheat and corn, and raising cattle.

I asked him about farming life and economics in the Dakotas and he echoed what I had heard in Kansas weeks before.

"There's no living in wheat anymore. The price is so low, then there's fuel, machinery." He jerked a thumb at his new pickup truck. "One of those things cost you thirty-four thousand dollars."

"How's the cattle market these days?"

"Cattle's a bit better, prices are supposed to be up this fall." He went inside to pay for his gasoline and emerged with a cup of coffee.

"Where did you say you were from?"

"I didn't. I'm from New Jersey."

"New Jersey. Huh." He shook his head and looked at Lucy, my dusty boots, and sunburned shoulders, not needing to ask the other questions. We sipped our coffee, side by side on the bench in comfortable silence for a couple of minutes. He stood. "Well, see you around sometime . . . probably would have to be here though, 'cause I won't be going to New Jersey." A broad grin creased his features, he wished me well, and got into his truck. He waved as he pulled out onto the blacktop and disappeared into the beauty of the Plains.

Back on the road, comfortably cool for the first time in weeks, I watched snow-white egrets flap out of the roadside ditches where they had been hunting for frogs. Their cousins, the great blue herons, fished on slender legs in ponds a little farther off the road. Had they made a deal? Egrets in the ditch, herons in the pond, tomorrow we switch? There were surely plenty of frogs as this was green, moist country, watered by a network of rivers: the Snake, Mud, Wolf, Turtle, and James. The land was level and fertile, with straight roads and ninety-degree turns that joined at rigidly east-west-north-south intersections. Was it possible to get lost in eastern South Dakota? I thought not.

At Kranzburg, running due east on Route 212 and not far from the Minnesota border, I stopped at a roadside rest area for lunch. On the end of a picnic tabletop, carefully arranged multicolored pebbles formed an arrow pointing to a chunk of white quartz at the other end of the table. *Curious.* I lifted the quartz and found the roach end of a joint. Pot smokers have better senses of humor than alcohol users. Had this been the site of a beer bash rather than a toke circle, the remains would have been a litter of bottles and crushed cans instead of this carefully arranged tableau that whispered, "Look what happened here."

Despite the bohemian nature of rest-area detritus, the roadside signs and bumper stickers of Route 212 made the political climate of the Dakota-Minnesota border not overly difficult to ascertain. PROTECT LIVESTOCK FROM PREDATORS—WEAR FUR one billboard read. UNBORN BABIES ARE PEOPLE TOO was the next. IT'S TIME TO ROTATE THE CROP—JOE THOMPSON FOR U.S. CONGRESS! Unless I missed my guess, the religious agricultural right populated these counties. Had there ever been any, the liberals were not in evidence. Perhaps it was their modest farmhouses that stood, gaping windows letting in the swallows, treeless and abandoned in the middle of the lush tilled fields of expanding agribusiness. Regardless of whether one was Democrat or Republican, left or right leaning, it was hard to make a living as a small farmer where corn, wheat, and sugar beets stretched, thousands of acres to a field, to the hazy white horizon. Those on the fringe, the smallholders and the liberals, had clearly vacated, tilled under by the plows of corporate farming, economies of scale, and Christian conservatism.

Across the border and into Minnesota, Lac Qui Parle and Yellow Medicine Counties were as sparsely populated as the country to the west, and the occasional communities looked as if whatever residents remained were trying to get out as rapidly as possible. Dawson and Wegdahl, little towns on the way to nowhere, housed more dead than living judging by the expansive graveyards, deserted sidewalks, and compressed number of homes and businesses, many of which were boarded up and falling in on themselves. There was an eerie sense of people who were no longer there, as well as of those who had been left behind: the elderly who sat silent and motionless on front porches that were shedding fist-sized scabs of old paint. The thruways were empty.

The heat was rising again, and there was something humming, unsettled and ominous, in the air. Was a storm brewing? I throttled Lucy across the outskirts of Granite Falls and past the smashed leavings of tornado. The intense heat of the previous day had apparently launched a thunderstorm when the cooler air of the evening had rolled in, a thunderstorm that had then spawned a funnel cloud. The twister roared through town just after dark, shattering trees, blasting out plate-glass windows, and peeling the roofs off businesses and homes. At one farm, a massive spreading oak was shorn off thirty feet above the ground, amputated in a fracture of yellow wood and matchsticked branches. At another, a violently truncated steel silo, the roof gone and the top folded in on itself, appeared as if a giant fist had come down directly upon it, squashing the metal like a giant beer can. In many ways, the people of Granite Falls had been lucky. It was late evening when the tornado touched down, most families were at home, and the heaviest damage had been in the business district. I passed a campground, green and beautiful, a mile and a half from Main Street, and was grateful that I had not made it to Granite Falls any earlier.

Tired, dusty, and road-weary, I stopped in Olivia for groceries and to consider camping options on a map spread over Lucy's tank. Although no state campgrounds were marked, there was a series of small lakes forty miles ahead, just west of the outer suburbs of Minneapolis. Surely I could find a spot to set up my tent there. I folded the map, put it away, and walked slowly toward the small grocery store. It had already been a four hundred mile day on Lucy and bipedal locomotion was a concerted effort. Thirty feet from the entrance a man in his seventies hustled by me, hurriedly reaching for the handle so that he could step back and hold the door open for me. I smiled, feeling sweaty, dirty, and distinctly undeserving of this ritual.

"Thank you."

"You betcha!" This small-town variety of chivalry reminded me that in places like Olivia, Minnesota, it didn't matter whether I deserved it or not, whether I was clean or filthy, whether I was a neighbor or a stranger, a gentleman always held the door for ladies. It was simply the way people treated one another.

My guess about the lakes was right, and forty-five miles later I pulled into Marion Lake Campground just south of Hutchinson. The woman in the office was the grandmotherly type and called me "dear." Although there were tent spaces available on the lakeshore she advised me to take one closer to the center of the campground and a cluster of motorhomes.

"Well, you know, dear," she said, "boys from town sometimes come out and have parties down by the lake. We call the police, of course, but it can be quite noisy before they get here." I set up my tent near the motorhomes and the bathhouse. As it turned out, there was no lakeside party but my tent location worked out well for other reasons.

Cloying humidity and that thick unsettled humming was still present in the early-evening atmosphere. Considering a swim I walked down to the lake, stood on the dock, and reconsidered as I looked into the glistening greenish frogspawn that coated the water. The surface appeared to be clear farther out, but I wasn't enthusiastic about paddling through a couple million embryonic amphibians to get there and decided on a cold shower instead. The lake was oval, perhaps half a mile across and two miles long, serene and strangely still. In the fading light of the evening, I looked at the horizon over the glassy surface, at the greenish black clouds that were building in great massed thunderheads, and thought about Granite Falls. *Oh shit.* Riding out storms in a fabric tent, especially storms that had a recent history of dropping tornados, did not seem like the brightest of ideas. I looked around . . . *options . . . options. What to do? I could get my tired ass back on Lucy, ride up to Hutchinson, and try to find a hotel.* I was exhausted and hungry, it had been a long day that had once again turned brutally hot in the afternoon, my tent was already up, my stuff unpacked, my site paid for, and Lucy was under her tarp. These were all very bad reasons to stay, considering what was blowing in over the lake, but I was also camped next to the concrete bathhouse. *If things get ugly, I can always shelter in there.* In the internal dialogue this sounded reasonable and I went back to my tent site, hammered the stakes a little farther into the ground with a smooth rock, perched on top of one of the picnic tables, ate a cheese and cracker dinner topped off with a can of spinach, and watched with morbid fascination as the thunderheads built into anvils thousands of feet high.

The remaining light shifted to greenish gray and disappeared altogether as I crawled into my tent after checking the tethers on the rain fly. The growing breeze could not shift the humidity, but it carried with it the silence of an oncoming storm. Not a single cricket or bird sang into the night sky. By flashlight I read a few lines of Whitman and dozed until ten-thirty, when the walls of the tent began to pop with the first spattering of raindrops. Thunder rolled in the distance, becoming louder and closer by the minute. By eleven the storm was shrieking its full fury. The tent poles bowed under the gale of the wind and the incandescence of purple-white lightning filled the small space in decreasing intervals. The roar of the storm was deafening. *Perhaps not packing up and heading for Hutchinson had been a mistake.* A tearing crack, the sound of a howitzer exploding over my head, had me wriggling as close to the ground as my sleeping bag would allow. *I need to move. Now.* I gathered up my sleeping bag, journal, book, and wallet and unzipped my tent for a dash to the bathhouse. Sheets of rain had dropped too quickly for runoff, and the campground looked as if the lake had crawled beyond its banks. A violet web of light flashed across the sky, illuminating the standing water. I had never seen such lightning before. These were not individual vertical bolts that leaped and flashed from cloud to ground and back again, but rather a lacework of electricity running horizontally across the sky; purple, white, and blue. Soaked in seconds, I stood and watched the play of light in stupefaction until another crash of thunder reminded me of the idiocy of standing upright in the heart of a massive electrical storm. I sprinted for the bathhouse, tore open the door, and curled up in a corner to wait it out. It was a fast-moving system, too violent to last long, and an hour later the flashes of lightning were less bright and the roar of thunder was a distant thing, already far to the east. I returned to my tent and was somewhat surprised to find it still tethered to the ground, wet but upright. After readjusting Lucy's tarp, which had half blown off, I crawled back into my damp sleeping bag. There were still rumbles of thunder and the occasional flash of lightning, but by 1 A.M. I was too tired to care.

The purist's attempt to stay on secondary roads got lost in the horror of negotiating suburban strip-mall traffic around the Minneapolis–Saint Paul metro area and I guided Lucy into the steel flow of the 494 and 694 beltways. Highway traffic around the Twin Cities was the ubiquitous urban madness moving at sixty miles an hour, but I was amazed and somewhat puzzled by the courteousness of most of the drivers and all of the truckers. Welcome to the Midwest where, even in the largest cities and heaviest traffic, people signal before changing lanes and leave a safe distance between their vehicle and the next.

Route 36 east brought me off 694 and into the narrow riverside streets of Stillwater. Although choked with traffic and the heavy burning fumes of a paving job that snarled movement through its narrow streets, Stillwater, as its name implied, was a place that invited lingering. Red brick buildings supported elaborately carved balconies that overlooked water's-edge streets, and small cafés and boutiques entreated sidewalk strollers to enter, sit down, just take a look. Unfortunately, the heat was rising again, as was the humidity, so instead of window-shopping I opted to keep moving, across the Saint Croix River and into the beckoning green hills of Wisconsin.

Route 63 took me north through the towns of Clear Lake, Turtle Lake, and Cumberland, before I leaned Lucy into the turns of Route 48, running east toward Rice Lake. Northwestern Wisconsin was hill and river farming country. A patchwork of fields and woodlots quilted the view where the road rose high enough to overlook a landscape stitched together in the shades of dusty-leaved poplars and tall oaks, emerald corn, and gold wheat. Red barns flanked angular symmetric houses with white verandas, and porch swings surveyed curving gravel drives. I wondered about the nature of the families who had settled there and how they had chosen the location for their farmhouses. Some stood exposed to wind and weather, sunblasted on hilltops where the views were striking and where every passing breeze held the scent of mown hay and growing corn. Others were tucked into sheltered hollows, where they were protected by tall trees from the burning rays of summer, but where the snow must fall into deep drifts when winter came. Did it say anything at all to note that some people hunkered down into hollows while others built with an eye to exposure?

Pulling into Rice Lake for gas and a granola bar, it was my own exposure that was beginning to concern me. The thick humidity was again building into the towering mountain ranges of purple and green streaked clouds that foretold another violent evening storm. The force of the wind made the station door difficult to close as I went inside to pay for my gas. The girl behind the register was young and had a monochromatic, powdered, perfectly oval face, dark blonde hair of a single chemical shade, and a bored, although not unfriendly, look in her heavy eyes. A small television on the counter behind her was tuned to the local news.

"What are they saying about the weather tonight?"

"Strong storms," she said, "and a possible tornado watch." She chewed her gum languidly and gave me change for a ten-dollar bill. I walked toward the door. "Have a good night," she said. Her voice lacked the smallest trace of irony.

Outside again, I pulled my rain jacket over my leather and rolled onto the "M" road headed north. Wisconsin was the first state where I encountered roads labeled with letters rather than numbers or names. Each county apparently started with "A" and alphabetized the roads until they ran out of letters. After that they doubled them up: "AA," "BB," and so on. Halfway through the alphabet, there must be ten "M" roads in Wisconsin, twice as many "A," "B," and "Cs," and half as many "X," "Y," and "Zs," but as they are all in different counties no one gets confused. No one except the tourists.

In the distance, thick bolts of lightning dropped straight out of the lowering cloudbank, followed almost immediately by thunder so intense that I could feel it through my sternum. I was only ten minutes out of Rice Lake, driving the line of an eastbound storm of Wagnerian proportions, when I decided that it was time to look for roofed shelter for the night. I estimated I had half an hour before the system was on top of me and real trouble began. Hunching down behind Lucy's windshield as the rain began to fall, I twisted her throttle and ran for the next community. Birchwood had a single motel; at forty-four dollars a night, had what looked like a flight of Valkyries not been blowing in, I would have kept driving. However, after one last hurried perusal out the motel office window, I dropped a credit card on the reservation desk and asked the woman to charge it.

Wrenching my luggage from Lucy's frame, I tied her tarp as tightly and as strongly as I could through her wheels and forks, gave her gas tank one final pat, and sprinted for the room. Five minutes later, walnut-sized hail joined the drenching rain and blasting wind. After changing into dry clothes, and tuning in the Weather Channel's tornado warnings for Rice Lake and northern Wisconsin, forty-four dollars did not seem so extravagant.

IN A HORRIBLE MOMENT OF UTTER dislocation, I opened my eyes to white walls, a particleboard ceiling, and the cling of bedsheets. No birds sang, the filtered light of morning sunshine through blue tent fabric was absent, and the scent of grass, loam, and dew-wet earth had been replaced by the chemical odors of detergent, bleach, and furniture polish. I had no idea where I was. Panic stiffened my hands and I struggled clumsily to unwind the bedclothes from my legs. Then . . . *oh, right . . . Lucy and road . . . the storm and a hotel. OK.* I rearranged the twisted blankets and lay back, attempting to relax in roofed luxury, but sleep was gone.

The morning was overcast, with thick gray clouds hanging so low and pendulous that they left my faceshield dappled with clinging mist. Route 70 swayed through forest and field, following the curvature of the hills, and skipping across the run of the Thornapple, Flambeau, and Wisconsin Rivers. The tangle of lakes at Arbor Vitae, Saint Germain, and Eagle River lent more mist to the atmosphere as well as flashes of steel-blue water glimmering behind the scrim of dark, wet pines. Wonderful old farmhouses flashed by, substantial yet strangely luminous walls built of bowling ball–sized, rose-colored stones set into gray mortar.

Iron Mountain had a good library and following a few e-mail updates to the family I also found a good coffee shop, where large windows flooded blond wood and black fixtures with light. I sat and nursed a latte for an hour, listening to the hiss of espresso machines and watching the street. These last few days I had been unaccountably tired. Was it the heat of the Midwest? Or was it just that the aggregation of miles and weeks on the road were starting to collect in entrenched body fatigue? It was in Alberta, with Dave and his family, when I had last slept in a bed for more than one night and eaten off a kitchen table rather than out of a saddlebag or at a roadside café. Since Sturgis, I had found myself swilling back coffee, the larger and stronger the better, almost as often as I stopped for gas. Lucy and I were both running on high octane. For her it was mechanical necessity, for me it was a chemical attempt to keep moving, to drag myself through the weariness, through the fifteen hundred miles of pavement from South Dakota to Ontario, where my family had their backwoods cottage. There, on the lake, I would sleep, rest, and slow to a standstill for a few days. I drained my latte and watched a mother and child, hand in hand, cross one of Iron Mountain's quiet streets. I did worry that in flying through the miles, forcing myself and my machine through ten- to twelve-hour days, that I was missing what I had come to see: the quiet beauty of rural towns, the patchwork of cultures that made up communities far from the interstates and the cities, and the relaxed pace of the forty-mile-an-hour secondary and tertiary roads, which connected one little town to the next to the wilderness beyond. Was I still feeling the roll of the land? Was I still seeing the gentle shift of forest to field and back to forest again? Or was I just pushing through the miles, pushing through the days? I wasn't sure anymore.

From Blaney Park, in the flat-topped hills of Michigan's Eastern Upper Peninsula, it was only a half-day's run through familiar country toward Sudbury, Ontario, and my family. The hamlets of Engadine, Gilchrist, Rexton, and Trout Lake dotted Route 540 like an archipelagic chain, just clearings in the dense woods, clusters of small homes, and possibly a single auto repair bay. The second belt of the Hiawatha National Forest, which cinched the northern waist of the Upper Peninsula in a greenish-black tangle of firs, was only thirty miles from the international bridge that joined the urban halves of Sault Ste. Marie on either side of the channel that connected Lake Huron with Lake Superior. By midmorning I was back in Canada.

Despite a soft campsite and seven hours of sleep the night before, I was still desperately tired. Although I expected an easy three-hour run up the Trans-Canada Highway, I stopped in Bruce Mines for a huge cup of coffee to fuel the final miles. A single motorcycle, an early-eighties Honda Gold Wing, was parked in the Tim Horton's lot and I pulled up alongside it, lowering Lucy onto her kickstand. Casually looking the bike over, I was surprised to see a small canine head pop up over the armrest of the passenger seat. The poodle was a tiny thing with a sharp, wet nose, tightly curled silver fur, and a sweet disposition. I patted her head, my two fingers wide enough to cover the entire top of her delicate skull. Her owner came back just as I turned to Lucy to retrieve my wallet, and the dog wriggled her whole body with the joy of seeing him. In his sixties, he was a big man with gray hair and a sparkling stud earring in his left lobe. He was from Bruce Mines, he told me, but had taken his bike and his dog, which always rode in the passenger seat, on several long trips, which included runs out to the Maritime Provinces.

"You don't worry about her jumping off?" I asked.

"Well, I started her off riding in the saddlebag"—he pointed to the hard luggage flanking the back wheel—"but once, I looked down and she wasn't there. I thought she'd jumped out so I pulled over and was going back to look for her on the road when she stuck her nose up from the passenger seat. She's ridden here ever since."

"Guess she wanted a better view."

"Guess so." He dropped a huge hand gently across her wriggling back. "She's real good company."

The Trans-Canada Highway is the only west-east road in south-central Ontario and I followed it through familiar landscape. It had been in Pennsylvania, close to fourteen thousand miles of pavement back, where I had last driven a road that was not new to me, and it felt good to recognize the names of the communities flashing on the signs: Iron Bridge, Blind River, Algoma Mills, and Spanish. I passed a roadside gallery owned and run by a collective of native artisans, where I had bought a bold graphic abstraction of a stylized sun rising behind two loons five years before. The loon print was in New Jersey, waiting to be hung on the wall of my next home, wherever that might be. It was a smooth run of pavement, and I could feel the images of the familiar, and the memories and nostalgia of tradition, gathering in a fine web of expectation. I knew exactly the structure of the next day: a morning swim, pancakes made by Mom or waffles made by Dad, the slow crank of the handle and the scratchy rendition of "When the Swallows Come Back to Capistrano" that I always played on my grandmother's seventy-eight upright phonograph. In the next week there would be hours in my grandfather's fishing boat; fishing more for the sake of the gentle rocking of the waves and the slow drift past cedars, white pines, and laurel undergrowth than for the trout and bass we pulled from the lake. Dad and I would talk about international politics, institutional development, and banking in a setting that was as far removed from such things as one could get. Mom and I would sit in the big chairs on the small deck that overhung the water and I would parry her acerbic questions about the complexities of my love life. We would drink fuzzy navel cocktails and cook dinner together as the loons began to sing on the lake. I loved it: the pace, the peace, the simplicity and the stability, both spatial and emotional. Another couple of hours and I would be there.

Lost in thoughts of rocking boats and casting lures, I found the heavy road construction that commenced just east of Espanola a rude shock. Like the Alcan, parts of the Trans-Canada are constantly under repair and rebuilding to widen, straighten, and turn what is still largely a two-lane thruway into a four-lane divided highway. The Espanola construction was vintage Alcan: the halted traffic, the wait for the convoy car, the clouds of swirling dust, and the slippery shift of miles of gravel and newly laid chip rock beneath Lucy's tires. Past the torn pavement and heavy equipment, however, it was a smooth run on Route 10 to Whitefish, across one corner of a reservation where Ojibwas make their home, and out to the marina dock where my family keeps the boat that takes us nine miles down the roadless edge of a lake to the point of land where my grandfather built a hunting shack sixty years ago.

Weary, covered in tiny motes of pulverized pavement and roadbed dust, I parked Lucy in front of the white stucco building that serves as general store, fishing license dispenser, boat repair and maintenance office, and home of the marina owner, Louis Dozie, and his family. Louis and one of his mechanics, a tall blond man named Ray, looked at me curiously as I swung out of the saddle. I pulled my helmet off, shook out my hair, and turned around. Louis has known me since I was a baby, and although I only make it up to the lake once a year, he always remembers me. He didn't, however, know anything about my motorcycles, or this trip. He stared.

"Jesus . . . is that you, Karen? What the *hell* are you doing on that thing?"

"I thought I'd come catch a trout. Have you left any in the lake for me?" Once an avid fisherman, Louis's interests were now more toward golf, but he still threw a line in from time to time.

"A few." He chuckled, shaking his head at the sight of the boots, the leather, and the bike. "It's always great to see you." He came over and wrapped his arms around me. "How long are you staying?"

Ray, also a Harley rider, was engaged in a love-hate relationship with a 1981 shovelhead that spent more time in parts on his shop floor than actually out on the road. He found me a place to park Lucy in one of the repair sheds. It smelled of motor oil and fish but it was dry and had a padlocked slide bolt on the door. Ray promised to keep an eye on Lucy for me and I left her in his capable hands for the week.

There is no telephone at our cottage and there was no way to reach my parents to ask them to come pick me up at the marina. Louis runs a boat-taxi service, however, and he called over one of the dock boys to run me down the lake. I sat in the bow, perching on my backpack and watching the familiar shoreline through the rainbow spray of water splashing off the prow. Water traffic is light on our end of the lake as most of the shoreline backs onto tens of thousands of Crown-owned acreage that was closed to sale or development fifty years ago. From a mile and a half away, if one hears a boat coming through the last set of narrows, chances are it's headed for our cottage. Both my parents were standing on the dock, grinning broadly, when I pulled in. Dad reached for my backpack and Mom for my hand as I paid the boy and thanked him for the trip. Mom pulled me into her arms.

"So you're still alive?" She was laughing and clearly relieved to see her daughter in one piece.

"Sure. No problems."

I thought that a week at the lake, off the bike and with my family, would be enough time to rest, tell some stories, and pull some fish from the water before heading south and east on the final leg back to the East Coast. A week stretched into ten days, however, when weariness turned into a pounding headache, a sore throat, and finally a raging fever. It was an ugly process that lasted for days and I spent my waking hours in hallucinatory half-light, swallowing ibuprofen and watching the flashing images of the Utah desert, California redwoods, and Albertan wilderness that swirled through my blurred vision. At night I woke soaked in sweat. Dad was going to take me into town to see a doctor, but on the third day white patches appeared on my tonsils: strep throat. My father is a cancer survivor with poor circulation and an immune system compromised years ago by heavy doses of chemotherapy, and he carries a supply of amoxicillin to forestall infection should he get injured or ill. He gave me his pills and three days later the fever finally broke.

While Dad went fishing, Mom and I spent afternoons sitting on the dock in beautiful cedar chairs that my brother and sister-in-law had given her. One afternoon, as the light was just beginning to shift the colors of the lake from deep blues and greens to the softer evening hues of silver and topaz, she gingerly broached a sensitive topic. I could hear the hesitation in her voice.

"So, how did it go . . . with Dave. And his family?" I had to give her enormous amounts of credit, and I am deeply grateful, for her ability to discuss a subject that she once found so bitterly painful.

"It went really well, Mom, really well." We sat and talked it through. I told her everything about my visit to Alberta, what I had learned from Dave regarding his relationship with Gloria, and pieces began to fall into place. My parents had never known why I was already four months old when they adopted me, while my brother had been a tiny infant when they adopted him. She asked my thoughts about what my relationship with Dave and Gloria's families might be in the future, and how they saw my arrival back into their lives. She asked the most simple questions, about such things as physical resemblances, as well as the most difficult ones about histories of disease and personal concepts of exactly what a family is. I believe that she had thought a lot about these things as I traveled the country and I admired her courage for wanting to talk about them directly. We are a Scandinavian family, my mother is Finn-Swede and my father is Danish, and such things as feelings and emotion, loss and renewal, connection and separation—most topics of the spiritual or familial sort—while undoubtedly felt, are simply not discussed. It is a cultural barrier, negative certainly, but one that is usually balanced by clearly expressed concepts of stoicism, loyalty, bravery, and responsibility. There are rare times, however, when bridges between the two sets of values are established, and they are incredibly powerful moments. Such was the moment sitting on the dock in the late afternoon sun with my mom as the loons began to sing.

43 | HEADED HOME

TWO DAYS LATER, MY PARENTS TOOK me back to the dock, to Lucy, and to the road. The boat trip up the lake was, as it always is on the summer's last trip to the marina, a bittersweet journey. I was looking forward to continuing with Lucy, and was much more rested and enthusiastic about traveling than I had been coming into Ontario, tired and ill, the week before, but I loved the lake and loved the brief periods of time that I was able to spend with my parents. It was a misty ride through the narrows and across the wide expanses of water that people called "bays." The cedars and the white and jack pines lining the shore were bluish, just tinged with green through the mist. Dad drove the boat at speed, with the running lights on, and with the surety of one who had studied that shoreline for the thirty-six years that he and my mother had been married.

Although they were going into town, too, for groceries, we said good-bye at the dock. My parents never say "I love you," but I could feel the reality of love in their warm hugs that were just a little longer than the usual quick squeeze, and in their final admonitions to "Drive safely." They followed me down the highway and into the town of Lively, where I pulled off to bring Lucy into the Harley dealership for a new battery. Turning into the driveway I waved, Dad honked his horn, and they were gone.

. . .

I've always liked the stretch of highway that runs between North Bay and Cobden. Wooded hillsides and long thin lakes mark a landscape that has changed little since the French *voyageurs* came upstream during the seventeenth and eighteenth centuries, exploring for their king and pursuing private wealth in traded furs. Where only the flow of the Ottawa River once linked villages that were little more than eddies at the bends in the bank—Mattawa, Deep River, and Chalk River—the highway now connects them to the centers of government, mass employment, and commerce: Ottawa to the east, Sudbury to the west. My favorite place on that stretch, which actually has a name, is Deux Rivières, a tiny community just north of Bisset Creek. It is the place where the river draining the Lac Maganasipi watershed joins the Ottawa at a misty, pooled junction of low hills, water, and thick black forests. The Ottawa banks the north side of the road while a small lake laps at the south. Running Lucy between the two, with the forest ahead at the end of the causeway, the feeling was one of riding the back of a skipping stone, skimming the plane of blue water to the shore beyond.

After Cobden the highway emptied out of the forest, following the broadening spill of the river into the open, farmed spaces of the Ottawa Valley. The traffic and the speed of the road increased as the forest thinned, the farms began, and the rumbling eighteen-wheelers moved corn and milk out, merchandise and machinery in. By Renfrew, dense fields of corn grew rank on rank. Butter-and-sugar and silver queen varieties were sold at roadside stands, while feed corn ripened in the fields for the dairy cows that dotted the open pastures in chessboard-colored herds. Substantial brick farmhouses built at the turn of the last century sat atop knolls or at the end of tree-lined drives, their roof peaks trimmed in green oxidized copper or white-wood lacework. I twisted the throttle, holding between sixty and sixty-five, keeping pace with the traffic, yet staying within the speed limit. The rumors about the Ontario Provincial Police were that they lacked a certain sense of humor, and that no matter how good the excuse, or how dazzling the smile, they could not be talked out of writing tickets; tickets that were generally expensive. It was an urban legend that I did not feel the need to verify and I kept Lucy to an easy, law-abiding lope.

In Antrim I pulled over for gas and spent a few minutes waiting in line at the register at the busy truck stop. By the time I got back to the pumps, three soldiers in cocked black berets were clustered around Lucy. They wandered off to their truck as I approached, said nothing, and simply stared as I put my wallet back in a saddlebag, pulled on jacket, gloves, and helmet, and fired her up. They made no attempt to hide their curiosity and did not get into their own vehicle until after I had left. It had been ten days since I had felt like a public curiosity and I honestly hadn't missed it. After months on the road I should have expected and made peace with what it meant to be a spectacle because of my machine and my gender, but in fifteen thousand miles of riding I never became oblivious of, or even quite used to, the constant stares and comments. If one wanted to slip into the vapor, if one had the desire to vanish anonymously down a nameless road, driving a motorcycle is not the way I would recommend a woman do it. People notice, comment on, and remember "a girl on a bike," and everybody has an opinion about what they are seeing. Sometimes I wished that I might find that nameless road, or that vapor of anonymity, that would swallow me whole.

At slower speeds I cut south on Route 15, closely following the bends of the Mississippi River. It wasn't *that* Mississippi, the pulsing main artery of the southern continent, but rather a slow brownish green flow perhaps thirty feet at its broadest, which drained out of Mississippi Lake, sixty miles south of the Ottawa River. Route 15 was gorgeous and Lucy threaded her way on a gridwork of narrow, curving rural roads; through Alfred, the "French Fry Capital" of Ontario and Grafton, the "Lilac Capital," as the afternoon shadows stretched into evening. Huge trees shaded the pavement and villages built with strong Victorian influences dotted the route. Silent churchyards, with marble stones surrounded by lush lawns, abutted equally still domestic yards filled with hollyhocks, gladioli, and roses; their colored exuberance bound by black wrought-iron fences.

The St. Lawrence River, the broad seaway that connects the Great Lakes with the open ocean, is at its narrowest where the international bridge joins

Ontario with New York near Prescott. The light was failing in a swirl of fading pinks and growing grays as I crossed the high, arching span of metal grating, and the dark had fully descended as I started hunting for a campground. Choices were limited and, too tired to go any farther than the outskirts of Ogdensburg, I found a KOA and disgustedly gave the cashier nineteen dollars to set up my tent on a bit of marshy grass. In the space beside mine a man in a pop-up camper noticed me fumbling with my tent poles, a small flashlight clenched between my teeth, and came over to offer help and a bright propane lantern. He and his wife and their two daughters had driven from Crystal Falls on Michigan's Upper Peninsula to drop one of the girls off at her first year of college in New York. It was a lovely thing, he said, to be able to turn some of the difficulties of a child's leave-taking into the celebration of a family camping trip. My tent set up, I handed him back his lantern.

"Thank you."

"We're glad we could help." He was alone. "The girls" had gone into town to buy groceries. I said nothing but appreciated that in this family, even in the absence of the others, "I" was expressed as "we."

The family from Crystal Falls was still asleep as I showered in the bath-house, packed up, and headed out. Only a young rabbit, short ears erect over his chubby baby face, watched me leave. The morning had the kind of gradually intensifying brilliance that whispers it is only a matter of time before the sun will break through and sweep away the mist. As expected, flashes of light broke through the thick curls of hanging fog as I traveled south on Route 68 through Flackville, crossed the Grass River, and slowly drove the streets of Canton where gracious turn-of-the-century houses, brick sidewalks, old trees, and wide lawns mutely displayed the understated elegance of a small college town.

Colton was the terminus of Route 68 and, past the blue flash of the Carry Falls Reservoir, it was Route 56 that ran south, merging into Route 3, twisting and contorting over the Raquette River, around Raquette Pond, and through the town of Tupper Lake. The western slopes of the Adirondacks is a landscape of hills and water, where wood-frame villages, built on the timber and mining industries, cluster on riverbanks and nestle between lakes. Long Lake is one of those: a hamlet of rambling homes, a gold sand beach, and old hotels with long verandas that overlook the water. It is also a sportfishing and float-plane base from where Cessnas and Beavers on pontoons take anglers through the chain lakes that rope the northwest corner of the Adirondack Park. I stopped in at the general store for a tire pressure gauge, as I had not been able to dig mine from the depths of my saddlebags since Ontario. I was engrossed in the small selection of automotive tools and parts when a blond, ruddy-faced man in his late forties came over to say hello.

"Touring?" He motioned to my jacket slung over my left arm.

"Yes."

"Where are you from?"

"New Jersey." I was only a state away from my point of origin and it was safe to tell the truth again.

"That's a nice drive!" It was, too. The green undulations of the Adirondacks spilled south until they reached the Delaware Water Gap in northwestern New Jersey, where the low-rolling eastern Appalachians of the mid-Atlantic states claimed their territory. When not spending holidays fishing with his family, the blond man was a motorcyclist, too, and he went on to tell me in some detail about the previous summer, when he had driven all the way out to Montana on his BMW.

"That trip was four thousand three hundred miles!" He was positively radiant in his memories of the road and a long solitary ride. "What's the longest trip you've done?" There was curiosity and a little challenge in his voice. Long-distance bikers are sometimes like mountain climbers: "How high have you gone? I've gone higher." It's a pissing match, a poker game, and the stakes are points of pride and an "ironbutt" reputation for having gone farther, lived in the wind, smiled through the bugs and the weather, and lived to tell the story.

"This one."

"Where've you been?"

"Alaska." I laughed as his face went slack with surprise. I had just won the "ironbutt" title.

"And here I thought I was the distance rider. How far is that?"

"It's a little better than fourteen thousand miles, but I've been doing a lot of backroads wandering and didn't go direct." Issues of hierarchical machismo solved, we stood in the aisle talking for a few minutes about the beauty of the high passes in Montana and the ride down the Alcan. He said he'd like to go see the Far North someday and I told him that he should, that it was the trip of a lifetime. He shook my hand, chuckled, and went to look at bass lures as I headed for the cash register with my gauge.

WITH THE ADIRONDACKS RISING TO THE west and the Green Mountains welling up in the east, I drove south following Route 22 through a series of valleys that hugged the Vermont border. Low-rolling farm country, woodlots, and fields brushed up against one another, corn and cattle and timber unevenly spaced over the hillsides. In Salem, population not quite a thousand, I stopped for lunch, a stuffed roasted green pepper from a supermarket deli, and sat at a picnic table with the sun-warmed brick of the store at my back. With a map spread out on the battered and graffiti-engraved surface, I looked closely at where I was on the tangle of roads that generally followed the orientation of the Hudson River, and at where I was going—or rather stopping—in the suburbs of Boston. It was less than four hundred miles from Salem, New York, to Carlisle, Massachusetts, where I would park Lucy for a couple of weeks as I searched for a new apartment and reclaimed my warehoused possessions. With a plastic forkful of green pepper halfway to my mouth, it struck me with stunning clarity that this was my last full day on the road. *Goddamn, is that possible? I guess so.* I looked around: at the parking lot, at my half-eaten pepper, at the street beyond. Here I was, as the end of this marvelous journey approached, still eating lunches in the lee of grocery stores. It was a good stuffed pepper, juicy with tomato sauce and ground beef, but I dropped what remained in the garbage can and strode across the street to a fancy French patisserie that catered to wealthy New York ladies who came up the Vermont border to "antique." It was time to begin the celebration.

Old silver gleamed on the sideboards, and flowers in cut-glass vases decorated each petite marble-topped table. A carved chest filled with lavender potpourri stood by the door and wrought-iron chairs reflected graceful frames on the highly polished floor. I took a table against the wall where I could see Lucy through the plate-glass windows and ordered a French roast coffee and a chocolate mousse laced with Chambord. The white porcelain pot arrived, along with a fragile cup and saucer, silver spoon, and a silver cream and sugar set. The mousse was served in a fat-bowled wine glass with a white doily and service plate beneath, fresh cream and a sprig of mint on top. I felt like asking for a last-day-celebration candle. In the elegance of the café, with its polished glass cases of handmade chocolates and cakes, I felt tattered and a little road weary, but also strong and experienced, accomplished and capable. What a magnificent journey this had been. Now that there was so little of it remaining, I resolved to do the last four hundred miles with reverence, to pay attention to every lift and curve, and to make a song of this last stretch of road that I could carry with me for life.

Back on 22 I noticed anew the sensuality of moving through space, riding the back of a motorcycle that swooped over hills and swung into corners like a bird on the wing. Fifteen thousand miles and I still loved that flying, floating feeling and could wonder at it afresh each time I called it to consciousness. Cambridge, Eagle Bridge, and Hoosic Falls passed in the amber light of the late summer afternoon. At Petersburgh I turned left onto Route 2 and fifteen minutes later entered my last state, Massachusetts.

Williamstown is a lovely community with narrow side streets and huge trees flanking the main boulevard. Williams College, a small liberal arts institution with a reputation for expensive, quality education, is at its heart. Unfortunately, some of the charm of the place was lost when a black BMW convertible with a pulsing stereo, driven by a trust-fund kiddie who couldn't have been more than twenty, pulled into traffic from a side street without stopping. Junior did not bother to slow or look for who might already be there, and as his left front panel came much too close to sideswiping Lucy, I moved rapidly from the closing space of the right lane toward the centerline, braking hard and pulling in behind his polished bumper as he accelerated through a yellow light. Although I thought seriously of chasing him down at the next intersection, I was tired and not really in the mood to explain the gross points of considerate driving to a kid with too much money and too little sense, so I let the aggravation slip. I also did not want to ruin my last night on the road with sustained irritation at someone else's idiocy. What I wanted was a gentle night to think, relax, and consider this journey, which was almost over, and I knew exactly where to go in western Massachusetts to find quietude and expansive vistas.

At a liquor store in North Adams I bought a sixteen-ounce bottle of beer, tucked it into my pack, and turned right off of Route 2 for the long hairpin turns that climb Mount Greylock. At just under three thousand five hundred feet, it is the highest peak in Massachusetts.

Standing slightly off the open summit is one of the Appalachian Mountain Club's "huts," Bascom Lodge, where I had worked in the summer of 1988. Although rustic in setting and remote from the mill valley bustle of Pittsfield and North Adams, there is nothing even vaguely hutlike about Bascom. Constructed by the Civilian Conservation Corps in 1937, it looks rather like a hunting lodge from the nineteen-teens; a structure that Teddy Roosevelt might have liked. Stone and timber walls, gabled dormers, and the chimney of a huge central fireplace stand overlooking unimpeded vistas that stretch south toward Connecticut, west to New York and north to Vermont and New Hampshire.

I pulled into the parking lot, took off my helmet, and looked at all that was familiar: the lodge, the white marble war memorial beacon that crowned the summit, the sloping grass interspaced by lichen-painted boulders. In the late summer evening, the view of the landscape below was an undulating tapestry of pale green pasture, vivid gold feed corn, and dark woodlots. Little had changed. It was as windswept and beautiful as I remembered it from that summer twelve years before, when I had come to Greylock in the last six weeks before beginning university to flip pancakes in the kitchen and clean the upstairs bunkrooms. I had come when my attempt to hike the entire Appalachian Trail had been cut short by uncontrolled tendonitis in my right ankle. Not yet ready to leave the woods and the camaraderie of other long-distance hikers, I had begged a job at Bascom Lodge because it stood near to where the Appalachian Trail crosses the moss-covered ridges of Greylock and was a place where I could see my friends, support myself, and still be within the embrace of the mountains.

The rhythmic pulse of an African drum came rolling down from the summit, stopping my stride toward the lodge. Turning, I followed the sound. In the slanting burnished-orange rays of the setting sun, a boy kneeled on a grass mat atop the war memorial's retaining wall. Between his knees he held a great drum, its skin stretched tight over a carved and painted wooden barrel frame, and pounded out a rhythm—now soft, now driving—that honored the sun as it slipped toward the horizon. Thirty feet away from his mat I found my own westward-facing perch on the wall, flipped the top off the beer, and listened to the music meld into the sky's own rhythm. Strands of horsetail clouds overhung us, reflecting gold and orange and vivid pink. I thought of the sunset rolling west across the continent. It had already left the Maritime Provinces in the deepening shades of evening. The shift and coloration of light would finish bronzing the eastern seaboard and New England before moving on to the heartland—Illinois, Iowa, Manitoba, and Saskatchewan—within the hour. An hour more and it would touch the high ranges of the Rockies. It was still full daylight in California and British Columbia, and the pink and orange light would take another five hours to reach Valdez, Girdwood, Anchorage, and Denali, but they, too, would see this setting sun in just a few hours. Would the roll of African drums go with it, music and light flowing together across the continent? The boy played for forty-five minutes and I sat alone within my thoughts for most of it, watching the shimmer of color and sound, lost in the music, until a man with a native face and a hawk's feather dangling from a braid in his long black hair asked if he could share the wall.

"Of course. Sit down." He introduced himself as David and said he had come with his children to see the concert that would be held in the lodge later that evening. We sat together in silence until the boy with the drum played his final rhythms, rolled up his mat, and joined us. His name was Chris and he worked at the lodge, he said, and for a few minutes the three of us talked of music and mountains.

"I come out every night," he said. "I never know what rhythms to play, they just come." We passed my beer around and talked quietly of the beauty of that place, the heartbeat thrum of drumming, and the journeys that each of us were on. Chris had just finished high school and was still deciding what he wanted to do when the snows came and the lodge closed. David was from Alaska. How strange and appropriate, that on my final evening, I should find myself sitting beside people like them. Life can be a spiderweb of experience, and where the threads cross one can see how the past, the present, and the future all mesh one into the other.

Chris was gone, headed downhill for the lodge and his evening duties, and David and I talked of Ninilchik, the pass through the mountains at Hope, and the communities of Homer and Girdwood. His twin nine-year-old girls laughed and ran over the summit, calling to one another, their voices high and childish in the mountain air. David said that his heart ached for Alaska, but that he was here in Massachusetts because, despite a failed marriage, he wanted to be near his children as they grew.

"One day," he said, "when they're older, I'll go back. Soon." Leaving David and his daughters with a promise to see them later at the concert, I walked to the lodge, registered with Chris to spend the night in one of the bunkrooms, and carried my pack up stairs that I had swept a thousand times more than a decade before.

The bunkroom was the same: white painted double-decker frame beds, dark hardwood floors glowing beneath many coats of sock-polished lacquer, and thin white curtains fluttering at the windows. Below, the sound of chairs being rearranged came up through the elaborate wrought-iron registers. I pulled a fleece jacket from my bag against the evening chill and went down to help.

At the heart of the evening's concert was a group called Tall Trees, who sang and drummed Abanaki, Ojibway, and Mohawk songs. On a large circular drum, four men beat the rhythm with long-handled, round-ended sticks as women, standing close behind, sang in high, shifting octaves; a weft of melody that wove into the warp of the drumbeat. I sat on the floor, back against the wall, and out of the crush of chairs arranged to leave enough space for the children to dance. The last song was the American Indian Movement Anthem, dedicated as a freedom song for Leonard Peltier.

The stars were bright and the Milky Way was a glittering, shifting, band of light and vibration against the stillness of the moonless night, as I closed the lodge's oak door and climbed to the summit. Wrapped in the heavy warmth of my leather jacket, I lay back on the grass and stared into the velvet blackness of the sky. It was a magnificent evening and I couldn't think of a better way to spend my final night on the road than there; in that place where past met present, where the sky and the mind opened to view, and where the rhythms of ancient peoples met those of the land.

In the early morning light I walked down to where Lucy waited behind the retaining wall of a parking lot and stood for a few minutes overlooking the low hills of the Berkshires. Thick cottony fog banks had poured into the hollows of the landscape and the aerial view was a mottle of green hilltops rising like turtles from a glacial gray lake. The last day was beginning. I took the curves slowly on the way down Greylock, consciously feeling the mass and force of the bike in the corners, and deliberately adjusting the angle of my spine in relation to acceleration. The laws of physics are glorious when they manifest in motorcycles and motion. The growing sunshine sifted gold dapples through the leaves and moist air, spotting the road under Lucy's tires. *Is it possible that this is the final morning?* It still felt so natural, so right, to be moving through the eastern slant of the sun, to be rolling through small towns that were just waking up.

Past the brick factory walls of North Adams, up the switchback loops of Route 2 over the Hoosac Range, and along the fall of the Cold River, Lucy and I swept down through Florida, Drury, and into Charlemont. I knew those turns well. When I worked at Bascom, my best friend used to drive out from Concord to see me. There was jazz on Friday nights at the Charlemont Inn and, as it was too long a drive to return to Mount Greylock when the music ended, we booked in together as Mr. and Mrs. D with an inn staff whom we somehow thought would notice or care that we shared a room. I am sure the clerk knew that we lied about our shared last name; our faces were too young, an ill-fitting silver ring was counterfeit on my left hand, and the carefully counted pile of one and five dollar bills was too neat on the front desk. It was, however, an excellent thing to sit in the August heat—a fan on, cold beer in hand, our feet propped on the windowsill of our second-floor room—and listen to the liquid notes of a saxophone rising through the humidity. In those moments we felt wild yet grown up, as if we were somehow renegades under aliases. I looked for the window on the second floor as I passed and wondered, a little ruefully, if I was still playing at being a renegade and wondered if the charade, if that is what it was, couldn't last just a bit longer.

An antiques barn outside of Shelburne advertised hot coffee and I pulled over for the midmorning jolt of caffeine and also to slow things down. In less than two hours it would be over. I wasn't ready. Three bikers, with their highly polished chrome and steel gleaming in the sun, pulled into the gravel parking lot as I sat on a veranda bench drinking my coffee and watching dust devils dance and swirl.

"Hey." One of them greeted me with a lifted chin and rakish smile as his bike fell to silence next to Lucy. He unbuckled his beanie helmet. "Is that yours?"

"Sure is."

Another motioned to the luggage. "Are you traveling?" I nodded. "East or west?"

"East."

"Too bad. We're going west, to Lake George, you could have come with us." He paused and then laughed. "Why don't you?" He was half joking but not quite. "One of the guys canceled out and we've got an extra space at the hotel. You could ride with us! We're good guys. It'll be fun!" I looked at him for a long, silent moment, smiling at the flippant invitation that I knew would become serious if I made it so. It would be so easy, *so easy* to just turn and ride out again toward what I knew: the open road, the easy friendship of other bikers, the miles humming under Lucy's tires. What was I going back to? I had no home of my own, my parents were still away at the lake, my biological family was scattered up the Western side of the continent, I was happily unemployed and my new job wouldn't start for another three weeks. Start, that is, if I decided to show up at all. Why not stay out, do something that I loved, ride west again until the cold weather settled in, maybe go south, and then decide what to do? The fantasy flickered bright and hot for a few seconds and then burned out. The circle was almost complete. It was time to end this run.

"No." I shook my head. "It's tempting, but I can't. I'm almost home." We talked for a few minutes of what a perfect thing it was to be out on a motorcycle on a beautiful road, and how they would spend the day driving to Lake George and the evening drinking cold beer together. Although I didn't say it, I knew that I would spend my evening in solitude. It was as it should be.

"Drive safe."

"Shiny side up." And they were gone, open throttles roaring west. I threw a leg across Lucy's back to finish my journey as I had started it: alone.

I TOOK THE LONG WAY HOME, down Monument Street from Concord's center, past the Old North Bridge and the yellow farmhouse with the Revolutionary War bullet still lodged in the door frame, past the vegetable farm where I worked one barefoot high school summer, and loped through the outskirts of Carlisle.

Carlisle is a village of forty-five hundred people. Once it produced milk and vegetables for the Boston and Lowell markets, and when my parents moved there in the late sixties it was still a farming community with space for some of the hippie ideals that they, among other new residents, brought with them: a food co-op, collective nursery school, and town sports leagues coached by parents. Everyone went to town meetings in those days, and everyone grew their own vegetables or bought them at the roadside stands of the farmers that we all knew: Mr. Clark, Mr. Swanson, Mr. Lapham, and Mr. Metivier. Things were different now. Carlisle had become a pricey suburban address, beautiful certainly, with much of the open space that I had roamed as a girl preserved by an active conservation commission; but the town had changed fundamentally in character over the past two decades. The farmers were gone. Some had retired and some had been forced out by exorbitant property taxes on land that had become ever-more desirable, not for the vegetables that it grew or the herds that it supported, but for the cachet of a fashionable address and the pretty myth of a New England village close to the economic beltways that surrounded Boston. Most of the fields now grew manicured lawns and homes, the cost of which effectively—and perhaps deliberately—barred Carlisle to middle- and low-income people by fences of wealth and privilege. The nursery school remained but the food co-op was gone, the soccer league had a hard time finding parents willing to spend time coaching their own children, and town meetings were filled only when issues of taxation came to the fore. Through the village center, where a marble Victorian war goddess stood behind her shield, past the town green and the tall steepled churches, I drove up my parents' driveway and into the shelter of their yard at a little past one in the afternoon.

For a moment I sat, Lucy idling beneath me and, like a whisper, the thoughts of the morning came back. *Go. Just keep going. Ride. There's so much yet to see. You know this life. Go live more of it.*

No. It was over. There were different roads that I needed to run in the coming year, a different life that I needed to create. I could always come back; the wind would welcome me into her arms, and the land would open up before me when the time was right to return. I hit the engine-stop button and reached down below Lucy's gas tank to turn the key to "off." The driveway was suddenly quiet. I took off my helmet, hung it over the mirror, dropped the kickstand, and leaned forward to lie across Lucy's frame, breathing in the smell of gasoline, hot oil, and road dust. Inhaling freedom.

"Well goddamn, Lucy, we did it."

Later that evening I sat alone on the deck with a bottle of my father's best scotch and a heavy-bottomed glass. What a great, mad, beautiful adventure it had been. I thought of what I had seen and flipped through the mental images as if they were photos in an album: the rich black earth of Iowa, the great spaces of Kansas where grain silos rose above the prairie like castles, balloons rising over the San Juan Mountains, swimming in Crater Lake, driving Route 16 alongside the icy froth of the Skeena River, White Pass into the Yukon, fishing on the Kenai Peninsula, the bears near Liard River, that beautiful—oh so beautiful—wolf in northern Alberta, the quiet spaces of Innisfail that surrounded a symphony of emotion, the Icefields Parkway, sunset in Glacier, flying into the Sturgis night, my family in Ontario, the greenness of the Adirondacks, and now here, the quietude of my girlhood home. And the people—such faces, such stories. There were the farmers of the Heartland who spoke of their lives and their communities. There were the native men who cared for their heritage, saw that it grew strong and straight, and who carved their history into the rosy trunks of old-growth cedars. There were the fisher-women, the adventurers, the bicyclists, the dog mushers, the motorcyclists, the small-business owners, the mothers, and the grandfathers. There were the individuals who had touched my trip and touched my life. I remembered Sue, the waitress in New York who gave me a kind word and made me believe in what I had begun. I remembered a woman dying in a field in Illinois who told me everything I needed to know about how fast the road, and life itself, can change. There were the Charleys in Nevada who reminded me to recognize the reemergence of the senses. There was Grant and Todd, pulling up fish and nurturing a friendship. There was the tiny Japanese woman, Kisiael, on her huge adventure. There was Dale, who allowed me to be free and irresponsible and to dance for just one night. There was the welcome and the warmth and the working through of all the pain, loss, discovery, and reunion with my bio-logical family: Gloria and her sons, Dave and Colleen and their daughters. How much each and every one of those people had taught me.

In the end, what had I learned? The North American continent is indeed a fantastic and varied landscape. I had seen only a fraction of it and it will take me a lifetime to see even a fraction more of what it offers. The Americans and Canadians that I sought as unique cultural entities I never found. Rather there was regionalism; ties that bound families and communities to the land and to one another by circumstance, by choice, and by love. The biological links that I sought to clarify were still emerging. In Gloria's and Dave's welcome and warmth and openness, and in my parents' acceptance and support, I had learned that the relationships that bind, the relationships that are critical in any family, are those of love, of commitment, of respect, and of communication. These are points of connection that are open to every family regardless of biology, regardless of the distance between members, and regardless of the schisms of time and emotion.

On the open road I had learned to accept each day for what it brought and each turn for what it revealed. I had learned something of strength and stamina, something of vulnerability and loneliness. I had learned when I had reached my limits, and when to push on. I had learned how to listen to both my machine and my inner voice, and to pay attention to what they suggested. Rather than looking to find myself, I learned how to lose myself in the road, to take each moment for what it was, and to open my eyes and heart to what surrounded me. In a great circling loop I had learned how a sense of self and heritage is necessary and that a stronger future can be built by confronting the past and all its present manifestations. I now know, better than I ever did before, that openness is more powerful than secrecy, that truth can bring love rather than recrimination, that there is little that cannot be explained or forgiven if asked, and that there are few things that cannot be found if searched for.